The London-spy compleat. In eighteen parts. By Mr. Edward Ward.

Edward Ward

The London-spy compleat. In eighteen parts. By Mr. Edward Ward.
Ward, Edward
ESTCID: T231166
Reproduction from Cambridge University Library
Vol. 2 entitled 'The London spy. For the month of November, 1699. The second volume. ...' and the imprint, "printed and sold by J. How", dated 1699. Each volume composed of parts and vol. 1 has a general titlepage; the parts have separate titlepages, with imprint "printed and sold by J. How", and pagination; the parts are variously dated: vol. 1, pt. 1 1700, pts. 2 and 6 1701, pts. 3-5 and 8-12 1699, pt. 7 1702; vol. 2, pt. 1 1699, pt. 2 1701, pts. 3-6 1700. In vol. 1, pts. 1- 2 and 6 are of the third edition; pt. 7 is of the second edition; in vol. 2 pt. 2 is of the second edition.
London : printed for, and by J. How, and sold by Eliphal Jaye, [1702].
2v. ; 2°

Eighteenth Century
Collections Online
Print Editions

Gale ECCO Print Editions

Relive history with *Eighteenth Century Collections Online*, now available in print for the independent historian and collector. This series includes the most significant English-language and foreign-language works printed in Great Britain during the eighteenth century, and is organized in seven different subject areas including literature and language; medicine, science, and technology; and religion and philosophy. The collection also includes thousands of important works from the Americas.

The eighteenth century has been called "The Age of Enlightenment." It was a period of rapid advance in print culture and publishing, in world exploration, and in the rapid growth of science and technology – all of which had a profound impact on the political and cultural landscape. At the end of the century the American Revolution, French Revolution and Industrial Revolution, perhaps three of the most significant events in modern history, set in motion developments that eventually dominated world political, economic, and social life.

In a groundbreaking effort, Gale initiated a revolution of its own: digitization of epic proportions to preserve these invaluable works in the largest online archive of its kind. Contributions from major world libraries constitute over 175,000 original printed works. Scanned images of the actual pages, rather than transcriptions, recreate the works *as they first appeared.*

Now for the first time, these high-quality digital scans of original works are available via print-on-demand, making them readily accessible to libraries, students, independent scholars, and readers of all ages.

For our initial release we have created seven robust collections to form one the world's most comprehensive catalogs of 18th century works.

Initial Gale ECCO Print Editions collections include:

History and Geography
Rich in titles on English life and social history, this collection spans the world as it was known to eighteenth-century historians and explorers. Titles include a wealth of travel accounts and diaries, histories of nations from throughout the world, and maps and charts of a world that was still being discovered. Students of the War of American Independence will find fascinating accounts from the British side of conflict.

Social Science

Delve into what it was like to live during the eighteenth century by reading the first-hand accounts of everyday people, including city dwellers and farmers, businessmen and bankers, artisans and merchants, artists and their patrons, politicians and their constituents. Original texts make the American, French, and Industrial revolutions vividly contemporary.

Medicine, Science and Technology

Medical theory and practice of the 1700s developed rapidly, as is evidenced by the extensive collection, which includes descriptions of diseases, their conditions, and treatments. Books on science and technology, agriculture, military technology, natural philosophy, even cookbooks, are all contained here.

Literature and Language

Western literary study flows out of eighteenth-century works by Alexander Pope, Daniel Defoe, Henry Fielding, Frances Burney, Denis Diderot, Johann Gottfried Herder, Johann Wolfgang von Goethe, and others. Experience the birth of the modern novel, or compare the development of language using dictionaries and grammar discourses.

Religion and Philosophy

The Age of Enlightenment profoundly enriched religious and philosophical understanding and continues to influence present-day thinking. Works collected here include masterpieces by David Hume, Immanuel Kant, and Jean-Jacques Rousseau, as well as religious sermons and moral debates on the issues of the day, such as the slave trade. The Age of Reason saw conflict between Protestantism and Catholicism transformed into one between faith and logic -- a debate that continues in the twenty-first century.

Law and Reference

This collection reveals the history of English common law and Empire law in a vastly changing world of British expansion. Dominating the legal field is the *Commentaries of the Law of England* by Sir William Blackstone, which first appeared in 1765. Reference works such as almanacs and catalogues continue to educate us by revealing the day-to-day workings of society.

Fine Arts

The eighteenth-century fascination with Greek and Roman antiquity followed the systematic excavation of the ruins at Pompeii and Herculaneum in southern Italy; and after 1750 a neoclassical style dominated all artistic fields. The titles here trace developments in mostly English-language works on painting, sculpture, architecture, music, theater, and other disciplines. Instructional works on musical instruments, catalogs of art objects, comic operas, and more are also included.

The BiblioLife Network

This project was made possible in part by the BiblioLife Network (BLN), a project aimed at addressing some of the huge challenges facing book preservationists around the world. The BLN includes libraries, library networks, archives, subject matter experts, online communities and library service providers. We believe every book ever published should be available as a high-quality print reproduction; printed on-demand anywhere in the world. This insures the ongoing accessibility of the content and helps generate sustainable revenue for the libraries and organizations that work to preserve these important materials.

The following book is in the "public domain" and represents an authentic reproduction of the text as printed by the original publisher. While we have attempted to accurately maintain the integrity of the original work, there are sometimes problems with the original work or the micro-film from which the books were digitized. This can result in minor errors in reproduction. Possible imperfections include missing and blurred pages, poor pictures, markings and other reproduction issues beyond our control. Because this work is culturally important, we have made it available as part of our commitment to protecting, preserving, and promoting the world's literature.

GUIDE TO FOLD-OUTS MAPS and OVERSIZED IMAGES

The book you are reading was digitized from microfilm captured over the past thirty to forty years. Years after the creation of the original microfilm, the book was converted to digital files and made available in an online database.

In an online database, page images do not need to conform to the size restrictions found in a printed book. When converting these images back into a printed bound book, the page sizes are standardized in ways that maintain the detail of the original. For large images, such as fold-out maps, the original page image is split into two or more pages

Guidelines used to determine how to split the page image follows:

• Some images are split vertically; large images require vertical and horizontal splits.
• For horizontal splits, the content is split left to right.
• For vertical splits, the content is split from top to bottom.
• For both vertical and horizontal splits, the image is processed from top left to bottom right.

THE
LONDON-SPY
COMPLEAT.

In Eighteen Parts.

By Mr. Edward Ward.

LONDON,

Printed for, and by *J. How*, and Sold by *Eliphal Jaye*, at the
Sign of the Candlestick, the lower-end of *Cheapside.*

THE
LONDON
SPY.

For the *Month* of *November*, 1698.

PART I.

By the *Author* of the Trip to *JAMAICA*.

Ned. Ward. Buried at Old St Pancras Church

The Third Edition.

LONDON,
Printed and Sold by *J. How,* in the *Ram-Head-Inn-Yard,* in *Fanchurch-street,* 1700.

Books Sold by J. How, *in the* Ram-Head-Inn-Yard *in* Fanchurch-Street; J. Weld, *at the* Crown *between the* Temple-Gates *in* Fleet-street; *and* Mrs. Fabian, *at* Mercers-Chappel *in* Cheap-side.

1. SOt's Paradife: Or the Humours of a Derby-Ale-Houfe: With a Satyr upon the Ale. Price Six Pence.

2. A Trip to *Jamaica*: With a True Character of the People and Ifland. Price Six Pence.

3. *Eclefia & Factio.* A Dialogue between *Bow-Steeple-Dragon*, and the *Exchange-Grafhopper*. Price Six Pence.

4. The Poet's Ramble after Riches. With Reflections upon a Country Corporation. Alfo the Author's Lamentation in the time of Adverfity. Price Six Pence.

5. A Trip to *New-England*. With a Character of the Country and People, both Englifh and Indians. Price Six Pence.

6. Modern Religion and Ancient Loyalty: A Dialogue. Price Six Pence.

7. The World Bewitch'd. A Dialogue between Two Aftrologers and the Author. With Infallible Predictions of what will happen from the *Vices* and *Villanies* Practis'd in *Court*, *City* and *Country*. Price Six Pence.

8. A Walk to *Iflington*: With a Defcription of New *Tunbridge*-VVells, and *Sadler's* Mufick-Houfe. Price Six Pence.

9. The Humours of a Coffee-Houfe: A Comedy. Price Six Pence.

10. A Frolick to *Horn-Fair*. With a Walk from Cuckold's-Point thro' *Deptford* and *Greenwich*. Price Six-Pence.

11. The Dancing-School. With the Adventures of the *Eafter*-Holy-Days. Price Six Pence,

12. The Firft Volume of the LONDON-SPY: In Twelve Parts.

13. The Firft, Second, Third, Fourth, Fifth, and Sixth Parts of the Second Volume of the *London-Spy*. Price Six Pence Each.

All Written by the fame Author.

THE
LONDON
SPY.

FTER a tedious Confinement to a Country *Hutt*, where I dwelt like *Diogenes* in his *Tub*, or an *Owl* in a *Hollow-Tree*, taking as much delight in my *Books*, as an *Alchimist* does in *Bellows*; till tired with Seven years fearch after Knowledge, I began to reckon with my felf for my Time; and examine what a *Solomon* my Diligent Enquiry into the uncertain Guefles of our Fore-Fathers had made me; but foon fell upon the Opinion of *Socrates*, and found my felf as much the Wifer, as if, like the Looby *Achilles*, I had fpent my hours at a *Diftaff*. This was no little Vexation to a Man of my Genius, to find my Brains loaded to no purpofe, with as many Antiquated *Tringum Trangums* as are lodg'd in the Whimfical Noddle of an old *Aftrologer*, and yet could make twice Ten no more than a *Junior Soph*, or a *Chalk Accountant*. Thefe Reflections put me into as great a Paffion with my felf, as a *Beau* when he dawbs his Clothes, or makes a falfe ftep in the Salutation of his Miftrefs: That I refolved to be no longer *Ariftotle's Sumpter-horfe*, or, like a *Tinkers Afs*, carry a Budget for my Anceftors, ftuff'd full of their frenzical Notions, and the mufty Conceits of a parcel of dreaming *Prophets*, fabulous *Poets*, and old doating *Philofophers*, but fhifted them off one by one, with a Fig for St. *Auftin* and his Doctrines, a Fart for *Virgil* and his Elegancy, and a T—d for *Defcartes* and his *Philofophy*. Till, by this means, I had Rid my Brains of thofe troublefome Crotches, which had rais'd me to the Excellence of being half Fool, and half Madman, by ftudying the weighty difference between *Up-fide-down*, and *Top-fide-turvy*, or to be more knowing, in fome fuch Nicety, then the reft of my Neighbours.

At laft, I thank my Stars, I turn'd my back-fide upon Times-paft, and began, like a wary Traveller, to look before me; and now having recover'd my Native Liberty, I found an Itching Inclination in my felf to vifit *London*; and to fhun the Cenfure of my Sober Country Friends, I Projected, for their Satisfaction, and my own Diverfion, this *Monthly Journal*, wherein I purpofe to expofe the *Vanities* and *Vices* of the *Town*,

as

as they shall by any Accident occur to my Knowledge, that the Innocent may see by Reflection, what I gain by Observation and Intelligence, and not by Practice or Experience. With this design I pursued my Journey, and the Second Day enter our *Metropolis*, with as much Wonder and Amazement, as the *Hatfield Fiddler*, did *Old Nicks* Palace in the time of the *Christmas* Holy-days. I had but just pass'd thro' *Aldgate*, like a *Ball* thro' the *Port* of a *Billiard-Table*, but by good Fortune met an old School-Fellow, who I found had laid down the *Gown* and took up the *Sword*; being Trick'd up in as much Gaiety, as a *Dancing-Master* upon a *Ball-Day*, or a Young *Sheriff* at a *County Assizes*. After we had mutually dispatch'd our Compliments to each other, and I had Awkwardly return'd, in Country Scrapes, his *All-a-mode* Bows and Cringes, he would needs prevail with me to Dine with him at a Tavern hard by, with some Gentlemen of his Acquaintance; which, I being an utter stranger in the Town, very readily Embrac'd; he enter'd the Tavern first, like a Young 'Squire attended with his Fathers *Chaplin*; for a Black Coat and Band are as great signs of a *Parson* or a *Pedagogue*, as a *Blew Frock* is of a *Butcher* or a *Tallow-Chandler*. Besides, my Hat by often handling, was tug'd into the Canonical Flap, that I look'd like a *Deacon* who had laid by his *Crape*, in order to the Re-baptising of his Soul in Clarret, without the danger of being seen *Staggering* in his *Faith*, to the Scandal of his Function.

As soon as we came near the Bar, a thing started up, all Ribbons, Lace, and Feathers, and made such a Noise with her Bell and her Tongue together, that had half a Dozen *Paper-Mills* been at work within three yards of her, they'd have been no more then so many *Lutes* to a *Drum*, or Ladies *Farts* to a Peal of *Ordinance*, which alarm'd Two or Three nimble heeld Fellows aloft, who shot themselves down Stairs with as much Celerity, as a *Mountebanks Mercury* upon a *Rope*, from the Top of a *Church-Steeple*, every-one Charg'd with a mouthful of *Coming, Coming*. This suddain clutter at our appearance, so surpris'd me, that I look'd as silly as a Bumpkin, Translated from the Plough-tail to the Play-house, when it Rains Fire in the *Tempest*, or when *Don John's* at Dinner with the *Subteranean* Assembly of terrible *Hobgoblins*: He that got the start, and first approach'd us, of these *Grey-hound-Footed* Emissaries, desir'd us to walk up, telling my Companion, his Friends were above. Then, with a Hop, Stride, and Jump, ascended the Stair-head before us, and from thence conducted us to a spacious Room, where about a dozen of my School-Fellows Acquaintance were ready to receive us: Upon our Entrance, they all started up, and on a suddain screw'd themselves into so many Antick Postures, that had I not seen them first Erect, I should have query'd with my self, whether I was fallen into the Company of *Men* or *Monkeys*.

This Accademical Fit of *Rigling Agility*, was almost over, before I rightly understood the meaning on't, and found at last, they were only showing one another how many forts of *Apes Gestures*, and *Fop's Cringes* had been invented since the first *French* Dancing Master undertook to teach our *English* Gentry to make *Scaramouches* of themselves; and Entertain their *Poor Friends*, and Pacify their *Needy Creditors*, with *Compliments* and *Congies*. When every Person, with abundance of Pains, had shown the ultimate of his Breeding, contending about a quarter of an

hour

hour who should sit down first, showing great want of a *Herald* to fix us in our proper places, which with much difficulty, being at last agreed on, we proceeded to a Whet of *Old H*——— sharpen our Appetites to our approaching Dinner. Tho', I confess (as to my own part) my Stomach was as keen already, as a *Grey-Hounds* to his Supper, after a Days Coursing, or a Miserly *Livery-Man's* who has Fasted three days to prepare himself for a *Lord-Mayors Feast*. The Honest Cook gave us no Leasure to tire our Appetites, by a tedious expectancy; for in a little time the Cloth was laid, and our first Course was usher'd up by the *Dominus Factotum*, in great order to the Table, which consisted of two *Calves-Heads* and a couple of *Geese*; I could not but Laugh in my Conceit, to think with what Judgment the *Caterer* had provided so lucky an Entertainment for so suitable a Company. After the Victuals was pretty well cool'd, in Complementing who should begin first, we all fell to; and Efaith I found by their Eating, they were no ways affronted at their Fare; for in less time then an *Old Woman can Crack a Nut*, we had not left enough to Dine the *Bar-boy*. The Conclusion of our Dinner was a Stately *Cheshire* Cheese of a Groaning Size, of which we devour'd more in three Minutes, than a Million of Maggots could have done in three Weeks. After Cheese comes nothing; then all we desir'd was a clear Stage and no Favour; accordingly every thing was whip'd away in a Trice, by so cleanly a Conveyance, that no *Jugler* by virtue of *Hocus Pocus*, could have handed away his *Balls with more Dexterity*; All our Empty Plates and Dishes were in an instant Chang'd into full Quarts of *Purple Nectar*, and *Unsullied Glasses*: Then a Bumper to the *King* in general, another to the *Church Establish'd* in particular, a third left to the Whimsey of the Toaster, till at last their *Slippery Engines of Verbosity*, coin'd Nonsence with such a facil fluency, that a parcel of *Alley Gossips* at a Christening, after the Sack has gone twice round, could not with their Tattling Tormentors be a greater Plague to a *Fumbling God-Father*, then their lame *Jests* and impertinent *Cunundrums* were to a Man of my Temper. *Oaths* were as plenty as *Weeds* in an *Alms-house Garden*, and in Triumph flew about from one to t'other, like *Squibs* and *Crackers* in *Cheapside*, when the Cuckolds all-a-row march in splendour thro' the City. But thanks to good Fortune, my Friend in a little time redeem'd me out of this Purgatory; who perceiving my uneasiness, made an apology for our going; and so we took our Leaves. I offer'd to pay my Proportion, but the whole Body of the Society stood up, *Contradicente*, with a Thousand Thanks to me for my good Company, tho' I sat all the time as silent as a Quaker, unmov'd by the Spirit at a *Hum Drum Meeting*. As we walk'd out, we were attended by the whole Family to the Door, with as many Welcomes at our Arses, as a Man has *Thank ye's* and *Lord bless ye's*, from a Gang of *Mumpers* for a Pennyworth of Charity.

But as soon as we were got clear of all our Noisie Flattery, I began to ask of my Friend, what sort of generous Gentlemen those were who had so kindly Treated us? He smil'd at my enquiry, and told me I could scarce guess by what measures they had buoy'd up such a seeming Grandeur. *Did you take notice (says he) of the Gentleman in a Blew Coat, Red-Stockins, Silver-hilted Sword, and Edg'd Hat, who sat at the upper end of the Table? He was a* Sword-hilt *maker by his Trade, but prov'd so very Ingenious at his Tools, that he has acquir'd the Art of Cutting Medals, or*

B   Stamps:

Stamps, *and is mighty great with most of the* Bankers *and topping* Goldsmiths *about Town; you may guess from thence, how he imploys his Talent: He keeps his Brace of* Geldings, *and a great many Brace of worse Cattle, living at the rate of a Thousand Pounds a Year, and passes, to those who know him not, for a Gentleman of good account in the* North *of* England, *and his Bills will pass as Currant in* Lombard-street, *as the best Merchants in the City.*

There was a handsome lusty young Fellow, who sat next him, with a Wheel-Barrow *full of* Periwig *on, and a whole Peice of* Muslin *about his Neck, and stunk as strong of* Orange-Flower-Water, *as a* Spaniard *does of* Garlick. *He was the other day but a* Wine-Copers Prentice; *and a brisk young Dame in the City, who was forc'd by her Father to Marry an Old Merchant for the sake of his Riches, maintains him in that Equipage you see, for supplying the Defects of her feeble Husband; and now he is grown so Prodigal, that he won't wash his Hands in any thing but* Juice *of* Oranges *and* Hungary-Water, *Dines every day at the* Tavern, *at the* Play-House *every Night, Stirs no where without a* Coach; *and has his* Fencing-Master, Dancing-Master, Singing-Master, French-Master, *and is as Compleat a* City Beau *(notwithstanding he was bred to the* Adds *and* Driver*) as you shall see in* Lombard-Street Church *of a* Sunday, *or in* Drapers-Garden *an hour before Dinner-time.*

If you observ'd, there was a little Demure Spark, in a Diminutive Cravat, and Fox-colour'd Wig, *with a* Hat *as broad as an* Umbrella, *whose level Brims discover'd it was carefully preserv'd in that order by a* Hat-Case *and* Smoothing-Iron: *He seems greatly to affect Antiquity you see by his Garb, tho' the Coat he has on has not been made above this two Months, yet he would have it in the Ancient Mode, with little* Buttons, *round* Cuffs, *narrow* Skirts, *and* Pockets *within two Inches of the bottom, as the most proper Fashion for his Business; and for all its so scanty, he makes it serve him for a* Cloak, *with which he Covers abundance of* Shame, *and a great deal of* Knavery. *He's an Incomparable* Herald, *and will give you an exact* Genealogy *of most good Families in* England; *and has the Art of making himself a* Kin, *when he sees it convenient. To be short with you, he is one of those gentile* Mumpers, *we call* Cadators; *he goes a Circuit round* England *once a Year, and under pretence of a decay'd Gentleman, gets both* Money *and* Entertainment *at every good House he comes at. And if he has Opportunity to handsomly convey away a* Silver Beaker, *or a* Spoon *or Two, he holds no long dispute with his Conscience about the Honesty of the matter. Then comes up to Town, and injoys the benefit of his Rural Labours.*

Another you needs must take perticular notice of, that pluck'd out a pair of Pocket-Pistols, *and laid them in the Window, who had a great Scar cross his Forehead, a Twisted Wig, and Lac'd Hat on; the Company call'd him* Captain; *he's a Man of considerable Reputation amongst* Birds *of the same Feather, who I have heard say thus much in his Praise, That he is as Resolute a Fellow as ever Cock'd* Pistol *upon the Road: And indeed I do believe he fears no Man in this World but the* Hang-man; *and dreads no Death but* Choaking. *He's as generous as a Prince, Treats anybody that will keep him Company; loves his Friend as dearly as the* Ivy *does the* Oak, *will never leave him till he has* Hugg'd *him to his Ruin. He has drawn in Twenty of his Associates to be* Hang'd, *but had al-*

ways

ways Wit and Money enough to save his own Neck from the Halter. He has good Friends at Newgate, who give him now and then a Squeese when he is full of Juice; and give him their Words to stand by him, which he takes as a Verbal Policy of Insurance from the Gallows, till he grows Poor thro' Idleness, and then (he has Cunning enough to know) he may be Hang'd thro' Poverty. He's well acquainted with the Ostlers about Bishopsgate-street, and Smithfield; and gains from them Intelligence of what Booties go out that are worth attempting. He accounts them very honest Tikes, and can with all safety trust his Life in their Hands, for now and then Gilding their Palms for the good Services they do him. He pretends to be a Disbanded Officer, and reflects very feelingly upon the hard usage we poor Gentlemen meet with, who have hazarded our Lives and Fortunes for the Honour of our Prince, the Defence of our Country; and Safety of Religion; and after all to be Broke without our Pay, turn'd out without any consideration for the dangers and difficulties we have run thro'; at this rate, Wounds who the Devil would be a Soldier? At such sort of Cant he is excellent, and utters himself with as little Hesitation, and as great a Grace, as a Town-Stallion when he Dissembles with his generous Benefactris, who believes all he says to be as true as the Gospel.

He that sat over against him, in the *Plate-button'd Suit* and *White Beaver-Hat*, is kind of an *Amphibious* Rascal, a Compound of two sorts of Villany: He is one half *Town-Trap*, and the other half *Sweetner*. He always keeps at his beck three or four handsome young Wenches, well Equip'd, and in good Lodgings, who are all *Modesty* without, and nothing but *Lewdness* within; who can seem as *Innocent* as *Doves*, and be as *Wicked* as *Devils*. Whose Education from their Cradles, under some skilful Matron in Iniquity, have made them pleasant *Companions*, taking *Bedfellows*, expert *Jilts*, incorrigible *Sinners* and *good* managers of a *bad Design*: Who had *Whores* to their *Mothers*, *Rogues* to their *Fathers*, *Bawds* to their *Tutors*; and under a deceitful Countenance, are so *Case-harden'd* in *Impudence*, that they never were sorry for any thing, but that they were too Young to be *Whores*, when they were old enough to endeavour it. These are his Working-Tools, who by their Beauty, Youth, and Airyness, insinuate into the affections of Young *Merchants, Shopkeepers, Prentices, &c.* whose Juvenal Fury carries them too often into the Ruinous Embraces of these Treacherous Strumpets; who when with their Wanton Tailes seem most obliging to their Admirers, their Mercenary Thoughts are projecting something to their Injury; like a *Water-lane Protestant*, who when at Church seems most Devout, is picking the Pocket of some over-Penitent Christian, who is so Zealous at his *Prayers* that he neglects to *Watch*; and whilst he has God in his Heart, has the Devil fumbling about his Breeches.

He accounts them rare Cattle if they Calve once in a Year, for there's never a Child they have but is worth two or three Hundred Pounds to him, besides by-Advantages he makes by their inspecting into the Affairs and Secrets of such who they can manage; and when the Filthiness of their Practice hath render'd them, like a *Path-way* by common *Treading*, Nasty and Infertile, he ransacks their Wardrobe, strips them of their Plumes, and Discards 'em; who are forc'd to fly to some common *Bawdy-House* for Refuge, and walk the Streets for Subsistance;
thus

thus fin on in publick Shame and Mifery, till the Gallows, or an Hofpital, at laft brings them to Repentance.

The other part of his Life is Tricking People out of their Money by falfe *Dice* and *Cards*, which he handles with more gainful Dexterity then the *German Artift*; and Preaches the *Parfon* with fuch a fraudulent deception of the Sight, that he will drain the Pockets of a large Company in fix Minutes as Clean as the *Royal-Oak Lotttery* fhall in fix Hours. He is often to be feen with a Country cloth Coat on, all over dirt, or according to the Weather, as if he had come a Fifty Mile Journey, tho' he's only Travell'd from *Salisbury-Court* to *Smithfield*, where he keeps the Market as conftantly as a *Toung Whore* does *Bartholomew-Fair*, or an *Old* one the *Sacrament*; Looking in his Ruftick Garb, as much like an honeft *Grafier*, as a *City Hypocrite*, in his Black Coat and Band, does like a *Good Chriftian*. He is conftant to no fort of Drefs, but changes his *Cloaths* as often as a Wimfical Woman does her Mind; and States-man like, always futes his Apparrel to his Project. Being a rare Tongue-pad and excellent at thefe following qualifications. He can out-Flatter a *Poet*, out-Huff a *Bully*, out-wrangle a *Lawyer*, out-Cant a *Puritan*, out-Cring a *Beau*, out-Face *Truth*, and out-Lye the Devil. The reft that you fee were a kind of *Supernumerary* Men, affiftants to the reft; who have not cunning enough to Project a piece of Roguery themfelves, but like a well-meaning Brother, will lend a Shoulder to the Villany: The former are your rare *Sycamore Rogues*, who flourifh and fpread finely for a Seafon; and the other are the *Catarpillars* than hang upon 'em.

But pray, Old Acquaintance, faid I, What is your Imployment in the World, that you are fo well acquainted with this Scandalous Society? Why I'll tell you, fays he, I ftudy'd a little Phyfick at the Univerfity, and fome fmall knowledge of Chyrurgery I gain'd fince I came to Town, which the narrownefs of my Fortune hath oblig'd me to the ufe of; and I have had moft of thefe Dark *Engineers* you faw, my Patients; for they are feldom free from *Clap, Pox, Thumps, Cuts*, or *Bruifes*; and pay as generoufly for their Cure, as an old *Maid* would do for a Nights Recreation with the Man fhe likes beft; parting with *Pounds* to their *Surgeon*, as freely as Fools did with their *Pence* to the *Wheel of Fortune*.

Come, fays my Friend, let us ftep into this *Coffee-houfe* here, as you are a Stranger in the Town it will afford you fome Diverfion. Accordingly in we went, where a parcel of Muddling *Muck-worms* were as bufie as fo many *Rats* in an old *Cheefe-loft*; Some Going, fome Coming, fome Scribling, fome Talking, fome Drinking, fome Smoaking, others Jangling; and the whole Room ftinking of Tobacco, like a *Dutch Scoot*, or a *Boatfwains Cabbin*. The Walls being hung with Gilt Frames, as a *Farriers-fhop* with *Horfe-fhoes*; which contained abundance of Rarities, viz. *Nectar and Ambrofia, May Dew, Golden Elixirs, Popular Pills, Liquid Snuff, Beautifying Waters, Dentrifices, Drops, Lozenges*, all as Infallible as the *Pope*, Where every one (as the famous *Saffold* has it) *above the reft, Defervedly has gain'd the Name of beft*. Good in all cafes, curing all Diftempers; every Medicine being fo *Catholick*, it pretends to nothing lefs than Univerfality: That indeed had not my Friend told me 'twas a *Coffee-houfe*, I fhould

have

have took it for *Quacks-Hall*, or the *Parlour* of some Eminent *Mounte-bank*.

When we had each of us stuck in our Mouths a Lighted Pipe of *Sot-weed*, we began to look about us, Do you mind (says my Friend) yonder old Sophister with an *Indian* Pipe between his his Meager Jaws, who sits staring at the Candle with as much stedfastness as a Country Passenger at *Bow-Steeple*, or a Child at a *Raree-show*; that's a strange Whimsie-headed Humorist; observe his Posture, he looks like the Picture of *Æsculapius* behind an *Apothecaries Counter*: And has as many *Maggots* in his *Noddle* as there are *Mice* in an old *Barn* or *Nuts* in a *Mumpers Doublet*. He has a wonderful Projecting Head, and has lately contriv'd one of the prettiest Pocket-Engines for the Speedy Blanching of *Haste-Nuts* and *Filbert-Kernels*, that ever was invented; he'll Crack and Skin Two, for a Squirrels One; and in few years by a little alteration, will improve it to the use of *Wall-nuts*. I'll assure you he's a Member of the *Royal-Society*, and had as great a hand for many Years together, in bringing the *Weather-glass* to perfection, as any of them. He puts great faith in the *Philosophers-stone*, and believes he shall one time or other be Rich as *Cræsus*, tho' he has almost Beggar'd himself in the search on't. And has as large a pair of *Bellows* in his *Laboratory*, as ever an *Alchimist* in Town. He try'd a very notable *Experiment* the other day, in setting Fire to a large *Hay-stack* he had in the *Country*, and order'd the Ashes to be brought to Town, from whence he propos'd to prepare a Medicine, call'd *Sall Graminis*, which should infallibly cure all Distempers in *Horses*, and be the rarest *Medicine* for *Cows*, *Sheep*, or *Oxen*, and all sort of Creatures that feed upon *Grass*, that any *Grasier* or *Farrier* can use in all such cases. But sending it up in an ill Season, the Ashes got wet in their Carriage, and quite lost their Vertue, that he was forc'd to sell them to a West-Country *Barge-man*, in order to Dung Land. But it's thought by the Wise, he might have Sold it in the Hay to as good an Advantage. He has abundance of Whims in him very Remarkable; he lives over against a Church, that when he dies he might not have far to Travel upon four Mens Shoulders. As soon as the Clock begins Nine, if he gets not his Shooes off before it has done Striking, in order for Bed, he is immediately seiz'd with such a violent Fit of the Gout, that he roars like a *Tower-Lion* at a Woman going with *Male-Child*. If he is not up just as the Clock strikes five in the Morning, he thinks himself Bedridden. If his Victuals be not brought to the Table whilst the Clock goes Twelve, he Eats nothing that Day; his Stomack is always at the *Meridian* height the same time as the Sun is; and if he finds by his Observation its Declin'd he is as much out of Humour for letting slip the Critical Minute, as a Married Lady (without Children to employ her thoughts) is for losing of her Lap-dog. He's a wonderful Antiquary, and has a Closet of Curiosities out-does *Gresham-Colledge*: He tells ye, that he has the Tooth-picker of *Epicurus*, which he always us'd after Eating; it is made of the Claws of an *American Humming-Bird*; and is to be us'd like a *Rake*, and will pick four Teeth at once. He has *Diogenes* Lanthorn, which he carry'd about *Athens* at Nooon day to seek for an Honest-man. He says he has some of *Heraclitus*'s Tears, which drop'd from him in a hard Winter, and are Frozen into Christal; they are set in a Locket, and every time any body looks upon it, they cannot forbear Weeping. Also a Tenpenny Nail drawn out of the *Ark*; and tho' it's Iron, toss it into a Tub of Water, and 'twill Swim like a Feather, He pretends to have one of

C

Judas's

Judas's Thirty Pence; and every time he looks upon't, he is ready to Hang himself. A mighty Collection of these sort of Trinkets, he tells the World he's Master of, and some give Credit to his Ridiculous Romances.

Mind that Spark who is just come in, Four Years since his Reputation was but slender; and in so little a time he has had Three Wives, and all good Fortunes to him, and now is look'd upon to be Worth Ten Thousand Pounds. 'Tis observ'd, said I, that Money is thrown into the very Mouths of Fortunes Minions: and some Men must grow Rich, if all the lucky accidents that Chance can give, will make them so. My Friend in pursuance to this particular, express'd himself to this purpose, That he believ'd there was some foul Play practic'd, because (says he) it is a thing so common in this City, for a Man to grow Rich by plurality of Wives, and send them one after another so Methodically to the Grave, as if he had a flight of Transferring them to another World, a little before their time: For I must confess, says he, I know an *Apothecary*, who if a Man will trust him with the Care of his Family, once in a Twelve months time he'll take an opportunity to do him such a piece of Service, if he gives him but the least item of his slender affections towards his *Help-mate*. And I have often heard him say, That Women are always the best Patients, especially if they die under his hands; for then, says he, let me make never so unreasonable a Bill, it's never disputed, but generously satisfied, with as good a will as a Married Man pays the Tax for the Birth of his first Child, or an Extravagant Heir the Charges of his Fathers Funeral.

Mind the little Blade in the Cloak, that's talking to a *Parson*; he's a *Bookseller* in this City, and has got an *Estate* by *Starving* of *Authors*. I'll warrant you the *Priest* has been Conjuring his Brains together, and has rais'd some wonderful Work to the Churches Glory and his own Fame. He has been providing a *Scourge* for the *Popes Jacket*, or a *Cudgel* for Antichrist; or else a mess of good *Protestant Porridge* to scald the Mouth of an Unbeliever; or some such business. But as to the *Wit-monger*, I'll tell you he's as honest a man as ever betray'd his Trust, or built his own Welfare upon the hazard of anothers Ruine; He was appointed Trustee for a Young Gentlewoman, and had the Charge of an *Estate* of between two or Three Hundred Pounds *Per Annum*, which he has very carefully secured to himself, by Marrying her to his Prentice, and obliging him upon that consideration to buy his Stock; whereby he became well paid for a great deal of *Waste-Paper*: So he is crept into the *Estate*, and they are got into his Books for it. There is abundance of such sort of *Plain dealing* practicable amongst our worthy Citizens; for you must know they do not always tell truth in their Shops, or get their Estates by their Honesty.

Being half Choak'd with the Steem that arose from their *Soot-colour'd Ninny-Broth*, their stinking Breaths, and Suffocating Fumes of their Nasty *Puffing Engines*, my Friend and I paid for our *Mahometan Gruel*, and away we came; and passing along *Leaden-hall-street*, I saw some Ships Painted upon the outside of a great Wall, which occasion'd me to enquire of my School-fellow what place that was? He told me 'twas the House
belonging

belonging to the *East-India Company*, which are a Corporation of Men with Long Heads and Deep Purses; who had purchas'd that with their Money, that no-Body ought to sell; and dealt in those Commodities to get Money, which it's pity any-Body should Buy. They are very Rich in *England*, and very Poor in the *Indies*. Were a *Schedule* of their *Effects* Drawn on one side, and their *Indian Debts* Scor'd on the other, it is believ'd more Bad Debts would arise upon the Reverse, Then are due to Trades-Men from all the Persons of Quality in Town, or perhaps then were ever found owing to either Army or Navy; which they have neither Will to Pay, or Power to Satisfy, to the great Honour of *Christianity* in so *Heathenish* a Country. There are two Companys now, and it's greatly hop'd by many honest Traders and Merchants in the City, that they may luckily prove the Breaking of each other; both have sent Ships to the *Indies*, and 'tis thought they will give one another a warm Salutation by the way, and maintain the Truth of the old Proverb, *That Two of a Trade can never agree.*

Pray take Notice (says my Friend) of that Gentleman that is steping into his Coach, I will tell you a pretty Story of him: There was a Poor Woman, not far from this Place, who Sold Earthen-ware, and had lately the good Fortune to have a Rich Relation Die, and leave her worth Forty Thousand Pounds; which he Hearing on (tho' a Man of Considerable Quality) thought it a Bait worth Snapping at; in order to which, he became one of her earliest Suitors, and was very Importunate with her to have the *Cracking* of her *Pipkin*; but she soon gave him a Repulse, and told him, Man was an *Earthen Vessel,* too brittle for her to deal in; and she had heard he had a great many *Flaws* in his *Fortune,* which she would not be at the expence of mending; and since she had never Receiv'd any Testimonials of his Affection before the happy Change of her Condition, she had Reasons to believe his desires tended to her *Money,* and not her *Person,* and therefore would not be made a *Lady* at so great an Expence. Adding his pretensions would be ineffectual, and hop'd he would give himself no further Trouble; assuring him, as her *Mind* was *Steadfast,* so would his *Pains* be *Fruitless.* Upon which, he feign'd a Melancholy humour; and Sighing like a Man at his *Wives Funeral,* told her his *Passion* was so great for her, that unless she gave him a more satisfactory answer, he would Drown himself in the *Tower-Ditch.* To which she reply'd, smiling, Perhaps, Sir, you propose that to your self which is not in your Power to do, you know not but Heaven has Decreed for you a *Dryer Destiny.* Upon which, he rose in a great Passion, crying, *Zounds, Madam! Do you think I'll Hang my self?* and so departed.

Now, says my School-fellow, we'll spend the Evening in a chearful Glass; here's a *Tavern* hard by, where a parcel of pleasant Companions of my acquaintance use, we'll see what diversion we can find in their Society. Accordingly we stept in, and in the Kitchen found half a dozen of my Friends Associates, in the height of their Jollity, as Merry as so many *Cantabrigians* at *Sturbridge-Fair,* or *Coblers* at a *Crispins Feast.* After a Friendly Salutation, free from all Foppish Ceremonies, down we sat; and when a Glass or Two round had given fresh Motion to our drowsy Spirits, and abandon'd all those careful Thoughts which makes Man's Life uneasie, Wit begot Wit, and Wine a Thirsty Appetite to each Succeeding

Glass:

Glaſs: Then open were our Hearts, and Unconfin'd our *Fancies*; my Friend and I contributing our Mites to add to the Treaſure of our Felicity. *Songs* and *Catches* crown'd the Night, and each Man in his Turn pleas'd his Ears with his own Harmony. Amongſt the reſt, we had one *Song* againſt *Muſick*, which, becauſe of it's being the firſt *Eſſay* in that Nature, I have thought it worth Inſerting.

A Song againſt *Muſick.*

MUSICK'S a Crotchet, the Sober think Vain;
　　The *Fiddle*'s a Wooden Projection;
Tunes are but flirts of a Whimſical Brain,
　　Which the Bottle brings beſt to Perfection.
Muſicians are Half-Witted, Merry, and Mad;
　　The ſame are all thoſe that admire 'em;
They're Fools if they Play, unleſs they're well Paid;
　　And the other are Block-heads to Hire-'em.

Chorus.

The *Organ*'s but Humming,
Theorbo but Thrumming,
The *Viol* and Voice
Is but Jingle and Noiſe,
The *Bagpipe* and *Fiddle*,
Goes Twedle and Diddle,
The *Hoit-boy* and *Flute*
Is but Toot a Toot Toot,
Your *Scales* and your *Cliffs*, Keys, Moodes, and dull Rules,
Are fit to pleaſe none but Madmen and Fools.

The Novelty of this Whimſie gave great Diverſion to the whole Company, except one, who was deſign'd by Nature a *Poet*, but having Fortune to his Nurſe, the Blind Maulkin, careleſs of her charge, dropt him from her Lap, bruis'd the Noddle of the tender Babe, and made his Fancy Ricketty; numb'd his Faculties, and ſo Eclips'd his Genius, that he dwindled into a *Muſician.*

Who being as angry as a *Tom-Turd-Man*, to hear his Profeſſion ſo diſparag'd, reſolv'd immediate Revenge upon the Author; calls for Pen and Ink, and went to work with as much Eagerneſs and Inveteracy as a *Parſon*, when he Writes an order to his *Attorney* to ſue a Pariſhoner for neglected Tythes. After ſome intervals of deliberation (wherein he ſat like a *Vertuoſa* at a *Philoſophical Lecture*) this following Crotchet ſtarted from his Brain, like *Æſops*-Mouſe from the Mountain, to the great Laughter of the whole Company.

A

A Song, by a *Musician* against *Poetry*.

POetry's Fabulous, Loose, and Prophane;
    For Truth you muſt never depend-on't;
It's Juvenal Froth of a Frenzical Brain,
    Hung with Jingling Tags at the end-on't.
Poets are poor, full of Whimſie and Flight,
    For Amorous Fops to delight in;
They're Fools if they Write, leſt they get Money by't,
    And they're Block-heads that pay 'em for Writing.

Chorus.

    Their ſoft *Panegyric*
    Is *Praiſe* beyond Merit;
    Their *Lampoon* and *Satyr*,
    Is *Spight* and *Ill-nature*;
    Their *Plays* and *Romances*,
    Are *Fables* and *Fancies*;
    Their *Drolls* and their *Farſes*,
    Are bald as our *Arſes*;
Their *Figures* and *Similies* only are fit,
To pleaſe the Dull Fool that gives Money for Wit.

This rais'd amongſt the whole Society ſuch an Evil Spirit of *Poetry*, That it began to have as much Power over us, as the *Devil* has over a gang of *Lapland* Witches. We now *(Ovid-*like*)* were ſo highly inſpir'd, we could ſcarce ſpeak without Rhyme and Meaſure; and ev'ry one, like a Country Fellow at a *Foot-Ball-Meeting*, was for ſhowing what he could do, or telling what he had done. Amongſt which, theſe follow-ing Verſes were lug'd out of a *Pocket-Library*, Written upon this Occa-ſion, as the Author inſinuated to the Company, That being bleſt with the Converſation of ſome Young Ladies, and one whoſe Wit and Beauty were aſpiring above the reſt, knowing he had ſome little fancy in Poe-try, told him ſhe took it very unkindly of him, that he never thought her worthy of his Muſes Notice. To which he reply'd, That he was at all times provided to oblige ſo Fair a Lady. Adding, If ſhe would be Pleas'd to lend him a Pen and Ink, he would take a Copy of her Perfections whilſt ſhe was there ready to ſit for her Picture; which ſhe very nimbly plac'd upon the Table, with a pleaſing expectancy of being at leaſt Flat-ter'd to her great Glory, as well as Satisfaction. Upon which, he Oblig'd her with theſe following Lines.

MAdam, how great and good your Vertues are,
    I can't well tell, nor truly do I care;
Nor can that Wit, which you from Plays have ſtole,
Admired be by any, but a Fool;   **D**   Who

Who may perhaps, thro' his weak Judgment, own
That you have *Sence*, 'cause he himself has none
Believe, I no such wrong Opinion hold;
I can discern false *Metal*, from true *Gold*.
Your Ill-tim'd Jests, so sharp in your Conceit,
Are spoild, for want of Judgment to Repeat;
Like an unskilful *Play'r* who lames each Line,
Which by the *Poet* Read, or Spoke, is fine.

If you have Wit, which you can boast your own,
Let it in some return to this be shown;
Or I, (Proud Lady fair) shall Justly think you've none.

    This he presented to the Lady, who upon the first glance, Blush'd at her Disappointment; run into her Closet, fir'd with Indignation and Revenge, soon shewing the pregnancy of her Wit, by the speediness of her Answer, which I have also given you.

TWO lively Figures, in one Piece you've shown,
    A True bred *Poet*, and an ill bred *Clown*:
Vertues not understood by you, I boast;
Such that in our Weak Sex are valu'd most;
As Truth, Good-nature, Manners, tho' not Wit;
Graces that never Crown'd a *Poet* yet.
To rail at a Weak Woman is a strain,
Does little Merit in its Wit contain,
It may be like a Scribler, but unlike a Man.
A Self opinion from your Lines I'll raise,
And Fancy you discover'd in my Face
Vertues beyond your Reach, and so above your Praise;
As envious *Beggars* spightfully disdain,
And rail at Blessings which they can't obtain.

    Tho' I'm abus'd, yet I'll good Natur'd be,
And beg for once you'll take Advice by me;
Much rather let your Wit in silence rest
Than lose a Friend, or Mistress, for a Jest:
Mix Manners and Good Nature with your Parts
And you'll deserve more Thanks, and win more Hearts.

    This being the product of a Female Genius, was very much admir'd by our whole assembly of *Poetasters*, who are always so favourable to the *Fair Sex*, to seem as much opinionated of what they Write, as a *Fond Father* is of the *Witty Sayings* of his own Progeney: It being as natural for a *Poet* to Doat upon *Woman*, as 'tis for a *Hound* to love *Horse-Flesh*. And I must confess when ever we rail at 'em, it is more for their *Vertues* than their *Vices*;
for

for the latter we are are as busie to seduce them to, as the rest of our Neighbours; and are very angry with them, but for denying us what they impart to others; or when by their Prudence they secure that Treasure to themselves, at which we want to be Nibling. A pretty Woman is but a piece of Heavens *Poetry*, wherein as many Changes are to be seen, as in *Ovids Metamorphosis*; And when ever she's attempted to be Read by our Earthly Sons of *Apollo*, she is found a Crabbed piece, and the measure of her *Verse* too long for Humane Scanning.

Another in the Company, being willing to Contribute something to our Mirth and Pastime, communicated to the Board this Poem in Manuscript, writ by a Fellow in *Bedlam*, who run Mad thro' Ambition, and fancy'd himself a *King*; but not being contented with the *Government* of his Sublunary Dominions, was Ambitious (as you will find by his *Lunatick Raptures*) of Conquering larger Territories above the Moon, or some where whither his Frenzy led him. Therefore as *Poetick Pill-Maker* says in his Learned Works, *Read, Try, Judge, and Speak as you find.*

The Madmans Flight

COuld I the Scepter of Heaven sway,
   And make Dame Nature my Commands obey,
The Ocean I'd Unbound, and Quench the Fiery Day.
Fearing no Thunder could from *Jove* be hurl'd,
I'd then in Darkness Ravage thro' the World:
Till met by Devils in Amazing throngs,
Who Poking stand with their Infernal Prongs;
Shrieking like Souls opprest, I'd bid 'em come;
And stare so fierce, I'd brazen out my Doom;
Knowing my Soul is too Divine an Air
For Fiends or Devils to torment or tear.
I'd forwards Press, and to repulse their Aim,
Would drive those Hellish Tribes from whence they came:

   Then mount to Heaven and kindle up the Sun
To see what Mischiefs I on Earth had done.
Behold, like Cruel Tyrants, with Delight
The Crimson Ills that stain'd the Sable Night.
My Power, like theirs, I'd build on others Fate;
And Glory in Black Deeds that made me Great.
When I thro' all the Purple Crimes had run,
That could be by Unbounded Greatness done,
Then the bright Chariot of the Sun I'd Seize,
And drive it where my God-like Soul should please.

   The Moon would I compel to be my Guide;
Thus Splendidly thro' Heaven would I ride,
There huff and strut, and kick the Gods aside.

In

In my Careir my Fury to expose,
I'd caft down Stars upon the heads of thofe
Whom either *Fate* or *Choice* had my Foes.

    And then the *Demons* of the Air to fcare,
The Clouds in fundry pieces would I tare,
And puff 'em up like Bubbles in the Air:
I'd joftle Clouds, Heavens Harmony confound,
And make each Flaming Orb dance nimbly round.
If any bold *Olympian* Cent'nel dare
Queftion my Office, or my Bufinefs there,
Or if againft me offer to Rebel,
I'd grafp his Air, and ftrike him down to Hell.

    Thus by Degrees would I the Gods Unthrone,
Till Heaven fhould at laft become my own.
Then to demolifh Earth's infernal Crew,
I'd Damn this Old World, and Create a New.

    This Frantick piece of Bombaft pleas'd wonderfully: No *Prophane Jeft*
to an *Atheift*, or *Bawdy Story* to an *Old Batchelour*, could have been more acceptable.   One commended the Loftinefs of the Fancy , another the Apt-
nefs of the Language; a Third the Smoothnefs of the Verfe; that the
Madman had like to have run away with the *Bays* from us all, had not one in
the Company been an *Author* in *Print*, to the great applaufe of the whole
Nation, who if he would have worn as much *Bays* as the common vogue
of the People has given him the Title to, his Head would have appear'd as
fine as a *Country Cafement* in the midft of *Chriftmas-Holydays*.

    By this time the Nimble Spirits of the reviving Juice, had fufficiently
enliven'd the Nobleft of our Faculties; and had feiz'd our Brains as their
proper Throne, to hold a Soveraign fway over the Dominions of the Flefh:
Driving out weak Reafon by a Power invifible, and making her become a
Subject till the next Morning.

    My Friend and I thought it high time to take our Leaves, which after
the Payment of our Clubs, we did accordingly, agreeing to give our felves
the Pleafure of two or three hours Ramble in the Streets.   Having fpent
the time at the *Tavern* till about Ten a Clock with Mirth and Satisfaction,
we were now defirous of prying into the dark Intrigues of the Town, to
experiment what Paftime the Night-Accidents, the Whims and Frolicks
of *Staggering Bravado's* and *Stroling Strumpets*, might afford us. An Account
of which we fhall give you in our next.

                         F I N I S.

THE
LONDON
SPY.

PART II.

By the Author of the Trip *to* JAMAICA.

𝔗𝔥𝔢 𝔗𝔥𝔦𝔯𝔡 𝔈𝔡𝔦𝔱𝔦𝔬𝔫.

LONDON,
Printed and Sold by *J. How,* in the *Ram-Head-Inn-Yard*
in *Fanchurch-Street,* 1701.

TO THE

READER.

PRefaces are now become so Common to every little Treatise, that I wonder there is not one to the Horn-Book. And indeed oftentimes, like Womens Faces, are found the most Promising and Inviting part of the whole Piece. But when a thing is usual, tho' never so Rediculous in the Eye of Reason, yet a Man, like him that spoiles his Stomach with a mess of Porridge before Dinner, may Plead Custom to excuse his Errour. I therefore hope it will be no offence to conform with others, and show my self a Fool in Fashion.

Some Authors are meer Beaus in Writing; and Dress up each Maggotty Flirt, that creeps from their Mouldy Fancy, with a fine Dedication, tho' to John-a-Nokes; and a long Preface to a little Matter, like an Aldermans Grace to a Scholar's Commons, thinking their Pigmy Products look as Naked without these Ornaments, as a Puritan without his Band, or a Whore without her Patches.

For my part I only use this preamble, as a Sow-Gelder does his Horn, that as by hearing of the latter, you may give a shrewed guess at his Business, so by reading of the former, you may rightly understand my Design, which I assure you in the first place, is not to Affront or Expose any body, for all that I propose is to scourge Vice and Villany, without level-
ing

To the Reader.

ing Characters at any Person in particular. But if any unhappy Sinner, thro' the Guilt of his own Conscience, shall prove himself such an Ass, to take that Burthen upon his own Shoulders, which Hundreds in the Town have as much Right to bear as himself, he has no reason to be Angry with me, but may Thank himself, or his Destiny, for making his tender Back so fit for the Pack-Saddle.

The first part of this Undertaking I pop'd into the cautious World, as a Skilful Angler does a new Bait among wary Fish, who have oft been prick'd in their Nibbling; and finding the Publick Snapping at it with as much Greediness as a News-monger at a Gazett, or a City Politician at a new Proclamation, makes me purpose to continue it Monthly, as long as we shall find Encouragement.

When I have taken a compleat Survey of the most remarkable Places, as well as the common Vanities and Follies of Mankind, both by Day and Night, I question not but the World will find it a Useful, as well as Diverting History. Wherein Young Gentlemen may see the Vices of the Town, without their dangerous experience; and learn the better to avoid those Snares, and practicable Subtleties, which Trappen many to their Ruin. In order to expose these the dark Misteries of Iniquity, in so Corrupt an Age, we have projected this Monthly Journal, as the best method we could take, which I hope all will Read with Pleasure, and some make profitable to themselves.

THE

THE
LONDON
SPY.

Ccording to the Wisdom of our Fore-fathers, we have craftily taken the Old Gentleman by the Fore-lock; for tho' we thought it Ten a Clock when we left the Blessings of dear *Hymen*'s Palace, yet, by the Night, it prov'd but the *Misers* Bed-time. The Modest Hour of Nine being now proclaim'd by *Times Oracle* from every *Steeple*; and the Joyful alarum of *Bow-Bell* call'd the weary Apprentices from their Work to their Paring-shovels, to Uhich their *Folded Shutters*, and Button up their *Lying Sanctuaries*, their Shops, till the next Morning, wherein there are more *Untruths* asserted in one day, then *False Oaths* taken in *Westminster-Hall* in a whole Term. Their Masters having more Canting Reservations to indemnifie their Consciences from the danger of Deceitful Protestations, than an Old Strumpet or a Plot Evidence; being more afraid of *Breaking*, than they are of *Damning*; for indeed, that Trader thinks he has made but an Ill Market that cannot safe himself.

The Streets were all adorn'd with dazling Lights, whose bright reflects so glitter'd in my Eyes, that I could see nothing but themselves. Thus walk'd amaz'd, like a wandering Soul in its Pilgrimage to Heaven, when he passes thro' the Spangled Regions.

My Ears were Serenaded on every side, with the Grave Musick of sundry *Passing Bells*, the ratling of Coaches, and the melancholly Ditties of hot bak'd *Wardens* and *Pippins*, that had I had as many Eyes as *Argos*, and as many Ears as *Fame*, they would have been all confounded, for nothing could I see but *Light*, and nothing hear but *Noise*.

We had not walk'd the usual distance between a *Church* and an *Ale-House*, but some Odoriferous *Civet-Box* perfum'd the Air; and saluted our Nostrils with so refreshing a Nose-gay, that I thought the whole City (*Edenborough* like) had been over-flow'd with an inundation of

B   Surrever-

Surreverence. By and by came thundering by us a rumbling Engine, in the Dark, which I took for a *Dead-mongers* Waggon, laden with a Stinking *Corps,* by reason of long keeping, driving Post-haste to the next Church-Yard, in order for interment: But was soon undeceiv'd by my Friend, who told me 'twas a *Gold-finders* Caravan, carrying Treasure to their *Land-bank* by the *Salt-Peter-Houses.* The Projectors of which Notable design (says my Friend) have at no small expence, discover'd the Fallacy of an old Proverb, and can (be your leave Sir) by found Reason and true Experience deny *Shitten Luck to be good Luck.* For after Two or Three Thousand Pounds disbursment, to turn a *T——d* into *Gunpowder,* they found their Project would not signifie a *Fart.* Which if their designing Noddles could have brought to perfection, our *Foes* then, like *Themselves* now, would have doubtless been in a very Stinking Condition.

As we stumbled along, my Friend bid me take Notice of a Shop, wherein sat three or four very provoking Damsels, with as much Velvet on their Backs, as would have made a *Burying-Pall* for a *Country-Parish,* or a *Holy-day Coat* for a *Physitian;* being Glorify'd at bottom with Gold Fringes, that I thought at first they might be Parsons Daughters, who had Borrow'd their Fathers *Pulpet-Cloths,* to use as Scarfs, to go a Visiting in; each with as many Patches in her *Market-Place,* as are *Spots* in a *Leopards* Skin, or *Freckles* in the Face of a *Scotch-man.*

I ask'd my Friend what he took them for, who answerd, They were a kind of First Rate *Punks* by their Riging, of about a Guinea purchase. I further queried, what reasons he had to believe them to be *Leachery Layers.* He reply'd, because they were siting in a *Head-Dressers Shop;* which, says he, is as seldom to be found without a *Whore,* as a *Bookfellers-Shop* in *Paul's* Church-Yard without a *Parson.*

Come, says my Friend, we'll call here hard by, at the *Widows Coffee-House,* and Drink a Dish or two, I have some Female Patients that use the House, who are a little in my Debt; and if the Lewdness of the Town has thrown a *Cully* in their way, they may chance to be able to make me Satisfaction.

Accordingly we blunder'd thro' a long dark Entry of an Ancient *Fabrick;* groping our way, like Subteranean Labourers in the Caverns of a Colepit, till we found the Stairs, which were rais'd as perpendicular as a Tilers Ladder, that had I not had the use of a Rope, which was nail'd along the Wall, as a Clue to Guide me, I cou'd have climb'd a Country May-pole, or have crawl'd up the Buttock-shrouds of one of his Majesties First Rates with less danger and difficulty. At last an old Weather-beaten *Cerberus* came to the Stair-head with a Candle, which to me was as wellcome as a Link in a dark Night to a stumbling Drunkard, or Moon-shine (when near Land) to a doubtful Mariner, saluting us with *Lord Gentlemen, why did you not call to be Lighted up? I protest, I thought there had been a Candle upon the Stairs, but my careless Baggage is so Lazy, she minds nothing as she should do; she's but lately come out of the Country, and runs staring about like a* Bumkin *in* Paul's Church, *or a* Libertine *in a* Conventicle.

With

With this fort of Talk fhe ufher'd us into the *Coffee-Room*; where, at the Corner of a long Table, next to her Elbow-Chair, lay a large old *Bible* open, with her Spectacles upon it; next to it a *Quarten-Pot*, two or three *Stone-Bottles*, a *Rowl* of *Plaster*, and a *Pip* of *Tobacco*, a *Handful* of *Fire* in a *Rusty Grate*, with a *Pint Coffee-Pot* before it, and a *Green Earthen Chamber-Pot* in the *Chimney-Corner*. Over the mantle Tree, Two *Bastard-dishes*, a *Patch-box* and a *Surreng*. On a little fhelf, amongst Viols and Galley-pots, half a dozen long Bottles of *Rosa Solis*; with an Advertifement of a rare *White-wash* for the *Face*, nail'd on one fide; and a brief account of the excellencies of Doctor *John C——fe*'s Pills for the Speedy Cure of a virulent *Gonorhea*, without lofs of Time, or hindrance of Bufinefs, on the other; a *Soldiers Simitar*, *Musket*, and *Cattooch-box*; behind the Door, a *Head-dreffers Block*, and a *Quart-Pot* (as terrible as a *Deaths-Head*, and an *Hour-glafs*) ftood frightfully in the Window. Alfo an old fafhon'd *Clock* in a *Cafe*, but as filent as a *Corps* in a *Coffin*. Next which hung the Reverend Print of the *feven Golden Candlestick*; and againft that a *Commode*, adorn'd with a Scar-let Top-knot, under it an Abftract of the Acts of Parliament againft *Drink-ing*, *Swearing*, and all manner of *Prophannefs*. A broken *Floor*, like an old *Stable*, Windows mended with *Brown-Paper*; and bare walls full of Duft and Cobwebs.

After I had walk'd about, and taken a compleat view of this antiquated *Sodom*, I fat my felf down; but of a fuddain felt fuch a trembling in the *Fa-brick*, that the Windows Jar'd, the *Fire-Irons* Jingled, in fhort all things in the Room feem'd to be in Motion, and kept time, with a tinkling noife, like a *Tambrel* in a *Moores Dance*; that had I not been furnifh'd with fome rea-fons to fufpect the contrary, I fhould have been under the frightful appre-henfions of an *Earthquake*. But in a little time the violent pulfation, that had given an *Ague* to the whole Houfe, was over, and all things were again reconcil'd to their former reft. Prefently after came down Stairs, from a loftier Apartment, referv'd for *Private Ufes*, a couple of Airy Youths; who, by their *Crop'd Hair*, *Stone Buckles* in their *Shooes*, Broad *Gold Hat-bands*, and no *Swords*, I took to be *Merchants Sons*, or the *Apprentices* of topping *Traders*. They ftay'd not above a minute in the Coffee-Room, but, Magpie like, ask'd what's a Clock? Then made their Honours after the neweft Fafhion, and fo departed.

My Friend by this time (knowing the Entertainment of the Houfe) had call'd for a Bottle of *Cock-Ale*, of which I tafted a Glafs, but could not con-ceive it to be any thing but a Mixture of *Small-Beer* and *Treacle*. If this be *Cock-Ale*, faid I, e'en let *Cocks-Combs* Drink it. Prithee give me a Glafs of *Brandy*, or fomething that will dart *Lightening* into my *Spirits*, and not fill my *Guts* with *Thunder*. With that the Reverend Doctrifs of Debauchery (after fhe had approv'd my choice, with a chearful fmile) fignified her Sympathifing Appetite, in thefe words, *Sir, you are of my mind, I think there's nothing like a dram of true* Nantes, *or fome fuch-like Comfortable Cor-dial; of the former indeed I have none, by reafon of its Scarcity, but I have an excellent Diftillation of my own preparing, which fome call* Aqua Veneris: *It will reftore an old Man of Threefcore, to the Juvenallity of Thirty, or make a Girl at Fourteen, with Drinking but one Glafs, as ripe as an old Maid of Four and Twenty. 'Twill make a Parfon Dance* Sallingers-round, *a Pu-ritan Luft after the Flefh, and a Married Man Oblige his Wife oftener in*

one

one *Night*, than without it he shall be able to do in *Seven*, I sell it to most *Citizens Wives* in *Town*, who are seldom without it in their *Closets*, to oblige their *Husbands* or *Gallants*. For tho' I say it, that should not, it's the best *Cordial* to strengthen a weak *Appetite*, drank a little before *Bed-time*, in the *World*. Here, *Priscilla*, *bring the Gentleman a Quartan*. Just as a Cup of *Corroboration* was moving round, who should bolt down Stairs from Fools Paradise above, but a couple of *Mortal Angels*, as nimble as Squirrels, with Looks as sharp, and Eyes as piercing as a *Tygers*; who, I suppose, after rumpling their Feathers in a hot engagement, had staid to rectifie their disorder'd Plumes, and make ready for a fresh Encounter: They presently saluted my Friend, as the *Devil* did Doctor *Edwards*, with your Servant Doctor. He return'd their Complement, and desir'd their Company; which they as readily Granted, as a Fortuneless *Jilt* her consent to Matrimony, or a poor *Sholar* his Company to a Treat.

By the help of *Paint*, *Powder*, and *Patches*, they were of a Wax-work Complexion: And thus drest, their under-Petticoats were *White Dimity* Flourished, like a *Turkey-work Chair*, or a *Fools Dublet*, with *Red*, *Green*, *Blew*, and *Yellow*. Their *Pin-up Coats* of *Scotch Plads*, adorn'd with *Bugle Lace*; and *Gowns* of Printed *Callico*: But their Heads drest up to as much advantage as a *Vintners Bar-keeper*, or a *Parsons Wife* upon an *Easter-Sunday*. These I suppose, Devil like, would play at small Game rather than stand out; and sooner condescend to the acceptance of a Shilling, then want Imployment.

By that time we had sip'd off our Nipperkin of my Grannums *Aqua Mirabilis*, our Airy Ladies grew so very *Mercurial*, they no longer could contain their feign'd *Modesty*, but launc'd out into their accustomary Wantonness; and show'd us as many whimsical Figaries, and diverting Pranks, as a young *Monkey* with a *Mouse* at his Tail, or an *Owl* upon a *Duck's* Back in the Water.

This Familiarity encourag'd my Friend to a further freedom, who took the boldness upon him to ask her if Trading had been so good of late, that she could pay the arrears due upon her last Misfortune. To which she reply'd, *The Lord confound your Devices, for a Twat Scouring Pimp, I owe you none till the breaking out of the next Fire. Did not I agree with you, when first we dealt together, to pay you one Cure under another; and therefore the last is not due till I next want your assistance? Pray Mr.* Emplastrum *don't you come that upon me neither, for I am sure I have paid you hitherto as generously as any Patient of my Quality that ever you gave* Pill *or* Bolus *to; and have done you, and your Profession, as much Service as any of my Function that Trades between* Aldgate *and* Temple-Barr. *You know when I was in keeping, I let you have Money to redeem your* Plaster-Box, *when I ow'd you not a Groat; and I have had nothing in return of my Kindness, as I know on, but a little* Roman Vitriol *for a Shanker, or a piece of* Orrice-root *for my Issue; therefore you need not be so sharp with me neither.*

This Impudence so silenc'd my Friend, that he look'd as Tame as a *City Cuckold* chid by his Wife; and as Dumb as a Statue: Being glad to appease her fury by calling for 'tother Quartan, which before we had Drank, who should grovel up Stairs, but, seemingly, a Sober Citizen, in

Cloke

Cloke and *Band*, about the Age of *Sixty*. Upon which the old *Mother* of the *Maids*, call'd hastily to *Priss*, and whispering ask'd her if there were any *Rods* in the House. I sitting just by, over-heard the Question: The Wench answer'd, *Yes, yes, You know I fetch'd six Penny worth but Yesterday*. Upon the Entrance of this grave *Formicater*, our Ladies with-drew themselves from our Company, and retir'd, like *Modest Virgins*, to their Secret Work-room of Iniquity; and left the old *Sinner*, in the *Winter* of his *Leachery*, to warm his *Grey-hairs* with a dram of Invigorating Cordial; whilst we pay'd our Reckoning, were lighted down Stairs, and left the Lustful *Satyr* (to the shame of his Age) a Prey to the two Strumpets; who, I believe, found himself in a much worse Condition then a *Breech* between two *Stools*, or *Lot* in *Sodom*, between the Merry Cracks his Buxom Daughters.

Time now, like a skilful Gamster, had just nick'd Seven; and each Parochial *Jack* of *Lanthorn*, was croaking about Streets the hour of Eleven. The Brawny Topers of the City began now to forsake the Tavern, and Stagger, haulking, after a *Poop-Lanthorn*, to their own Houses. *Augusta* appear'd in her Mourning-weeds; and the glittering *Lamps* which a few Hours before, sparkled like *Diamonds*, fix'd as Ornaments to her Sable Dress, were now dwindled to a glimmering *Snuff*, and burnt as dim as Torches at a Prince's Funeral. Strumpets in the Streets were grown a scarce Commodity, for the danger of the *Counter* had drove them home to their own poor sinful Habitations; where nothing Dwells but *Shame, Poverty* and *Misery*, the *Devil* and *Themselves*.

We now were at a stand which way to move; at last my Companion propos'd the *Dark-houses* at *Billings-gate*: Where, he told me, we need not question, amongst the various humours of the *Maritime Mobility*, but to find abundance of Diversion. Besides, when our Faculties should grow tired with our Pastime, and Nature, for the Refreshment of our drowsie *Microcosms*, should require rest, we could there have the conveniency of a Bed to repose our weary Members.

Accordingly we thither steer'd our Course; and by the way, I ask'd him what was the meaning when the *Old Leacher* came into the Coffee-Room, that *Mother Beelzebub* ask'd the Wench whether they had any *Rods* in the House? He smil'd at my Question; and told me he believ'd he should discover a new Vice to me which I scarce had heard of.

That Sober seeming Saint, says he, is one of that Classis in the Black School of *Sodomy*, who are call'd by Learned Students in the Science of Debauchery, *Flogging Cullies*. This unnatural Beast gives Money to those Strumpets which you see, and they down with his Breeches, and Scourge his Privities till they have laid his Leachery. He all the time begs their Mercy, like an Offender at a Whipping-Post, and beseeches their forbearance; but the more importunate he seems for their favourable usage, the severer Vapulation they are to exercise upon him, till they find by his Beastly Extasie, when to with-hold their Weapons.

We had not proceeded far towards our intended Harbour, but at the door of an Eminent Shop-keeper in *Grace-Church-street*, we heard, as we thought, the unsavory Squallings of some *Nocturnal Revellers*, call'd *Cats*, Summoning with their untunable *Bagpipes*, the Neighbouring *Mouse-hunters* to their merry meeting. But by the help of a Watchmans Lanthorn, who met us in our Passage, we discover'd a Hand-Basket; from whence we conceiv'd proceeded this ingrateful Discord. *Hey day*, says the Watchman, *What, in the Name of the Stars, have we got Here? The unhappy Fruits of*

some

some Bodies Labours I'll warrant you, who had rather get ten Bastards than Provide for one. He opens the Wicker Hammock, and finds a little lump of Mortality crying out to the whole Parish to lend him their assistance: With this Inscription, Written in a fair Hand, pin'd upon his Breast.

I was got by an Honest Poor Man,
    Who Sails in his Majesties Service ;
My Mother is call'd Whore Nan,
The Name of my Father is Jervice.
My Fathers first Letter is J,
    My Mothers with N does begin,
They put them together to try
    What it Spelt, and 'twas Luckily In.
Thus was I conceiv'd in Sin,
    There's no Body got without ;
And tho' I went Sinfully in,
    The Iniquity's now come out.
Have Mercy upon me I Pray ;
    And carry me out of the Weather,
For all that my Mother can say,
    The Parish must be my Father.

The unusualness of such a *Posie,* upon so unwelcome a *Present,* made us as Merry as a young *Comedian* over a *Lame Jest,* or a *Constable* at a *Bellmans* Verse. The Watch-man cough'd up a Phthisical Hem, as a Signal to his Associates of some Mischance, which was soon convey'd from one to t'other, till it alarm'd the Leader of the *Hour-grunters,* who soon came up, attended with his Twinkling Guard of *Superannuated Sauce-boxes ;* and presently *Saddled* his *Nose* with a pair of Glass'd Horns, to read the Superscription, and see to whom the *Squaling Packet,* was directed. But when he found the poor Infant lay driveling upon a whole Slabbering-bib of Verses, *Alack, alack,* says Father Midnight, *I'll warrant 'tis some poor Poets Bastard, Prithee take it up and lets carry it to the Watch-house Fire. Who knows, but by the Grace of Providence, the Babe may come to be a second* Ben Johnson *? Prithee* Jeffery *put the Lappit of thy Coat over it, I'll warrant 'tis so cold it can scarce feel whether 'tis a Boy or a* Girl. Away troop'd his Dark Majesty, with his Feeble Band of Crippled Parish Pensioners, to their Nocturnal Rendezvouz, all tick'l'd with the Jest, and as Merry over their hopeful Foundling, as the *Egyptian* Queen over her young Prophet in the Rushes.

We blunder'd on in pursuit of our Nights Felicity, but scarce had walk'd the length of a Horses Tedder, e'er we heard a Noise so dreadful and surprizing, That we thought the Devil was riding on Hunting thro' the City with a Pack of deep-mouth'd Hell-hounds, to catch a Brace of *Tally-men* for Breakfast. At last bolted out from the corner of a Street, with an *Ignis Fatuus* Dancing before them, a parcel of strange *Hobgoblins* cover'd with long Frize Rugs and Blankets, hoop'd round with Leather Girdles from their Crupers to their Shoulders ; and their Noddles button'd up into Caps of a Martial figure, like a *Night Errant* at Tilt and Turnament, with his Wooden-head lock'd into an Iron Helmet ; one Arm'd, as I thought, with a lusty *Faggot Bat,* and the rest with strange Wooden Weapons in their hands in the shape of *Clyster Pipes ;* but as long, almost, as *Speaking-Trumpets.* Of a sudden they Clap'd them to their Mouths, and made such a frightful Yelling, that I thought the World had been Dissolving, and the Terrible Sound of the last Trumpet to be within an Inch of my Ears. Under

Under these amazing Apprehensions, I ask'd my Friend what was the meaning of this *Infernal out-cry*? Prithee, says he, what's the matter with thee? Thou look'st as if thou wert Gally'd, why these are the *City Waites*, who play every Winters Night thro' the the Streets to rouse each lazy Drone to Family Duty. Lord Bless me, said I, I am very glad its no worse, I was never so scar'd since I pop'd out of the *Parsley-bed*. Prithee let us make haste out of the hearing of them, or I shall be forc'd to make a Close stool-pan of my Breeches. At which my Friend laugh'd at me: Why, what, says he, don't you love Musick? These are topping Tooters of the Town; and have *Gowns, Silver Chains*, and *Sallaries*, for playing *Lilla Burlera* to my Lord Mayors Horse thro' the City. Marry, said I, if his Horse lik'd their Musick no better then I do, he would soon fling his Rider for hiring such *Bug-bears* to affront his *Amblefhip*. For my part, when you told me they were *Waites*, I thought they had been the *Polanders*; and was never so affraid, but that their Bears had been Dancing behind them.

The next Scene the Night presented to our imperfect view, were a very Young Crew of deminutive Vagabonds, who march'd along in Rank and File, like a little Army of *Prester John*'s Countrymen, as if advancing in order to attack a Birdsnest. This little gang of *Tattermalions*, my Friend was almost as great a Stranger to as my self; and for our Satisfaction, to be better inform'd, we saluted them after this manner, *Pray what are you for a Congregation of Ragged Sprights? And whither are you Marching? We, Master,* reply'd one of the Pert Frontiers, *we are the City* Black-Guard, *Marching to our Winter Quarters the* Glass-House *in the* Minories. *Lord Bless you Masters, give us a Penny or a Half-penny amongst us, and you shall hear any of us (if you please say the Lords-Prayer Backwards;* Swear the Compass round; *give a new Curse to every Step in the Monument; call a Whore by as many proper Names as a Peer has Titles.* I find, said I, you are a parcel of hopeful Sprouts: However we gave the poor Wretches a Penny, and away they troop'd, with a Thousand God Bless ye's, as Ragged as Old Stockin Mops; and, I'll warrant you, as *Hungry* as so many *Cattamountains*: Yet seem'd as *Merry* as they're *Poor*; and as *Contented* as they're *Miserable*.

What a shame is it, said I, that such an infamous brood of Vagabonds should be train'd up in Vilany, Ignorance, Laziness, Prophanness, and Infidelity from their Cradles, in such a well Govern'd Christian City as this, where are so many grave Magistrates and Parish Officers, whose Care it ought to be to prevent such growing Evils; and yet to suffer such a Nest of Heathens to be Nurs'd up in Blasphemy, and contempt of Religion, under the very Walls of their Churches, to me 'tis very strange.

They are Poor Wretches, says my Friend, that are drop'd here by *Gypsies* and ▆▆▆try *Beggars*, when they are so little, they can give no Account of Parents, or Place of Nativity, and the Parishes caring not to bring a charge upon themselves, suffer them to Beg about in the Day-time, and at Night Sleep at Doores, and in Holes and Corners about the Streets, till they are so harden'd in this sort of Misery, that they seek no other Life till their Riper Years (for want of being Bred to Labour) put them upon all sorts of Villany: Thus, thro' the neglect of Church-Wardens and Constables, from Beggary they proceed to Theft, and from Theft to the Gallows.

As we were thus reflecting upon the Miserable condition of these unhappy Wretches, another *Midnight King of Clubs* was going his Progress round his scanty Dominions, attended with his whole Court of Ravenous Mobility, and popping on us unawares, his well-fed Majesty bid his Guard *De Core hault;*

hault; and with a Hem, claping his painted Scepter to the Ground as hard as a Paver does his Rammer, bid us stand and come before the *Constable*. We, like prudent Ramblers, obey'd the Voice of Authority; and with uncover'd Heads, pay'd Reverence to his awful Presence.

He Demanded of us, in an austere Voice, who and what we were; and had as many impertinent Questions at his Tongues end, as an *Apothecary* has hard *Words*, or a *Midwife bawdy Stories*. My Friend, in order to satisfie his worships curiosity, and make him something the wiser, answer'd his Foolish Examination, with as much Submission and Respect as a Proud Peevish Dunce in Authority could expect, or a Prudent Man, when at the Mercy of such a Cock's-comb, give.

He ask'd my Friend what was his Profession? He answer'd him a *Surgeon*. A Surgeon, says our Learned Potentate, in great derision; and why not a Chirurgeon I pray Sir? I could find in my heart to send you to the Counter, for presuming to corrupt the Kings English before me his Representative.

'Twas a mistake Mr. *Constable*, said I, pray Excuse it, and be not so severe with us, we are very sober civil Persons, and have been about Business, and going quietly to our own Habitations.

Civil and Sober, Persons, said he, how do I know that, Mr. *Prattle-Box?* You may be Drunk for ought I know, and only feign your selves Sober before my presence to escape the Penalty of the Act.

My Friend put's his Hand in his Pocket, plucks out a Shilling, indeed Mr. *Constable*, says he, we tell you nothing but the Naked Truth. There is something for your Watch to Drink: We know it is a late Hour, but hope you will detain us no longer.

With that, Mr. *Surlycuff*, directs himself to his right hand *Jannizary, Hem, bab*, Aminidab, *I believe they are Civil Gentlemen*: Ay, ay, said he, *Master you need not Question it; they don't look as if they had any* Fire-Balls *about 'em. Well, Gentlemen, you may pass; but Pray go Civilly home. Here* Colly *light the Gentlemen down the Hill, they may chance to stumble in the Dark, and break their Shins against* the Monument.

Thank you Sir kindly, said we, for your Civility, but we know the way very well, and shall need no Watchman: Your Servant Sir; good Night to you.

I am very glad, says my Friend, we are got out of the Clutches of this inquisitive *Coniwable*. This Grey-headed lump of grave Ignorance, takes as much Pride in being the most Officious Fool in his Parish, as a *Victualler* does to be one of the *Jury*, or a *Vintner* to be made an *Ensign* of the *Train-bands*. This is the most ill-natur'd Pragmatical Block-head, that ever was center'd in a circle of Lanthorns; and if he had said our *Heads* had been made of *Hackney-Turnips*, one Word in contradiction would have cost us a Nights Lodging in the *Counter*; for he makes no more of committing a Man, then a *Tavern-drawer* does of Killing the Cook. And his Thirsty Re●●e that attend him, are rare hard-mouth fellows at an Oath; and can Swear as heartily as a *Lancashire Evidence*, you were *Drunk*, tho' you Drank nothing but *Coffee* in three days before; and that you *Abused* the Constable, tho' you gave him not an ill word; and Swore abundance of Oaths, tho' your Communition (*Quaker* like) was nothing but *Yea, yea*, and *Nay, nay*.

The great good these Fellows do in the Streets, is to Disturb People every Hour with their Bawling, under pretence of taking care they may sleep quietly in their Beds; and call every old Fool by his Name seven times a Night, for fear he should rise and forget it next Morning; and often instead of preventing Mischief make it; by carrying honest Persons to the *Counter*, who

would

would fain walk Peaceably home to their own Habitations: And provoke Gentlemen, by their Sauciness, to commit those Follies 'tis properly their Business to prevent. In short, it is reasonable enough to believe, they play more Rogues Tricks than ever they detect; and occasion more Disturbances in the Streets than ever they hinder.

By this time we were come to *Billings-gate*; and in a narrow Lane, as dark as a *Burying-Vault*, which Stunk of stale *Sprats*, *Piss*, and *Sir-reverence*, we groped about, like a couple of *Thieves* in a *Cole-hole*, to find the Ent'rance of that *Nocturnal Theatre*, in whose delightful Scenes we propos'd to terminate the Nights felicity. At last we stumbled upon the Threshold of a *Gloomy Cavern*; where, at a distance, we saw Lights burning like Candles in a *Haunted Cave*, where *Ghosts* and *Gobblins* keep their Midnight Revels.

We no sooner enter'd, but heard such a number of *Female Tongues*, so Promiscuously engag'd in a mess of *Tittle-Tattle*, That had a *Water-man* knock'd down his Wife with his Stretcher, and been trying for the fact by a Parliament of *Fish-women*, they could not have exercis'd their nimble Instruments with more impatience.

We e'en turn'd our selves into the smoky *Boozing-ken* amongst them; where round the Fire sat a tatter'd Assembly of fat motherly *Flat-caps*, with their *Fish-Baskets* hanging upon their Heads instead of *Riding-hoods*, with every one her Nipperkin of warm *Ale* and *Brandy*; and as many *Rings* upon their *Thumbs* as belongs to a suit of *Bed-Curtains*. Every one as *Slender* in the *Waste* as a *Dutch Skipper* in the *Buttocks*; and look'd together, like a litter of *Squab Elephants*. Their *Noses* were as *Sharp* as the *Gnomon* of a *Dial*, and look'd as *Blew* as if they had been Frost-nip'd. Their *Checks* were as *Plump* as an Infants *Buttocks*, but adorn'd with as many *Crimson Carnosities* as the *Face* of a Noblemans *Butler*, who has Liv'd forty years in the Family; and plainly prov'd, by the depth of their colour, That *Brandy* is a Nobler *Die* than *Claret*. Their *Tongues* were, as loud as the *Temple-horn*, that calls the *Cuckold-makers* to their *Commons*: And every word they spoke was at least in the Pitch of double *Gammut*. Their chief clamour was against *High-heads* and *Patches*; and said it would have been a very good Law, if Queen *Mary* had effected her design, and brought the Proud Minks's of the Town to have worn *High-Crown'd-Hats* instead of *Top-knots*.

Then one looking over her Shoulder, and spying me behind her, accosts me after this manner; *God save you, honest Master, will you Pledge me? Ah Dame*, said I, *with all my Heart*. *Why then*, says she, *here's a Health to mine A——s; and a Fart for those that owe no Money*.

Lord help my poor Masters, says another, *they look as if they had disoblig'd their Wives or their Landladies, and they would not rise and let them in to Night*.

Come, come away, says my Friend, let's seek another Apartment: These Saucy tongu'd old Whores will tease us to Death. Which unhappy words one of them over-heard; and starting up like a *Fury*, thus gave her Lungs a Breathing.

You White-liver'd Son of a Fleet-street Bumsitter, *begot upon a Chair at noon-day, between* Ludgate *and* Temple-Bar. *You Puppily off-spring of a Mangy* Night-walker, *who was forc'd to Play the Whore an hour before she cry'd-out, to get a Crown to pay the Bawd her Midwife for bringing you, you Bastard, into the World. Who is it you call Whore?*

Away slunk my Friend and I into another Room, and left them to spend their Malignant Spirits by themselves; and were as thankful to Providence we escap'd so imminent a Danger, as it deliver'd from the rage of so many

D

Wild-

Wild-Cats. And indeed, if their *Tallons* were as sharp as their *Tongues*, they need not fear a Combat with all the Beasts of *America.*

We were now tumbled into Company compos'd of as many sorts of *Rakes* as you may see *Whores* at a *Buttock-ball.* One in a long Wig and Muff, looking as fretful as a *broken Gamster*, biting his Nailes as if he was ready to Curse aloud *Confound the Dice.* Another as dull as if the *Grey Mare* was the better *Horse*; and deny'd him Entrance for keeping late Hours. The next as brisk and lively as if just come of Age, had got his Means in his own Hands, bought his Time of his Master, and fear'd no colours : But thinking the day too short for his Fortune, resolves the Night shall make amends, by lengthening out his Pleasures.

Up in a Corner sat a couple of brawny Water-men, one Eating Broil'd Red-Herrings, and the other Bread and Cheese, and Onions, that had a Welchman Spew'd up his Cous-boby and Leek-Porridge into a Dutchmans Closestool-pan, it could not have produc'd a finner Nosegay to have Poison'd the Devil.

Then in blunders a Dunken Tar, as great in his Thoughts as an Admiral; and calls to the Boy in the Barr after this manner, *You Horse-turdly Spawn of a Fresh-water Lubber, why don't you hand me a Candle and* Induct *me to my* Cabbins *that I may* Belay *my self?* As the Boy lights him up Stairs, he Tumbles; and Curses *The Devil D——n the Ratlings of these Wood-n Shrouds, for I have broke my Shins against 'em, I had rather run up to the Cross-trees of the Main-topmast in a Storm, than six Rounds of these confounded Land-Ladders after the Drinking a Kan of* Phlip, *or a Bowl of* Punch.

Next this came in a spruce Blade with a pretended Wife, ask'd what time the Boats went off to *Gravesend*, The told him about four in the Morning. *Alas*, says he, *that will be too long to fit up: Can't my Wife and I have a Bed here? Yes, yes, Sir, if you Please*, reply'd the Pious Beldam, *God forbid else*; *we have several Couple above in Bed that wait for this Tide as well as you Sir.* So up they were lighted, Post-haste, to the old Trade of Basket-making.

After these Bolted in two Seamen, with a little crooked Fidler before them, short Pipes in their Mouths, Oaken Truncheons in their Hands, Thrum-Caps upon their Heads, and Canvas-Trunks upon their Arses. We had the good luck for these to Stagger into our Company, whose unpolish'd Behaviour, Apish Gestures, and Maritime Nonsense, added no small Pleasure to the Night; but gave us hopes of as much Mirth as a *London* Apprentice finds at a *Bartholemew*-Fair Popet-show, or a Country 'Squire among a gang of *Stroling-Comedians.*

The two Lousie Subjects of the Pickled God *Neptune*, having wash'd off their Brine, with a plentiful Dose of Fresh-water-Ale, began to be as brisk as a Town Rake that has shak'd off his Poverty, or a Court Libertine an old Mistress. In their Frolicks they happen'd to espy a Hook drove into the Mantletree, which they immediately converted to a very Comical use; laying violent Hands upon my little Lord *Crowdero*, and by the hind-slit of his Breeches, hung him upon the Tenter, who being sorely affrighted at this unexpected Elevation Shot that into his Trousers which made the Crooked Vermin out stink a Poll-Cat. In this condition, Pendant like a Play-house Machine, or a Brazen Cherub over a Church Branch; begging with humble Submission to be set safe upon *Terra Firma.* All the time dripping his Guts upon the Hearth, like a Roasting Wood-Cock; till at last, by righing broke the string of his Breeches, and down came our Broil'd Scraper into his own Sauce, upon his feeble instrument; and was a Sweet bit ready to be serv'd up to a weak Appetite.

This

This put the whole Company into such an extravagant fit of Laughter, That had we seen a *Bayliff* Bog'd, or a Fellow break his Neck at Foot-ball, it could not have been a greater Jest to the Spectators. Bus as soon as the Angry *Homunculus* had gather'd himself up from his own Dunghill, he gave the two *Tritons* such an untuneable Lesson upon his ill-ton'd Organ, That the whining of a *Dog-drawn Bitch* or the winding of a Cat-call, could not have oblig'd our Ears with less grateful Harmony. When he had thus given vent to his ungovernable indignation, he Cock'd the Arm of his *Hump Shoulder* upon his Hip, and away rowl'd the *Runlet of Gall*, and turn'd his unsavory *Bung-hole* upon the Company.

The *Tarpaulins* now began to talk to each other of their Travels; and of the sundry remarkable Accidents which had happen'd in their Voyages. One Swore *They once found it so excessive Hot going to* Guinea, *that they us'd no Fire to boil their Kettle, but drest all their Beef upon Deck in the Sun-shine And could Bake, Broil, Fry, or Stew, as well as in an* Admirals *Cook-room.*

Says the other, *I never was in so Hot a Climate as that, but I have been so many degrees to the* Northward *where it has been so Cold, it has Frozen our Words in our Mouths, that we could not hear one another speak, till we came into a warmer Latitude to Thaw 'em; and then all our Discourse broke out together like a Clap of Thunder, that there was never such a Confusion of Tongues ever heard at* Babel.

Says his Companion, *That's very strange, but I have known stranger things to be true. I once was sitting upon my Chest between Decks, Lousing an old Canves Jacket, and we had found by our Observation that day, we were within a few Minutes of being under the* Tropick *of* Cancer; *and on a sudden it began to Lower; and the* Larboard *Watch handed in our Sails, for fear of a* Tornado, *or a* Squale: *At last a Beam of Lightening darted thro' an open Port, melted one of the Guns, and went thro' a pair of Buck-skin-Breeches I had on, and Burnt the Lappets of a blew Shirt to Tinder, hiss'd as it came like a* Rattle-Snake, *but did my Body no manner of dammage.*

As our Salt-water Wits were thus Romancing, who should Stagger into our Company, but an old Acquaintance of my Friends, who (as I understand by his Talk) was an *Exchange Commodity broker :* A kind of *Mungril* Matchmaker, between *Cock-bawd* and *Pimp*; or rather a Composition of both. He made more a roaring than half a dozen Drunken *Porters*; and was as full of *Freaks* as a *Madman* at the Full of the *Moon*. He Guzzl'd, Rattl'd, Smoak'd, and Star'd like a Fury: And every time he spoke 'twas with so much Earnestness, that I thought his Eyes would have flown out of his Head in pursuit of his Words. All he talk'd was lowd Nonsense; and the heat of his Brain setting Fire to his Tongue, made every thing he said so wonderfully hot, it made the Ears of all People glow that heard 'em. At last he pluck'd out a Catalogue of what Fortunes he had now at his disposal, *viz.*

A Mercers Daughter in *Cornhill*, about Seventeen, who was unluckily Kiss'd by her Fathers Prentice, which being spread among the Neighbourhood, he is willing to give her two hundred Pounds advance, above an equality, to salve up the flaw, to any honest Young Shop-keeper, that will wink at a fault to better his Condition.

An old Maid that has liv'd thirty Years in an Aldermans family, who with her Wages, Ladies old Cloths, and Money got for private Service, is worth about three hundred Pounds; and thinks her self qualifi'd for keeping a *Victualers* Barr, is willing to bestow her self upon any honest Free-man, if clear in the World, tho' not worth a Groat.

A Young Buxom *Widow*, on the Back-side of the *Change*, who was Marry'd five Years, but never had a Child; is still in her Mourning; wonderfully

Pretty,

Pretty, and tollerably Honeſt: She is willing to diſpoſe of her ſelf to a brisk likely Man, within or without the Year: Is in a good Shop well Cuſtom'd; and needs no Money.

About half a Hundred *Exchange-Girles*, ſome Tall, ſome Short, ſome Black, ſome Fair, ſome Handſome, ſome Houſewiſely, ſome Homely, ſome Virtuous, but all with *White-Chappel* Portions; and will make very good Wives for thoſe who have more Money than Wit, and more Faith then Jealouſie.

A Vintners Daughter bred at the Dancing-School, becomes a Barr well, ſteps a Minuet finely, plays *John* come Kiſs me now, now, now, ſweetly upon the Virginals, makes a very graceful Figure, and is as Proud as ſhe's *handſome:* Will have a great many *Quart Pots*, old *Pewter*, *Linnen*, and other Houſehold-ſtuff to her Portion. But who ever Marrys her, muſt Rid her with a Curb, or ſhe may prove unlucky, to the Bane of her Rider.

When he had thus diverted us with his Catalogue of *Job*'s Comforters, which he pretended were upon Sale, and at his diſpoſal, my Friend began to put me in mind of the conſiderable Buſineſs we had upon *Change*, at *Greſham* Colledge, *Bedlam*, and other places, on the morrow, which occaſion'd us to think of Bed, tho' with as much indifferency as a Worn-out Stallion does of a Pretty Punk, or a new Married Women of her Prayers. For the Pleaſures of the Night were ſo engaging, and every various Humour ſuch a wakeful piece of Drollery, That a Mounte-bank and his Jack Pudding, or a ſet of Morrice-dancers, could not give more Content to a croud of Country Spectators, than the lively Action of what is here repeated did afford us. But to qualifie our ſelves the better for our next Task, we thought it neceſſary to take ſome Reſt: So, accordingly, were conducted to a Room which ſtunk as bad of Pitch, Tar, Sweat, and Tallow, as a Ship between Decks, when the Tars are in their Hammocks: But the unſeaſonableneſs of the hour forc'd us to be Content. And ſo good Night to ye.

F I N I S.

THE
LONDON
SPY.

For the *Month* of *January*, 1699.

PART III.

By the Author of the Trip *to* JAMAICA.

LONDON, Printed and Sold by *J. How*, in the *Ram-Head-Inn-Yard* in *Fanchurch-street*, 1699.

THE
LONDON
SPY.

THE
LONDON
SPY.

WHEN we had cool'd the Fever of our Brains with a plentiful Dose of that reviving Cordial, Sleep; and our wakeful Faculties having shaken off *Morpheus*'s Leaden Plummets from our drowsie Eye-lids (after a few Slug-a-bed Yawnes and Lazy Stretches) we found by the advancement of the Day it was high time to make our Resurrection. Accordingly, with mutual resolutions, we started from *Sluggards Paradise*, the Bed; and collected our scatter'd Garments in order for Equipping.

When with abundance of Rubbing, Scrubbing, Washing and Combing, we had made our selves tolerable Figures to appear by Day-light, we descended from our *Snoaring-Kennel*, so finely Perfum'd by the fusty Jackets of their Tarpaulin Guests, that it smelt as Odoriferously grateful, as a *Suffolk-Cheese* toasting over a Flaming *Pitch-barrel*. It's walls being adorn'd with as many unsavory *Finger-dabs* as an *Inns of Court Bog-house*. The Cieling Beautified, like a *Soldiers Garret*, or a *Counter Chamber*, with Smutty Names and Bawdy Shadows, Sketch'd by unskilful hands with Candle-flame and Charcole, The Bed, 'tis true, was Feathers, but most of them large enough to make *Pens* or *Tooth-Pickers*. An Earthen Chamber-Pot as big as a three Gallon *Steyn*, Glaz'd o'er with Green, and looks as fine as any *Temple Mug* or *Countrey Pudding-Pan*.

Having turn'd our Backsides upon these Cubicular Conveniencies, we creeping Cold, to a new kindled smoaky Fire, where we fortified our Appetites against the Contagious Breaths of *Funking Carmen*, with a Penny-worth of burnt Bread soften'd in a Mug of *Porters Guzzle*, improv'd with a slice of *Cheshure*. This we gobbled up (being hasty to be gone) with as much Expedition as a *Citizens Wife* does an *Islington Cheese-cake*, when Treated by her Husband. Then satisfied our *Tun-bellied Hostess*, and left her Infernal Mansion to the sinful Sons of Darkness, there to practice their Iniquities.

We now turn'd down to the *Thames-side*, where the frightful roaring of the *Bridge* Water-falls so astonish'd my Eyes, and terrify'd my Ears, That, like *Roger* in his *Mill*, or the Inhabitants near the Cataracts of *Nile*, I could hear no Voice softer than a *Speaking-Trumpet*, or the audible Organ of a

Scolding

Scolding Fish-woman. After I had feasted my Intellects with this surprizing Novelty, we turn'd towards *Billingsgate*; where a parcel of Fellows came running upon us in a great fury, crying out (as I thought) *Schollars, Schollars, will you have any Whores?* Lord *Bless me,* said I to my Friend, *What a wicked place is this, that a Man in a Black Coat cannot pass about his business without being ask'd in publick such an abominable Question?* Hauling and Pulling him about by his Arms, as if they would force him to commit Fornication in spight of his Teeth. Notwithstanding I told 'em we wanted no Whores, nor would we have any, yet they would scarce be satisfied. My Friend laugh'd heartily at my innocent Mistake, and undeceiv'd my Ignorance; telling me they were *Watermen,* who distinguish'd themselves by the Titles of *Oares* and *Scullers;* which made me Blush at my Error, like a *Bashful Lady* that has drop'd her Garter, or a *Modest Man* who cripples his Jest by a forgetful Hesitation.

After we had loos'd our selves, with much difficulty, from the unparallell'd Insolency of *Charon's* Progeny, we turn'd into a Crowd of *Thumb-Ring'd Flat-caps,* from the Age of Seven to Seventy, who sat Snarling and Grunting at one another, over their *Sprats* and *Whitings,* like a Pack of *Domestick Dogs* over the *Cook-maids* kindness, or a parcel of hungry *Sows* at a Trough of *Hogwash*; every one looking as sharp as a stroling *Fortune-teller*; that I fear'd they would have pick'd my Pocket with their Eyes, or have brought me under an *ill-Tongue* before I could have shot this dangerous Gulph, where the Angry Surges of a Tempestuous Tittle-Tattle run Mountain-high, dashing into my Ears on every side, that I was as glad when I had weather'd this Storm of Verbosity, as an *Insolvent Creditor* who has slip'd the Villanous gripes of a gang of *Protection Cursers.*

Having thus happily quitted the stink of *Sprats,* and the untunable Clamours of the Wrangling Society, we pass'd round the Dock, where some Salt-water Slaves, according to their well-bred Custom, were pelting of *Sons of Whores* at one another, about the *Birth* of their *Oyster-Boats.* One unhappily being acquainted how to touch the other in his tenderest Part, gaul'd his impatient Adversary with the provoking Name of *Cuckold*; which intolerable Indignity so fermented the Choler of the little *Snail-catcher,* that he resolved to show himself a Champion in defence of his Wife's Virtues; and leaping into the others Boat, there, like a true-bred *Cock,* made a vigorous assault upon his Enemies *Dunghill.* But a sad disaster attended the poor Combatants, for in their Scuffle they fell Overboard: But the Tide being half spent, the Water was not high enough to cool their Courage; for notwithstanding, they maintain'd an *Amphibious* Fight, and Battled, like *Ducks* and *Drakes,* in two Elements at once, till the *Cuckold* had bravely subdued his Antagonist, and made his poor Victim (half Drown'd and half Knock'd o'th' Head) Publickly acknowledge the unspotted Reputation of the Victor's Dutchess; who at the end of the Fray, having receiv'd Intelligence of her Lord and Master's Engagement, came down to the Dock-side Crown'd with an *Oyster-Basket,* and there, with an audible Voice, set up a passionate Justification of her own Honesty, to the great Diversion of the whole Auditory. Her *Leviathan-Shape* was a good testimony of her Virtues, for had our first She-Parent been but half so Homely, the Devil would have been Damn'd nine times deeper into the Infernal Abyss, before he would have Robb'd her of her Innocency, or frustrated *Adam* in the Blessing of his Help-mate.

From

From thence we mov'd on to a stately Fabrick, before which a parcel of Robuſt Mortals were as buſie as ſo many *Flies* upon a *Cow-turd*; ſome running about in *Circular Jſmcraks*, like ſo many *Turnſpits*, labouring in their *Jack-wheels*; others ſo deeply engag'd in hooping of Caſks, as if they were taking all Imaginable care that euery Tub ſhould ſtand upon its own bottom. Many Scales at work, and abundance of *Eagle-Ey'd Vermin* hovering about 'em, that I thought at firſt *Juſtice* might have reſided there, (till my Friend told me *No, no*) and theſe were her *Agents*, Ballancing the *Miſeries* againſt the *Sins* of the Nation. *Prithee Friend*, ſaid I, *What is that Grizly* Bachanalian, *with a Pen twiſted in his Hair, whoſe Face looks as if it had coſt as much the Dying as would have ſet up a Topping* Vintner? Says my Friend, He's one of thoſe Cormorants call'd a *Land-Waiter*: His buſineſs is to take care that no body cheats the King but himſelf. His Poſt is honeſtly worth a Hundred Pound a Year; but with the help of an *Open Hand* and a *Cloſe Mouth*, he can (without a Burthen to his Conſcience) make it worth thrice the Money. *What is he in the long Wig, with his Fox-skin Muff upon his Button, and his Pocket-book in his Hand?* Why he (replies my School-fellow) is a *Beau*, Prentice to ſome topping Merchant; and is taking the weight of his Maſters Goods, that he is not wrong'd in the Cuſtoms. He is very careful no body cheats him abroad, and his Maſter is forc'd to be as watchful Mr. *Finnikin* does not injure him at home: For a *Flattering Companion*, or a *Jilting Miſtreſs*, will at any time make him dip his fingers in the *Caſh*, to treat them with a *New Play*, or ſolace them with a *Bottle*.

Pray, ſays my Friend, take Notice of that Gentleman in the Camlet-Cloke, he will tell you from his own Experience, that any man may grow Rich from Humility and Induſtry; and that 'tis nothing but *Pride* and *Lazineſs* that begets *Poverty* and *Misfortune*. When he came firſt to Town he had but three Pence in the World, which he prudently laid out in a new Broom, that might ſweep clean, which he very dextrouſly apply'd, with his utmoſt Labour, to the Dirty Wharf, without bidding from any body; but had ſenſe enough to conſider it belong'd to ſome-body, who would at leaſt give him Thanks, if not Recompence his Trouble. The Maſter of the Wharf happening to eſpy him at his Task, gave him ſome ſmall encouragement to continue his cleanlineſs, which he practiced dayly with as much diligence as a *Tounger Brother* in the Courtſhip of a Fortune, till he had gain'd his end, and curry'd favour with the Merchant, who lent him his aſſiſtance by degrees, which the other improving, is now become a Man of a great Eſtate, and conſiderable Authority: But if any poor Man ask him for an *Alms*, he tells him there are Riches buried in the *Dirt*; and good Fortune in a *Broom*; and if he will *Sweep* as he was forc'd to do, he may come in time to be *Lord Mayor of London*; To which a croſs old *Mumper* reply'd, *If you had not got more by* Knavery *and* Uſury, *than ever you did by your* Honeſty *and* Induſtry, *you might have been Apprentic'd to your* Broom *till this time, and never have been made a Freeman.*

I now enquir'd of my Friend what they call'd this buſie ſpot, he told me 'twas the *Cuſtom-houſe*; and in that ſtately Edifice the Commiſſioners ſat, about whom I ask'd ſome Queſtions, but found my Friend too ſhie to give me ſatisfaction, ſaying, If I tell you Truth, I'm a Fool to my ſelf; if Falſe, unjuſt to my Friend; and make you become a Lyar to the World.

I shall therefore instead of what you expect, give you a proverbial Caution; *viz.* They are a parcel of Edg-Tooles, with whom there is no *Jesting*; and he that attempts to Eat Fire to please a Crowd, if he finds cause to complain he has Burnt his Mouth, makes himself but a Laughing-stock.

By the advice of my Companion, we turn'd back till we came to a place call'd *Pig-hill*, which resembling the steep descent down which *the Devil drove his Hogs to a Bad-market*, I suppose it is therefore honour'd with the aforesaid Title; in regard to which, they are always in a condition of turning the Stomach of a *Jew*, or Poisoning a *Scotchman*; and can satisfie an Epicurian Appetite, or save a Lady's Longing, with *Pigg* or *Pork*, in any hour of the Day, or any day of the Year; the Cooks, according to report, keeping many *Spaniel Bitches*, as *Wet-Nurses*, for the due suckling of their *Sowes Babbies*; which adds, they say, such a Sweetness to their Flesh, that they Eat as fine as any *Papy-dog*, and all such Persons who are admirers of this Luxurious food, may the whole Winter have it there ready drest, without the danger of Fly-sauce, which is more then in Summer I am able to promise you: All the Elements contribute to their Cooking of every Squeaker they dress; he is first scalded in Water, then dry'd in the Air, and half bak'd in the Sun; then Roasted by the Fire, afterwards dissected by a Cholerick Executioner, and his Quarters dispos'd on to several Gates of hungry Citizens, where Teeth are the Port-Cullice, as if the poor had been convicted of a Plot, and died a Traytor.

As we walk'd up the Hill as Lazily as an *Artillery* Captain before his Company upon a *Lords Mayors-day*, or a *Paul's* Labourer up a Ladder with a Hod of Mortar, we peep'd in at a *Gateway*, where we saw three or four Blades well drest, but with Hawkes Countenances, attended with half a dozen Ragamuffinly Fellows, showing Poverty in their Rags, and Dispair in their Faces, mix'd with a parcel of young wild Striplings like Runaway-Prentices: I could not forbear inquiring of my Friend about this Ill-favour'd multitude, patch'd up of such awkward figures that it would have puzzled a *More-fields Artist* well read in *Physiognomy*, to have discover'd their Dispositions by their Looks.

That House, says my Friend, which they are entering, is an Office where Servants for the Plantations, bind themselves to be miserable as long as they Live, without an especial Providence prevents it, &c. Those fine Fellows who look like Foot-men upon a Holy-day, crept into cast Suites of their Masters, that want Gentility in their Deportment, answerable to their Apparel, are *Kidnappers*, who walk the *Change* and other parts of the Town, in order to seduce People who want Services, and Young Fools cross in Love, and under an uneasiness of mind, to go beyond Seas, getting so much a head of Masters of Ships and Merchants who go over, for every Wretch they Trapan into this Misery. Those Young *Rakes* and *Tatterdemalions* you see so lovingly herded, are drawn by their fair promises to sell themselves into Slavery, and the *Kidnappers* are the Rogues that run away with the Money.

Now, says my Friend, I'll show you a Towering Edifice, erected thro' the Wisdom and Honesty of the City; as a very high Memorandum of it's being laid low, either by a Judgement from Heaven, for the Sins of the People,

People, or by the Treachery of the *Papists*, according to the a ssertion of the *Monument*; who I suppose as Ignorant of the matter as my self; for it was neither Built then, nor I Born; so I believe we are as equally able to tell the Truth of the Story, as a *Quack-Astrologer* is by the assistance of the Signs and Planets, what was the Name of *Moses*'s Great Grand-Father, or how many Quarts of Water went to the Worlds drowning. You'll be mightily pleas'd with the Loftiness of this Slender Column, for it's very height was the first thing that ever occasioned wry Necks in *England*, by the Peoples staring at the Top on't. To the Glory of the City, and the everlasting Reputation of the worthy Projectors of this most high and mighty *Babel*, it was more savingly than honestly Built, by the Poor *Orphans* Money; many of them since having beg'd their Bread; and the Charitable Elders of the City have given them a stone. Look ye now, you may see it; pray view it, and give me your Opinion.

What is it of no use but only to Gaze at? Yes, yes, says my Friend; Astrologers go often to the top on't, when they have a mind to play the Pimp, and see *Mars* and *Venus* in Conjunction; tho' the chief use of it is for the improvement of Vintners Boys and Drawers, who come every week to exercise their Supporters, and learn the Tavern-Trip by running up to the *Balcony*, and down again, which fixes them in a Nimble step, and makes them rare Light-heel'd Emissaries in a Months Practice. Do you observe the Carving, which contains the King and his Brother's Picture? They were cut by an Eminent Artist, and are look'd upon by a great many Impartial Judges to be a couple of extraordinary good figures: Pray what think you? I know you have some Judgement in Proportion.

Why, truly, said I, they are the only Grace and Ornament of the whole Building; but 'tis a thousand pities the Stones form'd into so Noble an order, should be so basely purchas'd, to the ruin of so many thousand Fatherless and Widdows; but I suppose it was politically done, to fix such a Testimonial of their Loyalty upon a Structure so unjustly rais'd, that the one might in some measure wash away the Stain of the other; and to prevent the high-flown Loyalists to reflect upon their Teachery to the poor *Orphans*, since they may pretend (tho' they cheated 'em of their Money) 'twas with a pious design of setting up the Kings Picture, in reverence to his Person, who all the world knows they had a wonderful respect for; and in honour to the City, which to besure was as dear to them as their Lives and Fortunes. Tho' I have heard their chief drift in this memorable Undertaking was, to get, Estates to themselves without mistrust; that they might enjoy them without molestation.

As you say, this Edifice, as well as some others, was not projected purely as a Memorandom of the Fire, or an Ornament to the City; but to give those corrupted Magistrates who had the Power in their hands, the opportunity of putting Two thousand Pounds into their own pockets, whilst they paid One towards the Building. I must confess all that I think can be spoke in praise of it, is, *'Tis a Monument to the City's shame, the Orphans Grief, the Protestants Pride, and the Papists Scandal; and only serves as a high-crown'd hat, to cover the head of the old fellow that shows it.*

When my Friend had thus Oblig'd me with a full Prospect of our

Metropolitan Maypole, we turn'd up *Gracechurch-street,* in order for *Gresham-Colledge,* where we met a Fellow in a Gown, with a piece of Prodigality, call'd a *Mace,* upon his Shoulder; and another, like one of *Justice's Sumpter-Horses,* laden with *Scales, Weights,* and *Measures;* a third Arm'd, like a *Roundheaded Cuckold,* marching to *Horn-fair,* with a *Pick-Ax.* These advanced in the Front, attended with a Troop of *Loyterers* in Gowns, who hobbled after with as much Formality as a parcel of *Gossips* at a *Christening,* to the Parish-Church, behind Mother *Grope* and her fine Mantle. They had Match'd themselves together with abundance of Discretion; mix'd *Fat* and *Lean, Fat* and *Lean,* like so many *Scotch* Runts in *Smith-field-market,* amongst the like Number of *Lincoln-shire* Oxen, that I thought it a lively representation of *Pharoh's* Dream, appearing to me as a true Emblem of *Plenty* and *Famine:* For one part of them look'd as if they had half eat up the other. By and by, they pitch'd down a Triangular Device, with as many Legs as *Tyburn;* and began of a suddain to be all as busie as so many *Sheriffs-men* at an Execution. I enquir'd of my Friend how these Mortals were Dignified or Distinguish'd, and what was the weighty affair they were so pryingly Engaged in? He told me these were a part of the worthy Members of the *Quest,* whose business was to Inspect *Weights* and *Measures,* taking care that every Shop-keepers *Yard,* be of the standard-length, whilst the Wife (sitting behind the Counter) laughs in her Sleeve all the time they're Measuring. Also to give warning for the mending of Pavements, and removing all *Neusances* under the penalty of a *Fine.* Their meeting is generally at a *Hall,* except they have a *Quest-house,* from whence they go to Church to Prayers, and return to be Drunk. They detect very few People in their Faults, for they Honestly take care not to injure their *Neighbours,* but inform them when they shall walk their Rounds, that they may remove their false *Weights* and *Measures* out of the way; and have larger ready to produce to conceal the Roguery. The Inhabitants of every *Precinct* are oblig'd to give 'em their Company at Dinner; where he that does not behave himself Generously, and purchase his Security at the expence of half a piece, shall be surely return'd upon the *Jury* the next Impannel. They have an old Custome of Brewing Spic'd-Ale; and he that does not take care to send his Wife a Jug-full, runs the hazzard by his Negligence, of raising an evil Spirit in his Family, that no Conjurer can lay in a Fortnight. They have as many several Offices amongst 'em, as are in a Noble-mans Family, *viz. Foreman, Controulor, Treasurer, Steward, Butler,* &c. They have a Groat a House from each Inhabitant, besides their Fines, with which they feast their Ingurgitating Stomachs, with Luxurious Excesses. The *Quest-mens* Generosity and the *Aldermans* Humility are commonly equal: The *Quest* contribute in every Ward, thro' Benevolence, their Crowns a peice, to give his Worship a Collation in respect to his Dignity.

From hence we pass'd, without any thing remarkable, till we came to *Wise-Acres-Hall,* more commonly call'd *Gresham-Celledge,* which we enter'd as gravly as a couple of Eleemosinary Smoakers into *M——u's* Shop, or a couple of sanctified *Harlots* into *B——s* Meeting-house; we step'd thro' a little Brick Court, and then came into a Spacious Quadrangle, where, in a Melancholy *Cloister,* we saw a Peripatetick walking, ruminating, as I suppose, upon his *Entities, Essences,* and *Occult Qualities,* or else upon the *Philosophers-stone;* looking as if he very much wanted it; his steps he measur'd out with that exactness and deliberation, that, I believe, had just such a

Number

Number fail'd by bringing him to the end of the *Cloister*, he would have been in a great Passion with his Legs; during his perambulation, his Eyes were fix'd upon the Pavement, from whence I conjecture, he could see as far into a Mill-stone as another; all the time we observ'd him, he took great care to follow his Nose, fearing, I suppose, if he had turn'd his Guide towards either Shoulder, he should have lost his way, and have wandred upon some other Stones out of that direct line to which he had confin'd his walk: His Countenance was Mathematical, having as many Lines and Angles in his Face, as you shall find in *Euclid*'s Elements; and look'd as if he had fed upon nothing but *Cursus Mathematicus* for a Fortnight; he seem'd to scorn the use of Gloves as much as *Diogenes* did his Dish, crossing his Arms over his Brest, and warming his Hands under his Armpits; his Lips quak'd as if he'd had an Ague in his Mouth; which tremulous motion I conceiv'd was occasion'd by his Soliloquies, to which we left him. My Friend conducted me up a pair of Stairs, to the Elaboratory-keeper's Apartment, and desir'd him to oblige us with a Sight of the Rarities; who very curtiously granted us the Liberty; opening his Ware-house of *Egyptian Mummies*, old musty Skeletons, and other antiquated Trumpery: The first thing he thought most worthy of our Notice, was the *Magnet*, with which he show'd some notable Experiments, it made a Paper of Steel-Filings Prick up themselves one upon the back of another, that they stood pointing up like the Bristles of a *Hedg-hog*; and gave such Life and Merriment to a parcel of Needle, they danc'd the Hey, by the motion of the Stone, as if the Devil were in 'em; the next things he presented to our view were a parcel of Shell-Flies almost as big as *Lobsters*, arm'd with Beaks as big as those of *Jack-daws*: Then he commended to our observation that wonderful Curiosity the *Unicorns* Horn; made as I suppose, by an Ingenious Turner, of the Tuskes of an *Elephant*; it is of an excellent Virtue; and, by report of those that know nothing of the matter, will expell Poison beyound the *Mountebanks Orvieton*: Then he carry'd us to another part of the Room, where was an *Aviary* of dead Birds, collected from the extream parts of *Europe, Asia, Africa*, and *America*; amongst which were an *East-India* Owle, a *West-India* Bat, and a Bird of *Paradise*, the last being Beautified with Variety of Colours, having no disernable Body, but all Feathers, feeding when alive upon nothing but Air, and tho' 'tis as big as a Parrot, 'tis as light as a Cobweb; it is reported by the Sage *Philosophers* of this Society, That a Feather of this Fowl, carry'd about you, is an infallible security against all Evil Temptation; for which Reason they have pretty well pluck'd it, to carry home Presents of it to their Wives and Daughters. Then he usher'd us among sundry sorts of Serpents, as the *Noy, Pelonga, Rattle-Snake, Alligator, Crocodile*, &c. That looking round me, I thought my self hem'd in amongst a Legion of Devils; when we had taken a survey of these Pincushion Monsters, we turn'd towards the Skeletons of Men, Women, and Monkeys, Birds, Beasts, and Fishes; Abortives put up in Pickle, and abundance of other Memorandums of Mortality; that they look'd as Ghostly as the Picture of *Michael Angelo*'s Resurrection; as if they had collected their scatter'd Bones into their Original order, and were about to march in search after the rest of the Appurtenances.

When we had taken this short view of the Wonders of the World, and had crost the hand of our Raree-show Interpreter with a piece of Silver, who like the Crooked Oratour to the Abby-Tombs, made a notable Haran-

gue

gue upon every Bauble in his Store-houſe, glutted with the Sight of theſe Ruſty Reliques, and *Philoſophical* Toys, we determin'd to ſteer our courſe towards *Bedlam*; ſo remov'd from *Maggotmongers-Hall*, to ſurvey *Madmans-Colledge.* In the midway, between both, my Friend bid me take notice of a Man who was Shuffling along in as much haſte as a Scrivener to make a Will, or a poor Quack to a rich Patient; That Man, ſays he, that walks like a *Mercury*, as if he had Wings to his heels, is a *Topping Vertuoſa*, and a Member of the *Royal Society*; he is by his Profeſſion a Labourer to a Phyſician, but has made himſelf, by a curious inſpection into the Myſteries of Univerſallity, a *Jack of all Trades*, and is thought by the Lear-ned, to be as knowing a *Philomat* as he that has peep'd ſeven years into a *Pitch-Barrel*; he's a wonderful Artiſt at the cleanſing of a foul Stomach, or the Sweeping of a Gut; and was one of the chief promoters of Mens Eaſe, who brought that ſavory Receptacle call'd a Cloſe-ſtool, to it's true perfection; he publiſhes a Weekly Paper for the improvement of Trade and Husbandry, wherein, for the benefit of the Publick, he has inſerted the moſt choice Receipts for the making of *Pancakes, Fritters, Puddings, Dumplins*, alſo to make *Porridge* or *Thick-milk*, that ever were extant; he like-wiſe, thro' his Wiſdom and Generoſity, has taught the World at the ex-pence of half a Crown to ſweeten a Dozen of Glaſs-Bottles, which you may buy new for two Shillings; alſo how at thirty Shillings charge we may improve an Acre of Land not Valluable at one Shilling, to be worth Twenty; amongſt the reſt, he is a *Joyner of Sexes*, and will Learnedly prove, upon ſuch Occaſions, *That Generation was the main end of our Crea-tion*; whatever Match he makes, he ſeldom fails of this double Reward, that is, to get Money on one ſide, and Curſes on t'other; for he is a Man of that Conſcience and Conſideration, that he generally takes care to couple thoſe who are worth Money, to ſuch who want it.

Thus we prattled away our time, till we came in Sight of a Noble Pile of Building, which diverted us from our former diſcourſe, and gave my Friend the Occaſion of asking me my Thoughts of this Magnificent Edifice: I told him, I conceiv'd it to be my *Lord Mayor's Palace*, for I could not imagine ſo ſtately a Structure could be deſign'd for any Quality inferior; he ſmill'd at my Innocent Conjecture, and inform'd me this was *Bedlam*, an Hoſpital for Mad-folks: In truth, ſaid I, I think they were Mad that Built ſo coſtly a *Colledge* for ſuch a Crack-brain'd Society; adding, It was pitty ſo fine a Being ſhould not be poſſeſſed by ſuch who had a Senſe of their Happineſs; ſure, ſaid I, it was a Mad Age when this was Rais'd, and the chief of the City were in great danger of loſing their Senſes, ſo contriv'd it the more Noble for their own Reception; or they would never have flung away ſo much Money to ſo fooliſh a purpoſe: You muſt conſider, ſays my Friend, this ſtands upon the ſame Foundation as the *Monument*, and the Fortunes of a great many poor Wretches lies Buri-ed in this Oſtentatious Piece of Vanity; and this, like the other, is but a Monument of the Cities Shame and Diſhonour, inſtead of it's Glory; come let us take a walk in, and view it's inſide.

Accordingly we were admitted in thro' an Iron-gate, within which ſat a Brawny *Cerberus*, of an Indico-colour, leaning upon a Money-box; we turn'd in thro' another Iron-Barricado, where we heard ſuch a ratling of *Chains*, drumming of *Doors, Ranting, Hollowing, Singing*, and *Running*, that

I

I could think of nothing but *Don Quevedo*'s Vision, where the Damn'd broke loose, and put Hell in an Uproar. The first whimsie-headed Wretch, of this Lunatick Family, that we observ'd, was a merry Fellow in a Straw Cap, who was talking to himself after this manner, *That he had an Army of Eagles at his Command*; then claping his hand upon his Head, *Swore by his Crown of Moon-shine, he would Battel all the Stars in the Skies but he would have some Clarret*: In this interim, came a Gentleman to stare at him with a Red face: *No wonder*, said his Aereal Majesty, *Clarret is so scarce; look there's a Rogue carry's more in his Nose than I, that am Prince of the Air, have had in my Belly this Twelvemonth.* If you are Prince of the Air, said I, why don't you command the Man in the Moon to give you some? To which he reply'd, *The Man in the Moon's a sorry Rascal, I sent to him for a dozen Bottles but t'other Day, and he Swore by his Bush, his Cellar had been dry this Sixmonths; but I'll be even with the Rogue, I expect a Cloud laden with Clarret to be sent me by the Sun every day; and if a Spoonful of Lees would save him from Choaking, the old Drunken Whores-Bird should not have a drop.*

We then mov'd on till we found another remarkable Figure worth our observing, who was peeping thro' his Wicket, eating of Bread and Cheese, talking all the while like a Carrier at his Supper, chewing his Words with his Victuals, all that he Spoke being in praise of Bread and Cheese; *Bread was good with Cheese, and Cheese was good with Bread, and Bread and Cheese was good together*; and abundance of such Stuff; to which my Friend and I, with others, stood listening; at last he Counterfeits a Sneeze, and shot such a mouthful of Bread and Cheese amongst us, that every Spectator had some share of his kindness, which made us retreat; he calling after us *Masters, Masters*; some went back to hear what he had to say, and he had provided them a plentiful Bowl of Piss, which he cast very successfully amongst them, crying out in a laugh, *I never give Victuals, but I give Drink, and you're Welcome Gentlemen.*

The next unhappy Object amongst this Shatter-brain'd Fraternity, was a Scholar of St. *John*'s Colledge in *Cambridge*, who was possess'd with Melancholy, but very inoffensive, and had the Liberty of the Gallery; this was a very Musical Man, which is thought to be one great Occasion of his Distemper: My Friend walk'd up to him, and introduc'd some talk, to divert himself with a few of his Frensical Extravagancies. Another Lunatick in his Intervals, who had the Liberty of ranging the House, catches hold of my School-fellows Arm, and express'd himself after this manner, *Do'st thou know, Friend, what thou art doing? Why thou art talking to a Madman, a* Fiddling *fellow, who had so many* Crotchets *in his Head, that he crack'd his Brains about his thorow* Bases. Prithee, says my Companion, what was the Occasion of Thy Distemper? To which he answer'd, *I am under this Confinement for the Noble Sins of* Drinking *and* Whoring; *and if thou hast not a care, it will bring thee into the same Condition.*

We peep'd into another Room, which smelt as strong of Chamber-lye, as a Bottle of *Sal Armoniac*, where a fellow was got as hard at work as if he'd been treading *Mortar*: What is it Friend, said I, thou art taking all this Pains about? He answer'd me thus, still continuing his Action, *I am Trampling down Conscience under my Feet, least he should rise up and fly in my Face; Have a care he does not fright thee, for he looks like the Devil;*

and

and is as fierce as a Lyon, but that I keep him Muzzled; therefore get thee gone, or I will set him upon thee. Then fell a Claping his hands, and cry'd, Halloo, halloo, halloo, halloo, halloo; and thus we left him Raving.

Another was holding-forth with as much Vehemence against Kingly-Government, as a Brother of Commonwealth-Doctrine railes against Plurality of Livings, I told him he deserv'd to be Hang'd for talking of Treason. Now, says he, You're a Fool, we Madmen have as much priviledge of Speaking our Minds within these Walls, as an Ignorant Dictator, when he Spews out his Nonsense to the whole Parish. Prithee come and live here, and you may talk what you will, and nobody will call you to Question for it: Truth is persecuted every where abroad, and flies hither for Sanctuary, where she sits as safe as a Knave in a Church, or a Whore in a Nunnery. I can use her as I please, and that's more than you dare do. I can tell Great Men such Bold Truths as they don't love to hear, without the danger of a Whipping-post; and that you can't do: For if ever you see a Madman Hang'd for Speaking Truth, or a Lawyer whip'd for Lying, I'll be bound to prove my Cap a Wheel-barrow.

We then took a walk into the Womens Appartment, to see what whimsical Figaries their wandring Fancies would have them to entertain us with-all.

The first that we look'd in upon, stood stradling with her Back against the Wall, crying, Come, John come; you're Master's gone to Change. I believe, the poor Fool's afraid of Forfeiting his Indentures. Did you ever see the like? Why, sure you wont serve your Mistress so, John, will you? Hark, hark, run you Rogue; your Master's come back to Shop. Yes, you shall have a Wife, you old Rogue, with Seven Hundred Pounds, and be Married Six Years, and not get a Child. Fy for shame, out upon't! A Husband for a Woman! A Husband for the Devil. Hang you, Rot you, Sink you, Confound you. And thus at last she run Raving on, to the highest degree of Madness.

Another was talking very merrily, at her Peeping-hole, to a crow'd of Auditors, most of them young Wenches. A foolish Girl, amongst the rest, ask'd the Madwoman how old she was? who reply'd; she was old enough to have Hair where the other had none. Which made the Young Creature betake herself to her heels to avoid the Mockery of the rest. In this interim came by a Beauish Blade, with his Wig very much Powder'd, Look, look, cries Bess of Bedlam, yonder goes a Prodigal Puppy, an Extravagant Rascal, that has got more Flower in his Wig, than my Poor Mother has in her Meal-Tub to make a Pudding with-all.

The next poor Object that happen'd under our Observation, was, a Meager old Grey-headed Wretch, who look'd as wild as an Angry Cat, and all her Tone was, The Wind is — blow Devil, blow; the Wind is — Blow, Devil, blow; a Seaman who was a staring at her, and listening to what she said, must needs be inquisitive how the Wind sat, asking her, Where is the Wind, Mother? She hastily replying, The Wind's in mine A—s; Blow Fool, blow: Being so pleas'd she had sold him a Bargain, that she fell into an Extravagant fit of Laughter, in which we left her.

Having pritty well tir'd our selves with the Frantick Humours and Rambling Ejaculations of the Mad-folks, we took a turn to make some
few

few Remarks upon the Loosness of the Spectators, amongst whom we observ'd abundance of Intriguing; Mistresses we found were to be had of all Ranks, Qualities, Colours, Prices, and Sizes, from the *Velvet-Scarf*, to the *Scotch-plad-petticoat*: Commodities of all sorts went off, for their wanted not a suitable *Jack* to every *Jill*. Every fresh comer was soon engaged in an Amour; tho they came in Single, they went out by Paires; 'tis a new *Whet-stone's Park*, now the old ones Plough'd up, where a Sportsman at any Hour in the Day may meet with Game for his purpose; 'tis a Conveniency to *London* as the *Long Cellar* to *Amsterdam*; where any Stranger may purchase a Purge for his Reins, at a small expence, and may have a Pox by chance flung into the bargain; All that I can say of it, is this, *'Tis an Alms-house for Madmen, a Showing-Room for Whores, a sure Market for Leachers, and a dry Walk for Loiterers.*

We needed now no Clock to give the Hour of the Day, our Stomachs, as true as those of the *Change*, went One; and after redeeming our Liberties from this Piss-burn'd Prison, at the expence of two-pence, we were led by our Appetites into a Cook's Shop, and when we had refresh'd Nature with a necessary supply of what she most coveted, we march'd towards the *Royal Exchange*, to which Traders were trotting in as much haste, as *Lawyers* to *Westminster*, or Butchers to *Smithfield*.

The Pillars, at the Entrance of the Front-*Porticum*, were adorn'd with sundry Memorandums of old Age, and Infirmity, under which stood here and there a *Jack in a Box*, like a Parson in a Pulpit, selling Cures for your Corns, Glass Eyes for the Blind, Ivory-Teeth for broken Mouths, and Spectacles for the weak-sighted; the Passage to the Gate being lin'd with Hawkers, Gardeners, Mandrake-sellers, and Porters; after we Crowded a little way amongst this Miscellaneous Multitude, we came to a *Pipping-Monger's* Stall, Surmounted with a *Chymist's* Shop, where *Drops*, *Elixers*, *Cordials*, and *Balsams*, had justly the preheminence of *Apples*, *Chesnuts*, *Pears* and *Oranges*; the former being Rank'd in as much order upon Shelves, as the Works of the Holy-Fathers in a Bishop's Library; and the latter being Marshal'd with as much exactness as an Army ready to engage; here is drawn up several Regiments of *Kentish-Pippins*, next some Squadrons of *Pearmain's* joyn'd to a Brigade of *Small-Nuts*, with a few Troops of *Booncritons*, all form'd into a Battalion; the Wings compos'd of *Oranges*, *Lemons*, *Pomgranates*, dry'd *Plumbs*, and *Medlars*; the Decade of these lower gross Bodies drawn over the *Helm*, are fitted by the help of *Ginger*, *Nutmeg*, and *Liqorish*, to stand upon the upper Shelf, under a Saleable-Title, to Cozen Madmen and Fools out of their Health, and their Money; and to let you know it's truly prepar'd, it is made by him who may write himself *Physician*, *Chymist*, *Apothecary*, *Confectioner*, and *Costermonger*.

We then proceeded, and went on to the *Change*, turn'd to the Right, and Jostled in amongst a parcel of Swarthy Buggerantoes, Preternatural Fornicators, as my Friend call'd them, who would Ogle a Handsome Young Man with as much Lust, as a True-bred English Whoremaster would gaze upon a Beautiful Virgin. Advertisements hung as thick round the Pillars of each Walk, as Bells about the Legs of a Morris-dancer, and an Incessant Buz, like the Murmurs of the distant Ocean, stood as a *Diapason*, to our Talk, like a *Drone* to a Bagpipe. The Wainscote was adorn'd

D with

with Quacks Bills inftead of Pictures; never an Emperick in the Town but had his Name in a Lacquer'd Frame, containing a fair Invitation for a Fool and his Money to be foon parted; and he that wants a dry Rogue for himfelf, or a Wet-Nurfe for his Child, may be furnifh'd here at a minutes Warning. After we had Squeez'd our felves thro' a Crowd of *Bumfirking-Italians*, we fell into a throng of Strait-lac'd Monfters in Fur, and Thrum Caps with huge Logger-heads, Effeminate Waftes, and Buttocks like a Flanders-Mare, with Slovenly Mein, Swinifh Looks, whofe upper lips were gracefully adorn'd with T—d-colour'd Whiskers, thefe with their Gloves under their Arm, and their Hands in their Pockets, were grunting to each other like hogs at their Peafe, thefe, my Friend told me, were the Water-Rats of *Europe*, who love no body but themfelves, and Fatten upon the Spoils, and Build their own Well-fare upon the Ruine of their Neighbours.

We had no fooner Joftled thro' this Clufter of Commonwealth's-men, but we were got amongft a parcel of Lank-hair'd Formalift's in Flat crown'd-Hats and fhort Cloakes, walking with as much State and Gravity as a Snail o're the Leaf of a Cabbage, with a Box of Tobacco-duft in one Hand, and the other imploy'd in charging their Noftrils, from whence it drops into the Muftachoes, which are always as full of Snufh, as a Beau's Wigg full of Powder; every Sentence they Spoke, was grac'd with a Shrug of the Shoulders; and every Step they took, was perform'd with as much leifure as a Cock ftrides; thefe, my Friend told me, were *Spaniards*: Says he, you may know them by the Smell, for they Stink as ftrong of Garlick as a *Polonian* Saufage

Thefe were confus'dly Jumbled among People of fundry Nations, as our Neighbouring Anticks, the French; who talk more with their Heads and Hands, than with their Tongues; who commonly Speak firft, and Think afterwards; ftep a *Minuet* as they walk, and fit as graceful on an Exchange-bench, as if in a great Saddle; their Bodies always dance to their Tongues, and are fo great Lovers of Action, that they were ready to Wound every Pillar with their Canes, as they pafs'd by, either in *Ters*, *Cart*, or *Saccoon*.

There likewife were the Lord's Vagabonds, the *Jews*, who are fo accurs'd for their Infidelity, that they are generally the Richeft People in all Nations where they Dwell; thefe, like the *Spaniards*, were fuch great confumers of the wicked Weed in Snufh, That their upper lips look'd as if they excreted thro' their Noftrils, and had forgot to ufe Bumfodder. Thefe, fays my Friend, are the Hawks of Mankind, the Spies of the Univerfe, the only Trade-Politicians, fubtle Knaves, and great Merchants.

Here were alfo a few Amber-Necklace Sellers, as my Friend call'd 'em; Men with Fur Caps, Long Gowns, and grave Countenances, feeming Wife in their Looks, Noble in their Garb, and Stately in their Carriage; retaining fomething of the old *Grecian* Grandure in their comely Deportment; amongft whom there was one very Handfome young Fellow, which my Companion bid me take particular Notice on, for fays he, that Spark in the Red Gown was very Familiar with fome of our Sweet lip'd Ladies of the City, and was very much Admir'd and Courted by feveral topping Benefactreffes at this end of the Town, to receive their Favors; till the Fool, proud of his Happinefs, muft needs boaft of their Kindneffes to the Difreputation of his humble Servants; that they all difcarded him with such

such hatred and contempt, That he is now become the Scorn and Ridicule of every Woman in the City.

Pray, said I, What Tall Sober-look'd Gentleman is that, in so grave a dress, in the Long Black Wig, and formal Hat, that stands as level in the Brim as a Pot-lid; he seems to be wonderfully reverenc'd by a great many much finer than himself? That Man, says my Friend, is the greatest Merchant we have in *England*; and those fellows that keep a Stern, and now and then come upon his Quarter with their Top-sails lower'd, are Commanders of Ships, who are soliciting for Employment; and he that plies him so close, they call *Honour and Glory*; who lately bore Command in the Service; he was originally a poor Fisherman, but did a very Notable Exploit, by the help of his Man *Jack*, that recommended him to a Commission; but either for want of Discretion or Honesty, is turn'd out; and I suppose rather than return to his Nets, he is willing to enter into Merchants Service.

The next Walk we went into, were a mixture of Two sorts of People, one of a Tall Stature, amongst whom were a parcel of Swords-men in Twisted Wigs, and lac'd Hats, with broad Faces, and flattish Noses, saluting one another commonly by the Title of Captain; but look'd as if they had been a great while out of Commission, for most of them were very much out of repair; some like Gentlemen without Estates, and others like Footmen out of places, many of them picking their Teeth, often plucking out large Tobacco Boxes to cram a wad in their Mouths, as if most of their Food was Minc'd-meat.

The other sort were a kind of lean Carrionly Creatures, with reddish Hair, and freckly Faces, being very much given to Scratching and Shruging, as if they held Lousiness no Shame, and the Itch no Scandal; stooping a little in the Shoulders, as if their Backs had been us'd to a Pedlars Pack; amongst them was a Poor Parson who came to the wrong place to look for a Benefice; these I found were a Compound of *Scotch* and *Irish*, who look'd as if they rather came to *Seek* for Business, than *Dispatch* any.

We now were come to the back Gate of the *Change*, on the East-side of which sat a parcel of Women, some looking like Jilts who wanted Cullies, and others like Servants who wanted Places.

We past by them, and Squeez'd amongst Coasters and English Traders, who were as busie in Out-witting one another, as if Plain-dealing was a Crime, and Cozenage a Vertue.

Take Notice, says my Companion, of that Camel-back'd Spark, he is dignified with the Title of my Lord, and has as many Maggots in his Head as there are holes in a Cullender; tho' the Rickets have crush'd him into that lump of Deformity, he has the Happiness, or Curse, I know not whether, to have a very handsome Woman to his Wife, whose prevailing Glances, have tempted such Custom to his Shop, that he can afford to spend three or four Hundred Pounds a Year in a Tavern, without doing himself a prejudice, which she very generously allows him to do out of her gettings, as some Censorious People are apt to imagine, as a gratuity for his Toleration for her Liberty of Conscience; she is never without a Shop-full

of

of Admirers, whom she poisons with her Eyes, and bubbles as she pleases: Give her her due; she is as Beautiful as an Angel, but as Subtle as the Devil; as Curteous as a Curtesan, but sharp as a Needle; very Free, but very Iltish; very Inviting, yet some say very Vertuous.

Now, says my Friend, we are got amongst the Plantation-Traders. This may be call'd *Kidnappers Walk*; for a great many of these *Jamaicans* and *Barbadians*, with their Kitchen-stuff Countenances, are looking as sharp for Servants, as a Gang of Pickpockets for Booty; but we have given these their Characters already in the *Trip to Jamaica*, therefore we shall speak but little of them here; I'll warrant you if they knew the Author was among them, they'd hustle you about, as the Whigs would a *Jacobite* at the Election of a Lord-Mayor; or the Quakers a Drunken Ranter that should disturb them at their Meeting.

Pray said I, what is the meaning of that Inscription in Golden Capitals over the Passage, *My Lord-Mayors Court*? my Friend reply'd, That was the Nest of City-Cormorants, who by saving a little out of many Mens Estates, raise great ones to themselves; by which means they teach Fools Wit, and bring Litigious Knaves to Repentance.

Within that Entry is an *Office of Intelligence*, pretending to help Servants to Places, and Masters to Servants; they have a knack of Bubbling silly Wenches out of their Money; who loiter hereabouts upon this expectancy, till they are pick'd up by the Plantation-Kidnappers, and Spirited away into a State of Misery and Whoredom

Now, says my Friend, let us walk on the middle of the Change, and view the Statue; this, says he, is the Figure of King *Charles*, and those are Stock-jobbers who are hovering about him, and are by report a pack of as great Knaves as ever he had in his Dominions; the rest are a mix'd multitude of all Nations, and not worth describing. Now I'll conduct you up Stairs, to take a view of the Fair Ladies, and so adjourn to the Tavern, and refresh our selves with a Bottle.

Accordingly we went up, where Women sat in their Pinfolds, begging of Custom, with such Amorous Looks and Affable Tones, that I could not but fancy they had as much mind to dispose of themselves, as the Commodities they deal in: My Eares on both sides were so baited with *Fine Linnen, Sir*, and *Gloves and Ribbons, Sir*, that I had a Milliner's and a Sempstress's Shop in my Head for a Week after: Well, says my Friend, what do you think of all these Pretty Ladies? I answer'd, I thought of them as I did of the Sex; I suppos'd they were all ready to obey the Laws of Nature, and answer the End of their Creation. Says he, This Place is a Nursery for Wives, the Merchant's Seraglio; for most that you see here, come under *Chaucer*'s Cha-racter of a Sempstress, and so we'll leave them:

> She keeps a Shop for Countenance,
> And S——— for Maintenance.

F I N I S.

THE
LONDON
SPY.

For the *Month* of *February*, 1699.

PART IV.

By the Author of the Trip to *JAMAICA.*

LONDON, Printed and Sold by *J.* How, in the *Ram-Head-Inn Yard* in *Fanchurch-street*, 1699.

Books Sold by J. How, *in the* Ram-Head-Inn-Yard *in* Fanchurch-Street; J. Weld, *at the* Crown *between the* Temple-Gates *in* Fleet-ſtreet; *and* Mrs. Fabian, *at* Mercers-Chappel *in* Cheap-ſide.

1. SOt's Paradiſe: Or the Humours of a Derby-Ale-Houſe: With a Satyr upon the Ale. Price Six Pence.

2. A Trip to *Jamaica*: With a True Character of the People and Iſland. Price Six Pence.

3. *Eclesia & Factio.* A Dialogue between *Bow-Steeple-Dragon*, and the *Exchange-Graſhopper*. Price Six Pence.

4. The Poet's Ramble after Riches. With Reflections upon a Country Corporation. Alſo the Author's Lamentation in the time of Adverſity. Price Six Pence.

5. A Trip to *New-England.* With a Character of the Country and People, both Engliſh and Indians. Price Six Pence.

6. Modern Religion and Ancient Loyalty: A Dialogue. Price Six Pence.

7. The World Bewitch'd. A Dialogue between Two Aſtrologers and the Author. With Infallible Predictions of what will happen in this Preſent Year, 1699. From the *Vices* and *Villanies* Practis'd in *Court*, *City* and *Country*. Price Six Pence.

8. A Walk to *Iſlington*: With a Deſcription of New *Tunbridge*-VVells, and *Sadler's* Muſick-Houſe. Price Six Pence.

9. The Humours of a Coffee-Houſe: A Comedy. Price Six Pence.

10 A Frolick to *Horn-Fair.* With a Walk from Cuckold's-Point thro' *Deptford* and *Greenwich.* Price Six-Pence.

11. The Firſt Volume of the LONDON-SPY: In Twelve Parts.

All Written by the ſame Author.

THE
LONDON
SPY.

**EING** now well tired with the days Fatigue, our thirsty Veins and drooping Spirits call'd for the assistance of a Cordial Flask. In order to gratifie our craving Appetites with this Refreshment, we stood a while debating whither we should Steer our Course, and what Tavern we should choose to enrich our Minds with unadulterated Juice. My Friend at last recollected a little Sanctified *Aminadsb* in *Finch-lane*, whose Purple *Nectar* had acquir'd a Singular Reputation amongst the Staggering Zealots of the Sober Fraternity, who are allow'd of late to be as good Judges of the comfortable Creature, as a *Proteſtant Prieſt*, or a *Latitudinarian* Fuddle-cap, who (as Rooks play) drink Wine on Sundays.

To this Salutiferous Fountain of Nature's choiceſt Juleps, our inclinations led us, tho' we knew the little Ruler of the Manſion intended it chiefly for Watering the Lambs of Grace, and not to ſuccour the Evil off-ſpring of a Reprobate Generation.

When we had entred our Land of Promiſe, which overflow'd with more Healthful Riches than either Milk or Honey, we found all things were as ſilent as the Mourning Attendants at a Rich Mans Funeral; no ringing of *Bar-Bell*, bawling of *Drawers*, or ratling of *Pot-lids*; But a general huſh ordered to be kept thro' the whole Family, as a warning to all Tiplers at their entrance, how they make a Noiſe to awake the Spirit, left it move the Maſters and Drawers to ſtand ſtill when you call 'em; and refuſe to draw you any more Wine, for fear the inward Man ſhould break out into open diſorder.

In the Entry we met two or three bluſhing Saints, who had been holding forth ſo long over the Glaſs, that had it not been for their flapping Umbrella's, Puritanical Coats, and diminutive Cravats, ſhap'd like the Roſe of a Parſons Hat-band, I ſhould have taken them by their Scarlet Faces, to have been good Chriſtians. They paſs'd us by as upright and as

ſtiff,

ftiff, as fo many Figures in a *Raree-fhow*; as if a touch of the Hat, had been committing of Sacriledge; or a Ceremonious Nod, a rank Idolatry.

A Drunken-look'd Drawer, difguis'd in a Sober-Garb, like a Wolf in Sheeps Clothing, or the Devil in a Fryars Habit, fhew'd us into the Kitchen, where we told him we were defirous of being, as Crickets covet Ovens, for the fake of warmth: Several of Father *Ramfeys* flouching Difciples fat hovering over their Half-pints, like fo many Coy Goffips over their Quarterns of Brandy, as if they were afraid any body fhould fee 'em; caft as many froward looks upon us Swords-men, as fo many Mifers would do upon a couple of fpunging Acquaintance; as if they took us for fome of the wild *Irifh*, that fhould have Cut their Throats in the beginning of the late Revolution.

However we bid our felves Welcome into their Company; and were forc'd for want of Room, the Kitchen being well fill'd, to mix higgle-de piggle-de, as the Rooks amongft the Crows upon the Battlements of a Church-Steeple: They leering at us under their Bongrace with as much contempt as fo many *Primitive Chriftians* at a couple of *Pagans*.

We, like true Proteftant Topers, who fcorn the Hypocrifie of Tipling by half Pints, as if we drank rather to wafh away our *Sins* than our *Sorrows*, appear'd bare-fac'd, call'd for a Quart at once, and foon difcover'd our Religion by our Drinking; whilft they, like true Puritans, gifted with abundance of holy Cheats, will never be Catch'd over more than half a Pint, tho' they'll drink Twenty at a Sitting.

The Wine prov'd extraordinary, which indeed was no more than we expeded, when we found our felves Surrounded with fo many Spiritual Mum-chances, whofe Religious Looks fhew them to be true Lovers of what the Righteous are too apt to efteem as the chiefeft Bleffing of Providence.

We had not fat long, obferving the Humours of the drowthy Saints about us, but feveral amongft them began to look as chearful, as if they had drown'd the terrible apprehenfions of Futurity, and thought no more of Damnation, than a Whore of a Twelve-months ftanding.

The Drawer now was conftantly imploy'd in replenifhing their Scanty Meafures; for once warm'd, they began to drink fo faft, 'twas the Bufinefs of one Servant to keep them doing. Notwifftanding their great averfion to external Ceremony, one pluck'd off his Hat, and ask'd his next Neighbour, *What do'ft thou think, Friend, this coft me? But before thou telleft me, let me Drink; and I hope thou underftand'ft my meaning.* This I fuppofe, was the Canting Method of paying more than ordinary Veneration to fome peculiar thoughts; which by this ftratagem were render'd Intelligible to each other: For I took Notice this Allegorical method of drinking fome obliging Health, was obferv'd thro' the whole Society, with reverence of uncover'd Heads, under a crafty pretence of examining into the price of each others Hat; and when they were defirous to Elevate their Lethargick Spirits with the circulation of a Bumper, one fills it, and offers the prevailing Temptation to his left Hand

Companion,

Companion in thefe words, faying, *Friend, does the Spirit move thee to re-ceive the good Creature thus plentifully?* The other replys, *Yea, Do thou take and enjoy the fruits of thy own Labour, and by the help of Grace I will drink another as full.* Thus did the liquorifh Saints quaff it about as merrily, after their precife Canting manner, as fo many Country Parfons over a Tub of Ale, when freed from the remarks of their cenforious Parifhioners, till, like reprobate Sinners, who have not the fear of Providence before their Eyes, they were deluded by Satan into a Wicked State of Drunkennefs.

By this time the fubtile Spirits of the Noble Juice had given in us frefh motion to the Wheels of Life, and Coroborated thofe fprings which impart Vigour and Activity to the whole Engine of Mortality; and my Friend muft needs be fo frolikfome to Tune his Pipes, and entertain us with a Song, in order to try whether thofe who were deaf to Reafon and good Manners, had any Ears towards Mufick with their Wine, which are ufually held to be fuch infeparable Companions, that the true Relifh of the one, can never be Enjoy'd without the affiftance of the other: And becaufe the words happen'd in fome meafure applicable to that prefent Juncture, I have thought it not amifs to infert 'em.

SONG.

WHY *fhould Chriftians be reftrain'd*
From the brisk enliv'ning Juice;
Heaven only has ordain'd
(Thro' Love to Man) for humane ufe?
Should not Claret *be deny'd*
To the Turks; *they'd Wifer grow;*
Lay their Alchoran *afide,*
And foon believe as Chriftians do.

CHORUS.

For Wine and Religion, like Mufick and Wine,
As they are Good in themfelves, do to Goodnefs incline;
And make both the Spirit and Flefh fo divine,
That our Faces and Graces both equally fhine:
Then ftill let the Bumper round Chriftendom *pafs,*
For Paradice *loft may be found in Glafs.*

Juft as my Friend had ended his Sonnet, in came the little Lord of the Tippling Tenement, about the height of a Nine-pin, with his Head in a Hat of fuch Capacious Dimenfions, that his Body was as much drown'd under the difproportion'd Brims of this unconfcionable Caftor, as a Pigmy under the Umbrage of a Giants Bongrace, or a Moufe crept into a Clofe-ftool-pan. He was button'd into a plain Veftment that touch'd no part of his Body but his Shoulders; his Coat being fo large, and his Carcafe fo little, that it hung about him like a Maukin upon a crofs-ftcik in a Country Peas-field: His Arms hung dangling like a Mobs Taffy mounted upon a Red-herring upon St. *David's*-day, and his Legs fo flender, they bid defiance to any Parifh Stocks.

B   He

He waited a little while the motion of the Spirit; and when he had com-pos'd his Countenance, and put himself into a fit posture for Reproof, he breaks into this following Oration, *Pray, Friend, forbear this Prophane hollow-ing and hooting in my House, the wicked Noise thou mak'st among my Sober Friends, is neither pleasing to them nor me; and since I find the Wine is too powerful for thy Inward-man, I must needs tell thee I will draw thee no more of it. I therefore desire thee to Pay for what thou hast had, and depart my House, for I do not like thy ways, nor does any Body here approve of thy rant-ing doings.*

We were not much surpris'd at this piece of Fanatical Civility, it be-ing no more than we expected; but the manner of his delivery, render'd his words so very diverting, that we could not forbear laughing him into so great a Passion, that the looks of the little Saint, discover'd as great a Devil in his Heart, as a Pious Disciple of his bigness could be well possess'd with: Then according to his Request, we paid our Reckoning, and left him in a condition of Vinegar and Crabs Eyes, upon a great ferment.

From thence (pursuant to my Friends inclinations) we adjourn'd to the Sign of the *Angel* in *Fanchurch-street*, where the Vintner, like a double-dealing Citizen condescended as well to draw Carmans Comfort, as the Consolatory Juice which Nature has bestow'd on more deserving Mor-tals. There my Friend had the good Fortune to meet with some of his Acquaintance with whom we Joyn'd, and made up, together, as pretty a Tippling Society, as ever were drawn into a Circumference, from the Noble Center of a Punch-Bowle; tho' [our] Liquor was the Blood of the Grape, in which we found that delectable Sweetness, that so many thirsty Pigs round a Trough-ful of Ale-grounds, could not have exprest more satis-faction in their Grunts, than we did in our merry Songs and Catches.

Time now taking the Advantage of our carelesness, prun'd his Wings, and fled with such Celerity, that he had brought the Noon of Night upon our Backs before our Thoughts had measur'd out a sufficiency of the Noble Creature to our craving Appetites; and as we were contending with the drousie Master for the other Quart, who should come in and put an end to our Controversie; but a Tall, Meagre, Carrionly *Cony-fum-ble*, and with him his Crazy Crew of Cornigerous Halberteers, who look'd, together, like *Judas* and his Accomplices, or a parcel of *Tom-T——d-Men* with their long Poles coming to Gauge a Vault. When he had given us a fair Sight of his painted Authority, which he stamp'd down upon the boards before him, with as much threatning Violence, as a *Jack-Adams* in a *Musick-house*, at the end of every strain, when dancing with a Quar-ter-staff; Then, with as much Pride as a Loobily Mayor of a Country Corporation, he open'd his Mouth, like *Balaam's* Ass, and thus Spake; *Look you, d'ye see me, Gentlemen? 'Tis an unseasonable time of Night for Peo-ple to be Tippling; every honest Man ought to have been in his Bed an hour or two ago.* That's true, said I, for no body ought to be up so late, but Constables and their Watches; at which some of the Company titter'd; which gave great offence to the Cholerick Conservator, who commanded us instantly to be gone, or he would commit us to the *Counter*. A Wine-Cooper in the Company, being well aquainted with this shred of Autho-rity, us'd importunate Solicitations for the Liberty of drinking another

Quart,

Quart, saying, *Pray Mr. Constable, don't be thus severe with us; 'twas but last Night you and I were drinking at a later hour together, I therefore hope you won't deny us the Priviledge your self has so lately taken.* This bitter Reflection, tost into the very Mouth of a Magistrate, had such an unsavory relish, that he could not swallow it; but commanded his Black-guard to take us to the *Poultry-Counter*, who presently fell on, like so many Foot-Pads; first secur'd our Weapons, and then led us along by the Elbows, in Triumph to the Rats-Castle, where we were forc'd to do pennance till the next Morning, in obedience to the Will of a Cucumber Cormorant, a Taylor good Lord! At whom I had flung a Remnant of hard words, which made the Cross-leg'd Nit-cracker more particularly my Enemy.

After we had pass'd thro' a spacious Porch, where Knaves in a forenoon may be seen in Clusters as thick as Pick-pockets round *Tyburn* at an Execution, or Beggars at a Hall Gate upon a Festival day, we came to a frightful Grate, more terrible than the Scene of Hell in *Circe*, where Oak and Iron were met in Conjunction to Eclipse our Liberty. After two or three knocks of Authority were given at the Gate, a single-headed *Cerberus*, in a fur Cap, let fall a Chain, from the Back of a Barricado, that made a more terrible ratling in our Ears, than the Tongue of a Scold, or a Clap of Thunder: Then with a Key much bigger than St. *Peters*, in which there was enough Iron to have made a Porridge-Pot, and consisted of more Wards than are Parishes in the City, he open'd the Wicket of the Poor-Mans Purgatory, into which they thrust us, one upon the back of another, like so many Swine into an Hogs-stie. The Turn-Key was so Civil to offer us Beds, but, upon such unconscionable terms, that a Salt Sinner might have hir'd a Feather'd Conveniency in a Bawdy-House, with a Downy Bed-fellow into the bargain, for less Money than they exacted for the Sheets; So, like good Husbands, we thank'd him for his Love, but refus'd his Courtesie.

After we had taken two or three turns in a Pav'd-yard, viewing the Strength and Loftiness of our Garrison by Star-light, we began to reflect upon the Mischance we had fallen under; and look'd as simple as so many Knight Errants forc'd into an Enchanted Castle. As we were thus ruminating upon our present Circumstances, we heard the Laughing of many Voices, mix'd with the confus'd wranglings of a different Society: We ask'd the under Turn-key the meaning of this promiscuous Noise; who told us, the Prisoners on the Common-side were driving away Sorrow; and making themselves merry with some of their Pastimes: Upon which we made it our choice to be of their Society, and desir'd admittance (accordingly) amongst 'em, as a means to pass away the tediousness of the Night with some diversion, and also that we might Judge the better of Confinement, and the hardships of a Prison.

When we first enter'd this Apartment, under the title of the *Kings-Ward*, the mixtures of Scents that arose from *Mundungus Tobacco*, foul Sweaty *Toes*, Dirty *Shirts*, the *Sh——t-Tub*, stinking *Breaths*, and uncleanly *Carcasses*, Poison'd our Nostrils far worse than a *Southwark* Ditch, a *Tanners* Yard, or a *Tallow-chandlers* Melting-Room. The Ill-looking Vermin, with long Rusty Beards swaddled up in Rags, and their heads some cover'd with Thrum Caps, and others thrust into the tops of old
Stockins;

Stockins; fome quitted their Play they were before engag'd in, and came hovering round us, like fo many Canibals, with fuch devouring Countenances, as if a Man had been but a Morfel with 'em, all crying out *Garnifh, Garnifh,* as a Rabble in an Infurrection, cry *Liberty, Liberty.* We were forc'd to fubmit to their Doctrine of Non-refiftance, and comply with their demands, which extended to the Sum of Two Shillings each. Having thus Paid our Initiation Fees, we were bid Welcome into the *Kings-Ward*; and to all the Priviledges and Immunities thereof. This Ceremony being ended, the Lowfie Affembly of Tatterdemallions, with their fingers in their Necks, return'd to their Sports, and were as merry as fo many Beggars in a Barn; fome of them form'd a high Court of Juftice, by whom a Criminal was to be try'd for Cracking his Lice between his Teeth, and Spitting out the Bloody Skins about the Ward, to the great Nufance of the good Subjects of *England* under Confinement in the *Poultry:* The Culprit mov'd the Court to allow him Counfel, which was granted; and there happening to be amongft them a Fat *York-fhire* Attorney who was committed for foul Practice, and extorting undue Fees, the Offender at the Bar chofe him as his Advocate, who indeed was very induftrious in the defence of his Client, till a couple of unlucky Rogues, who were privately appointed to manage the Defign, came on a fuddain, charg'd with their hands-full of Sir-reverence out of the excreting-Tub, mix'd up with Soot and Tallow, and as the poor Pleader was gaping to the Court, with abundance of intention, they flap'd it into his Mouth, as Poulterers do Pafte when they cram Capons; and what by the ftrength of his Jaws he bit off with his Teeth, and would not fuffer to be internally apply'd, they anointed his Face with, till they had made him ftink like a *Tom-T——d-Man,* and look as Beautiful as a Chimney-Sweeper.

This put the Court, as well as the other Spectators, into an exceffive laughter, to fee the poor Lawyer Spit, Splutter, Spew, and run about Swearing and Curfing, Raving and Crying, like a *Bedlamite* that had broke his Chains; they having hid the Bucket of Water, that he had nothing either to gargle his Mouth, or recover his Face to its Natural Complection: Every body was glad to efcape his fury, by keeping at a diftance; none came within the reach of his Arms, or the fcent of his Breath, which you may be fure ftunk as bad as a Houfe of Office; till at laft he feifes a Young fellow, who had no hand in the matter, and blow'd upon him like a Bear upon a Dog, till he had almoft poifon'd him; and fo befmeer'd him with Kiffes, that they look'd as like one another in the Face, as the two Images of St. *Dunftan's* Clock. In revenge of which, the Young Sufferer retir'd to the Stink-Tub, as a good fortrefs well ftor'd with Ammunition, there fifh'd for Pellats, which he caft fo thick upon his Adverfary, that he made him look and ftink like a Bogg'd Bayliff, and now and then a Random-Shot hit a ftander-by, which had like to have begot him more Enemies: what the Lawyer could gather from the Ground and pick off his Garment, he moft Manfully return'd, and fighting Cunning, being much upon the Dodg, an unlucky Bullet flew over his Shoulder, and fhot a broken Perfumer juft in the Face, whofe Noftrils being us'd to Odoriferous Scents, were the more Offended at the unfavory misfortune, which came with fuch angry force, from a provok'd Enemy, that the major part of his Face was eclips'd by the Stinking Meffenger of War.

Both

Both fides maintain'd the Battel with great bravery, till their Ammunition was quite fpent, which forc'd them to end their Quarrel in a few hard Words. But notwithftanding they gave equal Teftimonials of their undaunted Courage, yet I muft needs tell you, they both came off, faving your Prefence, in a very Shitten Condition.

When the foul mutiny was thus ended, which began in a Sir-reverence, a general Search was made after the Bucket of Water, in order to wafh off their Impurities with which, in the heat of Paffion, they had wofully defil'd each other; after a fedulous enquiry, they found the hidden Element, which by cleaning their Hands and Faces, they foon died of a Beaftly Complexion.

By this time moft of the *Pediculous* Inhabitants of thefe uncomfortable Confines, being well tired with the Paftimes of the Night, were fitting Naked in their Cabins over-hauling their Shirts, and preffing their Eight-leg'd Enemies to death between their Thumb-nails, wherefoe'er they found them; every now and then came a frightful figure from aloft, clawing his own flefh for madnefs, he was fo Loufie; turns his Buttocks o'er the edge of a Wooden Conveniency, lets fly, and away Scowres up again: At laft defcends a Fellow in a Mourning Surplifs, and in his hand a Wooden Porridge-difh, whofe hair ftood as if, *Medufa*-like, it had been turn'd into Snakes; whither fhould he trot, but to the Pail of Water, where the Dunghil-fcented Combatants had wafh'd off their Mire, and quaffs off a couple of Bumpers very favourly; but as foon as it was down, he found it left a very unpallatable Relifh behind it, which made poor drowthy *Barnaby* fall a Spitting and Curfing, the *Plague D—n the Pump, it is grown fo rotten, and makes the Water tafte fo ftrong of the Tree, that we fhall be all poifon'd.* This unlucky deception of the innocent miftaken Wretch, rais'd amongft my Friends and I a great deal of Merriment; who, like the reft of Mankind, were under a natural propenfity to laugh at mifchief. The fellow had got drunk in the Cellar, and went to Bed before the Prifoners began their Revels, and knew nothing of the feud had been rais'd by the dropings of the Fundament, which occafion'd him to be thus deceiv'd.

Now the whole Family were grown as filent as fo many Hogs when their Bellies are full, nothing being heard but Snoring, except now and then a Crack from the ftretching of a Loufes Skin, or an ingrateful Sound from the untunable Drone of a filthy Bag-pipe, which is never heard, but by the affiftance of a ftinking breath: With this of fort Mufick were our Ears entertain'd all Night; and that my Eyes might be oblig'd with anfwerable fatisfaction, I thought it now the only time to look about me, where I obferved Men lay pill'd in Cabins one upon another, like Coffins in a Burying Vault, poffeffing only the fame allowance above Ground, as the Dead do under, their Breadth and Length, and that's all. Other poor Currs, that wanted the conveniency of Kennels, (being fupernumerary to the Sleeping Huts) were lain fome upon Benches, as if they had been bred Courtiers Footmen: Others Coil'd underneath, like Dogs, and flept as found as Low-Country Soldiers: Some lay round the Fire, almoft cover'd with afhes, like Pottatoes roafting, with their Nofes in Conjunction with one anothers A———s, like Hogs upon a Dung-hil:

C

Thefe

These I suppose were tender Mortals, bred up at the Forge, and as great Enemies to cold weather, as the Mad Fellow that walks about the Town Naked. Another was crept into a Corner, and had whelm'd over his Head the Ashes Tub, and so made a Night-Cap of an Ale-firkin, to defend his head from the coldness of the weather.

With these sort of Observations we past away the dull hours of Confinement till the morning; and were all as glad to see day-light again, as a Man would be to see the Sun, that had tumbled by accident into a neglected Cole-pit: Our Fellow Sufferers began now to awake, stretch and yawn, and hawk up their Soot-colour'd Flegm, congeal'd in their filthy Stomachs, with unwholesome Belch and nasty *Oroonoko*. Every one stinking as he rows'd from his warm Den, like a Fox newly unkenneld. Now, I must confess, I was forc'd to hold my Nose to the Grate, and Snuff hard for a little fresh Air; for I was e'en choak'd with the unwholesome fumes that arose from their uncleanly Carcasses: Were the burning of Old Shooes, Dray-mens-Stockins, the diping of Card-matches, and a full Close-stool-pan, to be prepared in one Room, as a Nosegay to torment my Nostrills, it could not have prov'd a more effectual Punishment.

At last I heard the Keys begin to rattle, which tho they were Indifferent Musick over Night, they were very pleasing to my Ears in the Morning. The Turn-Key now, according to my wishes, let us into the Yard, where we drew a little new breath, and belch'd into the World those Pestilential Seeds which were drawn into our Bodies, from the three fatal Sisters *Filth*, *Poverty*, and *Laziness*.

We now thought it necessary to fortifie our Stomachs with a Mornings draught, and accordingly descended into the Cellar to the same purpose, where every Captive, that had either Money or Credit, was for posting with all Speed.

Now we were happily come into the Conversation of the Ladies, who (poor Creatures) in tatter'd Garments, and without Head-cloaths, look'd as if they were just deliver'd from the Rude hands of an unmerciful Rabble. One amongst the rest, who had something more than ordinary in her Person, to recommend her to our Notice, I drank to, and beg'd the favour of her Company, which without much importunity she granted; and after a little talk, I took the freedom to ask her what she was in for: She hesitated a little, at last told me she was at the suit of a Tally-man in *Hounds-ditch*, for things to the Value of four Pounds; and that he offer'd to Kiss it out, but she would not let him; for which reason he Arrested her, and had her run up to an Execution. But, I suppose, Madam (said I) you have heartily repented since, that you refus'd the offer. *No Sir*, she replyed, *rather than I would gratifie the desires of such unmerciful Rogues as either Tally-man, Pawn-Broker or Bailiff, I would Prostitute my self to the honest Porters in the Town. For I'd have you to know, Sir, I scorn to defile my body with such Vermin, such inhumane Knaves, that can't be content to cheat People out of their Money, but must Cozen them out of their Liberty too. Here are but Thirteen poor Wretches of us on the Common-side, and Twelve of 'em were brought in upon the Tally-account; and if Pro-*

vidence shew us no more Mercy than our Creditors, here they may keep us as examples of their Cruelty, to frighten others in their Books to turn either Whore or Thief, to get Money to be Punctual to their Payments, which many have been forc'd to do, to my certain knowledge, to satisfie the hungry demands of those Unconscionable Usurers.

I was mightily pleas'd with the Womans talk, because I thought it reasonable to believe there was abundance of truth in't. For People that are poor, to pay such unreasonable extortion as *Cent per Cent*, it's a Scandal to the Laws, an Enemy to the Publick Good, a great oppression of the Poor, a shame to Christianity; and all to gratifie the Miserly Lusts of insatiate Consciences.

I rose up and peep'd a little about to survey this Subteranean Boozing Ken; and found it divided by as many Paritions, as the *Temple-*House of Office, tho' I confess it smelt not quite so sweet: The Walls were Varnish'd with the slime of Snails; and had nothing to cover their Nakedness in the coldest of Weather, but a Tiffany Cobweb wherein hung Spiders as Big as Humble-Bees that had not been molested with a Broom since they were first enliven'd. The Tables and Benches were of Sturdy Oak, handed down thro' many many Ages to Posterity, and look'd of that venerable Antiquity, as if they had been faithful Servants to some great Man in the first year of Jubilee. Like undutiful Children, we Trod and Spit upon the bare Skin of our first Parent, Earth; for 'twas floor'd like a Barn, tho' it stunk like a Stable; for every Body Piss'd as they sat, without requiring the use of a Chamber-Pot.

By this time came down the Constable who committed us, with a Countenance as white as the head of a *Rumford-Calf*; and both his Sleeves arm'd with Spanish Needles of all sorts and sizes, with here and there a Remnant of Basting-Thread and Stitching-Silk, hanging upon his Coat and Stockins. His Shoes, behind in the Quarters, being polish'd with the Sweat of his Heels, of a Jet-colour, to show his Profession requires him to be often Slip-shod. By Virtue of his painted Rowling-pin, he remov'd us from the Plagues of *Scotland*, and carry'd us before our Betters, Sir *Milk* and *Mayeril*, to answer what Mr. *Stablecunt*, could alledge against us. When his Worship had set his Band to rights, and Dress'd his Countenance with abundance of Gravity, he betakes himself to his Elbow-Chair, plac'd within a Bar, to keep unmannerly Transgressors at their due distance, and also to secure his Corns from the careless affronts of whispering Constables, who are commonly proud to be seen standing between Justice and the People. Our business was soon dispatch'd; 'twas a case so familiar to his Worship, that he had it his at fingers ends, without consulting of *Keeble:* For all the charge delivered against us was Tippling at an unseasonable hour, and refusing to go home according to the command of Authority. But Mr. *Buckram* being highly displeas'd at some aggravating Words I had given him over Night, told his Wisdom I threaten'd him; and said I would make him pay five Pound an hour for Detaining of me. *How!* says Sir *Serious, Pray what are you, that you Value your Time at so precious a Rate, or that dare speak such affrightning words to the face of the Kings Representative?* I reply'd, An't please your Worship, I am a Gauger, and was out last Night about the Kings Business as well as Mr. Conſtable; and the King, for ought I know, has ſuſtain'd two or three hundred Pounds damage by my being detain'd from my Duty, for which I look upon it Mr. Conſtable muſt be anſwerable, for I aſſure him, I will give a report of the matter to the Commiſſioners.

This put his Gravity to his hems and ha's. *I muſt confeſs, Mr. Con-ſtable,* (ſaid he) *You did not do well to commit one of his Majeſties Officers; it was very unadviſedly done of you. Well, Gentlemen, paying your Fees, you may all go about your Buſineſs, I have nothing further to ſay to you.*

Had it not been for the aſſiſtance of a few Brains, and a little Con-fidence, I had been bound over to the Seſſions: But I bleſs my Stars, a lucky Providence prevented the misfortune; and reſtor'd us to our for-mer Liberty. Being now glad we had ſhak'd off the Yoke of Confine-ment at ſo eaſie a Rate, without paying for either Drunkenneſs, Swea-ring, or the like, which are as commonly accumulated upon any Tranſgreſ-ſors under our Circumſtances, as it is to find Canvas, Stay-tape, and Buck-ram in a Taylors Bill. As we had been fellow Sufferers together, there was no parting without a Glaſs; ſo we went to the *Roſe Tavern* in the *Poultry,* where Wine, according to its merit, had juſtly gain'd a Reputation; and there in a Snug Room, warm'd with Bruſh and Faggot, over a quart of Good Claret, we laugh'd at our Nights Adventure, and Curs'd the Con-ſtable. And that all others, who fall into his Clutches, may do the like, I have given them the ſame Words to their Aſſiſtance.

> *May Rats and Mice*
> *Conſume his Shreds,*
> *His Patterns and his Meaſures;*
> *May Nits and Lice*
> *Infeſt his Beds,*
> *And Care confound his Pleaſures.*
> *May his Long-Bills*
> *Be never paid;*
> *And may his Help-mate Horn him;*
> *May all his Ills*
> *Be Publick made;*
> *And may his Watchmen Scorn him.*
> *May Cucumbers*
> *Be all his Food,*
> *And Small-Beer be his Liquor;*
> *Luſtful Deſires*
> *Still fire his Blood,*
> *But may his Reins grow weaker.*
> *When old, may he*
> *Reduced be,*
> *From Conſtable to Beadle,*
> *And live until*
> *He cannot feel*
> *His Thimble from his Needle.*

After

After we had drank a refreshing Glass, my Friend and I took leave of our Companions; and concluded to take a turn in *Guild-hall,* which he told me was a fine Place; and my Lord Mayors chosen Dining-room, upon his Day of Triumph. As I came out of the Tavern, Bumpkin-like, I could no more forbear staring at *Bow-Steeple,* than an Astrologer could looking at a *Blasing-star,* or a Young Debauchee, at a fine *Woman:* But I wonder'd the Projector of such a Noble Pyramid, should form so mean a Model for the Church; which compar'd together, are just the reverse of St. *Andrews Holborn,* the one being like a Woman with a Beautiful Face joyn'd to a deform'd Body, and the other, like an old Pigmy's head upon a young Giants Shoulders. But, pray, said I, what is the meaning of that terrible Monster upon the Top, instead of a Fane, or Weather-cock? Why that (says my Friend) is a Brazen Dragon, exalted as an Emblem of the Churches Persecution: The *Dissenters* once look'd Devilishly a Squint at it, but now they dread it no more, than *More* of *More-hall* did the Dragon of *Wantly.*

From thence we Jostled thro' a parcel of busie Citizens, who blunder'd along with as much speed towards the *Change,* as Lawyers in Term time towards *Westminster-hall,* till we turn'd down *Kings-street,* and came to the Place intended; Which I enter'd with as great astonishment, to see the Gyants, as the *Morrocco* did *London,* when he saw the Snow fall. I ask'd my Friend the meaning or design of setting up those two Lubberly preposterous Figures, for I suppose they had some peculiar end in't? Truly, says my Friend, I am wholly Ignorant of what they intented by 'em, unless they were to show the City what huge Loobies their Forefathers were, or else to fright stubborn Apprentices into obedience: for the dread of appearing before two such Monstrous Loggerheads, will sooner reform their manners, or mould 'em into a compliance of their Master's Will, then carrying 'em before my Lord Mayor, or the Chamberlain of *London*; for some of them are as much frighted at the Names of *Gog* and *Magog,* as little Children are at the terrible sound of *Raw-head* and *Bloody-Bones.*

Pray, said I, what are yon cluster of People doing, that seem all as busie as so many Fools at the Royal Oak Lottery? Truly, said my Friend, you are something mistaken in your comparison; if you had said *Knaves,* you had hit it, for that's the S——s C—-t; and I must needs give 'em that Character, That I never yet knew one *Fool* among them, tho' they have to do with a great many. All those Tongue-padders who are Chattering within the Bar, are Picking the Pockets of those that stand without. You may know the Sufferers by their pale Faces; the Passions of Hope, Fear, and Revenge, hath put them into such disorder, they are as easie to be distinguish'd in a Croud by their Looks, as an Owle from a Hawk, or a Country Esquire from a Town Sharper.

He's a very comely Gentleman, said I, that sits upon the Bench; and puts on as pleasing a Countenance, as if, like a God, he view'd with Pleasure the Jars and Discords of contending Mortals, that Fret and Fume beneath him.

My Friend reply'd, He might well look merrily who sits the playing
D
of

of so many great Games, and is sure always to be on the Winning-side. For you muſt know, ſays he, theſe Courts are like Publick Gaming-Tables, the Steward's the Box-keeper, the Councel and Attorneys are the Sharpers, and the Clients the Fools that are bubbled out of their Money.

Pray what is that Croud doing at the other end of the Hall? That, my Friend told me, was the Court of Conſcience, whoſe buſineſs it is to take care that a Debtor, of a Sum under forty Shillings, ſhall not pay Money faſter than he can get it. 'Tis a very reaſonable Eſtabliſhment, without Jeſting, for the prevention of poor Peoples ruin, who lie at the Mercy of a parcel of Raſcally Tally-men, and ſuch like Unconſcionable Traders, who build their own Well-fare upon the Miſeries and Wants of others. There are ſeveral other Courts held here, beſides what we now ſee ſitting, but this I think does the moſt good of any of 'em, except to the Lawyers; and they look upon it with as evil an Eye, as the Devil look'd over *Lincoln*.

Pray, ſaid I, whoſe graceful Pictures are theſe, that are ſo great an Ornament to the Place? My Friend reply'd, They were the grave Sages of the Law. Sure, ſaid I, he was no skillful Artiſt that painted 'em. Do but ſee how black he has made ſome of the Palms of their Hands. Poh, poh, crys my Friend, I find you are no Judge of Painting; Why it muſt be ſo, that's nothing but the Shadow, don't you ſee the Light ſtrikes full upon the back of the hand, and conſequently the inſide muſt appear Dark; That's true (ſaid I) I thank you for making me ſo much the Wiſer: I muſt confeſs it is an Art I have no knowledge in. Pray whoſe Pictures are thoſe at the upper end? Thoſe, reply'd my Friend, are the King and the Late Queen *Mary*; and thoſe in black Gowns, with the Purſe before them, are ſuch who have been Chancellors. Bleſs me! ſaid I, Painting is a fine Art: How ſtedfaſtly all thoſe in black look upon the King? But, to my thinking, all thoſe who come after in Red, Squint with one Eye upon his Majeſty, and the other wiſtfully upon the Purſe and Mace.

Away, away, ſays my Friend, that's nothing but your fooliſh fancy, I ſhall apply the old Proverb to you, *As the Fool thinketh, the Bell clinketh.* We have ſeen all we can ſee here at this time, I'll go and ſhow you St. *Pauls*, and by that time, I reckon you'll have got you a good Stomach to your Dinner.

According to my Friends Propoſal, we ſteer'd our Courſe towards the famous Cathedral; and as we paſs'd along *Cheapſide*, we met an old fellow with a Noſe (bleſs my Eye-ſight!) 'twas as long almoſt as a Rowling-Pin, and I am ſure as big at the end as a Foot-ball, beſet with Carbuncles and Rubies, no *Princes* Noſe could have appear'd more Glorious; and look'd as freſh as the Gills of an angry Turky-cock; and was ſo rare a fence for his Mouth, that whoever fights him, muſt firſt knock off the Gnomon of his Face, or he could never propoſe to do his Teeth any Dammage. I wonder (ſaid I) he ſhould be ſo fooliſh to walk the ſtreets in publick: Certainly if he would keep private, and only ſhow himſelf in *Bartholomew* Fair, amongſt the *Arabian* Monſters, he might make his Noſe worth two or three hundred Pound a year to him. Says my Friend, It's nothing now, to what it is ſome times; you ſee it in the Wane: He's

forc'd

forc'd to have it par'd every full Moon, it grows so fast. I see by its Redness it has been done lately; I'll warrant you he has had a Pound or two of Stakes cut off on't within this day or Two. I vow, said I, 'tis very strange; methinks my Nose begins to swell at the very thoughts of him. Sure this is *Tom Jolly*, the Song was made on, is he not?

No, says my Friend, This is a good honest fellow, a Tally-man, and is a true Toper of Claret; he will sit Twelve hours in a Tavern before he can fill his Nose, when he has replenish'd which, he Staggers home; and the Bottle-end being Spungy, he Squeezes it again into his Mouth and has the pleasure of Drinking on't a second Time; and will live longer, they say, by sucking his Nose, than a Bear can by licking his Paws. Marry, said I, that may well be, for if you tell me Truth, his Nasal Runlet affords much the better Liquor.

We had not gone much further, but we met with a fellow stark Naked from the Wast upward, arm'd with a lusty Cudgel; I concluded he must be either Fool or Madman, to expose his bare flesh to the sharp Pinches of so cold a Season; But however, I enquir'd of my Friend if he knew the meaning of his ridiculous Whimsie? Who Reply'd, He had heard he was a Man of good Parts and Learning; and from thence did believe he was a kind of self-will'd *Philosopher*, who had a mind to broach some new Principles, and make People believe he first left off his Cloaths to keep him Warm, and ever since has refus'd to put 'em on for fear he should catch Cold by wearing 'em. But I fancy has made but few Proselytes; he has gone in this manner many years, till his Skin is by the Weather as hard as the outward part of a Draymans Shooe. I met him the last Snowy day we had, going into the Fields (instead of a Mouthful) to take his Belly-full of fresh Air; and esteems it much better walking then, than at Mid-summer.

By this time we were come to *Cheapside*-Conduit, pallisado'd in with Chimney-sweepers Brooms. These we pass'd, and enter'd into *Pauls* Church-yard; where our Eyes were surpris'd with such a Mountainous heap of Stones, that I thought it must require the assistance of a whole Nation for an Age to remove 'em from the Quary, and pile 'em upon one another in such admirable Order, and to so Stupendious a height.

We turn'd to the Right, where Booksellers were as Plenty as *Pedlars* at a Fair,: and Parsons in their Shops as busily searching after the Venerable Conceits of our Worm-eaten Ancestors, as if they came thither for want of Brains, or a Library, to patch up a Seasonable Discourse for the following Sunday.

Pray, says my Friend, take Notice of that old Lanthorn-Jaw'd Peri-patetick, so thoughtfully perambulating in his Ware-house of Roman Saints, Religious Heathens, and Honest Sociable Moralists. He looks so like a Modern Polititian, as if thro the whole Course of his Life he had Studied nothing but a *Machiavel*. In all seasons of the Year you may find him walking in his Shop; and (like a *Spanish* Farrier, that Shooes Horses in his Cloak) he is never to be seen without his hanging Coat, at all Times, and in all Business For as the Satyr in the Fables, could

with

with the same breath, blow Hot and Cold; so is his *Irish* Mantle possess'd of the like qualities; for he wears it in the Winter to keep him Warm, and in the Summer as an Umbrella to skreen his wither'd Carcase from the scorching Sun-beames. Tho he has but a small Head, he has a great deal more Brains than a Goose; and never gave any body an Occasion to call him Fool that ever dealt with him. He's so far a true bred *Englishman*, as to be a great Enemy to the intrest of *France*; for he rails mightily against Taverns, and never drinks Wine but when he's treated. He's a little too Cunning to be too Honest, and too Miserly to be Generous; Loves nothing more than his Money, and hates nothing so much as to part with it: Calls Generosity, Folly; Charity, Extravagance; Over-reaching, Wisdom; Nigardliness, Discretion; and Unconscionable Extortion, but a lawful Interest. Since *Winchester* quarts were thrown out of fashion, he never has been known to Drink strong Drink but once, and then treated by his Apprentice, who had found at the Door a piece of Money, and being upon his Masters Ground, he claim'd the right; and after some little Contest about the matter, they agreed to spend it.

It now being about Three a Clock, we concluded to go into *Pauls*, an Account of which, I shall give in my next.

F I N I S.

THE
LONDON
SPY.

For the *Month* of *March*, 1699.

PART V.

By the Author of the **Trip** *to* **JAMAICA.**

LONDON,
Printed and Sold by *J. How*, in the *Ram-Head-Inn-Yard* in
Fanchurch-street, 1699.

Books Sold by J. How, *in the* Ram-Head-Inn-Yard *in* Fanchurch-Street; J. Weld, *at the* Crown *between the* Temple-Gates *in* Fleet-ftreet; *and* Mrs. Fabian, *at* Mercers-Chappel *in* Cheap-fide.

1. SOt's Paradife: Or the Humours of a Derby-Ale-Houfe: With a Satyr upon the Ale. Price Six Pence.

2. A Trip to *Jamaica*: With a True Character of the People and Ifland. Price Six Pence.

3. *Ecclefia & Factio*. A Dialogue between *Bow-Steeple-Dragon*, and the *Exchange-Grafhopper*. Price Six Pence.

4. The Poet's Ramble after Riches. With Reflections upon a Country Corporation. Alfo the Author's Lamentation in the time of Adverfity. Price Six Pence.

5. The London Spy, the Firft, Second, Third, Fourth, Fifth, Sixth, Seventh, Eighth, Ninth, Tenth, and Eleventh Parts. To be Continued *Monthly*. Price Six Pence Each.

6. A Trip to *New-England*. With a Character of the Country and People, both Englifh and Indians. Price Six Pence.

7. Modern Religion and Ancient Loyalty. A Dialogue. Price Six Pence.

8. The World Bewitch'd. A Dialogue between Two Aftrologers and the Author. With Infallible Predictions of what will happen in this Prefent Year, 1699. From the *Vices* and *Villanies* Practis'd in *Court*, *City* and *Country*. Price Six Pence.

9. A Walk to *Iflington*: With a Defcription of New *Tunbridge*-VVells, and *Sadler's* Mufick-Houfe. Price Six Pence.

10. The Humours of a Coffee-Houfe: A Comedy. Price Six Pence.

All Written by the fame Author.

THE
LONDON
SPY.

IN our Loitering Perambulation round the out-fide of *Pauls*, we came to a Picture-fellers Shop, where as many Smutty Prints were ftaring the Church in the Face, as a Learned Debauchee ever found in *Aretine*'s Poftures. I Obferv'd there were more People gazing at thefe loofe Fancies of fome Leacherous Graver, than I could fee reading of Sermons at the Stalls of all the Neighbouring Bookfellers. Amongft the reft of the Spectators, an old Citizen had mounted his Spectacles upon his Nofe, and was bufily peeping at the Bawdy Reprefentation of the Gentleman and the Milk-Maid. Pray Father, faid I, what do you find in that Immodeft Picture worth fuch ferious Notice? *Why, I'll tell you, Young Man, fays he, I cannot without wonder behold in this Painting the Madnefs and Vanity of you Young Fellows, with what Confidence you can take a Bear by the Tooth, without the Dread of the Danger.* I rather believe, faid I, you gratified fome fenfual Appetite, by giving Titilation to your Vitious Thoughts, from the Obfcenity of the Action. To which he reply'd, *Indeed Mr.* Inquifitive, *you are much miftaken; but if thy Head had been where his Hand is, I fhould have view'd it with much more Pleafure, To have thought in what a pretty Condition thy Nofe had been;* And away he fhuffled, with Compaffion towards his Corns, as ftiff as a *Tork-fhire* Bullock into *Smithfield* Market, very Merry at his Jeft; and chattering to himfelf like a Magpy that has Bilk'd a Gunner.

We Walk'd a little further, and came amongft the Mufick-fhops, in one of which were fo many Dancing-Mafters Prentices, Fidling and Piping of *Bories* and *Minuets*, That the Crowd at the door could no more forbear Dancing into the Shop, than the Merry Stones of *Thebes* could refufe capering into the Walls, when Conjur'd from Confufion, into order, by the Power of *Orpheus*'s Harmony. Amongft 'em ftood a little Red-fac'd Blade, beating Time upon his Counter, with as much Formality, as if a *Bartholemew* Fair Confort, with affiftance of a *Jack-pudding*, had been Ridiculing an *Italian* Sonetta in the Ballcony, to draw People into the Booth; and was as Prodigally Pert, in giving his Inftructions to the reft, as a Young Pedagogue Tutoring a Difciple in the hearing of his
Father.

Father. We added two to the Number of Fools; and ftood a little, making our Ears do Pennance to pleafe our Eyes, with the conceited Motions of the Heads and Hands, which mov'd too and fro with as much deliberate Stiffnefs, as the Two Wooden Horologifts at St. *Dunftan's*, when they ftrike the Quarters.

We left thefe Jingle-Brains to their Crotchets, and proceeded to the Weft End of the Cathedral; where we paft by abundance of Apples, Nuts, and Ginger-bread, till we came to a Melancholly Multitude, drawn into a Circle, giving very ferious Attention to a Blind Ballad-finger, who was Mournfully fetting forth the wonderful ufefulnefs of a Godly Broad-Side, proper to be ftuck up in all Righteous and Sober Families, as a means to continue the Grace of God before their Eyes; and fecure even the little Lambs of the Flock, from the Temptations of *Satan*. After he had prepared the Ears of his Congregation, with a tedious Preamble, in Commendation of his Divine Poem; being mounted upon a Stone, above his Blew-Apron Auditory, he began with an Audible Voice to Lirick it over, in a Pfalm Tune, to the great fatisfaction of the Penitent Affembly; who Sigh'd and Sob'd, fhook their Heads and Cry'd; fhowing a Greater Sorrow and Contrition for their Sins, (which I believe indeed were great) than the Pious Affembly at *Megs's* Dancing-School, when the Reverend Doctor holds-forth upon Death and Judgment. At laft he came to the Terrible Words of Hell and Damnation, which he Sang out with fuch an Emphafis, that he put the People a trembling as if they had all been troubled with a *Tertian Ague*: Who liking not the harfh found of fuch Inharmonical Bugbear-Words, began to fneak off, like a Libertine out of a Church, when the Parfon galls the old Sores of his Confcience, by preffing too hard upon his Vices. Many Charitable Chriftians, bought his Religious Sonnets, becaufe he made 'em himfelf; wondering how a Blind-man fhould fee to Pen fuch marvellous good things; and remember to Sing them by Heart, without the help of his Eye-fight.

From thence we turn'd in thro' the Weft Gate of St. *Paul's* Church-Yard; where we faw a Parcel of Stone-Cutters and Sawyers fo very hard at work, that I Proteft, notwithftanding the Vehemency of their Labour, and the Temperatenefs of the Seafon, inftead of ufing their Handkerchiefs to wipe the Sweat off their Faces, they were moft of them blowing their Nailes. Blefs me! Said I to my Friend, fure this Church ftands in a Colder Climate than the reft of the Nation, or elfe thofe Fellows are of a ftrange Conftitution, to feem ready to Freez at fuch Warm Exercife. *You muft Confider*, fays my Friend, *this is Work carry'd on at a National Charge; and ought not to be haften'd on in a hurry; for the greateft Reputation it will gain when its Finifh'd, will be, That it was fo many Tears in Building.* From thence we mov'd up a Long Wooden Bridge, that led to the Weft Porticum of the Church, where we intermix'd with fuch a Train of Promifcuous Rabble, That I fancy'd we look'd like the Beafts driving into the Ark, in order to Replenifh a New Succeeding World.

The firft part that I Obferv'd of this inabruptable Pile, were the Pillars

lars that fustain'd the Covering of the Porch. I cannot but conceive faid I, that Legs of this Vaft Strength and Magnitude, are much too big for the Weight of fo fmall a Body it fupports. In anfwer to which, my Friend repeats me this following Fable.

There was a Little Carpenter, and he hew'd himfelf a Mighty ftrong Stool out of the whole Timber, to fit and Smoke a Pipe on at his Door: A Paffenger coming by, feeing fuch a Difproportion between the Man and his Seat, took an Occafion to ask him, *Why he had made fuch a huge Clumfy Stool for fuch a Pigmy of a Man*? He replyed, *He will it himfelf, and car'd not whether any Body elfe did or not*: Adding, *He intended it to ferve the Childrens Children of his Grand Children: And befides, the ftronger it is*, fays he, *if any Body finds fault, the better able it is to bear their Reflections*.

From thence we enter'd the Body of the Church; the Spacioufnefs of which we could not difcern for the Largenefs of the Pillars. What think you now, fays my Friend? Pray how do you like the Infide? I'll tell you, faid I, I muft needs anfwer you as a Gentleman did another, who was a Great Admirer of a very Gay Lady, and ask'd his Companion whether he did not think her a Woman of Extraordinary Beauty? Who anfwer'd, *Truly he could not tell, fhe might be fo for ought he knew; for he could fee but very little of her Face for Patches*. Poh, Poh, fays the other, *You muft not quarrel at that, fhe defigns them as Ornaments*. To which his Friend reply'd, *Since fhe has made them fo large, fewer might have ferv'd her turn; or if fhe muft wear fo many, fhe might have Cut 'em lefs*; and fo I think by the Pillars.

We went a little further, where we Obferv'd Ten Men in a Corner, very bufy about Two Mens Work; taking as much care that every one fhould have his due proportion of the Labour, as fo many Thieves, in making an Exact divifion of their Booty. The wonderful piece of difficulty, the whole Number had to perform, was to drag along a Stone of about three Hundred Weight, in a Carriage, in order to be hoifted upon the Moldings of the Cupula, but were fo fearful of difpatching this Facile Undertaking with too much Expedition, that they were fo long in hauling on't half the length of the Church, that a couple of Lufty Porters in the fame time, I am certain, would have carry'd it to Paddington, without Refting of their Burthen.

From thence we approach'd the Quire, the *North*-fide, by the entrance of which, being very much defac'd by the Late Fire, occafion'd by the Carelefnefs of a Plumber, who had been mending fome defective Pipes of the Organs; which unhappy Accident has given the Diffenters fo far an opportunity to reflect upon the ufe of Mufick in our Churches, that they Scruple not to vent their Spleen, by faying, 'Twas a Judgment from Heav'n upon their Carvings, and their Fopperies, for difpleafing the Ears of the Almighty with the Prophane Tootings of fuch abominable *Cat-Calls*. Tho' fome of the moft Learned amongft 'em, and in particular Mr. *Baxter*, were of a different Opinion, as to the ufe of grave Mufick in Holy Places; and fo highly extoll'd and commended to all Chriftians the Ufefulnefs of it, that in his *Chriftian Directory*, he expreffes thefe Words,

viz.

viz. As Spectacles are a Comfortable Help to the Reading of the Divine Scriptures, so Musick Serves to Exhilerate the Soul in the Service of Almighty God.—

Afternoon Prayers being now ready to begin, we pass'd into the Quire, which was adorn'd with all those graceful Ornaments, that could any ways add a becoming Beauty to the Decency, Splendor, and Nobility of so Magnificent a Structure; which indeed consider'd abstractly from the whole, is so Elegant, Awful, and well-compos'd a Part, that nothing but the Glorified Presence of Omnipotence can be worthy of so much Art, Grandure, and Industry as shines there, to the Honour of God, and Fame of Humane Excellence.

When Prayers were over, which indeed was Perform'd with that Harmonious Reverence, and Exhilerating Order, Sufficient to reclaim the Wickedness of Men, from following the Untunable Discord of Sin; and bring them over to the Enlivening Harmony of Grace and Goodness; We then return'd into the Body of the Church, happily intermix'd with a Crow'd of Good Christians, who had concluded, with us, their Afternoons Devotion.

We now took Norice of the vast distance of the Pillars from whence they turn the Cupula, on which, they say, is a Spire to be Erected three Hundred Foot in heighth; Whose Towering Pinacle will stand with such Stupendious Loftiness above *Bow-Steeple* Dragon or the *Monuments* Flaming Urn, that it will appear to the Rest of the Holy Temples, like a Cedar of *Lebanon* among so many Shrubs, or a *Goliah* looking over the Shoulders of so many *Davids.*

As we were thus gazing with great Satisfaction, at the Wondrous Effects of Humane Industry; raising our Thoughts by degrees, to the Marvellous Works of Omnipotence, from those of his Creatures, we Observed an Old Country fellow leaning upon his Stick, and staring with great amazement up towards Heaven, thro' the Circle from whence the Arch is to be turn'd: Seeing him fix'd in such a ruminating Posture, I was desirous of knowing his Serious Thoughts, in order to discover which, I ask'd him his Opinion of this Noble Building; and how he lik'd the Church? *Church!* reply'd he, *'tis no more like a Church than I am. Adsheart! Its more by half like a great Goose Pye I have seen at my Landlords; and this Embroider'd hole in the middle of the Top is like the Place in the upper Crust where they put in the Butter.* I could not forbear laughing at the odness of Slouch's Notion; and hoping to hear something further from him that might give us a little Diversion, we continued his Company. Prithee, said I, honest Country-man, since thou do'st not believe it to be a Church, what place do'st thou take it to be? *Why* says he, *I'll warrant you now thou think'st me to be such an Arrant Fool I can't tell, but thou art mistaken; for my Vather was a Trooper to* Oliver Cromwel, *and I have heard him say, Many a time, he has set up his Horse here; and do you think the Lord will ever Dwell in a House made out of a Stable?* That was done, said I, by a parcel of Rebellious People, who had got the upper-hand of the Government; and car'd not what Murder, Sacriledge, Treason, and Mischief they Committed: But it was a Church before it was converted to that Heathenish

use

use, and so it is now. *Why then*, says *Roger*, *I think in good Truth the Cavaliers are as much to blame in making a Church of Stable, as the* Roundheads *were, in making a Stable of a Church; and there's a* Rowland *for your* Oliver; *and so good-by to you.* Away he trudg'd, like the true Offspring of Schismatical and Rebellious Ancestors; expressing in his looks no little Malice and Contempt towards the Magnificency of the Building, which they have been always ready to deface, when they have had any opportunity.

We now began to Stifle our Sober and more Elevated Thoughts and Contemplations; and form in our selves a sutable Temper, to a different Undertaking; which was to observe some Disconsolate Figures which were wandring about the Church like Mice in an empty Barn, or Snails in a Vintners Cellar; as if their Mellancholy thoughts had tempted them foolishly to look for what they were assur'd they should not find; Some of them look'd as pale as if troubled with the Hypochondry, and fancy'd themselves to be walking in some Subteranean Cavern, far remote from that Transitory World in which they had once been Sinners. These had their Eyes cast down, as if they had great regard to their Footsteps, as if they were under some Melancholy Apprehension (if they took not great care) of sliping into a Bottomless-Pit, from whence there is no Redemption.

Others walking with their Arms Across, staring about with their Eyes directed altogether upwards, as if they were so deeply fallen in Love with the Beauty of the Building, that their Senses were Ravish'd with each Masterly stroak of the skillful Stone-Cutter. Amongst the rest, here and there a Lady, who look'd as Wild and Wanton, as if (tho she was admiring the Church) she thought more on a Gallant than she did on her Devotions; and would rather sing a Song, than say her Prayers; or see a Play, than hear a Sermon.

The next that we remark'd, were a kind of a Cuckoldy Row of penurious Citizens, consisting in Number of about half a dozen; who, I suppose, had taken Sanctuary in the Church to talk Treason with safety, or because it was Cheaper walking there, then sitting in a Coffee-house: Their Heads, Tongues, Hands, and Eyes, were all eagerly in Motion, showing they were extraordinary intent upon some wonderful Projection. At last I conjectur'd from words which I over-heard, they were some of the shallow-brain'd *Cullies*, who were drawn in by the *Land-Bank*, and were fumbling out a Method of licking themselves whole, by cheating of other People. These I thought, like the Money-Changers ought to have been whip'd out of the Temple.

There was nothing offer'd worth our further Observation, except a parcel of Wenches fit for Husbands, playing at Hoop and Hide among the Pillars, who were full able enough, and, I suppose, willing, of an Evening to help the young Work-men home with their Tools, if they would venture to thrust them into their Custody. This revelling of Girls I thought was very indecent; and ought to be carefuly prevented, lest the New Church be polluted far worse than the Old one; and instead of a Stable be defil'd with worse Beasts than Horses.　　From

From thence we made our Egress on the South-side; and quitted the Consecrated bounds of this Holy Leviathan; and cross'd a Dirty Kennel to take a view of a Parcel of Cleanly Beau Prentices, who were walking in their Masters Shops with their Perriwigs just Comb'd out of Buckle, well drudg'd with the Barbers Powdering Puff, the extravagant use of which, made them appear so Party-Colour'd, That their upper Parts look'd like Millers; and their Coats, from the Wast downwards, hanging in as many folds as a Watermans Dublet, to show there was more Cloth in the Skirts of one Tunica, than any of their Ancestors wore in a whole Suit. But thus much may be said in excuse of 'em, They may the better afford it, because they are *Woollen-Drapers*.

By this time we were come to an Arch, where we turn'd in, on the left hand of which many Scutcheons were hung out, as if Funerals were more in Fashion at this End of the Town, than any part I had yet seen. Had I been skill'd in Heraldry, I might have Blazon'd the Vanity of a great many Noble Families, who are apt to Boast of their Coates of Arms, tho' there are blots which denote *Treason* in one, *Cowardice* in another, *Illegitimacy* in a third, and *Murder* in a fourth, &c. Yet the Vulgar understanding them not, they are sometimes Reverenc'd for that Painted Distinction which they ought to be Asham'd of. I ask'd my Friend the meaning of all these Gawdy Hierogliphicks being hung out in so private a Thorough-fare. You are Mistaken, says he, this is a Place of Great Business, for most Persons who Travel in Dead Mens Shooes are Necessitated to come this way, and ask leave of those who never knew one of their Family, whether they shall Enjoy that which no Body has any Right to but themselves: And that Shop where you see so many Good Colours flung away upon Paper, like so much Gold upon Ginger-bread, belongs to a *Herald Painter*, who indeed (give him his due) is as honest a Man as ever guided Pencile; and has taken as much pains, at his own expence, to detect a Knave, and prevent the Publick's being Cheated, as ever his Neighbour did to subdue a Stubborn Conscience, and make it pliable to his Own and the Nation's Int'rest: This is his Office, who upon just grounds laid open the Funeral Interloper, the Robber, instead of Preserver, of the Dead; the Cozener of the Living, the Corrupter of Gentlemens Coachmen, the Invader of Tradesmens Properties, the Undervaluer of poor Mens Labour, the Fool of an Embalmer, and the Knave of an Undertaker.

Pray, said I, whose great House is that on the Right-hand, which, tho' it looks so stately, it appears as plain as a Physicians Coach, or a Gouty States-mans Horse-Litter? Why that, reply'd my Friend, was a large Trap set by the Government to Catch the *Popular Weasle*, so much talk'd of, who stood so long tottering in the beginning of the Revolution, between Hawk and Buzzard, but at last he snap'd at the Bait, and was taken; and from a Man of a Discontented Conscience, is become as well satisfied since, as if *De Jure* and *De Facto* had never been a point in Question. This is the Seat of him, to his everlasting praise be it spoken, who serv'd his Followers as *Saul* did the *Gentils*, and became a Convert to the Faith in Fashion: There being this Difference to be consider'd, The one got a Better Name, and a Worse Living; The other a Better

Living,

Living, but a Worſe Name. He has been Baited Fifty times worſe than ever the *Tygar* was; for every Scribling Mungrel in the Town has had a fair ſnap at him, till at laſt they *Uncas'd* him, but all to little purpoſe, for his Caſe ſince is ſo well amended, that there are but three Dangers which he ſtands in fear of, *viz.* The Coming of King *J——s*; the Scolding of his Wife, and a Conſumption.

That place, ſays he, on the Left-hand, is a Spiritual Purgatory, to torment *Fornicators* and *Adulterers*: Where they bring many Sinners to *Pennance*, but very few to *Repentance*. And uſe to Excommunicate People Out of the Church, for not Going thither. That me thinks, ſaid I, is like forcing a Man to Forbear ſuch Victuals which he cannot endure to Eat, or Debaring him of ſuch Company, which he always hated to keep. This Liberty of Conſcience, ſays my Friend, has been a Deviliſh Thorn in their ſides; for in the Joyful days of Church-Perſecution, they us'd to have two or three Brace of Diſſenters every Morning for Breakfaſt, but now the Office is dwindled into ſuch a Vacancy of Buſineſs, that their Neighbouring Vintner deſpairs of ever being made an Alderman; for the *White-horſe* Alehouſe has run away with moſt of his Cuſtomers.

Pray, ſaid I, whither does that Paſſage lead, where thoſe Country Fellows ſtand gaping and ſtaring about? That, reply'd my Friend, is *Doctors Commons*; and they are come to Town about the Probat of ſome laſt dying Will and Teſtament, Adminſtration, Caveat, or ſome ſuch Buſineſs. It's wonder none of the Spiritual Cormorants have ſeiz'd them yet, for they are generally as quick-ſighted as Hawkes, and love as dearly to Prey upon a Country Curmudgion, as a Hound does upon Horſe-fleſh. In that Court Live the Learned Readers of the Law Civil, who made ſuch a terible buſtle with the Poor Word *Abdication*; but after all their Debates and Conſultations, could not, with the aſſiſtance of their Magick, Conjure up any other Puzzling *Crambo* ſo proper for their purpoſe; and at laſt did approve that the Word might ſtand, inſtead of a better.

We adjourn'd from thence back into *Paul's* Church-Yard, and turn'd Weſtward into a famous ſtreet, wherein a Noble Poſtern was preſented to our View, the ſtatelineſs of its Appearance made me inquiſitive with my Friend what they call'd this Edifice; to what purpoſe Built, and to what Uſe Converted. Who told me it was call'd *Ludgate*, rais'd both as an Ornament and Security of the City. And thro' a Charitable Compaſſion to Unfortunate Citizens, it is made a Commodious Priſon for Freemen; furniſh'd with ſuch Conveniencies, and ſo plentifully ſupply'd with Proviſions, by the Gifts of Good People, and other Certain Allowances, that many live far better in it, than ever they did out on't; and are ſo fallen in Love with their Confinement, that they would not change it for Liberty.

After we had ſhot the Arch, we turn'd up a ſtreet, which my Companion told me was the *Old-Baily*. We walk'd on till we came to a great pair of Gates; it being a Remarkable place, according to my uſual Cuſtome, I requeſted my Friend to give me ſome further knowledge of the matter, who Inform'd me 'twas *Juſtice-Hall*, where a Dooms-day Court was held once a Month, to Sentence ſuch Canary-Birds to a Penitential Pſalm,

who

who will rather be Choak'd by the Product of Hempfeed, for living Roguifhly, than exert their Power in Lawful Labour, to purchafe their Bread Honeftly. In this narrow part of the Street, into which we are now paffing, many a fuch wretch has taken his laft walk; for we are going towards that famous Univerfity, where, if a Man has a mind to Educate a hopeful Child in the Daring Science of Padding, the Light-finger'd Subtlety of Shop-lifting, the excellent ufe of Jack and Crow for the filently drawing Bolts, and forcing Barricadoes; with the knack of Sweetening; or the moft ingenious dexterity of Picking Pockets, let him but enter him in this Colledge on the Common-fide, and Confine him clofe to his ftudy but for three Months, and if he does not come out Qualified to take any Degree of Villany, he muft be the moft honeft Dunce that ever had the Advantage of fuch Eminent Tutors.

From thence my Friend led me thro a Place call'd *Gilt-fpur-ftreet*, and brought me to a fpacious Level, which he told me was diftinguifh'd by the Name of *Smithfield-Rounds*, which entertain'd our Noftrils with fuch a Savory Scent of Roaft-meat, and furpris'd my Ears with the Jingling Noife of fo many Jacks, that I ftar'd about me like a Country Bump-kin in *Spittle-fields* amongft fo many Throfters-Mills; and feeing fuch a bufie Number of Cooks at work, I thought my felf in the Kitchin to the Univerfe; and wonder'd where the Gluttons could Live who were to devour fuch vaft Quantities of fundry forts of Food, which run fo merrily round before Large Fires, in every Greafy Manfion. We foon deliver'd our fqueamifh Stomachs from the Surfeitng Fumes that arofe from their Rotten-roafted Diet, which made the ftreet ftink like a *Hampfhire* Farmers Yard, when fingeing of a Bacon-Hog.

And from thence we proceeded to the Rails, where Country Carters ftood Arm'd with their Long Whips, to keep their Teams (upon Sale) in a due *Decorum*, who were drawn up into the moft fightly order, with their fore-feet mounted on a Dung-hill, and their Heads drefs'd up to as much advantage as an Inns-of-Court Sempftrefs, or the Miftrefs of a Boarding-School: Some with their Manes Frizzled up, to make 'em appear high Wither'd, that they look'd as Fierce as one of *Hungefs's* Wild-Boares. Others with their Manes Plaited, as if they had been rid-den by the Night-Mare: And the Fellowes that attended 'em made as uncooth Figures as the Monfters in the *Tempeft*. Amongft thefe Cat-tel, here and there, was the Conductor of a Dung-Cart, in his Dirty Sur-plice, wrangling about the Price of a Beaft, as a wary Purchafer; and that he might not be deceived in the Goodnefs of the Creature, he muft fee him ftand Three fair pulls at a Poft, to which the poor Jade's ty'd, that he may exert his Strength, and fhow the Clown her Excellencies; for which he ftroafes him on the Head, or claps him on the Buttocks, to recompence his Labour

We went a little further, and there we faw a parcel of Poor rag-ged Rapfcallions, mounted upon Scrubbed Tits, fcowring about the Rounds; fome Trotting, fome Galloping, fome Pacing, and others Stum-bling; blundering about in that Confufion, that I thought them, like fo many Beggars on Horfe-back, Riding to the Devil; or a Parcel

of

of *French* Proteſtants upon *Dover* Road, ſcrambling Poſt-haſte up to *Pick-a-dilly*

Pray Friend, ſaid I, what are thoſe Eagle-look'd Fellows in their Narrow-brim'd White-Beavers, Jockeys Coats, a Spur in one heel, and Bended Sticks in their Hands, that are ſo buſily peeping into every Horſes Mouth, and ſaunter about the Market like Wolves in a Wilderneſs, as if they were ſeeking whom they ſhould Devour? Thoſe Blades, ſays my Friend, art a ſubtle ſort of *Smithfield*-Foxes, call'd *Horſe-Courſers*, who Swear every Morning by the Bridle, They will never from any Man ſuffer a Knaviſh Trick, or ever do an Honeſt one. They are a ſort of *Engliſh Jews*, that never deal with a Man but they Cheat him; and have a rare faculty of Swearing a Man out of his Senſes; Lying him out of his Reaſon, and Cozening him out of his Money. If they have a Horſe to ſell that is Stone-blind, they'll call a Hundred Gods to Witneſs he can ſee as well as you can. If he be down-right Lame, they will uſe all the Aſſeverations that the Devil can aſſiſt 'em with, that it's nothing but a Spring-hault. If he be as rotten as a Town-Stallion who has been Twenty times in the Powdering-Tub, they will warrant, upon their Souls Damnation, he's as Sound as a Roach. And if he be Twenty Years Old, they'll Swear he comes but Seven next Graſs, if they find the Buyer has not Judgment enough to diſcover the Contrary.

I perceive, ſaid I, this is a Market for Black Cattle as well as Horſes: Yes, reply'd my Friend, if we had come in the Morning, you would have ſeen the Butchers as Buſie in handling the Flanks and Arſes of Oxen, as now the Jockeys are in fumbling about the Jaws of Horſes: But now the Market is almoſt over: yet you may ſee ſome *Welſh* Runts and *Scotch* Carrion, which wait for the coming of *Shore-ditch* Butchers, who buy 'em up for the *Spittle-fields* Weavers, and the Poorer ſort of *Hugonites*, who have taken poſeſſion of that part of the Town; and, like the *Scots*, have no great kindneſs for Fat Meat, becauſe they never us'd to Eat any in their own Country.

Come, ſays my Friend, now we are here, we'll take a turn quite round, and then we ſhall eſcape nothing worth obſerving. In order to compleat our Circular Walk, we mov'd on; but had as many Stinking-whiffs of *Oroonoko* Tobacco blown into our Noſtrils, as would have cur'd an Afflicted Patient of the Tooth-ach, or put a Nice Lady into a gentle Salivation.

By this Time we were come to an Arch, about the middle of the Row, where a parcel of Long-leg'd Loobies were ſtuffing their Lean Carcaſes with Rice Milk and Furmity, till it run down at each corner of their Mouths back into their Porridgers, that each of them were a true Copy of *Martin Barnick's* Feeding the Cat with Cuſtard: We paſs'd by theſe devouring Gang of Milk-ſops, and came up to the Corner of a narrow Lane, where *Money for Old Books* was writ upon ſome part or other of every Shop, as ſurely as *Money for Live Hair*, upon a *Barbers* Window. We took a ſhort turn into it, and ſo came back, where we ſaw a Couple of poor Schollars, with diſconſolate Looks, and in Thredbare Black Coats,

Selling

Selling their Authors at a Penny a Pound, which their Parents perhaps had Purchased with the Sweat of their Brows. And a Parson almost in every Shop, searching the Shelves with as much Circumspection to find out a Book worth Purchasing, as ever Cock us'd upon a Dunghill of Rubbish when he's scraping for an Oat worth Pecking.

Being now pretty well tired with our Days Journey, we concluded to Refresh our selves with one quart of Claret, before we walk'd any further; and being near the Sign of Honours Fountain, the Crown, the Representation of which Royal Diadem, I thought no Vinter would presume to distinguish his House by, unless he had Wine in his Cellar fit to bless the Lips of Princes; to experience the Truth of which Notion, we step'd in, where the Jolly Master, like a true Kinsman of the *Bacchanalian* Family, met us in the Entry with a Manly Respect; and bid us wellcome. We desir'd he would show us up staires into a Room forward; accordingly in his own proper Person, like a Complaisant Gentleman Usher, he conducted us into a large stately Room; where, at first Entrance, I discern'd the Masterly Stroakes of the fam'd *Fuller*'s Pencil, the whole Room being Painted with that commanding Hand, that his Dead Figures appear'd with such Lively Majesty, that they begot Reverence in us the Spectators, towards the Awful Shadows; our Eyes were so Delighted with this Noble Entertainment, that every Glance gave new Life to our weary Senses.

We now beg'd him to oblige us with a Quart of his Richest Claret, such as was fit only to be drunk in the presence of such Heroes, into whose Company he had done us the Honour to Introduce us. He accordingly gave directions to his Drawer, who return'd with a Quart of such inspiring Juice, that we thought our selves Translated into one of the Houses of the Heavens, and were there Drinking-Immortal Nectar, amongst Gods and Goddesses. My Friend, like my self, was so wonderfully pleas'd at this Obliging Usage, that he was very Importunate with me to Scribble a few Lines in Commendation of our Present State of Happiness, which to gratifie his desire, I Perform'd; and Present to the Reader.

WHO can faith Blessings, when they're found, resign?
An Honest Vintner, Faithful to the Vine;
A Spacious Room, Rare Painting, and Good Wine?

Such Tempting Charms what Mortal can avoid?
Where such Perfections are at once Enjoy'd,
Who can be Dull, or who be ever Cloy'd?

If you would Love, see there fair Pallas stands;
How Chaste her Looks? How Fine her Breasts and Hands?
Her Eyes raise Wonder, and your Heart Commands.

If you to Wit or Musick would aspire,
Gaze at the Nine, that Blest Harmonious Quire,
They'll Kindle in your Thoughts new sparks of Fire.

If

If to the Warlike Mars *you'd be a Friend,*
And learn to bravely Conquer or Defend,
See Ajax *and* Ulysses *there Contend.*

If neither Love *or* Arms *your Temper Suit;*
Nor wish to be Wife, Musical, *or* Stout ;
Here Wine *will make you truly Bleſſ without.*

By this time we had Tippled off our Salubrious Juice ; and Buſineſs denying us leiſure to Renovate our Lives with t'other Quart, we took our leaves, with a promiſe to recompence this reſpectful Uſage, at a better Opportunity. We'd not gone above Ten Strides from the Door, but we ſaw a Cluſter of Tun-belly'd Mortals, with Malignant Aſpects, Arm'd with ſturdy Oak, of an unlawful ſize, looking as ſharp upon every Paſſenger, as if, Canibal-like, they were juſt ready to devour 'em. I enquir'd of my Friend, what he took theſe ill-favour'd Crew to be, whoſe Bull-Dog Countenances, and Prepoſterous Bodies, ſpoke 'em betwixt Men and Monſters? Theſe Fellows, ſays my Companion, which you ſeem to be ſo much Amaz'd at, are nothing but Serjants, who are waiting to give ſome body a Clap on the Shoulder: This Corner is their Plying-place, and is as ſeldom to be found without Rogue, as *Grays-Inn-Walks* without a Whore, or *New-gate-Market* without a Basket-Woman. We mov'd on from thence, till we came to the Corner of a Street, from whence a parcel of Nimble-Tongu'd Sinners leap'd out of their Shops and ſwarm'd about me like ſo many Bees about a Honey-ſuckle, ſome got me by the Hands, ſome by the Elbows, and others by the Shoulders : and made ſuch a Noiſe in my Ears, that I thought I had Commited ſome Egregious Treſpaſs unawares, and they had ſeiz'd me as a Priſoner : I began to ſtruggle hard for my Liberty, but as faſt as I Loos'd my ſelf from one, another took me into Cuſtody. Wounds ! ſaid I, what's the matter? What wrong have I done you ? Why do you lay ſuch Violent hands upon me? At laſt a Fellow, with a Voice like a Speaking-Trumpet, came up cloſe to my Eares, and ſounded forth, *Will you buy any Cloaths*? A Pox take you ſaid I, you are ready to Tear a Mans Cloaths off his Back and then ask him whether he'll buy any. Prithee let mine alone and they will ſerve me yet this Six Months. But they ſtill huſtled me backwards and forwards, like a taken Pick-pocket in a Crow'd, till at laſt I made a Looſe, and ſcamper'd like a Reſcu'd Priſoner from a Gang of Bailiffs; my Friend ſtanding all the while and laughing at me. Pray ſaid I, what's the meaning of theſe unmannerly Clip-Nits uſing Paſſengers with this ſhameful Incivility? Certainly 'tis greater Pennance for a Man to walk thro' this Confounded Wardrobe, than 'tis to run the Gantlet. But what is the meaning they did not treat you after the ſame manner? You muſt Know, ſays he, they can diſtinguiſh a Country Man as well by his Looks, as you can a Parſon by his Robes; and being a parcel of unlucky Vermin, they teiz a Stranger to the Town as much to make themſelves Sport, as to promote the Sale of their Goods ; and if they had got you up a little higher, they would have handed you quite thro the Lane ; for its like a Gulf, when you're a little way enter'd, the Current will carry you thro' The Maſters of thoſe Shops will give you as much Wages for one of thoſe Tongue-pading Sweetners, who ſtand Sentinel at their

D

Doors,

Doors, as an Illiterate Mountebank will allow to a good Oratour, *i. e.* fifty Shillings, or three Pounds a Week. They are like the Jack-all to the Lyon, they Catch the Prey for the Master; and if once they get you but into their Shops, they as certainly cheat you before you get out again, as you go in with Money in your Pocket: For they will out-Wheedle a Gipsie, out-Swear a Common Gamster, out-Lie an Affidavit-Man, and out-Cozen a Tally-Man. They will make up New Cloaths, and sell 'em for Second-hand, and get more Money by 'em, then the Topingst Taylor in Town ever got by a Young Heir, when he made his Cloaths upon Credit. They are a Pack of the sharpest Knaves about *London*; and are as great a Grievance to the Publick, as the *Royal-Oak* Lottery. Since they have serv'd me so affrontively, and you have given me such a hopeful Character of 'em, I'll lend them a few of my good Wishes, to Revenge my self of their Rudeness to me.

MAY *the Cockroach and Moth,*
  Eat such holes in their Cloth,
 That the Prime-Cost may never return-in;
But must all be laid by,
For a Black Rusty Dy,
Fit for Dead-mongers Lacquays to Mourn-in.

 May their Second-hand Stocks,
 Of Coats, Breeches, and Cloakes,
Hang by till they're quite out of Fashion;
 And like Userers Bags,
 May they Rot into Rags,
And Provoke the Damn'd Knaves to a Passion.

 May their Taylors ne'er Trust,
 Nor their Servants prove Just;
And their Wives and their Families vex 'em:
 May their Foreheads all Ake,
 And their Debters all Break;
And their Consciences dayly Perplex 'em.

 With their Whores may they Sport,
 Till their Noses fall short,
And have none but a Quack to come Nigh 'em;
 And in Fluxing become,
 Lame, Deaf, Blind, and Dumb,
That a Man may walk Quietly by 'em.

Having thus taken our Farewel of these Hempen-look'd Tormenters, we Strol'd along till we came into a Corner, where the Image of a Bear stood out upon a Sign-post, perk'd upon his Arse with a great Faggot-Bat in his Claws, that he look'd like one of the City Waites playing upon the Double Curtell. Beneath the Effiges of his Ugliness, a parcel of Swine lay Couchant in the Dirt, attended with a Guard of Lousie Ragamuffins, with one Hand in their Necks and the other in their Codpieces, looking like some of the Devils Drovers, who had brought his Hogs to a fair

Market;

Market; smelling as Frouzily together, as so many Flitches of Rusty Bacon, or *Bruins* Bed-chamber in the *Bear-Garden*.

We Jogg'd on from thence, to relieve our Noses from their Sweaty Feet and Nasty Jackets, that out-stunk a Dog-kennel, and cros'd over, Fetlock Deep in Mud and Filthiness, to the Sheep-Pens: Where a parcel of Dirty Mungrels did the Drudgery of their worse look'd Masters; and reduc'd each stragling Innocent to his proper Order and *Decorum*. Butchers were here as Busie as Brokers upon Change; and were groping their Ware, with as much Caution, to know whether they are Sound and Wholesome, as a Prudent Sports-man would a New she-Acquaintance of a Loose Conversation. Money, in every House seem'd to be a plentiful Commodity; for every Russet-colour'd Clown was either Paying or Receiving, to the great uneasiness of such who pass'd by and wanted it. We walk'd on till we came the end of a little stinking Lane, which my Friend told me was *Chick-Lane*; where Measly Pork, and Neck-Beef stood out in Wooden Platters, adorn'd with Carrots, and Garnish'd with the Leafs of Mary-golds: Where, Carriers and Drovers sat in Publick View, stuffing their Insatiate Appetites, with greasie Swines Flesh, till the Fat Drivel'd down from the Corners of their Mouths, as Spittle from the Lips of a Changeling.

Having now seen all the Market could afford, we crost the Rounds, and went into a Lofty Cloister, which my Friend told me was the *Lame-Hospital*: Where a parcel of Wretches were hopping about, by the assistance of their Crutches, like so many *Lincoln's-Inn-Field* Mumpers, drawing into a Body to attack the Coach of some Charitable Lord: Women were here almost as Troublesome as the *Long-Lane* Clickers, and were so importunate with us to have some Dealings with them, that we had much ado to forbear handling their Commodities. I look'd about me, and could not forbear taking Notice of two things, *viz*. The Prettyness of the *Place*, and the *Homeliness* of the *Women*. Sure, said I, the Noblemen never come to this *Seraglio* to choose themselves Mistresses; for, I protest, I can scarce see one among them all handsome enough to make a Wife for a Parson. As many Names were Pencill'd out upon the Walls, as if there had been the Genealogy of the Twelve Tribes, or a publick Register of all the Topping Cuckolds in the City. I ask'd my Friend the meaning of this Long Catalogue of Esquires and Worships, who told me, they were the Names of the Benefactors, Ostentatiously set up, that every Passenger may see what a Number of Charitable Lord Mayors and Aldermen we have had in our Famous Metropolis: And indeed it was Politically enough done of the Governours; for its a great Encouragement for others, who Glory in their Good Deeds, to do the like:' Who, if it was not for seeing their Names in great Letters, to Vainly beget amongst Men an Opinion of their Peity, would no more dispose of a Groat to Charitable Uses, than they would give a Portion to a Daughter who has pleas'd herself in the Choice of a Husband, without the Consent of her Father, You may Imagine by the Number of the Names, it is largly Endow'd, there being several other Branches belonging to the same Foundation, as *Kingsland* Hospital, and St. *Thomas's* in *Southwark*. And Pray, said I, what are these Hospitals for? My Friend answering, for the receiving of Sick and Lame Soldiers and Seamen,

and

and other Poor Wretches, that can make Intereſt; and here they keep 'em upon Water-gruel and Milk-porridge, till they are either Dead or Well; and then they turn them either into this Wide World, or the Next, about their Buſineſs.

We went from thence (thro a Narrow Entry, which led us by a a parcel of Diminutive Shops, where ſome were buying Gloves, ſome ſmoking Tobacco, others drinking Brandy) into a famous Piazza, where one was Selling of Toys, another Turning of Nut-crackers, a third, with a pair of Dividers, marking out ſuch a parcel of Tringum-Trangums, to underſtand the Right Uſe of which, is enough to puzzle the Brains of an *Eſculapius*. From hence we paſs'd into another Cloiſter, whoſe Ruſty Walls and Obſolete Ornaments denoted great Antiquity; where abundance of little Children, in Blue Jackets and Kite-Lanthorn'd Caps, were very buſy at their ſeveral Recreations. This,ſays my Friend,was Originally founded by *Edward* the Sixth,for the Education of Poor Children; but has been largely improv'd ſince by additional Gifts; and is one of the Nobleſt Foundations in *England*. No Youth can have the Advantage of a better Education; and are afterwards provided for according as they're Qualified, being ſent either to Sea, Trades, or the Univerſity. There is a Ridiculous Story reported, and Credited by many People, which is, *That a Gentlewoman poſſeſt of Great Riches, when ſhe came to Die, gave her whole Eſtate to the Hoſpital, leaving behind her a poor Siſter, for whom ſhe Neglected to make any Proviſion, who having the Expectancy of the Eſtate after the others deceaſe, and finding her ſelf unhappily diſappointed, and Reflecting too deeply upon her Unfortunate Condition, and the unkindneſs of her Siſter, broke her Heart; and upon her Death Bed raſhly pronounc'd the Curſe of ſome Diſtemper always to attend the Hoſpital: ever ſince which time it has not been freed from the* Itch: But I look upon this Tale to be very Fabulous; for indeed it would be very wonderful that ſo many hundred Children, tho' look'd after with all the Cleanlineſs imaginable, ſhould at any time be all free from thoſe Diſtempers to which they are chiefly Incident.

After we had taken a Turn round the Cloiſter, we made our Egreſs towards *Newgate Street*, in order to pay a Viſit to *Phyſicians-Colledge*, and ſome other Neighbouring Places, an Account of which, for wont of Room, I ſhall defer till my Next.

F I N I S.

THE
LONDON
SPY.

For the *Month* of *April*, 1699.

PART VI.

By the Author of the Trip *to* JAMAICA.

The Third Edition.

LONDON,
Printed and Sold by *J. How*, in the *Ram-Head-Inn-Yard*
in *Fanchurch-Street*, 1701.

THE LONDON SPY.

WE now proceeded to survey, *Phyficians-Colledge*, which we found Illuftrated with fo Loft and large a *Porticum*, that when we had enter'd it, we were no more in Proportion to the fpacious Lanthorn o'er our Heads, than a Cricket to a Bisket-Bakers Oven, or *Tom-Thumb* to the Pudding-Bowl. Pray, faid I, what is the ufe of that great Painted Tub that ftands upon Wheeles? It looks as if it was defign'd as a Whimfical Cottage for fome Maggot-Brain'd *Diogenefs*: I hope there are no fuch fantafti-'cal Humorifts among this Learned Society? No, no, reply'd my Friend, you are very much befide the Cufhion; that Engine is a kind of a *Syrringe*, defign'd to cure fuch Houfes by Injection, that are under an Inflamation: From whence a Learned Phyfician of thefe times, took up a New Notion of curing a *Gonorhea*, till by the Practice of his upftart Meafures, he has Pox'd half the Town, to the great fatisfaction of his Fraternity, but fo much to the Plague and Terrour of his Patients, that it is believ'd fallen Nofes will be as Fafhionable about *Soho* and *Pickadilly* in a little time, as Scars amongft Prize-Fighters, or fhort Snouts among Ladies Lap-Dogs. Pray, faid I, explain your Allegory; I do not readily underftand what you mean by your *Syrringe*, &c. Why, if you muft have it in plain terms, fays he, that which I term'd fo, is a Device to caft Water into Houfes that by accident have taken *Fire*; from whence, I fuppofe, the Doctor undertook to extinguifh, after the like manner, all *Venereal* heats ftruck by Humane *Stones* and *Steel*, into the *Tinder-Box* of Generation.

There are a Couple of fine Statues, plac'd oppofite to each other, pray who do they Reprefent? The one, fays my Friend, is the Kings, and the other that Worthy Charitable good Chriftian Sir *John Cutler*, who, as a means, I fuppofe, the better to fecure his own Health, and Long Life, by the faithful affiftance of this Anti-mortal Society, was in his Life-time fo great a Benefactor to this Learned Corporation, that when the Fire in

Sixty

Sixty six, had confum'd their Colledge in *Amen-Corner*, and the Ground being but a Leafe, he lent them Money to Purchafe this Foundation, and to Build thereon this ftately Edifice, which they, thro' the miftaken hopes they had of his Generofity, receiv'd from him as a Gift, and to exprefs their Gratitude, for fo Bountiful a Donation, have Publickly return'd him thanks, for what the Mudling *Crafus* never intended to perform, Dedicating feveral Books to him, wherein, like poor Poets, they exprefs'd their unparalell'd Veneration to fo Liberal a Patron, till at laft their flatteries had fo prevail'd upon the franknefs of his humour, that he thank'd them kindly for their thanks, and prais'd them highly for their praifes; but told them plainly, He fear'd there was a Mifunderftanding between them, for that he had not given them a Groat, as he knew on, but only affifted them at an unhappy Juncture, with the Lent of fome Money, to recover their ancient Grandure, then buried in Afhes, which he expected in a little time they would make a juft Return of. This Difappointment fo aftonifh'd the *Gallenian* Fraternity, that they look'd as Difconfolate one upon another, as fo many broken Gamefters at a Hazard-table, hoping his Worfhip would take it into his further Confideration, and not give them fo bitter a Pill to Purge out the grateful Relifh of fo fweet an Expectancy as they had been under. A little time after this Conference had pafs'd between 'em, the pale-fac'd Mafter of the Ceremonies conducted the old Gentleman to the next World, in Mercy to his Surviving Relations, who have fince demanded the Money of the Colledge, the dread of Refunding which, having put fome of them into as Loofe a condition, as if they had lately fed upon nothing but their own Phyfick.

What Priviledges, faid I, extraordinary are Granted to them in their Charter, above what are held by other Phyficians, who are not of their Society? Many, reply'd my Friend, and thefe in particular, *viz.* No Perfon, tho' a Graduate in Phyfick of *Oxford* or *Cambridge*, and a Man of more Learning, Judgment, and Experience than one half of their Members, fhall have the liberty of Practifing in, or within feven Miles of *London*, without Licenfe under the Colledge Seal, or any other part of *England*, if they have not taken fome Degree at one of the Univerfities; they have alfo power to adminifter an Oath, which they know by Experience, is as Practicable to be broke the next day as 'tis to be taken; they can likewife Fine and Imprifon Offenders, in the Science of Phyfick, and all fuch who prefume to Cure a Patient, when they have given 'em over, by more excellent Meafures than ever were known by their Ignorance, they have alfo the Priviledge of making By-Laws, for the Intereft of themfelves, and Injury of the Publick, and can purchafe Lands in Right of their Corporation, if they could but find Money to pay for 'em, they have authority to examine the Medicines in all *Apothecaries* Shops, to Judge of the Wholefomnefs and Goodnefs of many Drugs and Compofitions they never yet underftood; they are likewife exempt from troublefome Offices, as *Jury-men*, *Conftables*, &c. Being no ways oblig'd to keep Watch or Ward, except with a Rich Patient, where they are affur'd to be well paid for their Labour; they have alfo the liberty to Kill as many as they pleafe, provided they do it *Secundum Artem*, and no Law fhall call them to account. They are freed from the bearing of *Arms*, or providing of *Ammunition*, except *Pill*, *Bolus*, or *Potion*, or fuch as Deftroy the Bodies of Sick Perfons they know not how to Cure: Any Member of the Colledge,

edge may Practice Chirurgery, if he will but take pains to understand it; They lately Committed a more able *Physician* than themselves, without Baile or Main-prize, for Male-Practice, in Curing a Woman of a dangerous Ulcer in her Bladder, by the use of *Cantharides*, which they affirm not fit for Internal Application, tho' the Patients Life was sav'd by taking on't; which shows they hold it a greater Crime to *Cure* out of the Common Method than it is to *Kill* in it: And in Prosecuting their Antagonist for the contempt of *Gallen* and *Hipocrates*, they charg'd him with Evil Practice, for doing that Good which they themselves wanted either will or knowledge to perform, and made themselves all Fools in attempting to prove the other a Knave, who procur'd his Discharge at the *Kings-Bench-Bar* without a Tryal, and now sues them for false Imprisonment; and has inform'd against 'em in the *Crown-Office*, as common Disturbers.

They rail mightily in their Writings against the Ignorance of *Quacks* and *Mountebanks*, yet, for the sake of *Lucre*, they Licence all the Cozening Pretenders about Town, or they could not Practice; which shows it is by their Tolleration that the People are cheated out of their Lives and Money; and yet they think themselves so Honest, as to be no ways answerable for this Publick Injury; as if they could not Kill People fast enough themselves, but must depute all the Knaves in the Town to be Death's Journymen. Thus do they License what they ought carefully to Suppress; and Practice themselves what they Blame and Condemn in others; And that the Town may not be Deceiv'd by *Apothecaries*, they have made themselves *Medicine-Mongers*, under a pretence of serving the Publick with more faithful Preparations; in order to perswade the World to a belief of which, they have Publish'd Bills, where, in the true *Quacks* Dialect, they tell you the Poor shall be supply'd for nothing; but whoever is so Needy as to make a Challenge of their Promise empty handed, will find, according to the *Mountebanks* saying, *No Money, No Cure.* The disposal of their Medicines they leave to a Boy's Management, who scarce knows *Mercurius Dulcis* from *White-Sugar*, or *Mint-Water* from *Aqua fortis*: So that People are likely to be well serv'd, or Prescriptions truly observ'd, by such an Agent.

From thence my Friend conducted me to *Bridewell*, being Court day, to give me the Diversion of seeing the Letchery of some Town Ladies cool'd by a Cat of Nine-tailes: But in our Passage thither meeting with some remarkable Accidents, I think it may contribute something to the Readers satisfaction to give a Rehearsal of them.

As we came down *Ludgate-hill*, a couple of *Town Bullies* (as I suppose by their Behaviour) met each other, *Damn ye, Sir*, says one, *why did you not meet me Yesterday Morning according to Appointment? Damn you, Sir, for a Cowardly Pimp*, reply'd the other, *I was there, and waited till I was Wet to the Skin, and you never came at me. You lie like a Villain*, says to'ther, *I was there, and stay'd the time of a Gentleman; and draw now, and give me Satisfaction like a Man of Honour, or I'll Cut your Ears off. You see*, says the Valiant Adversary, *I have not my Fighting Sword on, and hope you are a Man of more Honour than to take the Advantage of a Gentleman. Then go home and fetch it*, says *Don Furioso*, like a Man of Justice, *and meet me within an Hour in the* Kings-Bench-Walks *in the* Temple, *or the next time*

I see you, by Jove's *Thunder-bolts, I will Pink as many Eylet-holes in your Skin, as you have Button-holes in your Coat; and therefore have a Care how you Trespass upon my Patience. Upon the Reputation of a Gentleman, I will Punctually meet you at your Time, and Place;* reply'd the other, and so they Parted.

Bullies, *like Dunghill-Cocks, will strut and Crow,
But few or none dare stand the sparring Blow,
So does the Peevish Mungril take delight
To snap and snarl, show Teeth, but dare not Bite;
Oft Mischief makes, but still the danger shuns;
He Creeps and Fawns, or else turns Tail and Runs:
So Cowards often do their Swords Unsheath,
But Cow'd and Daunted with the fear of Death,
Thus Tamely show their Blades, as fearful Curs their Teeth.*

We mov'd on till we came to *Fleet-Bridge*, where Nuts, Ginger-bread, Oranges and Qysters, lay Pil'd up in Moveable Shops that run upon Wheeles, attended by Ill-looking Fellows, some with but one Eye, and others without Noses. Over against these stood a parcel of *Trugmoldie's*, in Straw-Hats and Flat-Caps, selling Socks and Furmity, Night-Caps and Plumb-Pudding. Just as we pass'd by, a Feud was kindling between two Rival Females, who from the Brimstone of *Lust*, had blown up such a Fire of *Jealousie* between 'em, that one call'd the other Adulterous Bitch; and charg'd her with Lying with her Husband, and Robbing her of his Love: Then falling into Tears, express'd herself further in these Words, *Have I lent you the Money out of my Pocket, the Gown off my Back, and my Petticoat off my Arse, to be thus ungratefully rewarded? You know, Hussie, I have given you the very Bread out of my Mouth; but before you shall take my Bedfellow from my Belly, you Whore, I'll Tare your Eyes out;* and then, with Teeth and Nails, made a Violent assault upon her Rival, who Roar'd out for help, and crying out she was quick with Child, the Mobb hearing her plead her Belly, were moved to Compassion, and so parted 'em, their Coifs having receiv'd the greatest Dammage in the Fray.

Just as the Squabble was ended, before the Rabble was dispers'd, who should be stumbling along upon his Hide-bound Prancer, but one of the *Horse Mountebanks*, who seeing so rare an opportunity to hold forth to a Congregation already assembled, Spurs up his Foundred *Pegasus*, and haults into the middle of the Crowd, plucks out a Pacquet of Universal *Hodg-Podg*, and thus begins an Oration to the Listening Herd.

Gentlemen, you that have a Mind to be mindful of preserving a sound Mind in a sound Body, that is, as the Learned Physician, Doctor Honorificabilitu-dinitatibusque *has it,* Manis Sanaque in Cobile Saniquorum, *may here, at the expence of Two-pence, furnish himself with a parcel, which tho' it is but small, yet containeth mighty things, of great Use, and Wonderful Operation in the Bodies of Mankind, against all Distempers, whether* Homogeneal *or* Complicated; *whether deriv'd from your* Parents, *got by* Infection, *or proceeding from an ill Habit of your own Body.*

In the first Place, Gentlemen, *I here present you with a little inconsiderable Pill to look at, you see not much bigger than a Corn of Pepper, yet in this Di-*
minutive

minutive Panpharmica, so powerful in effect, and of such excellent Vertues, that if you have Twenty Distempers lurking in the Mass of Blood, it shall give you just Twenty Stools, and every time it Operates it carries off a Distemper; but if your Blood's Wholesome, and your Body's Sound, it will work with you no more than the same quantity of Ginger-bread. I therefore call it, from its admirable Qualities, Pillula Tondobula, which signifies, in the Greek, The Touch-stone of Nature: For by taking of this Pill you will truly discover what state of Health or Infirmity, your Constitution is then under.

In the next Place, Gentlemen, I present you with an excellent outward application, call'd, a Plaister; good against all Green Wounds, Old Fistula's and Ulcers, Pains and Aches, Contusions, Tumours or Kings-Evil, Sprains, Fractures, or Dislocations, or any Hurts whatsoever, receiv'd either by Sword, Cane, or Gun-shot, Knife, Saw, or Hatchet, Hammer, Nail, or Tenter-hook, Fire, Blast, or Gunpowder, &c. And will continue its Vertue beyond Credit; and will be found as useful seven Years hence as at this present Moment, that you may lend it to your Neighbours in the time of Distress and Affliction; and when it has perform'd Fourty Cures, 'twill be ne'er the Worse, but still retain its Integrity. Probatum Est.

The next unparalell'd Medicine contain'd in this my little Two-penny Beneficence, is an admirable Powder, good to fortifie the Stomach against all Infections, Unwholesome Damps, Malignant Effluvia's that arise from Putri'd Bodies; and the like. It also is a rare Cordial to strengthen and chear the Heart under any Misfortune; and will procure such an Appetite, being drank a little before Dinner, that a Man of an ordinary Stomach may Eat a Pound of Suffolk Cheese, and twice the quantity of Rye-Bread, and still have as good an Appetite to a Sirloin of Roast Beeff, as if he had not eat a bit in a Fortnight. This most excellent Preparation is also the most powerful Antivermineous Medicine ever given in England, Scotland, France or Ireland; and if either your selves, or your Children are troubl'd with that Epidemical Distemper, Worms, which destroy more Bodies than either Plague, Pestilence, or Famine, give, or take this infus'd in a little warm Ale, instead of Wormseed and Treacle, and you will find these devouring Vermin, these Deaths Agents, that Burrow in our Bodies, as Rabbits in a Warren, come creeping out at both Ends, like Lice out of a Beggars Dublet when he hangs it in the Sunshine. It is also a most rare Dentrificis, and cleanses all foul, and fastens all loose Teeth, to a Miracle. This Powder I call my Pulvis Lubberdatus, because in my Travels I first gave it amongst the Dutch when I was a Student at Leydon: Where, Gentlemen, I would have you to know, I took my Degrees, altho' I expose my self to the Worlds Censures, by appearing thus Publick, for the Good of my own Countrey, which at all times (it's well known) I have been very ready to serve.

The last, and most useful Medicine prepar'd throughout the whole Universe, is this my Orvieton, whose Vertues are such, it will, equally with the Unicorns-Horn, expel the Rankest Poison. It is absolutely Necessary for all Persons to carry in their Pockets, for who knows how the Passions of Love, Fear, Anger, Despair, Jealousie, or the like, by the subtle insinuation of Satan, who is watchful of all opportunities, may prevail upon you to offer violence to your most pretious Lives, by taking Rats-bane, Mercury, Arsnick, Opium, and the like. Why, who, I say, would be without a Medicine, to relieve themselves under such Misfortunes, which would not only hurry 'em to Death, but to Damnation? It is also the best Sudarifick,

in

in all Colds and Feavers that ever can possibly be taken; working out the distemper by gentle Perspiration, and fortifies the Heart against all Fainting and Swooning, also the Brain against all Dizziness and Swimming; and is, upon the word of a Physician, the greatest Cordial the most Eminent Doctor can Prescribe, or Patient take.

I do assure you, Gentlemen, the Colledge of Physicians offer'd to admit me as a Member of their Society, if I would make but a discovery only to themselves of this most excellent and admirable Secret; No, hold you me there a little, Gentlemen, (said I) I shall then make you as Wise as my Self, and should I do that, pray who would be a Fool then? Why truly my self, for I would have you to know, Gentlemen, I have more manners than to reflect upon such a learned Society.

This piece of Impudence so tickled the Ears of the Brainless multitude, that they began with as much eagerness to untie their Purses, and the Corners of their Handkerchiefs, and were as free of their pence, as they would be to buy Apples by the Pound, or see a Poppet-show; that it was as much as ever the Doctor could do to deliver out his Physick fast enough; his industrious Lies taking as well with the Mob, as a Treasonable Ballad, or a disgusted Statemans Pamphlet, upon the turn of a Government. Thus they continued flinging away their Money, of all Ages, from Sixty to Sixteen; many of them looking as if they could scarce command as much more till next Saturday Night they received their Wages; Till either the Doctor broke the Crow'd of their Money, or the Crowd the Doctor of his Physick, I know not whether; but away Trotted he on Horse-back with their Pence, whilst his Patients were glad to Trudg away on foot with his Pacquets.

Pray, says my Friend, what do you think? Is it not a Shame to our English Physicians to suffer such a parcel of Ignorant, Illiterate, and Impudent Vagabonds to Cozen poor Innocent Wretches out of their Money Publickly in the Streets, who want it themselves to purchase Bread and Necessaries? I can't imagine what can be urg'd as an excuse for the Tollorating such Rascals to drain the Pockets of the Poor by preposterous Lies, jumbled into a Senseless Cant, to perswade the People to believe them really that, to which they are only a Scandal. And as a means to disswade the Publick from their foolish Opinion of these Emperical Vagabonds, or their Medicines, which are only made from a parcel of perish'd Drugs, ground promiscuously together, without Art or Rule, and so made up into sundry sorts of species, to allure the Ignorant; I have here given a true portraicture of such a Scandalous Fellow, who makes it his Business to Cheat the common-people by his lying Assertions, and fallacious Insinuations, not only out of their Money, but often out of their Health, which is far more valuable.

A Character of a Quack.

A Shame to Art, to Learning, and to Sence;
A Foe to Vertue, Friend to Impudence;
Wanting in Natures Gifts and Heaven's Grace,
An Object Scandalous to Human Race;

A Spurious Breed by some Jack-Adams got;
Born of some Common Monstrous God-knows-what:
Into the World no Woman sure could bring
So vile a Birth, such an Unman-like thing.
Train'd from his Cradle up in Vices School,
To Tumble, Dance the Rope, and Play the Fool.
Thus Learn'd he stroles with some Illit'rate Quack,
Till by long Travels he acquires the Knack,
To make the sweepings of a Drugsters shop,
Into some unknown Universal slop.
On which some senseless Title he bestows,
Tho' what is in't, nor Buy'r or Seller knows.
Then Lazy grown, he doth his Booth forsake,
Quitting the Rope and Hoop, and so turns Quack.
Thus by base means to Live, does worse pursue;
And Gulls the Poor of Life and Money too.

From thence we took a turn down by the Ditch-side, I desiring my Friend to inform me what great Advantages this costly Brook contributed to the Town, to Countervail the Expence of Seventy-four Thousand Pounds, which I read in a very Credible Author was the Charge of its making: He told me he was wholly unacquainted with any, unless it was now and then to bring up a few Chaldron of Coles to two or three pedling *Fewel-Merchants,* who sells them never the cheaper to the Poor for such a Conveniency: And as for those Cellars you see on each side, design'd for Ware-houses, they are render'd by their dampness so unfit for that purpose, that they are wholly useless, except for Lightermen to lay their Tailes in, or to harbour Frogs, Toads, and other Vermin. The greatest good that ever I heard it did, was to the Undertaker, who is bound to acknowledge he has found better Fishing in a muddy Stream, than ever he did in clear Water.

We then turn'd into the Gate of a stately Edifice, my Friend told me was *Bridewell,* which to me seem'd rather a Princes Palace, than a House of Correction, till gazing round me, I saw in a large Room a parcel of Ill-looking Mortals stripp'd to their Shirts like Hay-makers, pounding a Pernicious Weed, which I thought from their unlucky-aspects, seem'd to threaten their Destruction. These, said I, to my Friend, I suppose are the Offenders at work; pray what do you think their Crimes may be? Truly said he, I cannot tell you; but if you have a mind to know, ask any of them their Offence, and they will soon satisfie you. Prethee, Friend, said I, to a Surly Bull-neck'd Fellow, who was thumping as lazily at his Wooden-Anvil as a Ship-Carpenter at a Log in the Kings-yard at *Deptford,* What are you Confin'd to this Labour for? My Hempen Operator, leering over his Shoulder, cast at me one of his hanging Looks, which so frighten'd me, I step'd back, for fear he should have knock'd me on the Head with his Beetle, *Why, if you must know,* Mr. Tickle-Taile, says he, taking me, as I believe, being in Black, for some Country Pedagogue, *I was committed hither by Justice* Clodpate, *for saying I had rather hear a Blackbird Whistle* Walsingham, *or a Peacock Scream against Foul Weather, than a Parson talk Nonsense in a Church, or a Fool talk Latin in a Coffee-House: And I'll be Judg'd by you that are a Man of Judgment, whether in all I said*

C

there

there be one Word of Treason to deserve a Whipping-Post. The Impudence of this Canary-Bird so dash'd me out of Countenance, together with his unexpected Answer, that like a Man Surfeited with his Mistresses Favours, I had nothing to say, but heartily wish'd my self well out of their Company; and just as we were turning back to avoid their further Sawciness, another calls to me, *Hark you Master in Black, of the same colour of the Devil, can you tell me how many thumps of this Hammer will soften the Hemp so as to make a Halter sit Easie if a Man should have occasion to wear one?* A third crying out, *I hope, Gentlemen, you will be so Generous to give us something to Drink, for you don't know but we may be hard at Work for you?* We were glad with what expedition we could, to escape their Impudence. Going from the Work-room to the Common-side, or place of Confinement (where they are lock'd up at Night,) thro' the frightful Grates of which uncomfortable Appartment, a Ghastly Skeleton stood peeping, that from his terrible Aspect, I thought some power Immortal had Imprison'd Death that the World might Live for ever. I could not speak to him without dread of danger, least when his lips open'd to give me an answer, he should poison the Air with his contagious Breath; and Communicate to me the same Pestilence which had brought his infected Body to a dismal Anatomy: Yet mov'd with pity towards so sad an Object, I began to enquire into the Causes of his sad appearance, who, after a Penitential Look, that call'd for Mercy and Compassion, with much difficulty he rais'd his feeble Voice a degree above silence; and told me he had been Sick Six-weeks under that sad Confinement, and had nothing to comfort him but Bread and Water, with now and then the refreshment of a little small-beer. I ask'd him further, what Offence he had Committed that brough him under this unhappiness? To which he answer'd, He had been a great while discharg'd of all that was charg'd against him, and was detain'd only for his Fee's; which, for want of Friends, being a Stranger in the Town, he was totally unable to raise. I ask'd him what his Fees amounted to; who told me *Five-Groats*. 'Bless me! Thought I, what a Rigorous Uncharitable thing is this, that so Noble a Gift, intended, when first given, to so good an End, should be thus perverted! And what was design'd to prevent People's falling into Misery, thro' Laziness or Ill-Courses, should now be corrupted by such Unchristian Confinement, as to Starve a poor Wretch because he wants Money to satisfie the demands of a Mercenary *Cerberus*, when discharg'd of the Prison by the Court! Such severe, nay Barbarous Usage, is a shame to our Laws, and unhappiness to our Nation, and a scandal to Christianity.

From thence we turn'd into another Court, the Buildings being like the former, Magnificently Noble; where straight before us was another Grate, which prov'd the Women's Appartment: we follow'd our Noses and walk'd up to take a view of their Ladies, who we found were shut up as close as Nuns; but like so many Slaves, were under the Care and Direction of an Over-seer, who walk'd about with a very flexible Weapon of Offence, to Correct such hempen Journy-women who were unhappily troubled with the Spirit of Idleness. These smelt as frowsily as so many Goats in a Welsh Gentlemans Stable, or rather a Litter of piss-tail Children under the care of a Parish Nurse; and look'd with as much Modesty as so many *Newgate* Saints Canoniz'd at the *Old-Baily*; being all as Merry over their shameful Drudgery, notwithstanding
their

their miserable Circumstances, as so many Jolly *Crispin's* in a Garret, or *Vulcan's* in a Cellar o'er the merry Clinks of their Anvil. Some seem'd so very Young, that I thought it strange they should know Sin enough at those Years to bring them so early into a State of Misery: Others so Old, that one would think the dread of the Grave, and thoughts of Futurity, were sufficient to reclaim 'em from all Vice had they been train'd up never so Wickedly, some between both, in the Meridian of their Years, and were very pretty, but seem'd very Lewd, that *Messalina*-like, they might be Tired, but never Satisfied. *Pray, Sir,* says one of them, *how do you like us? You look very wistfully at us? What do you think of us?* Why, truly, said I, I think you have done something to deserve this Punishment, or else you would not be here. *If you'll believe me, without Blushing, I'll tell you the Truth: I happen'd to live with an Old Rogue of a Haberdasher, and when my Mistress was out of the way, he us'd to tickle my Lips with a Pen-feather, and at last she Catch'd us, and had me before Justice Over-doe, who Committed me hither, where I have had more Lashes of my Back, than ever my Belly deserv'd.*

Don't believe her, *Master*, crys another, *She's as arrant a Strumpet as ever arm'd her Living at two-pence a Bout; and was Committed hither for Lying so long on her Back that her Rump grew to the Bed-Cloaths till she could not rise again. She's one of* Posture Moll's *Scholars, and can show you how the Water-men shoot* London-Bridge, *or how the Lawyers go to* Westminster. *What do you think,* replys the other, *this Buttocking Brimstone came hither for? I'll tell you, Master, says she, because I believe you have no good Guess with you, 'twas for Picking a Country-man's Pocket of his Pouch, and hiding on't in a Oven; but when she came to be search'd, the Fool having forgot to take up the strings, was discover'd in her Roguery, and sent here to be Lash'd, and does not she deserve it, Sirs, for trusting Money in a Box, that has neither Lid nor Bottom to it?* I could not but wonder to hear this Impudence from Women, more especially when I consider'd they were under such Shame, Misery, and Punishment, which a Man might reasonably imagine would work upon the most corrupted Minds to abominate those base Practices which brought 'em to this Unhappiness.

Being now both tired with, and amaz'd at, the Confidence and loose Behaviour of these Degenerate Wretches, who had neither Sence of Grace, Knowledge of Virtue, Fear of Shame, or Dread of Misery, my Friend Reconducted me back into the first Quadrangle, and led me up a pair of Stairs into a spacious Chamber, where the Court was sat in great Grandure and Order. A Grave Gentleman, whose Awful Looks bespoke him some Honourable Citizen, being mounted in the Judgment-Seat, Arm'd with a Hammer, like a *Change-broker* at *Loyd's Coffee-House*, and a Woman under the Lash in the next Room, where Folding-Doors were open'd, that the whole Court might view the Punishment; at last down went the Hammer, and the Scourging ceas'd; that I protest, till I was unde-ceiv'd, I thought they had sold their Lashes by Auction; the Honourable Court, I observ'd, were chiefly attended by fellows in Blew Coats, and Women in Blew-Aprons. Another Accusation being then deliver'd by a Flat-cap against a Poor Wench, who having no Friend to speak in her behalf, Proclamation was made, *viz. All you who are willing that* E——th *T——ll, should have present Punishment, Pray hold up your Hands:* Which was

done

done accordingly. And then She was immediately order'd the civility, of the House, and was forc'd to show her tender Back, and tempting Bubbies to the Sages of the Grave Assembly, who were mov'd by her Modest Mein, together with the whiteness of her Skin, to give her but a gentle Correction.

Finding little knowledge to be gain'd from their proceedings, and less Pleasure or Satisfaction from their Punishmens, my Friend and I thought it better to retire, and leave them to be Flog'd on till the Accusers had all satisfied their Revenge, and the Spectators their Curiosity.

Now, says my Friend, Pray give me your thoughts of what you have seen, whether you think this sort of Correction is a proper method to reform Women, from their Vitious Practices, or not? Why truly, said I, if I must deliver my Opinion according to my real Sentiments, I only conceive it may make many Whores, but that it can in no measure reclaim 'em: And these are my Reasons:

First, If a Girl of Thirteen or Fourtten years of Age, as I have seen some such here, either thro' the Ignorance, or Childishness of their Youth, or Unhappiness of a stubborn Temper, should be guilty of Negligence in their Business, or prove Head-strong, Humoursome, or, Obstinate, and thro' an Ungovernable Temper, take Pleasure to do things in disobedience to the Will of their Master and Mistress, or be guilty of a trifling Wrong or Injury, thro' inadvertency, they have Power at home to give them Reasonable Correction, without exposing 'em to this Shame and Scandal, which is never to be wash'd off by the most reform'd Life imaginable, which unhappy stain makes them always shun'd by Vertuous and Good People, who will neither entertain a Servant, or admit of a Companion under this Disparagement; the one being fearful of their Goods, and the other of their Reputation, till the poor Wretch by her Necessity is at last drove into the hands of Ill Persons, and forc'd to betake herself to bad Conversation, till she is insensibly Corrupted, and made fit for all Wickedness.

Secondly, I think it a shameful Indecency for a Woman to expose her Naked Body to the Sight of Men and Boys, as if it was rather design'd to feast the Eyes of the Spectators, or stir up the Beastly Appetites of Leacherous Persons, than to correct Vice, or reform Manners; therefore I think it both more Modest, and more Reasonable they should receive their Punishment only in the view of Women, and by the hand of them own Sex.

Thirdly, As their Bodies by Nature are more tender, and their Constitutions allow'd more weak, we ought to shew them more Mercy, and not Punish them with such Dog-like Usage, unless their Crimes were Capital.

I believe, reply'd my Friend, you are aiming to Curry Favour with the fair Sex: This Lecture to a Town Lady, if you had a Mind to be wicked, would save you Money in your Pocket, tho' indeed, what you have urg'd

seems

seems no more than reasonable: I think, I have now show'd you all this place affords; so we'll take our Leaves on't, but I hope you will give us a few Lines upon it, and then we'll seek some new Diversion. I could not but Gratifie my Friends Request, and what I did to Oblige him, I here present unto the Reader.

On Bridewell.

'Twas once the Palace of a Prince,
  If we may Books confide-in,
  But given was, by him long since,
For Vagrants to reside-in.

The Crumbs that from his Table fell,
  Once made the Poor the Fatter;
But those that in its Confines dwell:
  Now feed on Bread and Water.

No Ven'son now whereon to Dine;
  No Frigasies, or Hashes,
No Balls, no Merriment, or Wine:
  But Woful Tears and Slashes.

No Prince or Peers, to make a Feast:
  No Kettle Drums, or Trumpets,
But art become a shameful Nest
  Of Vagabonds and Strumpets.

Where once the King, and Nobles sat,
  In all their Pomp and Splendor:
Grave City Grandeur, Nods its Pate,
  And threatens each Offendor.

Unhappy thy Ignoble Doom,
  Where Greatness once resorted;
Now Hemp and Labour fills each Room,
  Where Lords and Ladies sported.

We now departed *Bridewell*; and willing to refresh our selves with the smoaking of one Pipe, turn'd into a Neighbouring Coffee-house, where glancing upon an old *Flying-Post*, we put our selves in Mind of my Dame *Butterfield's* Invitation to her *Essex* Calf and Bacon, with her Six Brass Horns, to accomodate Sports-men with the delightful harmony of Hunting: And believing a Relation of this unusual Feast might be Welcome to the Publick, my Friend and I agreed to move with the Stream; and give our selves a Country Walk to the Place appointed: I am sensible it is something of a Digression, or rather a Deviation from the Title: But tho' the *Feast* was in the *Country*, yet the *Guests* were *Londoners*; and therefore what we observe among 'em may be reasonably admitted.

Fearing Time should be Elaps'd, and cut short our intended Pastime, we Smoak'd our Pipes with greater Expedition, in order to proceed on our

D   Journey,

Journey, which we began about Eleven a Clock; and marching thro' *Cheap-side*, found half the People we either met, or over-took, equip'd for Hunting; walking backwards and forwards, as I suppose, to shew one another their Accouterments. The City Beaus in Boots as black as Jet which shin'd, by much rubbing, like a stick of Ebony, their Heels arm'd with Spurs, the travelling Weapons to defend the Rider from the Laziness of his Horse, carefully preserv'd Bright in a Box of Cotton, and dazzled in the Eyes of each beholder like a piece of Looking-glass; their Wastes hoop'd round with *Turkey*-Leather Belts, at which hung a Bagonet, or short Scymitar, in order to cut their Mistresses Names upon the Trees of the Forrest: In the right Hand a Whip, mounted against the Breast like the Scepter of a Kings Statue upon the *Change*; adorn'd with twisted Wigg's and Crown'd with edg'd Casters; being all over in such Prim and Order, that you could scarce distinguish them from Gentlemen. Amongst 'em were many Ladies of the same Quality, ty'd up in Safeguards so be-knotted with two-penny Taffaty, that a Man might guess by their Finery, their Fathers to be Ribbond-Weavers. We crowded along, mix'd among the Herd; and could not but fancy the major part of the Citizens were Scampering out of town to avoid the *Horse-Plague*. We mov'd forward, without any discontinuance of our Perambulation, till we came to the *Globe* at *Mile-End*, where a *Pretious Mortal* made us a *Short-hand* Complement, and gave us an Invitation to a Sir-Loine of Roast Beeff, out of which Corroborating Food we renew'd our Lives; and stengthening our Spirits with a Flask of rare Clarret, took leave of my Friends Acquantance; and so proceeded.

By this time the Road was full of Passengers, every one furnish'd with no small Appetite to *Veal* and *Bacon*. Citizens in Crowds, upon *Pads*, *Hackneys*, and *Hunters*; all upon the *Tittup*, as if he who Rid not a Gallop was to forfeit his Horse. Some Spurring on with that speed and chearfulness, as if they intended never to come back again: Some Double, and some Single. Every now and then drop'd a Lady from her Pillion, another from her Side-Saddle, some showing the Milky-way to Bliss, others their *Bugbears* to the Company, which, tho' it made them Blush, it made us Merry: Sometimes a Beau would tumble and dawb his Boots, which, to shew his Neatness, he would clean with his Handkerchief. *Horses*, *Coaches*, *Carts*, *Waggons*, and *Tumblers*, all Occupy'd by *Men*, *Women*, *Children*, *Rich*, *Poor*, *Gentle*, and *Simple*, having all *Travelling Conveniences* sutable to their Quality. In this Order did we March, like *Aaron*'s Proselites, to Worship the Calf, till we came to the New-rais'd Fabrick, call'd *Mobs Hole*, where the Beast was to be Eaten. The House was surrounded with the Mobility, that it look'd like the *Welsh-Cow-keepers Camp*, consisting of a number of both Sexes, of all sorts and sizes, sufficient, instead of one, to have Eaten all the *Calves* in *Essex*. We press'd hard to get into the House, which we found so full, that when I was in, what with the smell of Sweat, Stinking Breaths, and Tobacco, I thought there was but a few Gasps between this Place and Eternity. Some were Dancing to a Bag-pipe, others Whistling to a Base-Violin, two Fidlers scraping *Lillaburlero*, my Lord Mayors Delight, upon a couple of Crack'd *Crowds*, and an old *Oliverian* Trooper Farting upon a Trumpet. My Friend and I being willing to get as far out of the Noise as we could, climb'd up into a Garret, where we found a single Lady, in her Safeguard,

rectifying

rectifying her Commode from the abuses of the Wind; I thought my self oblig'd in Civility, to make some little use of so fair an Opportunity; and accordingly Welcom'd her to *Mobs Hole*; and at last talk'd her into so compliant a humour, that I perceiv'd she was as willing to give us her Company, as we could be to ask it; till we had brought our selves in danger of intailing that Trouble and Expence upon our selves, which, to tell you the truth, we thought it prudence to avoid; so by a cooler sort of treatment than we first began with, we gave her delicious Ladyship some Reasons to believe she might go a little further and fare better; accordingly she took her leave, and squeez'd down Stairs, to shew her Mar-malet-Looks and Inviting Airyness upon the Parade, where Tag, Rag, and Bob-taile, were promiscuously Jumbled amongst City Quality, from Beau to Bobby, and the Merchants Lady to the Thumb-ring'd Ale-Wife.

Being now left by our selves, in a Room not much bigger than a Hogs-Head, furnish'd with nothing but a little Bed-stead, and that of an un-easie height to sit on, that notwithstanding our tedious walk of Seven long Miles, at our Journeys End we could find no Resting-place; but either to lie down like Dogs, or lean like Elephants; finding as much dif-ficulty to get a little Drink, by reason of their number, as the Rabble at a Conduit that runs Wine upon a States Holy-day: When with abun-dance of Pains, and as much Patience, we had Liquor'd our Throats with two or three slender-Body'd Mugs of Country Guzzle, we jostled down two narrow Pair of Stairs, and encreas'd the numberless Throng of gazing Animals, who were differently dispos'd to divers Exercises, some Craming down *Veal* and *Bacon*, to allay the fury of their Cormorant Ap-petites, having no Table-Cloath, but Grass; or Seats, but Ground; others Projecting better for their Ease, had made a Table of a Horse-block, and blow'd their Noses in the same Napkins with which they wip'd their Fingers; some were Climb'd into an Arbour on the top of an old Tree, where they sat Hooping and Hollowing, like so many Owls, but could get no body near 'em, to bring 'em either Drink or Victuals: Some Ladies in their Coaches Mask'd, who, I suppose, wanted to give some Cully a cast home that would pay the Coachman, others on Horse-back, bare-fac'd, conducted thither by their Fathers Prentices, and many Hundreds of both Sexes on Foot, some Smoaking, some Drinking, others Cursing and Swearing, thro' want of that Refreshment, which the more Industri-ous Spectators had very Painfully procur'd. In the Interim we were thus walking, to take Notice of the sundry Humours and Transactions of the buzzing Multitude, came four Merry Dames in a Coach, and lighted by me, one trick'd up like an Old Maid with a Gold Chain about her Neck, Patches on a Wrinkled Face, and her Ill-shap'd Carcase splendidly set off with very Gay Apparel, her Eyes looking Angry with a hot Rheum cast up into her Head by the staleness of her Virginity, the rest wore Mo-therly Countenances, and look'd as if they had understood Trap this Twenty Years, I Welcom'd them to *Mobs Hole*, and began to entertain 'em, with some talk applicable to the present Juncture; at last the old Gentlewoman, whom I suppos'd a Maid, took the freedom to ask me, *What it was a Clock by my Watch? Truly, Madam,* said I, *I have not one about me; but if you please to turn about, and look at the Sun with those Vir-gins Eyes of yours, a Lady of your Judgment may understand the Hour of the Day by his distance from the Horizon.* Says another of 'em, *May be the Gen-*

tlemans

the mans Watch is down, and he is ashamed to show it us. To which I Reply'd, Indeed, Madam, if it be, I can see nothing in your Ladyships Face that will wind it up again. Why, Sir, says a third, does Faces use to wind up Watches? Yes, Madam, answer'd I, such as such as I carry about me, which is made without Wheeles; and will give such a Lady as you are, a better time of the Day when it's Standing, than other Watches do by their Motion. Bless me! Sir, says the Forth, yours is the strangest Watch that I ever heard on; I wish you would be so kind to let a Body see it. Truly Madam, says I, 'tis without a Case; and until so be pluckt out in Publick Company, otherwise I would be very willing to oblige you. She Replying, if it were for ty to hear it is so much out of Order; but if it wants nothing but a Case, you don't know but I may present you with one, if I think 'twill fit. I found, I should be over-talk'd upon this Subject, and was glad to make an excuse to quit their further Conversation; and from thence went into the Kitchen, built up with Furzzes in the open Aire, to behold their Cookery; where the major part of the Calf was Roasting upon a Wooden Spit: Two or three great Slivers He had lost off his Buttocks, his Babs par'd to the very Bone, with holes in his Shoulders each large enough to bury a Sevil Orange, that he look'd as if a Kennel of Hounds had every one had a Snap at him. Under him lay the Flitch of Roasted Bacon, of such an Ethiopean Complexion, that I should rather have guess'd it the side of a Blackamore: It looking more like a Canibals Feast, than a Christian Entertainment. My Appetite was so far from coveting a Taste, that I had a full Meal at the very Sight of their Dainties; and I believe, for the future, shall have as great a kindness for Veal and Bacon as an Anabaptist Preacher has for the Church Liturgy. Being soon Glutted with the view of this unusual piece of Cookery, we departed thence, and hearing a great bustle in the upper Room of an Out-House, we went up Stairs to see what was the matter where we found a poor Fidler Scraping over the Tune of Now Ponder well you Parents Dear; and a parcel of Country People Dancing and Crying to't. The Remembrance of the Uncles Cruelty to the poor Innocent Babes, and the Robbin Red-Breasts Kindness, had fix'd in their very Looks such Signs of Sorrow and Compassion, that their Dancing seem'd rather a Religious Worship, than a Merry Recreation. Having thus given our selves a Prospect of all that the place afforded, we return'd to Stratford, where we got a Coach, and from thence to London.

FINIS.

THE
LONDON
SPY.

For the *Month* of *May*, 1699.

PART VII.

The Second Edition.

By the Author of the Trip to *JAMAICA.*

LONDON, Printed and Sold by *J. How*, in the *Ram-Head-Inn-Yard*, in *Fanchurch-Street*, 1702.

THE
LONDON
SPY.

WHEN our *Stratford* Tub, by the affiftance of its Carrionly Tits of different Colours, had out-run the Smoothnefs of the Road, and enter'd upon *London-ftones*, with as frightful a Rumbling as an empty Hay-Cart, our Leathern-Conveniency being bound in the Braces to its Good-Behaviour, had no more Sway than a Funeral Herfe, or a Country Waggon, That we were jumbled about like fo many Peafe in a Childs Rattle, running at every Kennel-Jolt a great hazard of a Diflocation: This we endured till we were brought within *White-Chappel-Bars*, where we lighted from our ftubborn Caravan, with our Elbows and Shoulders as Black and Blew as a Rural *Joan*, that had been under the Pinches of an angry *Fairy*. Our weary Limbs being rather more Tir'd, than Refrefh'd, by the Thumps and Toffes of our ill-contriv'd Engine, as unfit to move upon a Rugged Pavement, as a Gouty Sinner is to halt o'er *London-Bridge* with his Boots on. For my part, faid I, if this be the Pleafure of Riding in a Coach through *London-ftreets*, may thofe that like it enjoy it; for it has fo loofen'd my Joints in fo fhort a Paffage, that I fhall fcarce recover my former Strength this Fortnight; and indeed, of the two, I would rather choofe to cry *Mous-Traps* for a Livelyhood, than be oblig'd every day to be drag'd about Town under fuch Uneafinefs: And if the Qualities Coaches are as troublefom as this, I would not be bound to do their Pennance for their Eftates. You muft Confider, fays my Friend, you have not the right knack of humouring the Coaches Motion; for there is as much Art in Sitting a Coach finely, as there is in Riding the Great Horfe; and many a younger-Brother has got a good Fortune by his Graceful Lolling in his Chariot, and his Genteel Steping in and out, when he pays a Vifit to her Ladyfhip. There are a great many fuch Qualifications amongft our true *French-bred* Gentlemen, that are Admir'd amongft our nicer Ladies now-a-days, befides the fmooth Dancing of a Minuet, the making a Love Song, the neat Carving up a Fowl, or the thin Paring of an Apple.

Pray,

Pray, Friend, said I, don't let us trouble our selves about how the Ladies choose their Husbands, or what they do with their Gallants, but Consider how we shall get to the other end of the Town, for my Pedestals are so Crippl'd with our Whimsical Peregrination, that I Totter like a founder'd Horse, or an old Sinner when his Corns are tender. To which, says my Friend, You have exprest such a dislike to a Coach, that I know not which way to get you thither, if you cannot walk it, except you can make your Supporters carry you down to the *Bridge* and there we may take Water at the *Old-Swan*, Land at *Salisbury-Court*, and then we shall be properly plac'd to proceed on our further Ramble.

I accordingly submitted to my Friends Advice; and hobbled down to the Water-side, with as much uneasiness as a Badger walks upon even Ground, or a Bear down-hill, where a Jolly Grizzle-Pated *Charon* handed us into his Wherry, whips off his short Skirted Doublet, whereon was a Badg, to show whose Fool he was, then fixes his Strecher, bids us Trim the Boat, and away he Row'd us; but had not Swom above the length of a West-Country Barge, before a scoundrel crew of *Lambeth* Gardeners attacked us with such a Volley of saucy Nonsence, that it made my Eyes stare, my Head ake, my Tongue run, and my Ears tingle: One of them beginning with us after this manner, *You couple of treacherous Sons of* Brid-well B——s, *who are Pimps to your own Mothers, Stallions to your Sisters, and Cock-Bawds to the rest of your Relations; Who were begot by Huffling, spew'd up, and not Born; and Christen'd out of a Chamber-pot; How dare you show your Ugly Faces upon the River of* Theames, *and fright the Kings Swans from holding their heads above Water?* To which our well-fed Pilot, after he had clear'd his Voice with a Hem, most manfully Reply'd, *You Lousie starv'd Crew of Worm-pickers, and Snail-Catchers; You Offspring of a Dunghill, and Brothers to a Pumkin, who can't afford Butter to your Cabbage, or Bacon to your Sprouts; You shitten Rogues, who worship the Fundament, because you live by a Turd; who was that sent the Gardiner to cut a hundred of Sparragrass, and dug twice in his Wives Parsley-bed before the Good-man came back again? Hold your Tongues, you Knitty Readishmongers, or I'll whet my Needle upon mine A——s and sow you Lips together.* This Verbal Engagement was no sooner over, but another Squabling Crew met us, being most Women, who, as they past us, gave us another Salutation, *viz. You* Taylors! *Who Pawn'd the Gentlemans Cloake to buy a Wedding-Dinner, and afterwards sold his Wives Cloathes for Money to fetch it out again? Here,* Timothy, *fetch your Mistress and I three hap'worth of boild Beeff, see first they make good Weight, and then stand hard for a bit of Carrot.* To which our Orator, after a puff and a pull up, being well skill'd in the Water-Dialect, made this return, *You, Durty Salt-Ass'd-brood of Night-walkers and Shop-lifies, which of you was it that ty'd her Apron about her Neck, because she would be Kiss'd in a Nightrail; and recon'd her Gallant a shilling for fouling of Linnen, when she had never a Smock on? Have a care of your Cheeks, you Whores, we shall have you Branded next Sessions, that the World may see your Trade in your Faces. You are lately come from the Hemp and Hammer. O Good Sir* Robert *Knock, Pray, good Sir* Robert *Knock.* The next Boat we met, was freighted with a parcel of City Shop-keepers, who being eager, like the rest, to show their acuteness of Wit, and admirable breeding, accosted us after this manner, *viz. You Affidavit Scoundrels, pluck the straws out of the heels of your shooes. You* Oats's *Journey-man, Who are you going to swear out of an Estate at* Westmin-fter-Hall?

fter-Hall, tho' you know nothing of the matter? You Rogues we shall have you in the Pillory when Rotten Eggs are plenty. You are in a safe Condition, you may Travel any where by Water and never fear Drowning. Thus they run on, till our Spokes-man stop'd their Mouths with this following Homily, *You Cuckoldly Company of Whistling, Pedling, Lying, Over-reaching Ninny-Hammers,* who were forc'd to desire some handsom Batchelor to Kiss *your Wives, and beg a Holiday for you, or else you would not have dar'd to come out to Day. Go make hast home, that you may find the Fowles at the fire. If I had but as many Horns on my Head, as you are forc'd to hide in your Pockets, what a Monster should I be. You little think what your Wives are providing for you against you come home. Don't be Angry Friends, it's many an honest Mans Fortune.* Said I, this is a rare Place for a Scold to exercise her faculties, and improve her Talant; for I think every body I meet is a new Accademy of ill Language. I observe 'tis as great a Penance for a Modest Man to go a Mile upon the River, as 'tis for him to run the Gantlet thro' an Alley where the good House-wives are Picking Okum; bad Words being as much in Fashion amongst such Gossips, as Curses at a Gaming-Ordinary; and good Words us'd as seldom, as Plain-Dealing among Courtiers.

By this time we were come to our propos'd Landing-Place, where a Stately Edifice (the Front supported by Lofty Columes) presented to our view. I enquired of my Friend what Magnanimous Don *Cressus* resided in this noble and delightful Mansion? Who told me No-body, as he knew on, except Rats and Mice; and perhaps an Old Superanuated *Jack-Pudding,* to look after it, and to take Care that no decay'd Lover of the Drama, should get in and steal away the Poets Pictures, and sell 'em to some Upholsters for *Roman Emperours,* I suppose there being little else to lose, except Scenes, Machines, or some such Jimcracks. For this, says he, is one of the Theatres, but now wholly abandon'd by the Players; and 'tis thought will in a little time be pull'd down, if it is not bought by some of our dissenting Brethren, and converted into a more Pious use, that might in part attone for the sundry Transgressions occasion'd by that Levity, which the Stage of late have been so greatly subject to. Here we took our leaves of the Lady *Thames,* wondering she should have so sweet a Breath, considering how many stinking Pills she swallows in a Day, each Neighbouring Tail, in contempt of her Pride, defiles her peacefull Surface, whose unsavory droppings, the Courteous Dame with Patience wears, to adorn her smooth Countenance, instead of Patches.

Being now Landed upon *Terra Firma,* we steer'd our Course up *Salisbury-Court,* where every two or three steps, we met some Old figure or another, that look'd as if the Devil had Rob'd 'em of all that natural Beauty, which (in being our Makers Image) we derive from our Creator; and had infus'd his own Infernal Spirit in their Corrupt Carcasses: For nothing could be read but Devilism in every Feature. Theft, Whordome, Homicide, and Blasphemy peep'd out at the very Windowes of their souls; Lying, Perjury, Fraud, Impudence, and Misery were the only Graces of their Covntenance.

One with slip-Shoes, without Stockings and a dirty Smock, visible thro' a Crape Petticoat, steping from the Ale-house to her Lodgings with a parcel of Pipes in one hand, and a Gallon pot of Guzzle in

B

the

the other; yet with her Head dreſt up to as great an Advantage, as if all the Members of her Body were ſacrific'd to all Wickedneſs, to keep her ill-look'd Face in Finery. Another, I ſuppoſe, taken from the Oyſter-Tub, and put into Whores Allurements, made a more cleanly appearance, but became her Ornaments as a Cow would a Curb-bridle, or a Sow a Hunting-ſaddle. Then, every now and then, would bolt out a Fellow, and whip Nimbly croſs the Way, being equally fearful, as I imagine, both of Conſtable and Serjeant: And look'd as if the dread of a Gollows had drawn its Picture in his Countenance. Said I to my Friend, what can theſe People be, who are ſo ſtigmatiz'd in their Looks, that they may be known as well from the reſt of Mankind, as *Jews* from *Chriſtians?* They ſeem to me ſo unlike Gods Creatures, that I cannot but fancy them a Colony of Hell-cats, planted here by the Devil, as a Miſchief to Mankind. Why, truly, ſays my Friend, they are ſuch an abominable Race of degenerate Reprobates, that they admit of no Compariſon on this ſide Hells Dominions. All this part quite up to the ſquare, is a Corporation of Whores, Coiners, Highway-men, Pick-pockets, and Houſebreakers; who, like *Bats* and *Owles*, skulk in obſcure holes by Day-light, but wander in the Night in ſearch of oppertunities wherein to exerciſe their Roguery.

When we had taken a Gentle Walk thro' the abominable *Sodom*, where all the ſins invented ſince the fall of *Lucifer* are daily practiſed, we came into the Common Road, *Fleet-ſtreet*, where the Ratling of Coaches, loud as the Cataracts of *Nile*, robb'd me of my Hearing; and put my Head into as much diſorder as the untuneable Hollows of a Rural Mob at a Country Bull-baiting. Now, ſays my Friend, we have a rare oppertunity of repleniſhing our Boxes with a pipe of fine Tobacco; for the greateſt Retailer of that Commodity in *England* lives on the other ſide the way; and if you dare run the hazard of croſſing the Kennel, we'll take a pipe in the ſhop, where we are likely enough to find ſomething worth our Obſervation. Indeed, ſaid I, you may well ſtile it a hazard, for when ever I have occaſion to go on the wrong ſide the Poſt, I find my ſelf in as much dread of having my Bones broke by ſome of theſe conveniences for the *Lame* and *Lazy*, as an unlucky Prentice to a Crabbed Maſter, is of a ſound beating after a ſtollen Holyday. But however, when we had waited with much patience for a ſeaſonable Minute, to perform this dangerous ſervice, we at laſt ventured to ſhoot our ſelves thro' a vacancy between two Coaches, and ſo enter'd the ſmoaky Premiſſes of the famous *Fumigater*: Where a parcel of Ancient Worſhipers of the Wicked Weed were ſeated, wrap'd up in *Iriſh* Blankets, to defend their Wither'd Carcaſſes from the Malicious Winds that only blows upon Old Age and Infirmity; every one having fortified the great Gate of Life with *Engliſh* Guns, well charg'd with *Indian* Gunpowder; their Meagre Jaws, Shrievel'd Looks, and Thoughtful Countenances might render them Philoſophers, their Bodies ſeeming ſo very Dry and Light, as if they had been as hard Bak'd in an Oven as a Sea-bisket, or Cur'd in a Chimney like a flitch of Bacon; fumbling ſo very often at a Pan of Small-coal, that I thought they had acquir'd the Salamanders Nature, and were ſucking Fire thro' a Quill for their Nouriſhment. They behav'd themſelves like ſuch true Lovers of this prevailing Weed, that I dare engage Cuſtom had made their Bodys incapable of ſupporting Life

by

by any other Breath than Smoak. There was no Talking amonst 'em; but *Puff* was the period of every Sentence; and what they said was as short as possible, for fear of losing the Pleasure of a Whiff, as *How d'ye do?* Puff. *Thank ye*, Puff. *Is the Weed Good?* Puff. *Excellent*, Puff. *It's fine Weather*, Puff. *G——d be thanked*, Puff. *What's a Clock?* Puff. *&c.* Behind the Counter stood a Complaisant Spark, who I observ'd show'd as much Breeding in the Sale of a Penny-worth of Tobacco, and the change of a Shilling, as a Courtiers Footman when he meets his Brother *Skip* in the middle of *Covent-Garden*; and is so very Dextrous in discharge of his Occupation, that he guesses from a Pound of Tobacco to an Ounce, to the certainty of one single Corn: And will serve more Penny-worths of Tobacco in half an Hour, then some Clouterly *Mundungus-sellers* shall be able to do in half Four and Twenty. He never makes a Man wait the Tenth part of a Minute for his Change, but will so readily fling you down all Sums, without Counting, from a Gunea to three Penny-worth of Farthings, that you would think he had it ready in his Hand for you before you ask'd him for it. He was very generous of his Small-beer to a good Customer; and I am bound in Justice to say thus much in his behalf, That he will show a Man more Civility for the taking a Penny, than many Stiff-rump Mechanicks will do for the taking of a Pound.

By this time the Motion of our Lungs had consum'd our Pipes; and our Boxes being fill'd, we left the Funking Society in a stinking mist, parching their Intrals with the drowthy Fumes of the pernicious Plant. Which taken so incessantly as it is by these Immoderate Skeletons, render them such Slaves to a Beastly Custom, that they make a Puff at all business, are led astray by following their Noses, burn away their Pence, and consume their time in Smoak.

We now departed hence, my Friend conducting me to a place call'd *White-Fryers*, which he told me was formerly of great Service to the honest Traders of the City; who, if they could by *Cant*, *Flattery*, and *Dessimulation* procure large Credit amonst their Zealous Fraternity, would slip in here with their Effects, take Sanctuary against the Laws, compound their Debts for a small matter, and often times get a better Estate by Breaking, than they could propose to do by Trading. But Now a late Act of Parliament has taken away its Privilidge; and since Knaves can neither Break with Safety nor Advantage, it is observ'd there is not a quarter so many Shopkeepers play at *Bo-peep* with their Creditors, as when they were encouraged to be Rogues by such cheating Conveniences.

We thus enter'd this Debtors Garrison, where, till of late, says my Friend, Old Nick broach'd all his Wicked Inventions, making this Place the very Theatre of Sin, where his most Choice Villanies were dayly represented. As we pass'd thro' the Gate-way, I observed a stall of Books, and the first that I glanc'd my Eye upon, happen'd to be dignified and distinguish'd by this venerable Title, *The Comforts of Whoring, and the vanity of Chastity; Together with a Poem in Praise of the Pox*. Bless me, Thought I, sure this Book was Printed in Hell, and Writ by the Devil; for what Diabolical Scibler upon Earth could be the Author of such unparallel'd Impudence? I was so surpriz'd by the Title, that I was

quite

quite thoughtless of inspecting into the Matter, but march'd on till we came into the main street of this neglected Asylum, so very thin of People, the Windows broke, and the Houses untenanted, as if the Plague, or some such like Judgement from Heaven, as well as Executions on Earth, had made a great Slaughter amongst the poor Inhabitance.

We met but very few Persons within these Melancholly Precincts, and those by the Ariness of their Dresses, the forwardness of their Looks, and the affectedness of their Carriage, seem'd to be some Neighbouring *Lemons*, who lay conveniently to be squeez'd by the Young Fumblers of the Law: Who are apt to spend more time upon *Phillis* and *Cloris*, than they do upon *Cook* and *Littleton*. Having taken a Survey of these Infernal Territories, where Vice and Infamy were so long Protected, and Flourish'd without Reproof, to the great Shame and Scandal of a Christian Nation; I shall therefore bestow a few Lines upon this Subject, which I desire the Reader to accept on.

On *White-Fryars*.

THE Place where Knaves their Revels kept,
  And bid the Laws Defiance;
Where Whores and Thieves for safety Crept,
Is of her filthy Swarms clean Swept,
Her Lazy Crew that skulk'd for Debt,
  Have lost their chief reliance.

The Vermin of the Law, the Bum,
  Who gladly kept his distance,
Does safely now in Triumph come,
And if he finds the Wretch at home,
He Executes the fatal Doom,
  Without the least Resistance.

Villains of ev'ry black degree,
  Were on this Spot collected;
Oaths, Curses, Lyes and Blasphemie,
Pass'd Currantly from He to She,
Made Virtue stare to Hear and See,
  What Vices here were acted.

A soil where Sin could only Grow,
  And devil'sh Dark Opinion;
A Looking-glass on Earth to show,
How Fiends and Devils live below,
That Mankind might the Discords know,
  That dwell in Hells Dominion.

The Streets were Stain'd, and Houses Lin'd
  With Bloodshed, sin and sorrow;
So Wicked it was hard to find
One Christian with an upright Mind;
But seem'd to be a place design'd,
  To perish like Gommorha.

           The

The sodden Sinners here that liv'd,
  With Pox, look'd pale as Tallow,
By whom no God was e'er believ'd,
Or Man amongst 'em ever Thriv'd,
But that Curs'd Wretch who dayly striv'd,
  To be the Basest Fellow.

To Thieve, Pick-pockets, Whore, and Cheat,
  Where all their chiefest Study;
And He, or She that was unfit
For any Rogu'ry, or Deceit,
Such a poor Rascal had no Wit,
  And She a silly Dowdy.

Pox, Poverty, Dirt, Rags, and Lice,
  By most were car'd about-'em;
They were too Nasty to be Nice,
And all their dayly Exercise,
Were Whoring, Drinking, Cards, and Dice,
  No Living here without-'em.

No Orders did they mind, or Hours,
  But free of all Restrictions,
Each Tipling-House kept Open-doors,
At Midnight, for Sots, Rogues, and Whores,
To Curse and Wrangle at All-Fours,
  And vent their Maledictions.

But now the Wicked Scene withdraws,
  And makes an Alteration;
It's Purg'd and Cleans'd by wholesome Laws,
And is become a Sober Place,
Where Honesty may show it's Face,
  Without Disreputation.

My Friend conducted me from thence, thro' the little Wicket of a great pair of Gates, which brought us into a stately part of that Learn'd Society the *Temple* : This, says my Friend, is called the *Kings-Bench* Walks, and here are a great many sorts of People, that are now walking to waste their time, who are well worth your Notice, we'll therefore take two or three turns amonst 'em, and you will find 'em the best living Library, to instruct you to read Mankind, that ever you met with.

Pray, said I, what do you take those Knot of Gentlemen to be, who are so Merry with one another? They, reply'd my Friend, are Gamsters, waiting to pick up some young Bubble or other as he comes from his Chamber; they are Men whose Conditions are subject to more Revolutions than a Weather-cock, or the uncertain Mind of a Fantastical Woman. They are seldom two Days in one and the same Stations, they are one day very Richly drest, and perhaps out at Elbows the next; they are Persons who have often a great deal of Money, and are as often with-

C

out

out a Penny in their Pockets; they are as much Fortunes Bubbles, as young
Gentlemen are theirs; for what ever benefits she beſtows upon 'em with
one Hand, ſhe ſnatches away with t'other; their whole Lives are a Lottery, they read no Books but Cards, and all their Mathematicks is to truely
underſtand the Ods of a Bet; they very often fall out, but very ſeldome
Fight, and the way to make 'em your Friends, is to Quarrel with them;
they are Men who have ſeldome occaſion to pare their Nails, for they
moſt commonly keep them ſhort by Biting of them. They generally
begin every Year with the ſame Riches, for the Iſſue of their Annual Labours, is chiefly to inrich the Pawn-Broker. They are ſeldome in Debt,
becauſe no-Body will Truſt 'em; and they never care to Lend Money, becauſe they know not where to Borrow it. A Pair of Falſe Dice, and a
Pack of mark'd Cards ſets 'em up; and an Hours Unfortunate Play
Commonly breaks 'em. They are nearly related to Madmen; for they
have generally more Raving Fits in a day than a *Bedlamite*, at which times
they are as profuſe of their Oaths, as a young Scholar is of his Latin.
They generally Die Inteſtate; and go as Poor out of the World as they
came into it.

As Marriners with hopes their Anchors weigh,
But if croſs Winds, or Storms they meet at Sea,
They Damn their Stars, and Curſe the Low'ring Day.

So Gamſters when the Luck of one prevails
Above anothers, than the Loſer rails,
Damns Fortune, and in Paſſion bites his Nails.

You have given me a very pretty Character of 'em. But pray what ſort
of Blades are thoſe in antiquated piſs-burnt Wigs; whoſe Cloaths hang
upon their Backs as if they were not made for 'em; who walk with
abundance of Circumſpection? I'll tell you, ſays my Friend, they are
a Kind of hangers on upon the Warden of the *Fleet*, and the Marſhal of
the *Kings-Bench*. They pretend to have an Intereſt with them in the
procuring of Liberty for Priſoners remov'd by *Habeas Corpus*: Who cun-
ningly, by theſe Stratagems, dive into your Circumſtances, and report
'em to the Warden or Marſhal, who know the better how to deal with
you, and Screw you up to the utmoſt doit you are able to afford him. They
are a kind of Solicitors in this ſort of buſineſs; who, whilſt they are
pretending to ſerve you, are ſubtly contriving a Treacherous way to pick
your Pocket; and if any Perſon makes his eſcape, they are very diligent
in their Enquiries after him; and if they make Diſcovery, do privately
diſpatch Intelligence to the Keepers aforeſaid, for which they are rewarded. Theſe are a parcel of as honeſt Fellows, as ever Cut the Throat of
a Friend, or Robb'd their own Father. For a Crown, or half a Piece,
they will give any Bailiff a Caſt of their Office, in Dogging, or Setting,
even thoſe of their own Acquaintance, to whom they profeſs their greateſt
Friendſhip. They are alſo very Servicable Agents in a bad Cauſe, if they
can Say or Swear any thing that will do your buſineſs a Kindneſs; they
will at any time, for a ſmall Fee, ſtrain a point to your aſſiſtance. They
are generally Tradeſmen, brought into Poverty by Negligence and their
own Profuſeneſs; and by Poverty and Impriſonment, arriv'd to the unhappy knowledge of theſe Shameful Undertakings. They are Men whoſe

Liberty

Liberty is owing to a long Confinement, or the Keepers Clemency; and when ever they die, the Warden or Marſhal make Dice of their Bones, to ſecure themſelves from the Suit of their Creditors.

> *Sure none like Man, will their own kind annoy,*
> *Hawks, will not Hawks, or Wolves, will Wolves deſtroy:*
> *But theſe inhumane Sharks, worſe Beaſts than they,*
> *On their own Fellow Creatures baſely Prey;*
> *Surely at laſt ſuch Deſtin'd are to Starve,*
> *Who can no better Life than this deſerve.*

I Obſerve, ſaid I, there are another ſort of Men, that appear ſomething like Gentlemen, with Meagre Jaws and Dejected Countenances; each walking ſingly, and look'd as Peeviſhly, as if the blind Jilt and he, thro' a mutual diſlike, were frowning on each other.

Thoſe you muſt know, ſays my Friend, are Gentlemen in diſtreſs, ſome coming to their Eſtates ſo Early, before they had Senſe enough to preſerve 'em, have been Bubbled by the Town Paraſites, Taverns, Whores, and Sharpers, till reduc'd to Miſery, and made the ſad Examples of their own Extravagance; and are now waiting with a hungry Belly, to faſten upon ſome old Acquaintance for a Dinner, who dreads the ſight of one of 'em, as much as a Debtor does a Bailiff: But becauſe he knew his Family and him in Proſperity, is willing now and then to give him a Meal, or relieve him with the Gift of a Shilling, which he takes with as humble an acknowledgement, as a poor Parſon does a Benefice from his Patron, or a Tradeſman the Payment of a Bill from a Courtiers Steward.

> *How Vain is Youth? How Ripe to be Undone,*
> *When Rich be-times, and made a Man to ſoon?*
> *Humour his Folly, and his Pride commend,*
> *You make him both your Servant and your Friend.*
> *But if with Councells you the Wretch ſhall Aid,*
> *He tells you, to Adviſe is to Upbraid;*
> *That Good your Admonitions are, 'tis true,*
> *But ſtill, no more than what before he knew;*
> *Prays you to hold your Tongue; he Scorns to Learn of you.*

There's another ſort among 'em who were born Gentlemen, and bred up in Idleneſs, whoſe Parents had the Care, by way of prevention, to ſpend their Eſtates themſelves, and leave their Iſſue nothing to truſt to. Theſe, ſome of them, are Pentioners to the Petecoat, ſome *Boretto*-Men at the *Groom-Porters*; ſome Flatterers, and Soothers, who ſupport themſelves by bringing others into the like Unhappineſs; and thoſe amongſt them of the meekeſt Spirits, are *Relation-Puniſhers*, who have Patience enough to bear a reproof at Dinner, without ſpoiling their Appetites.

> *Unhappy Wretch, by Chance and Bounty Fed;*
> *To nothing Born, and yet to nothing Bred;*
> *Thou'rt Fortunes Pentioner, whom Men Receive*
> *Sometimes for Sport, and ſometimes to Relieve:*

Mechanicks,

Mechanicks, in thy Company, look Great,
And Magnifie, by thee, their happier State
Each Man that knows thee, doubly Guards his Purse,
Thou'rt like Infection shun'd, and that that's worse,
A Burthen to the World, and to thy self a Curse.

As my Friend and I was walking upon the Grand Parrade, I obferv'd abundance of Mask'd Ladies, with rumpled Hoods and Scarfs, their Hands charg'd with Papers, Band-Boxes, and Rowls of Parchment, frisk in and out of their Staircafes, like Coneys in a Warren bolting from their Burrows. Said I, to my Friend, do you think all thefe Women are Madam *Blackacres*, and come hither about Law bufinefs, that we fee triping backwards and forewards fo very Nimbly? No, no, reply'd my Companion, thefe are Ladies that came to receive Fees inftead of giving any. They have now extraordinary bufinefs upon their Hands with many of the young Layers, tho' nothing in Relation to the Law; for you muft know, thefe are *Nimphs of Delight*, who only carry Papers in their hands for a blind; who are fuch confiderable Dealers they can afford to give Credit for a whole Vacation, and now, in Term time, they are induftrious in picking up their Debts. You are now, I'll affure you, in one of the greateft places of Trade in Town, for Dealing in that fort of Commodity; for moft Ladies, who for want of Fortunes difpair of Husbands, and are willing to give themfelves up to Mans ufe, without the dull confinement of Matrimony, come hither to be truely Qualified for their generous Undertaking, and by that time fhe has had a Months Converfation with the airy blades of this Honourable Society, fhe will doubtlefs find her felf as well fitted for the Imployment, as if fhe had had a Twelve-months Education under the moft experienc'd Bawd in Chriftendome; and if you ever chance to meet with any of our Trading Madams, and ask them *who Debauch'd 'em*, it's ten to one but her Anfwer will be, *a Gentleman of the Temple.* But whether it be matter of Fact, that thofe Sins are lay'd to their charge, or whether it is only the Ambition of the Jilt, to have you think fhe facrific'd her Virginity to the ufe of fo worthy a Society, I won't prefume to determine: Tho, I confefs, I think it reafonable to believe, that our forward Ladies are more apt to Dedicate their Honours to an Inns-of-Court than elfe where, for three Reafons. *Firft*, As they are the Flower of our Gentry. *Secondly*, As the greatnefs of their Number affords variety of Choice. And *Thirdly*, As they have the beft Conveniencies for Confummating Debauchery without dread or danger.

Could Youth thofe early Hours to Study bend,
Which on the Tempting Sex they Vainly fpend;
How fparkling would his happy Genius fhine?
How ftrong his Nerves? His knowledge how Divine?
To Adams firft perfections he'd attain;
And by degrees Loft Paradife Regain.
But that which Plagues and Bitters Humane Life
Is Woman, whether Miftrefs or a Wife,
Mother of Sin, Difeafe, of Sorrow and Strife.

Pray, faid I, what Noun Subftantive Flat-cap of a Houfe is this, fo very different from all the reft of the Buildings? My Friend told me

'twas

'twas the *Kings-Bench-Office*, where, says he, they Sell broken Latin much dearer than Phyſicians do their Viſits, or Apothecaries their Phyſick. Time, you know, has been always vallued as a precious Commodity by all Men, but here they Sell their Minutes at as Extravagant a Rate, as Great Men do their Protection, and won't let four Fingers and a Thumb run once croſs a Slip of Paper, but by Virtue of a *Hocus Pocus* Cuſtom, call'd *The Fee's of the Office*, they'll conjure two or three Half Crowns out of your Pocket, and won't put their Tongues to the trouble of giving you either a why or a wherefore for it.

Being wonderfully pleas'd with the Proſpect of the *Thames*, the Beauty of the Buildings, and the Airineſs and Spaciouſneſs of the Court, I began to look about me with no little Satisfaction; and gazing round, I eſpied a Sun-Dial, ſubſcrib'd with this Motto, *Be gone about your Buſineſs.* Pray, ſaid I, to my Companion, What wonderful Myſtery lies hid in thoſe Words, for ſurely ſo Learn'd a Society, would never have choſe a Sentence for this purpoſe, but what ſhould be very Significant, and I cannot for my Life underſtand the meaning on't; for certain they intend ſomething extraordinary by it, not inteligible to a common Capacity. Truely, ſaid my Friend, 'tis ſomething than that no-body could ever find out, for I never could hear it would admit of any other Application or Conſtruction, than what is render'd by the Literal Sence. No! ſaid I, then I think whoever plac'd it here, deſerves to be Bogg'd for putting ſuch an affront upon ſo honourable a Society; for I remember, when I was a School-Boy, thoſe very Words were the Burthen of a Ballad: Poh, poh, ſays my Friend, you only Jeſt with me. Upon my Word, ſaid I, 'tis very true, and I can my ſelf Repeat ſome Stanza's of it, which are theſe.

F IE! *You great Looby, John;*
Pray-now let me alone.
If you won't let me Reſt,
Now a Body is Dreſt,
Be gone about your Buſineſs.

Never Stir, let me Go,
Don't you Rumple me ſo;
Hold your Hand, you great Cur,
If you think I'm a Whore,
Be gone about your Buſineſs.

Nay, I Vow and Proteſt,
I will not be in Jeſt;
Why, you ugly Damn'd Devil,
If you will not be Civil,
Be gone about your Buſineſs.

O Dear! Nay, I Vow.
Why, where are you now?
O L—d I'm undone;
You will kill me anon,
Go on about your Buſineſs.

Certainly,

Certainly, says my Friend, if the Benchers had ever heard this Merry Ditty, they would not have thought it confistent with their Gravity, to have chose the *Chorus* for a Motto; I cannot but conceive they have shew'd a Blind Side, in putting so Dull a piece of Imperative *Fustian* in so Publick a Place, as if they defign'd to conjure Loiterers out of the Walks, as a Jugler does his Balls from under his Cups, with a *Presto be gon*. I think it's a great Difhonour to a Learn'd Society, that they could find no apt Phrase, to serve so Poor a purpose; but to be so sadly Puzzled at so ordinary a Task, as to use so Bald and Naked a Sentence, such a Thred-bare Scrap of Englifh too, which is now become the common Jeft, and Ridicule of every mean Mechanick.

From thence we went towards the Hall, and turn'd in at a dark Entry that brought us into a Cloifter or Piazza; where a parcel of Grave Blades Gown'd and Banded, with Green Snap-Sacks in their Hands, were so busily talking Alphabetically, about *A.* Marrying of *B.* and how they begat two Sons, *C.* and *D.* and how *C.* being the Elder Brother, Married *E.* by whom he had two Daughters, *F.* and *G.* &c. So that I thought they had been examining into the Genealogy of the Chrift-crofs-row; I liftening all the while with great Attention, expecting I fhould have heard the Original Rife of every individual Mark, or Letter, and how they begot one another, from *A.* to *Z.* thro' out the Alphabet, till my Friend told me 'twas their method of Stating a Cafe, which made me blufh at my Ignorance. Heads, Tongues, Feet, and Hands, were here all moving, which occafion'd me to fancy, their reading so much Law French, had infpir'd them with the Gallick Grace of so much Action in their talk.

We left thefe debating the weighty difference between *John* of *Oaks* and *John* of *Stiles*, and march'd forward, till we came into the Inward *Temple*, as my Friend inform'd me, where we had a fine Profpect of a Stately Hall, and Pleafant Fountain; here we alfo found walking fundry forts of Peripateticks, fome, I believe, thro' good Husbandry, having chofe the Broad Stones for the prevention of the Rough Gravel wearing out their Shoe-Soles, others for the Eafe of their Corns, and fome Country Clients, with Gray Coats and Long Staves, I fuppofe defired to walk there by their Lawyers, whilft their bufinefs was difpatched, becaufe they fhould not fpoil their Chamber-Floors with their Hob-nails. Here and there amongft 'em was a creeping old Fellow, with fo Religious a Countenance, that he look'd as if he had fpent more Pounds in Law, than ever he Read Letters in the Gofpel; and had paid in his time as much Money for Declarations, Pleas, Orders, and Executions, Subpena's, Injunctions, Bills, Anfwers, and Decrees, as ever it Coft him in the Maintenance of his Family.

Now, says my Friend, I believe we are both tired with the Labours of the Day; let us therefore Dedicate the latter part purely to our Pleafure, take a Coach and go fee *May-Fair.* Would you have me, said I, undergo the Punifhment of a Coach again, when you know I was fo great a Sufferer by the laft, that it made my Bones rattle in my Skin, and has brought as many Pains about me, as if troubled with the Rheumatifm. That was a Country Coach, says he, and only fit for the Road; but *London* Coaches are hung more loofe, to prevent your being Jolted by the roughnefs of the Pavement. This Argument of my Friends prevail'd upon me, to venture my Carcafe a fecond time to be Rock'd in a *Hackney* Cradle.

So

So we took leave of the *Temple*, turn'd up without *Temple-Bar*, and there took Coach for the General Rendezvouz aforementioned.

By the help of a great many Slashes, and Hey-ups, and after as many Jolts and Jumbles, we were drag'd to the *Fair*, where the harsh sounds of untunable Trumpets, the Catterwauling Scrapes of Thrashing Fidlers, the Grumbling of beaten Calves-Skin, and the discording Toots of broken Organs set my Teeth an Edge, like the Filing of a Hand-saw, and made my Hair stand as Bolt-upright, as the Quills of an Angry *Porcupine*.

We order'd the Coach to drive thro' the Body of the Fair, that we might have the better View of the Tinsey Heroes and the gazing Multitude; expecting to have seen several Corporations of Stroling Vagabonds, but there prov'd but one Company, amongst whom Merry *Andrew* was very busie in Coaxing the attentive Crow'd into a good Opinion of his Fraternitie's and his own Performances; and when with aboundance of Labour, Sweat, and Nonsence, he had drawn a great cluster of the Mob on his Parade, and was just beginning to encourage them to *Walk in and take their Places*, his unluckey opposite, whose boarded Theatre entertain'd the Publick with the wonderful activity of some little *Indian* Rope-dancers, brings out a couple of chattering *Homunculusses*, drest up in *Scaramouch* Habit; and every thing that Merry *Andrew* and his Second did on the one side, was mimick'd by the little Flat-nos'd Comedians on the other, till the two Diminutive Buffoons, by their Comical Gestures had so prevail'd upon the gaping Throng, that tho' Merry *Andrew* had taken pains with all the wit he had to collect the Stragling Rabble into their proper order, yet like an unmannerly Audience, they turn'd their Arses upon the *Players*, and devoted themselves wholly to the Monkeys, to the great vexation of *Tom-Fool*, and all the Struting train of imaginary Lords and Ladies. At last out comes an Epitome of a careful Nurse, drest up in a Country Jacket, and under her Arm a Kitten for a Nurslin, and in her contrary hand a piece of Cheese; down sits the little Matron, with a very Motherly Countenance, and when her Youngster Mew'a, she Dandled him, and Rock'd him in her Arms, with as great signs of affections as a loving Mother could well show to a disorder'd Infant, then bites a piece of the Cheese, and after she had mumbled it about in her own Mouth, then thrust it with her Tongue into the Kittens, Just as I have seen some Nasty Old Sluts feed their Grandchildren. Past these were a parcel of scandalous *Boosing-Kens*, where Soldiers and their Trulls were Skipping and Dancing about to the lamentable Musick, perform'd upon a crack'd Crow'd by a blind Fidler. In another Hut, a parcel of *Scotch* Pedlars and their *Moggies*, Dancing a *Highlanders* Jig to a *Horn-pipe*. Over against them the *Cheshire-booth*, where a Gentlemans Man, was playing more tricks with his heels in a *Cheshire* round, then ever were show'd by the mad Coffee-man at *Sadlers* Musick-house. These Intermixt with here and there a *Poppet-show*, where a Sencelefs Dialogue between *Punchenello* and the *Devil* was convey'd to the Ears of a Listning Rabble thro' a Tin Squeaker, being thought by some of them as great a piece of Conjuration as ever was perform'd by Dr. *Faustus*. We now began to look about us, and take a view of the Spectators; but could not, amongst the many Thousands, find one Man that appear'd above the degree of a Gentlemans Vallet, nor one Whore that could have the Impudence to ask a man above Six-pence wet and Six-pence dry, for an hour of her Cursed Company. In all the Multitudes that ever I beheld, I never in my Life fee fuch a Number of Lazy, Loufie-look'd Rafcals, and fo hateful a Throng of Beggarly, Slutifh Strumpets, who were a Scandal to the Creation, meer Antidotes againft Leachery, and Enemies to all Cleanlinefs. As we were thus rambling thro' the Fair, a Coach overtakes us, wherein were a Couple of more tollerable Punks, whofe Silken Temptations, and Airy Deportment, gave them a Juft Title to a higher Price than the White-Apron Bang-Tails, who were Sweating in the Crow'd, could in Confcience pretend to; an Arch Country Bumpkin having pick'd up a Frog in fome of the adjacent Ditches, peeping into the Coach as he pafs'd by, and being very much affronted that they hid their Faces with their Masks, Ads blood, Says he, you look as ugly in thofe black Vizards as my Toad here; e'en get you altogether, toffing on't into the Coach: At which the frightned Lady-birds Squeak'd out, open'd the Coach Doores, and leap'd among the throng, to fhun their loathfome Companion.

The Adjacent Mob being greatly pleas'd at the Country-Mans Unluckinefs, fet up a Laughing Hollow, as loud as a Huzza, to make good the Jeft, which Occafion'd the Coach-man to look back, who knowing nothing of the Matter, and feeing his Fair out of the Coach, thought they were about to bilk 'im, Alights out of the Coach-Box, in a great Fury Seizes one of them by the Scarf, and accofts them in thefe Words; *Z—nds, you B—ches, what would you Bilk me? Pay me my Fair, or by Gog and Magog you fhall feel the Smart of my Whipcord before you go a Step further.* The poor Harlot's endeavour'd to fatisfie their Angry Charioteer, that they were Women of more Honour, than to attempt fo Ill an Action; telling him, as well as their furpize would give them leave, the Occafion of their Lighting, which would not convince the chollerick Whore-driver, who refus'd either to quit his hold, or fuffer them to go again into his Coach, till they had paid him Eighteen-pence which he demanded as his Fair, but in the Sequel of the matter, they had it not to give him, prefuming to have met with fome Cully in the Fair, that might have ferv'd their purpofe: So that rather than to ftand a Vapulation, one of them took Notice of his Number, and gave him her Scarf as a Pledge, but he refus'd to carry them back, I fuppofe for fear they might call upon fome *Bully* or other that might make him deliver up his fecurity, without any other redemption than a Thrafh'd Jacket. Thus were the unfortunate Madams difmounted of their Coach, and were forc'd to Mob it on foot with the reft of their Sifters.

There being nothing further that occur'd, or to be feen, worth Notice, only a Turkey Ram, with as much Wooll upon his Tail as would load a Wheel-barrow, and a Couple of *Tigers*, grown now fo common they are fcarce worth Mentioning, I fhall therefore conclude the account we give you of *May-Fair*, in thefe following Lines.

'Tis *a fad Rendezvouz of the Wicked'ft of Wretches,*
Poor Rogues without Money, and Whores without patches,
A Sodom for Sin, where the worft Jack of Dandy,
May S——— thro, the Fair with a Gallon of Brandy.

F I N I S.

THE
LONDON
SPY.

For the *Month* of *June*, 1699.

PART VIII.

By the Author of the Trip to *JAMAICA.*

LONDON,
Printed and Sold by *J. How*, in the *Ram-Head-Inn-Yard* in
Fanchurch-street, 1699.

THE
LONDON
SPY.

FOR want of Glaffes to our Coach, having drawn up our Tin Safhes, pink'd like the bottom of a Cullender, that the Air might pafs thro' the holes, and defend us from Stifling, we were convey'd from the Fair, thro' a fuffocating Cloud of Dufty Atoms, to St. *James's* Pallace, in Reverence to which we alighted, and difcharg'd our Grumbling *Effedarius*, who ftuck very clofe to our Backfides, and Mutter'd heavily, according to their old Cuftome, for t'other Six-pence, till at laft moving us a little beyond our Patience, we gave an Angery Pofitive Denial to his Unreafonable Importunities; and fo parted with our Unconfcionable Carrion-Scourger, who we found, like the reft of his Fraternity, had taken up the Miferly Immoral Rule, *viz. Never to be fatisfied.*

We pafs'd thro' a Lofty Porch into the firft Court, where a parcel of Hob-nail'd Loobies were gazing at the Whales Rib with great amazement; being bufily confulting what Creature it could be that could produce a Bone of fo unufual a Magnitude. Who fhould come by in this Interim, but a *Fingallian* Conjurer, pofting to (as my Friend fuppofed) Duke *Humphery's* Walk in the *Park*, to pick his Teeth, and Loiter away his Suppertime. But feeing the Country Hobbies ftand gaping at this puzzling Rarity, he put in amongft the reft, to deliver his Judgment of this amazing Object. *I Pray you Sir* (fays one of the Countrymen to him) *what fort of a Bone do you take this to be?* To which the Captain, after taking a little Shufh, moft Judicioufly replyed, *By my Shoul, Egra, I believe it is the Jaw Bone of the Afh, wid which* Shampfon *Kill'd the* Philifchines: *And it ifh nail'd up here dat no body fhou'd do any more Mifchief wid it.* I wonder, faid another of the Plough-Jobbers, how he could ufe it, 'tis fuch a huge unweildy Weapon? By my Shoul, reply'd *Teague, Let Shampfon look to dat his nown felf, for it ifh none of my Bufinefs.*

From thence we went thro' the *Pallace* into the *Park*, about the time when the Court Ladies raife their extended Limbs from their
downy

downy Couches, and Walk into the Mall to refresh their Charming Bodies with the Cooling and Salubrious Breezes of the Gilded Evening. We could not possibly have Chose a Luckier Minute, to have seen the delightful *Park* in its greatest Glory and Perfection; for the brightest Stars of the Creation, sure (that shine by no other Power than humane Excellence) were moving here, with such awful State and Majesty, that their Graceful Deportments bespoke 'em Goddesses. Such merciful Looks were thrown from their engaging Eyes upon every admiring Mortal, so free from Pride, Envy, or Contempt, that they seem'd, contrary to Experience, to be sent into the World to compleat it's Happiness. The wonderful works of Heaven were here to be Read in Beauties Characters. Such Elegant Compositions might be observ'd in the sundry Frames of Woman, that it's impossible to conceive other, than such Heavenly Forms to be perfected after the Unerring Image of Divine Excellence. I could have gaz'd for ever with unexpressible Delight, finding in every Lovely Face, and Magnificent Behaviour, something still New to raise my Admiration, with due respect to the Creator, for imparting to us such shews of Celestial Harmony in that most fair and curious Creature, Woman.

W*Oman (when Good, the best of Saints)*
　　That Bright Seraphick Lovely She!
　　Who nothing of an Angel wants,
But Truth and Immortality.

Whose Silken Limbs, and Charming Face,
　　Keeps Nature Warm with Am'rous Fire,
Was She with Wisdom Arm'd, and Grace,
　　What greater Bliss could Man desire?

How Smoothly would our Minutes slide?
　　How Sweetly Lovers must accord?
Had she but Wit herself to guide,
　　Or Prudence to Obey her Lord.

Few Troubles would our Lives annoy,
　　Could Man in Wav'ring Beauty trust;
But her Misguidance mars the Joy,
　　Thro' want of Wisdom to be Just.

Adam no Paradise had Lost,
　　Had Eve not Disobedient been;
Her wand'ring inclinations cost
　　The Price of Happiness for Sin.

How Blest a Marry'd State would be,
　　Were but her Temper and her Love,
From Lust and Revolution free,
　　How great a Blessing would she prove!

But Pride of being Great and Gay,
　　Tempts her to deviate, by degrees,
From Virtue's Paths, and run astray,
　　For Gawdy Plumes, and Lolling Ease.

Thus

Thus once defil'd she soon growes Lewd,
Like Angels fall'n from Purity,
Pursuing Ill, disdaining Good;
And Envies what she cannot be.

Could Beauty in her Dressing-Glass
The Charms of Innocence but see,
How Virtue Gilds her awful Face,
She'd prize the darling Rarity.

For she that's Lovely, Just, and Kind,
Does Blessings to a Lover bring;
But if her Honour's once resign'd,
Tho' Fair she's but a Poys'nous Sting.

Tho' I was greatly affected with the Majestick Deportment of the Female Sex, Each looking with a Presence as well worthy of *Diana's* Bow, or *Bellona's* Shield, as the Golden Apple of *Venus*, yet I could by no means reconcile my self to the Sheepish Humility of their Cringing Worshippers, who were guilty of so much Idolatry to the Fair Sex, that I thought the Laws of the Creation were greatly transgressed, and that Man had dwindled from his first Power and Authority into Pusilanimity and Luxury; and had suffered deceitful Woman to cozen him of his Prerogative. For the Men look'd so Effeminate, and shew'd such cowardly tameness by their Extravagant Submission, as if they wanted Courage to Exercise their Freedom which they had a Just Title to use. It seem'd to me as if the World was turn'd Top-Side-turvy; for the Ladies look'd like undaunted Heroes, fit for Government or Battle, and the Gentlemen like a parcel of Fawning Flattering Fops, that could bear Cuckoldom with Patience, make a Jest of an Affront, and swear themselves very faithful and humble Servants to the Petticoat: Creeping and Cringing in dishonour to themselves, to what was Decreed by Heaven their Inferiors: as if their Education had been amongst Monkeys, who (as it is said) in all Cases give the preheminence to their Females.

Having thus seen what the Mall afforded, we stept over its boarded Bounds into Duke *Humphery's* Walk, as my Friend inform'd me, where he show'd me abundance of our Neighbouring Bull-Factors, distinguishable by their Flat Noses and Broad Faces, who were walking away their leisure hours beneath the Umbrage of the Lime-Trees; and were crawling about backwards and forwards, like so many Straggling Caterpillars in a Grove of Sycamores, who for want of other Food, are ready to devour the very Leaves that bred them; So these look'd as sharp as if they were ready to swallow their best Friends for want of other Subsistance. This Walk, says my Friend, is a rare Office of Intelligence for a Woman as rich as Lewd, to furnish her self with a Gallant that will stick as close as a Crablouse to her *Nunquam Satu*, if she will but allow him good Cloaths, three Meals a Day, and a little Money for *Usquebaugh*. If she likes him, when she has him, she need not fear Losing him as long as she's worth a Groat; for they are very constant

B

ftant

ftant to any Body that has Money, and will meafure out their Affections by her Generofity: and fhe will furely find (at her own coft) that
nothing but her Poverty will make him look out for a frefh Miftrefs.
The worthy Gentlemen who chiefly frequent this Sanctuary, are Non-
Commiffion Officers. I mean not fuch who have left their Commiffions,
but fuch as never had any; and yet would be very angry fhould you
refufe to Honour them with the title of Captain, tho' they never fo
much as traild a Pike towards the deferving on't.

From thence we walk'd into the *Parade*, which my Friend told me,
us'd, in a Morning, to be cover'd with the Bones of Red-herrings, and
fmelt as ftrong about Breakfaft time as a Wett-Salters fhop at Mid-
fummer. But now, fays he, its perfum'd again with *Englifh* Breath, and
the Scent of *Oroonoko* Tobacco no more offends the Noftrils of our Squea-
mifh Ladies, who may now pafs backwards and forwards free from all
fuch Neufances; and, if with Child, without the danger of being frighted at a terrible pair of Whifkers.

From thence we walk'd up to a *Canal*, where Ducks were frifking
about, and ftanding upon their Heads; fhowing as many Tricks in their
Liquors as a *Bartholomew-Fair* Tumbler. Said I, to my Friend, His Majefties Ducks are wond'rous Merry. He replying, Well they may, for
they are always Tippling. We then took a view of the fam'd figure
of a *Gladiator*, which indeed is well worthy of the place it ftands in;
for the exactnefs of its Proportion, the true placing and expreffing of the
exterior Mufcling, Veins, and Arteries, fhow fuch a perfection of Art,
that Juftly deferves our Admiration. Behind this Figure upon the foot
of the Pedeftal, my Friend and I fit down to pleafe our Eyes with the
profpect of the moft delightful Aquaduct, and to fee its Feather'd Inhabitants, the Ducks, divert us with their fundry Paftimes. In which
Interim, who fhould come up to the front of the *Gladiator*, but two or
three merry Buxom Ladies, who I fuppofe by their Exceptions againft
the Statue, were Women of no little Experience, but very competent
Judges of what they pretended to be Judges of. One of them more
forward to Araign the Artift than the reft, (not knowing we were
behind) exprefs'd herfelf with abundance of Scorn and Contempt, after
this manner, *viz. Is this the fine proportion'd Figure I have heard my Huf-
band fo often brag on? Its true, his Legs and Arms are ftrong and manly:
But look, look, Coafin, what a Bauble it has got!* With that my Friend
ftarts up, You muft confider Ladies (fays he) in the time when this
was made, Women did not wear their Confciences fo large as they do
now adays. At which, like a company of merry Wagtails, they run a-
way Tittering and Laughing.

We arofe from thence, and walk'd up by the Decoy, where Meanders
glid fo fmoothly beneath their Ofier Canopies, that the calm Surface
feem'd to exprefs nothing inhabited this Watry-Palace but Peace and
Silence. I could have wifh'd my felf capable of living obfcure from
mankind in this Element like a Fifh, purely to have enjoy'd the pleafure of fo delightful a fluminous Labyrinth, whofe Intricate Turnings
fo confound the Sight, that the Eye is ftill in fearch of fome new Difco-
verie, and never fatisfied with the tempting variety fo Artificially order'd in fo little a Compafs.

We

We turn'd up from thence into a long Lime-Tree-Walk, where either Art or Nature had carefully preserv'd the Trees in such exact proportion to each other, that a Man would guess by their appearance they all aspire in Heighth, and spread in Breadth to just the same Dimensions, and confine the leaves and Branches to an equal Number. Beneath whose shady Influence were pensive Lovers, whispering their Affections to their Mistresses, and breathing out despairing Sighs of their desir'd Happiness. Here also were the tender Off-spring of Nobility handed by their fresh-look'd Nurses, to strengthen and refresh their feeble Joints, with Air and Exercise, suitable to their childish weakness, and some having started more forward in their Infancy were accompany'd with their Tutors, showing such manliness in their Presence, and such Promises of Vertue in their propitious Looks, at Ten or a dozen years of Age, that they seem'd already fortified with Grace, Learning and Wisdom against the Worlds Corruptions.

The Termination of this delectable Walk was in a Knot of Lofty Elms, by a Pond side; round some of which were commodious Seats, for the tired Ambulators to refresh their weary Pedestals. Here a parcel of old-worn-out *Cavaliers* were conning over the *Civil-Wars*, and looking back into the History of their past Lives, to moderate the Anxiety and Infirmity of Age with a pleasing reflection of their Youthful Actions.

Amongst the rest, a Country Cormudgeon was standing with his back-side against a Tree, leaning forward on his Oaken companion, his Staff; and staring towards the top of a high adjacent Elm: Pray, said I, Friend, what is it you are so earnestly looking at; who answered me, *At yonder Birds-nest.* I further ask'd him what Birds-Nest is it? who reply'd, *What a foolish Question you askin me! Who did you ever know any thing but Rooks build so near the Kings Palace,* Whose Innocent Return put my Friend and I into a Laughter. I ask'd if he did not think they were very noble Trees? *Yes, zure, says he, if the Kings Trees should not be Noble, pray whose should?* I mean, said I, don't they Thrive and spread finely? *They have nothing else to do, says he: I know one: Every thing Thrives that stands upon Crown Land, zure, and so does my Landlord.*

Having now seen chiefly what the Park afforded, we set our selves down beneath the pleasant Umbrage of this most stately Arbour, by the Pond side, where I compos'd this following Acrostick on Saint James's Park at the Readers Service.

S ure Art and Nature, no where else can show
A Park where Trees in such true order grow.
I n Silver streams the gentle Isis here
N o Banks o'er flowes yet proudly swells so near,
T hat makes the pleasing Cup just brimming full appear.

I n Sumers longeſt days, when Phebus takes
A Pride to pierce the thickeſt Shades and Brakes,
M ay Beauties walk beneath a Verdant Skreen,
E xempt from Duſt, and by the Sun unſeen:
S o thick of Leaves each Plant, ſo green the Graſs,
S ure Mortal never view'd a ſweeter place.

P revailing Ladies meet in Lovely Swarms,
A nd bleſs each day its Umbrage with their Charms.
R ev'rence the Stuarts Name for this herea'ter,
K ing James the Firſt Club'd Wood, His Grand-ſon Charles found Water.

When by an hours enjoyment we had render'd the Beauty of the *Park* but dull and flat to our pall'd Appetites, we began to think of ſome new Object that ought to Feaſt and Refreſh our tired Senſes, with Pleaſures yet untaſted. Accordingly we took our leaves of the *Park*, with the ſame willingneſs as Lovers turn their Backs upon their Miſtreſſes, when by a vigorous repetition of Embraces to engage her Affections, he has turn'd the delight into a Servile Drudgery. We went thro' a narrow Paſſage that directed us towards *Weſtminſter*, in order to take a view of that Ancient and renown'd Structure the *Abby*, to which I was an utter ſtranger. When we came in ſight of which, I could not behold the outſide of the Awful Pile without Rev'rence and Amazement. 'Twas rais'd to that Stupendious Heighth and Beautified with ſuch Noble Ornaments, wherein the bold ſtroaks of excelling Artiſts will always remain Viſible : The whole ſeeming to want nothing that could render is truly Venerable. We paſs'd by that Emblem of Mortaſity the Charnel-houſe, where Poets, Prieſts, Pimps, and Porters, lay their empty heads together, without envy or diſtinction. And on the North ſide, enter'd the Magnificent Temple with equal Wonder and Satisfaction; which entertaind our Sight with ſuch worthy Monuments and aſtoniſhing Antiquities, that we knew not which way to direct our eyes, each object was ſo engaging. We took a general Survey of all that's to be ſeen in the open parts of the Church, where almoſt every Stone gives a brief Hiſtory of the Memorable Actions due to thoſe Pious Aſhes to whom the Table appertaineth. By this time the Bells began to Chime for Afternoon's Prayers, and the Quire was opened, into which we went, amongſt many others, to pay with rev'rence that Duty that becomes a Chriſtian: Where our Souls were elevated by the Divine Harmony of the Muſick, far above the common pitch of our Devotions, whoſe Heavenly Accents have ſo ſweet an Influence upon a Contrite Heart, that it ſtrengthens our Zeal, fortifies the looſe Imagination againſt wandring Thoughts; and gives a Man a taſte of Immortal Bleſſings upon Earth, before he is throughly prepar'd for the true Reliſh of Celeſtial Comforts.

When we had given our Souls the Refreſhment of this Enlivening Exerciſe, we made an entrance into the Eaſt-end of the *Abby*, which was Lock'd, and paid a viſit to the Venerable Shrines and Sacred Monuments of the dead Nobility: where the Memorable Virtues, and Magnanimous Actions of our Heroick Princes are faithfully convey'd to their
Poſterity,

Posterity, by the sundry Inventions of our Ingenious Ancestors, as Epitaphs, Effigies, Arms, Emblems, and Hieroglyphicks.

When we had satisfied our selves with a view of these ancient Curiosities, we ascended some stone steps, which brought us to a Chappel, that may Justly claim the Admiration of the whole Universe, such inimitable Perfections are apparent in every part of the whole Composure, and looks so far Exceeding Humane Excellence, that a man would think it was knit together by the fingers of Angels, pursuant to the directions of Omnipotence.

From thence we were conducted by our little Guide, to King *Charles* the Seconds Effigies; and as much as he excell'd his Predecessors in Mercy, Wisdom, and Liberality, so does his Effigies exceed the rest in Liveliness, Proportion, and Magnificence.

Having now satisfied our Curiosities with a Sight of what was chiefly admirable, we came again into the Body of the Church, where my Friend and I began to consider of some few things which we did not think were consistent with Reason, or the Glory of that Power to whom the Holy Pile is dedicated, which are these:

1. *That the Parish Poor of St.* Magarets *should be suffered Bto eg within the Abby, even in Prayer-time.*

2. *That those who are chosen as peculiar Agents in the Service of God, should be permitted to Sing in the Play-house.*

3. *That the Monuments should lye Defac'd, some with their Hands off, and some with their Feet off, Lying by them without Reparation.*

4. *That Women should have* Hebrew, Greek, *and* Latine *Epitaphs, who never understood a Word of the Languages.*

5. *That* Ben. Johnson *should want a Tomb; and lye buried from the rest of the Poets.*

6. *That the Monument of Esquire* Thin, *whose Death was so remarkable, should be without any Inscription.*

Having now satisfied our Senses with the sight of the sundry Curiosities contain'd within this Reverend Building, being Term time, we steer'd our course towards *Westminster-Hall*: But just as we came out of the North Porticum of the Abby, a company of Trainbands were drawn up in the Yard, in order to give their Captain a parting Volley. I could not forbear Laughing to see so many Greasy Cooks, Tun-bellied Lick-spiggots, and fat wheesing Butchers, sweating in their Buff Dublets, under the Command of some fiery fac'd Brewer, whose Godgel-Gut was hoop'd in with a Golden Swash, which the Clod-scull'd Hero became as well as one of his Dray-Horses would an Embroider'd Saddle. When the True Blue Officer (over thoughtful of Hops and

Glaines)

Grains) had by two or three Miftaken Words of Command hufled his Couragious Company into Clofe Confufion, inftead of Order, he bid 'em *Make Ready*; which made half of them change Colour, and fhow as much Cowardice in cocking of their Muskets, as if half a dozen Turks had fac'd 'em and frighted 'em with their Whiskers. Then the noble Captain advancing his filver-headed Cane, formally held up between both his hands, gave the terrible Word *Fire*, ftooping down his head like a Goofe under a Barn-door, to defend his Eye-fight from the flashes of the Gunpowder. In which Interim, fuch an amazing clap of Thunder was fent forth from their Rufty Kill-Divels, that it caufed fear and Trembling amongft all thofe that made it: for which the little Boys gave 'em the honour of a great hollow; and away trudg'd the foundred Soldiers home to their Wives, well fatisfied.

We then March'd forwards towards the *Palace-yard*, which we found as full of Hackney-Coaches, as *Greys-Inn-Walks* of Hackney Whores on a Sunday after Sermon; ftanding rank and file in as much order, as if they had been Marfhal'd by the *Fleet-ftreet* Deadmonger ready for a Funeral. When we had made more Turnings and Windings amongft the Coaches, than ever were known in Fair *Rofamonds* Bower, we arriv'd at the Hall-Gate, within-fide of which, innumerable crowds of Contending Mortals were fwarm'd at every Bar, where the black Syrens of the Law, with Silver Tongues and Gilded Palms, were Charming the Ears of the Judges with their Rhetorical Mufick. We firft gave our attention at the *Commonpleas*, where my Friend and I were much delighted, fometimes with Elegant Speeches from the Bench, as well as the pleafing Eloquence and powerful Reafonings at the Bar.

There happen'd an Old Yeoman to be a witnefs in one Caufe, that had fworn very heartily, and knowingly in a matter of great Antiquity, fo that the Councel on the Oppofite fide, ask'd him *How old he was?* To which he anfwered, at firft gravely in thefe words. *I am old enough to be your Father; and therefore I hope, young man, you will give that refpect to my Gray Hairs that is due to 'em?* That, reply'd the Councel, *is no Anfwer to my Queftion. I defire to know how many years old you account your Self; for I am very apt to believe you have Sworn pofitively to fomethings that are beyond your knowledge. I would have you confider, Sir*, fays the old Gentleman, *I am of a very great Age: I am in my fourfcore and Seventeenth year, and yet, I thank God for it, I have Memory and Senfe enough left ftill to make a Knave an anfwer.* with that the Court burft into a Laughter, which dafh'd the Lawyer out of Countenance, and made him afham'd of making any further Interogatives.

From thence we mov'd towards the upper end of the Hall, thro' fuch a crowd of Jerry Black-acres, that we were fhov'd about like a couple of Owles, falln into a great company of Rooks and Jackdaws. As we were thus Squeefing along, towards the Chancery-Barr, a couple of Country Fellows met, and Greeted one another, after the following manner. *How d'ye Neighbour?* fays the one, *Is your fewt ended yet?* *No trowly*, fays the other, *nor can any Body tell when it wool. To Speak the truth, Neighbour, I believe my Returney's a Knave. How fhid a be then*, reply'd the firft, *for thou feeft there are fo many of 'em here, that it's impoffible they fhid live honeftly one by another* We

We were now got to the *Chancery*, where so many smooth Tongues were so vigorously contending for Equity, that we found by their Long Harangues, and strenuous Arguments, it was not to be obtain'd with little difficulty. Whilst we were giving our attention to that engaging harmony, which flow'd with such a careless fluency from their well-tun'd instruments of Oratory, a cause was call'd on, wherein a Taylor happen'd to be a chief witness; the Council on the other side knowing his Profession, took an occasion to give him this Caution, *viz. I understand Friend you are by Trade a Taylor: I would advise you to use more Conscience in your Depositions than you do in your Bills, or else we shall none of us believe you.* Truly Sir, says the Taylor, *our Trade I must confess does lye under a great Scandal; but if you and I were in a Room together, and the Devil should come in and ask for a Thief and a Lyar, I wonder which of us wou'd be most frightned?*

We adjourn'd from thence to the *Kings-Bench-Bar*, where two Pleaders very eagre in dispute, were mixing their Arguments with some Reflections one upon another. A Country man happening to stand just by us, seem'd mightily pleas'd to hear 'em at such variance: at last, being unable to contain himself any longer, breaks out into these Words, *viz. Well said Efaith; this I hope will make the old Proverb good, That when Knaves fall out, Honest men will come by their Right.* A little after one of the Council, In a heat, happen'd to rashly say, *If what he had offer'd was not Law, he'd Justify the Law to be a Lottery.* Upon which, says the Country-man, *I wish heartily it was so, for then it would be put down by the late Act of Parliament; and I should fling away no more Money at it; for I am sure it has kept me and my Family as poor as Job this fifteen years.*

From thence we walk'd down by the Semstresses, who were very nicely Digitising and Pleating Turnovers and Ruffs for the young Students, and Coaxing them with their Amorus looks, Obliging Cant, and Inviting Gestures, to give so extravagant a Price for what they Buy, that they may now and then afford to fling them a Nights Lodging into the Bargain.

We now began to take notice of the Building, which to me seem'd as Noble as 'twas Ancient: And looking upwards, could do no less than greatly admire the Timber Roof, being finely built after the Gothick Order. But that which was chiefly to be obferv'd in it was, the Cleanliness thereof, it being as free from Dust and Cobwebs, as if 'twas rais'd but Yesterday. Which, says my Friend, occasions some People to conjecture it is built with *Irish* Oak, to which is ascrib'd this Miraculous Virtue, *viz.* That no Spiders, or any such sort of Nauseous, or Offensive Insect, will ever breed or hang about it. And, said I, are you apt to give Credit to this Vulgar Error; and attribute it's Cleanness to any Quality of the wood? No, says he, I am apt to believe all such notions to be Vain and Fabulous; and that its continuing free from all such Nasty Vermin, proceeds from another Reason. Pray, said I, lets hear your conjecture concerning it? For I assure you, I look upon it to be very strange that a Wooden Roof of such Antiquity, should be so very free of all that Filth which is most commonly collected in such old Fabricks: Why then, says he, I'll frankly tell you my Opinion, which

If it seems incongruous to your Reason, I hope you will be so friendly as to excuse my weakness. You must consider, says he, that the young Lawyers are unhappily liable to abundance of Mischances, and often require the use of Mercury to Repair their Members, some subtle particles of which being emitted with their Breath, ascend by their Volatility to the top of the Hall, where it Condenses it self, and lyes sublim'd upon the Beames; and so by its Poisonous Quality renders the Roof obnoxious to all Vermin. For this is certainly true, That let any Person who has taken a Mercurial dose, but breathe upon a Spider, and it will die immediately. This, said I, from a Surgeon is well enough; for men of your Profession may take the Liberty of talking like Apothecaries, and not be Censur'd for it. But I think you have fitted me with a piece of as dark Philosophy as any's to be found in *Aristotle's* Master-Piece. Meeting with nothing further, much worth our observation, I think it may not be improper to conclude our Remarks of this Place, with the Character of a Pettyfogger:

He's an Amphibious Monster, that partakes of two Natures, and those Contrary; He's a great Lover both of Peace and Enmity; and has no sooner set People together by the Ears, but is Soliciting the Law to make an end of the Difference. His Mother was a Scold, and he begot at a Time when his Father us'd the Act more for Quietness sake than Procreation. His Learning is commonly as little as his Honesty; and his Conscience much larger then his Green-Bag. His affections to the Law proceed from the Litigiousness of his Ancestors. Nor is there any thing he abhors so much as Poverty in a Client. He is never more Proud then when he has a Fee for a topping Councel; and would make any body believe Sergeant such a one and he are as great as the Devil and the Earl of *Kent*. He gets Money in Term time by sitting in a Tavern, for every Client that comes in he makes pay Six-pence for a Glass, till he has sold a Quart or two at that rate, and puts the overplus in his Pocket, he seems always as busie as a Merchant in Change-time; and if ever a Cause is carried that he's concern'd in, he tells you its owing to his management. He's a great lover of Veal, thro' the respect he has for Calves-skin: And admires the wonderful works of the Bee, more for the wax then honey. He's a man of so much Justice, that he loves all things should be done according to Law; and calls every body Fool that pays a debt till he has forc'd the Creditor to prove it in some of the Courts at *Westminster*. Unlike the rest of Mankind, he hates peace in his Neighbourhood; and looks upon it that he sits Rent-free, if he be but happily seated among wrangling Neighbours. Catch him in what Company soever, you will always hear him stating of Cases, or telling what notice my Lord Chancellor took of him, when he beg'd Leave to supply the deficency of his Councel. He always talks with as great assurance as if he understood what he only pretends to know: And always wears a Band, for in that lies his Gravity and Wisdom. He concerns himself with no Justice but the Justice of a Cause: And for making an unconscionable Bill, he out-does a Taylor. He is so well read in Physognomy, that he knows a Knight of the Post by his Countenance: and if your Business requires the Service of such an Agent, he can pick you up one at a small Warning. He is very understanding in the Business of the *Old-Baily*; and knows as well how to fee a Jury-man as he does a Barrister. He has a rare knack at putting in Broomstick-Bail; and knows a great many more ways to keep a man out of his Money then he does to get it him. He's very diligent in Business where Money's to be got, and runs backward and forward as nimbly, between the Lawyer and the Client, as a Rocket upon a string between two Posts. Tricks and Quirks he calls, the cunning part of the Law; and that Attorney that practices the most knavery, is the Man for his Money. His study is abroad, his Learning all Experience, and his Library in his Pocket, which is always stuffed with as many Papers as Poet *Bays's* in the *Reherfal*. He puts more faith in the Law, then he does in the Gospel; and knows no other Religion than to get Money, he thinks nothing a breach of Charity but Starving of of a good cause; and has often that Text of Scripture in his Mouth, *viz. The Labourer is worthy of his hire*: Which is as much as to say he would not waste time to read a Chapter in the Bible without being paid for it. He's also a great News-monger, all publick Reports must occur to his knowledge, for his business lies most in a *Coffee-house*, and the greatest of his Diversion is in reading the News-papers. He is commonly a great Smoaker, and will walk half a Mile to a Tobacconists where he thinks he may have six corns more then ordinary for his Penny. Meet him wheresoever in Term time, and ask him whither go you? And his answer shall be, *To Westminster*. And indeed you may find him in the Hall much oftner then he that has ten times the business there; for he is one of those that love to hear how other Peoples matters go, tho' it does not at all concern him. There's nothing that he abominates more, then to be thought Negligent; and has no other Vertue to boast on truly, but his diligence; for no man shall be more watchful in another's Ruin than himself. In short, He's a Catterpillar upon Earth, who grows fat upon the fruits of others Labour. A meer Horse-Leach in the Law, that when once he is well fasten'd, will suck a poor Client into a deep Consumption

Having thus taken Notice of most things Remarkable in the Hall, we made our Exit from thence, and crost the Pallace-Yard, on the East side of which lay the Reliques of *Westminster* Stone Clock-Case, in a confused heap of Ruins. There's nothing, says my Friend, concerns me more, than to see any piece of Antiquity Demolish'd. It always puts me in mind of the Ignoble Actions of the Sanctified Rebells in the late Domestick Troubles, who made it their Business to deface old Images; and with Sacrilgious hands throw down the Urns, and spoile the Monuments of the Dead : A Base and Inglorious Revenge, to gratifie their Chollerick Zeal, by Robbing their own Native Country of its Ancient Beauties; a Crime abominated by the most Savage and unpolish'd People in the whole Universe, and that *Christians* should be Guilty of such barbarity that is held detestable amongst the worst of *Heathens*, it's very strange. I speak not this, says he, to reflect upon the destruction of this old Steeple, which was wholly useless when they had remov'd the Clock to St *Pauls*, which indeed is far more worthy of so Ponderous a Bell, that affords so grave a Sound, than the Place it stood in.

The Common People have a Notion (but of no Authority as I know on) that this Bell was paid for by a Fine Levy'd upon some Judge, for

the

the Unlawful Determination of some weighty Affair, in which he suffer'd himself to be Brib'd to Partiality; and that it was converted to the use of a Clock, with this moral intent, That when ever it struck, it might be a warning to all succeeding Magistrates, in the Courts at *Westminster*, how they do Injustice. But if it were so, the Judges and Lawyers in this more Religious Age, are so free from Corruption, that they need no other Motives or Memorandums to discharge their Trust with Unbias'd Honesty, than the Unerring Dictates of their own good Consciences, so that my Loudmouth'd Name-sake might very well be spared to a better purpose, and hang within the hearing of all the Cuckolds in the City, to call their Wives twice a day to Prayers, that they may ask Forgiveness for the great Injury they did their Husbands the last opportunity: And also to proclaime, by the Gravity of its Sound, the Greatness of that Huge, huge, huge Cathedral, which is big enough to hold a great many more Souls than *Westminster-Abby*, tho' it is not half so handsome; and that's all, says my Friend, that can be said on't.

From the Palace-Yard we mov'd on Progressively, till we came to the Tennis Court, but could not for my Life imagine what place that could be, hung round with such a deal of Net-work; at last, thinks I, I have heard of such a place as a Plot-Office: I fancy this must be it, and those are the Projectors Nets to catch such *Jacobite* Fools who are drawn into the design. But however, not well satisfied with my own Notion, I thought it proper to enquire of my Friend before I told him my Sentiments, lest thro' an Innocent mistake I should give him just occasion to Laugh at my Ignorance; and he inform'd me twas a conveniency built for the Noble Game of Tennis, a very delightful Exercise, much us'd by Persons of Quality; and is attended with these two extraordinary good Properties, it is very Healthful to him that plays at it, and is very Profitable to him that keeps it. And rightly considered, its a good Emblem of the World: As thus: The Gamsters are the Great Men, the Rackets are the Laws, which they hold fast in their hands, and the Balls are we little Mortals which they bandy backwards or forwards from one to t'other as their own Wills and Pleasure direct's 'em.

We pass'd by this, and went forward to *White-hall*, whose Ruins we view'd with no less Concern, then the unhappy fate of such a Noble Structure must needs beget in each considerate Beholder, Especially when they reflect upon the honour it had to entertain the best and greatest of Princes, in their highest State and Grandeur, for several preceding Ages; and now at last to be consumed by Flames near so much Water, who cannot grieve to see that Order, which the hands of Artists, at the cost of Kings, had improv'd to that Delight and Statelyness lie dissolv'd in a heap of Rubbish. Those spacious Rooms where Majesty has sat so oft, attended with the transcending Glories of his Court, the Just, the Wise, the Brave, and Beautiful, now huddled in Confusion, and nothing more can boast themselves but dirt and ashes; as if the Misfortunes of Princes were visited upon their Palaces, as well as Persons, to manifest to the World more clearly, that an overruling Power, and not Accident, decreed their Sufferings.

After we had taken a survey of the Ruins, and spent some melancholly choly thoughts upon the tatter'd Object, that lay in Dust before us, we walk'd on thro' several out Courts, till we came into a place my Friend told me was *Scotland-yard*, where Gentlemen Soldiers lay basking in the Sun, like so many lazy Swine upon a warm Dunghill. I stood a little while Ruminating on the great unhappiness of such a Life, and could not restrain my Thoughts from giving a Character of that unfortunate Wretch, who in time of War hazzards his Life for Six-pence a day, and that perhaps ne'er paid him ; and in time of Peace has nothing to do but to keep Guard and Loiter.

A Foot Soldier is commonly a Man who for the sake of wearing a Sword, and the Honour of being term'd a Gentleman, is coax'd from a Handicraft Trade, whereby he might live comfortably, to bear Arms for his King and Countrey, whereby he has the hopes of nothing but to live Starvingly. His Lodging is as near Heaven as his Quarters can raise him; and his Soul generally as near Hell as a Profligate Life can sink him. To speak without swearing he thinks a Scandal to his Post; and is very Proud of that Cloth, which Wiser People are asham'd of. He makes many a Meal upon Tobacco, which keeps the inside of his Carcase as nasty as his Shirt. 'He's a Champion for the Church, because he fights for Religion, tho' he never hears Prayers except they be Read upon a Drum-head. He's often times seen to stand Centinel over an Oister-tub, in the absence of his flat-cap Mistress, who has him more at Command then his Officer. He often leads a Sober life against his will; and when ever he gets Drunk, it is in a Bawdy-house. He can never pass by a Brandy-shop with two-pence in his Pocket; for he as Naturally loves Strong-Waters as a Turk does Coffee. He is generally belov'd by two sorts of Companions, *viz.* Whores and Lice; for both these Vermin are great Admirers of a Scarlet Coat. No man Humbles himself more upon the commiting of a fault, for he bowes his Head to his Heels, and lies bound by the hour to his good Behaviour. He is a Man of Undaunted Couraged, and dreads no Enemies so much as he does the Wooden-horse, which makes him hate to be Mounted, and rather chooses to be a Foot Soldier. He's a man, that when upon guard, always keeps his word; and obeys his Officer as Indians do the Devil, not thro' Love but Fear, He makes a Terrible figure in a Country Town; and makes the old Women watch their Poultry more than a Gang of Gipsies. He seldom wants the two good Properties of Begging and Thieving, without which he would be but a poor Traveller. When once he has been in a Battle, it's a hard matter to get him out of it ; for where-ever he comes he's al-ways talking of the Action, in which he tells you he was posted in the greatest danger; and seems to know more of the matter than the Ge-neral. Scars, tho' got in Drunken Quarrels, he makes Badges of his Bravery; and tells you they were Wounds receiv'd in some Engage-ment, tho perhaps given him for his Sawciness. He's one that Loves Fighting no more than other Men ; tho perhaps a dozen of Drink and an af-front, will make him draw his Sword; yet a Pint and a good Word, will make him put it up again. Let him be never so many Campagnes in *Flanders*, he contracts but few Habits of a *Dutchman*, for you shall of-tener see him with his Fingers in his Neck than his Hands in his Pockets. He has the Pleasure once a Week, when he receives his Subsistance, of boasting he has Money in his Breeches, and for all he's a Soldier ows no Man a Groat, which is likely enough to be true, because no body

will

will truſt him. Hunger and Louſineſs are the two Diſtempers that af-
flict him; and Idleneſs and Scratching the two Medicines that Palliate
his Miſeries. If he ſpends Twenty years in Wars, and lives to be Fourty,
perhaps he may get a Halbert; and if he Survives Threeſcore, an Hoſpital. The Beſt end he can expect to make, is to Die in the Bed of Honour; and the greateſt Living Marks of his Bravery, to recommend him
at once to the Worlds Praiſe and Pitty, are Cripled Limbs, with which
I ſhall leave him to begg a better Lively-hood.

> To a Coblers Aul, or Butchers Knife,
> Or Porters Knot, Commend me;
> But from a Soldiers Lazy Life,
> Good Heaven pray defend me.

F I N I S.

THE LONDON SPY.

For the *Month* of *July,* 1699.

PART IX.

By the Author of the Trip *to* JAMAICA.

LONDON,

Printed and Sold by *J. How,* in the *Ram-Head-Inn-Yard* in *Fanchurch-street,* 1699.

THE
LONDON
SPY.

A S soon as we turn'd out of *Scotland-yard* into the common Road, I espied a famous, Edifice diametrically opposite to the Gate we pass'd thro'; the freshness of the Bricks, and form of which Building, shew it of a Modern Erection. Perpendicularly over the main Door, or Entrance, was place'd a Golden Anchor, which occasion'd me to enquire of my Friend, to what Publick Use this Noble Fabrick was converted. In answer to which, says he, This is the place where so many Letters have been directed which were put into the Gazet, concerning a discovery of many Abuses and Irregularities committed in His Majesties Navy; and great Encouragements were offer'd to the Authors of those Letters, to Appear and Justifie what Illegal and Unwarrantable Practices they could charge upon any Person or Persons commission'd in that Service under the Government. And pray, said I, what became of that matter at last, about which there was so great a Bustle? You must be careful, says my Friend, how you ask Questions in such Affair's; and it behoves me to be as Cautious how I Answer any. But to divert you from your Enquiries, I'll tell you a Story, *viz. A Merry Cobler, as he sat Stitching in his Stall, was Singing a piece of his own Composition to indulge his Chearful Humour, wherein he very often repeated these following Words, viz.* The King said to the Queen, and the Queen said to the King. *A Passenger coming by, who was mighty desirous of knowing what it was the King and Queen had said to one another, stood listening a considerable time, expecting the Cobler to have gone on with his Ditty, wherein he should have satisfied his Longing Curiosity: But the Musical Translator continu'd a Rehearsal only of the same Words, till he had tired the Patience of his Auditor; who at last stepp'd up to the Stall, and seriously ask'd the Drolling Sole-mender what it was the King said to the Queen, and the Queen to the King?* The Busie Crispin *Snatches up his Strap, and lays it, with all his Might, cross the Shoulders of the Impertinent Querist, Passionately expressing himself in these Words, viz.* How now, Sawce-Box! It's a fine Age we live in, when such Cocks-combs as you must be prying into

into matters of State! I'd have you to know, Sirrah, I am too Loyal
a Subject to betray the Kings Secrets; and pray get ye gone, and don't
interrupt me in my Lawful Occupation, left I stick my Aul in your
Arse, and mark you for a Fool that meddles with what you have no-
to do with. *The Cobler being an Old Sturdy Grizzle, the Fellow was forc'd
to bear both with this Correction and Reproof: And Shruging his Shoulders,
was glad to sneak off about his Business.* I know, said I, how to apply
the Moral of your Story; and shall therefore be very Careful how I
trouble you with any such Questions for the future, that are either improper for me to Ask, or inconsistent with your safety to directly Answer.

By this time we were come to the Door of the most Eminent
Coffee-House at the end of the Town which my Friend had before pro-
pos'd to give me a Sight of. Accordingly we blunder'd thro' a dark
Entry, where the Black-guard of Quality were playing their unlucky
Tricks, and Damning each other in their Masters Dialect, Arm'd with
Flambeaus against the approaching Night, that the Grandure of the Great
and Fortunate, may not be hid by Darkness; but shine in their proper
Sphere above lesser Mortals, by a distinguishable Lustre. At the end
of the Entry, we ascended a pair of Stairs, which brought us into an
Old-fashion'd Room of a Cathedral Tenement, where a very Gaudy
Crowd of Odoriferous *Tom-Essences* were walking backwards and forwards, with their Hats in their Hands, not daring to convert 'em to
their intended use, left it should put the Fore-tops of their Wigs into
some disorder. We squeez'd thro' the Fluttering Assembly of Smiling
Peripateticks, till we got to the end of the Room, where at a small Table,
we sat down, and Observ'd, tho' there was abundance of Guests, there
was very little to do; for it was as great a Rarity to hear any Body
call for a dish of *Politicians Porridge*, or any other Liquor, as it is to
hear a *Spunger* in a Company ask what's to Pay, or a *Beau* call for a
Pipe of Tobacco; their whole Exercise being to Charge and Discharge
their Nostrils; and keep the Curles of their Perriwigs, in their proper
Order. The Clacking of their Snush-box-Lids, in opening and shut-
ting, making more Noise than their Tongues; and sounded as Terrible in my Ears, as the Melancholy Ticks of so many Death-Watches.
Bows and Cringes of the newest Mode, were here exchang'd 'twixt
Friend and Friend, with wonderful exactness, being the finest Accademy
for a Painter to learn to draw the Sign of the *Salutation* for a Tavern,
in the whole Universe. They made a humming like so many Hornets
in a Country Chimney, not with their Talking but with their Whispering over their New *Minuets* and *Bories*, with their Hands in their
Pockets, if freed from their Snush-Box, by which you might understand they had most of them been Travellers into the *Seven Provinces*,
from whence they deriv'd that Custom. Amongst 'em were abundance
of Officers, or Men who by their Habit appear'd to be such; but look'd
as tenderly, as if they carried their Down Beds with them into the
Camp, and did not dare to come out of their Tents in a Cold Morning, till they had Eat a Mess of Plum-Panada for Breakfast, to defend their Stomachs from the Wind. Yet thro' a Principle of undana-
ted Courage, must signalize their Affections to their Country, in un-
dergoing the Fatigue of a *Flanders* Campaign, to the great terrour of
their

their Lady Mothers; and to as much purpofe otherways, as if they had fpent their time at *Hipollitoes* and the Play-Houfe, or ftaid at home to have been a *Guard de Core* to the *Bellfa's*, to protect 'em from being Plunder'd of their Virginities by the Town Stallions, which ought to have been preferv'd, as a recompence for thofe who truly deferv'd their Favours, by hazarding their Lives in the Nations Service; for as nothing more then the Noble Paffion of Love will Animate a Soldier with Bravery, fo, undoubtedly, is Beauty the greateft Reward of Victory. At the ends of this Principal Room were other Apartments, where, I fuppofe, the *Beau*-Poiltiques retired upon extraordinary Occafions, to talk Nonfence by themfelves about State Affairs, that they might not be Laugh'd at.

Having fat all this while looking about us, like a couple of *Minerva's* Birds among fo many *Juno's* Peacocks, admiring their Gaity; we began to be thoughtful of a Pipe of Tobacco, which we were not affur'd we could have the Liberty of Smoaking, left we fhould offend thofe fweet-Breath-Gentlemen, who were always running their Nofes in the Arfe of a *Civet-Cat*. But, however, we ventur'd to call for fome Inftruments of Evaporation, which were accordingly brought us, but with fuch a kind of unwillingnefs, as if they would have much rather been rid of our Company; for their Tables were fo very Neat, and fhin'd with Rubing, like the upper Leathers of an Aldermans Shooes, and as brown as the Top of a Country Houfe-Wifes Cupboard. The Floor as clean Swept as a Sir *Courtly's* Dining-Room, which made us look round, to fee if there were no Orders hung up to impofe the forfeiture of fo much *Mop-Money* upon any Perfon that fhould Spit out of the Chimney Corner. Notwithftanding we wanted an Example to encourage us in our Porterly Rudenefs, we order'd 'em to light the Wax-Candle, by which we ignify'd our Pipes, and blew about our Whiffs with as little concern, as if we had been in the Company of fo many Carmen; at which feveral Sir *Foplins* that were near us, drew their Faces into as many Peevifh Wrinkles as the *Beaus* at the *Bow-ftreet* Coffee-houfe, near *Covent-Garden* did, when the Gentleman in Mafquerade came in amongft 'em with his Oyfter-Barrel Muff, and Turnip-Buttons, to ridicule their Foppery. But, however, we (regardlefs of their grimaces, by which they exprefs'd their Difpleafure) puff'd on our unfavory Weed, till we had clear'd one corner of the Room, and feparated the *Beaus* from the more Sociable Party, and made 'em fly to a great Window next the Street, where there was fuch Snifting and Snuffing, that the reft of the Company could fcarce keep their Countenances.

Juft in this Interim, whilft the Gaudy knot of Effeminate *Philogi-nians* were looking into the Street, who fhould chance to come by, on the other fide the Way, but the old Dumb *Father-Red-Cap*, who cafting up his Eyes, and efpying fuch a parcel of Elegant Figures ftanding at the Window, made a full ftop over-againft the Coffee-houfe, and began according to his Cuftome, to fhow his Antick Poftures, and Buffoonery-Actions, Dancing the Soldiers Dance, and playing abundance of Fools Pranks, to engage Paffengers to tarry and behold his Apifh Geftures; and when he had Collected a Promifcuous Multitude of Trades-men, Soldiers, Porters, Chimny-Sweepers and Footmen, round about him, he

fronts

fronts his Flaxen-Wigg'd Spectators at the Coffee-house who were stroaking down their stragling Hairs, and sweetening the Common-Shore of their insipid Brains by their several Fumigations, and begins to mimick the *Beau*, rendering himself immediately so intelligible to the Rabble, by his apt Signs and ridiculous Postures that the Crowd set up a hollow, and the Eyes of the whole Mob were directed to our squeamish *Tobacco-Haters:* Whilst the poor Deaf Comedian perceiving the Mob well-pleas'd, persisted in his Whim, and Buffoon'd with excellent Humours the Strut, the Toss of the Wig, the Carriage of the Hat, the Snush-Box, the Guiding of the Foretop, the Hanging of the Sword, and to each Action form'd so suitable a Face, that the most Grave Spectator could not forbear Laughing. This put our Orangery Sparks to the Blush, and made them retire from their Casements: By which time our Smoaking had given encouragement to others to pluck out their Boxes, and betake themselves to the like Exercise, that we Smoak'd the *Beaus* almost as bad as unlucky School-Boys us'd to do the *Coblers*, till they sneak'd off one by one, and left behind 'em more agreable Company. We could then discern there were some Great Men by the Grandure of their Looks, the Awfulness of their Presence, and Gracefulness of their Deportment. And several Officers with Old English Aspects, whose Marshall Faces were adorn'd with weather-beaten Wrinkles, cross'd with Hacks and Scars, those rugged Beauty Spots of War, which they wore as true marks of their undaunted Bravery. Having by this time ended our Pipes, we wound up our Diversion with a Fashionable Mess of *Turkish* Sobriety; after which we Scribbled down these following Lines in a Slate-Book, and so departed.

Here Persons who for Places Wait,
Their Faithless Courtiers greet:
And Men of Sence, made Fools by Fate,
Their Crafty Patrons meet.

Here Pension'd Spies, like Saints appear,
Who do Mens Hearts inspect;
And whisper in the States-man Ear,
What they abroad Collect.

Here News by subtle Tongues is spread,
To try the Listening Crowd;
But what is Truth's a Secret made,
Whilst Lyes are Talk'd aloud.

Beau Fools in Clusters here Resort,
And are so saucy grown,
They'll ask my Lord, What News from Court?
Who Smiles, and Answers, None.

To be Inform'd few caring less;
But ask, as 'tis the Mode;
No Knowledge seek, but how to Dress;
Their Taylor is their God.

Here Flatterers meet their Empty 'Squires;
And praise their shallow Sence;
The Idiot in return admires
His fawning Eloquence.

And that he further may Enjoy
A Man of such Desert,
He steps to Lockets, cross the Way,
And Treats him with a Quart.

The Gamester does this Bubble set;
And seems his mighty Friend;
Hence draws him to a Tavern Treat,
That's Fatal in the end.

Both such who Serve and Plague the State,
Do hither make their Way;
And Crowds of Humane Vultures wait,
To Catch their Silly Prey.

Having now squeez'd back thro' a long dark Entry full of Rap-scalionly Skip-*Jacks*, into the open Street, my Friend bid me take Notice of two great Taverns on the other side the Way. In those Eating-Houses, says he, as many Fools Estates have been Squander'd away, as ever were swallow'd up by the Royal-Oak-Lottery; for every Fop, who with a small Fortune attempts to Counterfeit Quality, and is Fool enough to be-stow Twenty Shillings worth of Sawce upon Ten Penny worth of Meat, resorts to one of these Ordinaries; where a Man that's as Rich as *Cræssus* may out-live *Heliogabalus*, and spend more Money upon a Dinner, than a Sergeant at Law can get in a whole Issuable Term.

As we were thus talking, a Squadron of Horse march'd by in order to relieve the Guard; my Friend ask'd me my Opinion of their appear-ance, and how I liked the Sight of so many brave English-men on Horse-back; which, says he, has not been seen in these Parts, till of late, this many Years? Truly, said I, I think they look more like Soldiers, and become their Post much better in their Old Coats, then the Butter-boxes did in all their Finery; and indeed it's more Natural for us to think they would do their own Country greater Service upon occasion, and would hazzard their Lives with more heartiness, than it is reasonable to expect any Foreigners would do for us. *Dutch-Men*, for ought I know, may Fight in defence of *Holland*, or a *French-Man* for the Security of his own Nation: But when ever the Necessities of *England* shall force her upon either of their Assistances, she will find to her Sorrow, she has but a broken Reed to rely on.

By this time they were pass'd by us, so we mov'd on till we came to the *Subterranean* Ware-house of an Eminent Dealer in Old Boots, Shooes and Slippers, Spurs, Spatter-dashes, and Gambages; the front of his Translating Cavern, being adorn'd with such sundry sorts of Lea-thern-Conveniences, that I could not but think he was the only Humane

Farrier,

Farrier, appointed to Shooe all the inferiour Quality at this end of the Town. My Friend and I having propos'd, some time before, in a few days, to Ride down to *Tunbridge*, the well-furnish'd Palace of this *Coblerious Cæsar*, put us in mind of laying hold of this Opportunity, to fit our selves with some Accouterments at best hand, of which we were destitute; accordingly we descended to the Cabbin, by very steep Gradations, with abundance of caution, where otherwise the Hillocks of Dirt upon the Stairs, for want of the use of a Pairing-shovel, might have indanger'd our Necks; and the Jamb above us, without Humbling our Carcasses, threaten'd us with a Broken Head; but with Care and Gentleness we got safe to the Bottom, where the Grizly *Crepidarian* sat Uniting of Dissenting Soles, who by their Stubborn Disagreableness, had broke the Threds of Unity, and separated themselves, to their Makers dishonour, from their upper Leathers: As soon as he saw us, he bid us Welcome, Dismounting his Glass Adjutants, who Rid a Cock-horse on his Nose, lays by his Work with as much chearfulness as an Old Whore does the Practice of Piety, upon the reception of a Visitant; and ask'd us, *What we wanted?* We told him Boots; who presently furnish'd us with all sorts and sizes; amongst which parcel, after a little search, we pitch'd upon such that pleas'd us, and sat down upon a Stool hew'd out of the whole Timber for Durations Sake, in order to try 'em on; In which interval, a Ragged *Irish-man* (which in this Town is said to be a wonder) came down and desir'd him, in his Irish Accent, to show him a Pair of Shooes; *Crispin* being a little busie in giving us his Attendance, believing us the better Customers, happen'd thro' Carelesness to hand him a couple of Shooes which were not Fellows, *Teague* draws on one, and it fitted him very well, but when he try'd the other, he found it was much too little, and quite of another sort; *By my Shoul, dear Joy,* says he, *the Maas Futs that wore these Brogues were not Fellows: Prithee let me see another Pair.* The *Cobler* looking upon the Shooes, and finding his mistake, and casting his Eye upon the Fellows Feet, discover'd his Stockins to be of different Colours: *I thought Master,* says he, *you would have had your Shooes as you have your Stockins, one of one sort, and one of another; but however, if these wont do, I'll see further if I can fit you.* Accordingly hands him another Pair with the Toe of one (as is usual) thrust into the other. The *Irish-man* puts on his old Shooes again, in a great Passion, and takes his leave in these Words, *By Chreest and Shaint Patrick, ye are a Sheating Knave. De you tink E will buy a Pair of Brogues dat de Little one ish big enough to hold de Great one in ish Bally? How, by my Shoul, can you tink dey will fit my Futs, dat are bott' of a smallness?* And away he trips up Stairs in his aged Pumps, made Sandals by much wearing, that they were forc'd to be Lac'd on with Pack-thread; and so march'd off in a great fury, to relieve his Pedestals, at the next Conveniency, leaving us to Chatter with our Drolling *Mundungus* Puffer, who fitted us with what we wanted, at reasonable Rates, like a Man of Conscience, without using half so many Lyes and Canting Reservations as a Sober Citizen in his Shop, but gave us a hearty Welcome into the Bargain, and so we parted.

When we had Crawl'd up again into the Street, like a couple of Gentlemen Soldiers out of a Two-penny Ordinary, the first Object with which our Eyes were affected, was the Brazen Statue of that Pious Prince King *Charles* the First on Horse-back, whose Righteous Life, Unhappy

happy Reign, unjuſt Sufferings, unparallell'd Martyrdom, ſhall bury
Monuments, out-live Time, and ſtand up with Eternity; I could not
without the higheſt Concern, and deepeſt Reflections on his great Miſ-
fortunes, behold the Image of that Good Man, in whoſe Artful Effigy
may be ſeen the Piety, Majeſty, Mercy, Patience and Innocency of the
Matchleſs Original, the Cauſeleſs Diſturbance of whoſe Reign, and the
Barbarous Uſages of whoſe Perſon, will ſtick as Thorns, I hope, in the
ſides of Faction, till they are Cruſh'd into that Anarchy, from whence
they had their firſt beginning. Thus did we ſtand a while Ruminating upon the ſad Cataſtrophe of this unhappy Prince, till at laſt his
Venerable Statue inſpir'd me with theſe following Lines, which I hope
the Unprejudic'd Reader will Receive with Candour.

> Great were thy Wrongs, thy Patience ſtill as great;
> When Faction Rul'd the Church, and Knaves the State;
> Hard were thy People's Hearts, but harder yet thy Fate.
>
> Balm thou applyd'ſt, while they ſtill vex'd thee ſore,
> The more their Crimes, thy Mercy grew the more;
> Thy God-like mind was Rich, altho' thy Treaſure Poor.
>
> The Laws they ſmother'd in Rebellious Night,
> And trod dark Paths, whilſt thou purſu'dſt the Light,
> As they encreas'd their Shame, thy Glories ſhone more bright.
>
> Had'ſt thou in Rage thy Victories purſu'd,
> And took delight in ſhedding Rebels Blood,
> Thoud'ſt been ſecure; but wer't alas, too Mild and Good.
>
> Contempt of all thy Favours they return'd;
> Tawn'd at thy Power, and at thy Perſon ſpurn'd;
> Merry o'er others Spoils, whilſt all true Subjects Mourn'd.
>
> The Canting Pulpiteer, by Dreames made Wiſe,
> Turn'd Goſpel Truths into Audacious Lies;
> And taught the Blood of Kings a holy Sacrifice.
>
> Unlearn'd Mechanicks, full of nought but Noiſe,
> Were turn'd, thro' Grace, Expounders of the Laws;
> And juſtify'd Rebellion to be Heavens Cauſe.
>
> When Right, thro' want of due Aſſiſtance fail'd,
> And Wrong, thro' miſſ-led Multitudes prevail'd,
> The Trayt'rous Torrent grew too ſtrong to be Repell'd.
>
> Thus the Mad Crow'd, who could no Ills Foreſee,
> Of all Reſtraint endeavouring to be Free,
> Took off thy Head, becauſe themſelves would Headleſs be.

From Charring-Croſe we turn'd up towards the Strand, at the Entrance
of which, I obſerv'd an Ancient Stone Fabrick, in the Front of it
I beheld, with ſatisfaction, the handy-work of our Fore-Fathers, in

C

whoſe

whose fully'd Antiquity I could discern much more Beauty than my Genius can discover in any Modern Building. What a thousand Pities, said I, is it that so Noble a Palace, which appears so Magnificent and Venerable, should not have the old Hospitality continued within-side, answerable to its outward Grandure. Truly, says my Friend, it is a great Scandal to the present Age, That Quality should so Degenerate from their Ancestors; and instead of imitating the Liberality of their Grandsires, in Relieving the Distresses of their Neighbours, Supplying the Wants of their Poor Friends and Relations, and (to the Honour of themselves and Country) giving Charitable Entertainments to Strangers and Travellers, now squander away their Estates in Whoring, Gaming, and External Foppery, to the disgrace of so Flourishing a Nation, the Scandal of that Dignity to which God hath rais'd 'em, and to the Ruin of Themselves and Families. For it may be Observ'd, that when Great Men, who are indeed no more than Heavens Stewards for the Poor, discharg'd their Duty to those unhappy Wretches, who by the disabilities of Nature, or the Contingent Mutabilities of this Life, were reduc'd to Necessity, they added to their own Fortunes, by an Improvement of their Estates, and whilst they supported in their Houses a Commendable Hospitality, they were always attended with such Prosperity, that their Riches were preserv'd by Providence from any Chance or fatal Devastation. Whereas I could instance on the contrary (could it be done without Reflection) many Families now in being, who are brought to Beggary from very Plentiful Estates, who neither signaliz'd their Loyalty to the Crown, their Affection to their Country, their Kindness to their Low Relations, their Charity to the Poor, or Good to the Publick, by any expensive Act, as ever was made manifest, but worm'd out of their Patrimony by the fraud of Gamesters, the subtleness of Lewd Women, Emulation of Gaity, and the Treacherous Delusions of Hyppocrites and Flatterers. Methinks, said I, you have Preach'd a very Notable Sermon; this would rather have become the Mouth of a *Clergy-man*, than a Man of your Youth and Airiness. You must consider, says he, we *Libertines* have our Sober Intervals, as well as the Grave *Puritan* in private has his Comfortable Refreshments; for the difference between us, lies only in this particular, We Do seldom what they Practice, and they Practice seldom, what we often Do.

We mov'd on along the *Strand*, as Leisurely as a couple of *Vallet de Chambres* out of Place, in search of a Dinner; meeting nothing remarkable till we came to the *New-Exchange*, into which *Seraglio* of Fair Ladies, we made our Entrance, to take a pleasing view of the Cherubimical Lasses, who, I suppose had Drest Themselves up for Sale, to the best advantage, as well as the Fipperies and Toys they Deal in; and indeed, many of them look'd so very Amiable, so inticingly Fair, that had I been happily furnish'd with some superfluous Angels, I could willingly have dealt among the Charming Witches, for some of their Commodities; but as Curs'd Cows have short Horns, I could only Walk by, and Lick my Lips at their handsome Faces, as a Hungry Beggar, when he stares into Cooks Shops as he Stroles down *Pigg-Hill*; and was forc'd so to content my self. The chiefest Customers, I observ'd they had, were *Beaus*, who I imagin'd, were Paying a double Price for Linnen, Gloves, or Sword-knots, to the prettiest of the Women, that they might

go

go from thence and Boaſt among their Brother Fops, what ſingular Favours
and great Encouragements they had receiv'd from the Fair Lady, that Sold
'em. Finding nothing elſe amongſt 'em worth obſerving, I digeſted a little
of their Shop-Language into a Song, and ſo proceeded.

> Fine Lace or Linnen Sir,
> Good Gloves or Ribbons here;
>   What is't you pleaſe to Buy-Sir?
> Pray what d'ye ask, for this?
> Ten Shillings is the Price;
> It Coſt me Sir, no leſs,
>   I Scorn to tell a Ly-Sir.

> Madam, what is't you want,
> Rich Fans, of India Paint?
>   Fine Hoods or Scarfs, my Lady?
> Silk Stockins, will you Buy,
> In Grain or other Die?
> Pray Madam, pleaſe your Eye;
>   I've Good as e'er was made-ye.

> My Lady, feel the Weight,
> They're Fine, and yet not Slight,
>   I'd with my Mother truſt-'em;
> For Goodneſs and for Wear,
> Madam, I Vow, and Swear,
> I ſhow'd you this ſame Pair,
>   In hopes to gain your Cuſtome.

> Pray tell me in a Word,
> At what you can afford,
>   With Living gain to Sell-'em;
> The Price is One Pound Five,
> And as I hope to Live,
> I do my Profit give,
>   Your Honour's very Welcome.

> Knives, Penknives, Combs or Sciſſars,
> Tooth-Pickers, Sirs, or Tweeſers,
>   Or Walking Canes, to Eaſe-ye.
> Ladies d'ye want fine Toys,
> For Miſſes, or for Boys?
> Of all ſorts, I have Choice,
>   And pretty things to pleaſe-ye.

> I want a little Babe,
> As pretty a one as may be,
>   With Head-Dreſs, made of Feather,
> And now I think again,
> I want a Toy from Spain,
> You know what 'tis I mean:
>   Pray ſend 'em home together,

Having

Having taken a Satisfactory survey of this Jilts Acadamy, where Girles are admitted at Nine Year Old, and Taught by Eleven, to out-Chatter a Magpie, out-Wit their Parents, and by the the improving Inftructions, and taking Example of their kind Miftreffes and Neighbouring Correfpondents, are made as Forward and as Ripe in thought before they are out of their Hanging-fleeves, as a Country Wench is at Five and Twenty.

We then took our Leaves of this Cloifter of kind Damfels, fo turn'd up by the *Half-Moon-Tavern*, and proceeded towards *Covent-Garden*, where we over-took abundance of Religious Lady-birds, Arm'd againft the Affaults of *Satan*, with *Bible* or *Common-Prayer-Book*, marching with all Goodfpeed to *Covent-Garden*-Church; Certainly, faid I, the People of this Parifh are better Chriftians than ordinary, for I never obferved upon a Week Day, fince I came to *London*, fuch a Sanctified Troop of Females flocking to their Devotions, as I fee at this part of the Town. Thefe, fays my Friend, are a Pious fort of Creatures that are much given to go to Church, and may be feen there every Day at Prayers, as Conftantly as the Bell rings; and if you were to walk the other way you might meet as many Young-Gentlemen, from the *Temple* and *Grays Inn*, going to Joyn with them in their Devotions; we'll take a Turn into the Sanctuary amongft the reft, and you fhall fee how they behave themfelves. Accordingly we ftep'd into the Rank, amongft the Lambs of Grace, and enter'd the Tabernacle with the reft of the Saints, where we found a parcel of very Handfome Cleanly well-Dreft Chriftians, as a Man would defire to Communicate with, of both Sexes, who ftood Ogling one another with as much Zeal and Sincerity, as if they Worfhip'd the Creator in the Creature, and Whifpering to their next Neighbours, as if according to the Text, they were confeffing their Sins to one another; which I afterwards underftood, by my Friend, was only to make Affignations; and the chief of their Prayers, fays he, are that Providence will favour their Intrigues. When the Parfon had made an End of what with much Earneftnefs, to little purpofe, he had con'd over to his amorous Congregation, we made our *Exit* from thence, and went thro' the Market, where a parcel of Jolly Red-Fac'd Dames in Blew Aprons, and Straw-Hats, fat felling of their Garden-Ware, who ftunk fo of Brandy, Strong-Drink, and Tobacco, that the fumes they belch'd up, from their overcharg'd Stomachs, o'ercame the Fragrancy that arofe from their Sweet Herbs and Flowers: This Market, fays my Friend, and that Church, hides more faults of kind Wives and Daughters, among the Neighbouring Inhabitants, than the pretended Vifits either to my Coufin at t'other end of the Town, or fome other diftant Acquaintance: For if the Husband asks, *Where have you been, Wife?* or the Parent, *Where have you been, Daughter?* The Anfwer, if it be after Eleven in the Forenoon, or between Three and Four in the Afternoon, is, *At Prayers*: But if Early in the Morning, then their excufe is, *I took a Walk to* Covent-Garden-Market, *not being very Well, to refrefh my felf with the Scent of the Herbs and Flowers*; Bringing a Flower, or a Sprig of Sweet Bryar, home in her Hand, and it confirms the matter.

Now, fays my Friend, we are fo near, I'll carry you to fee the *Hummums*, where I have an honeft old Acquaintance, that is a Cupper,

and

and if you will be your Club towards Eight Shillings, we'll go in and Sweat, and you shall feel the effects of this Notable Invention: With all my Heart, said I, you know, I am always conformable to whatever you propose; so accordingly he Conducted me to the House, thro' which we pass'd into a long Gallery, where my Friends Acquaintance receiv'd him with much Gladness; I had not walk'd above once the length of the Gallery, but I began to find my Self as warm as a Cricket at an Oven's Mouth: My Friend telling him we design'd to Sweat, he from thence introduc'd us into a Warmer Climate. Pray Friend, said I, what Latitude do you think we are in now? You must consider, says he, we are making a short Cut to the *East-Endies*, and are now in about Twenty Three and Thirty, that's just under one of the *Tropicks*; but this heat is nothing to what you'll find when you come under the Equinoctial, where I can assure you we shall find ourselves in a very little Time. We now began to unstrip, and put our selves into a Condition of enduring an Hours Baking, and when we had reduc'd our selves into the Original state of Mankind, having nothing before us to Cover our Nakedness, but a Clout no bigger than a Figleaf, our Guide led us to the end of our Journy, the next Apartment, which I am sure, was as hot as a Pastry-Cooks Oven to Bake a White-Pot, that I began immediately to melt, like a piece of Butter in a Basting-Ladle, and was afraid, I should have run all to Oyl by that time I had been in six Minutes; the bottom of the Room was Pav'd with Free-Stone; to defend our Feet from the excessive Heat of which, we had got on a pair of new-fashion'd *Brogues*, with Wooden Soles, after the *French* Mode, Cut out of an Inch Deal Board, or else like the Fellow in the *Fair*, we might as well have walk'd cross a Hot Iron-Bar, as ventur'd here, to have Trod bare-Foot; as soon as the Fire had tapt us all over, and we began to run like a Conduit-Pipe, at every Pore, our Rubber arms his Right Hand with a Gauntlet, of course hair Camblet, and began to curry us with as much Labour, as a *Yorkshire-Groom* does his Masters best Stone-Horse; till he made our Skins as Smooth, as a Fair Ladies Cheeks, just wash'd with *Lemon-Posset*, and greas'd over with *Pomatum*: At last, I grew so very Faint, with the expence of much Spirits, that I beg'd as hard for a Mouthful of fresh Air, as *Dives* did for a drop of Water; which our attendance let in at a Sash-Window, no broader than a *Deptford* Cheese-cake; but however, it let in a Comfortable Breeze that was very Reviving: When I had foul'd about as many Callico Napkins, as a Child does double Clouts in a Week, our Rubber draws a Cystern full of Hot Water, that we might go in, and Boil out those gross Humours that would not be Emitted by Perspiration. Thus almost Bak'd to a Crust, we went into the hot Bath to moisten our Clay, where we lay softening ourselves like *Deer's*, Humbles design'd for Minc'd-Pies, till we were almost Parboil'd; I talking by Accident of a Pain that sometimes affected my Shoulder, occasion'd by a fall from my Horse, my Friend, by all means advis'd me to be Cup'd for it, telling me 'twas the best Operation in the World, for the removal of all such Grievances; being an utter Stranger to this sort of *Phlebotomy*, was a little unwilling to undergo the experience of it; but by the Perswasions of my Friend, and my Friend's Friend, I at last consented, upon which the Operator fetch'd in his Instruments, and fixes three Glasses at my Back, which by drawing out the Air, stuck to me as close as a Cantharides-Plaifter to the Head of a Lunatick, and Suck'd as hard as so many Leeches at a Wenches Fundament, troubled with the *Hemorhoides*, till I thought they would have Crept into me, and have come out on t'other side, when by Virtue of this *Hocus Pocus* Stratagem, he had Conjur'd all the ill Blood out of my Body, under his Glass Juggling-Cups, he plucks out an ill-favour'd Inftrument, at which I was as much frighted, as an absconding Debter is at the Sight of a Bill of *Middlesex*, takes off his Glaffes, which had made my Shoulder as weary as a Porters Back under a heavy Burthen, and begins to Scarifie my Skin, as a Cook does a Loin of *Pork* to be Roasted; but with such Ease and Dexterity, that I could have suffer'd him to have Pink'd me all over as full of Eylet-holes, as the Taylor did the Shooemakers Cloak, had my Malady requir'd it, without Flinching; when he had drawn away as much Blood as he thought Neceffary, for the removal of my Pain, he cover'd the Places he had Carbonaded, with a new Skin, provided for that purpofe, and heald the Scarifications he had made in an Inftant, then taking me up like a Scalded Swine, out of my Greafie Broth, and after he had wip'd o'er my Wet Buttocks with a dry Clout, telling us we had Sweat enough, he reliev'd us out of our Purgatory, and carried us back into our Dreffing Room, which gave us such Refreshment, after we had been thus long ftewing in our own Gravy, that we thought our felves as happy as a Couple of *English* Travellers, Tranfported in an Inftant, by a miracle from the *Torrid Zone*, into their own Country. Our expence of Spirits, had weakned Nature and made us drowfie; where having the conveniency of a Bed, we lay down and were rubb'd like a couple of Race Horfes, after a Courfe, till we were become as Cool as the Affections of a Paffionate Lover after a Nights Enjoyment. When we had refresh'd our feeble Carcaffes, by a plentiful dram of Doctor *Stephens* Cordial, so full of Gold, that it look'd as tempting as Gilded *Ginger-bread*, to the Eyes of a froward Infant, and had taken an hours repofe, to reconcile the fermented Humours of our Bodies to their orderly Motion, we then got up, and began to cover our Indecencies, with thofe Habiliments the Taylor had contriv'd to hide our Nakednefs; to put on which to the beft advantage, our Rubber gave us his Affiftance, during which time he alfo entertain'd us with feveral delightful Stories; which he told in fuch apt Words, and with fuch agreeable Humour, that he made my Guts Shake with Laughing, like a Trodden Quagmire: And that the Reader may be partaker of our Mirth, I have here made a recital of fome of his fhort Comedies, in which himfelf was the principal Actor.

It happen'd fays, he not long ago, that a very fine Lady of the Town, came in to clean her Skin, and fupple her Induftrious Joints, as I suppofe, and make her tender Limbs the more Pliable, and fit for the exercife of Love, which she was doubtlefs that Night to be engag'd in; Being at the Charge of a Crown Bath Extraordinary, Enrich'd with Effences and Sweet-Herbs, to add fuch a fragrancy to her Body, that might render her moft Putefcent parts, as Sweet as a Calves Noftril; when she had put herfelf into this Order, and made herfelf a fuitable Companion for the Niceft Bedfellow, she commanded her little *Mercury* that attended her, to call a Coach, and away she went. Immediately after, came in a very Toping Beau from the Tavern, pretty well Loaded with

Wine,

Wine, and using to Sweat in the Room, which the Lady had just quitted, being very Humoursome, would not be perswaded to go into any other, so that they were forc'd to show him the same Apartment. One of the Rubbers going into the hot Room where the Gentleman was to Sweat, and turning one of the Cocks, found that the Stoaker had been Negligent, and that the Hot-Water was all Run-off, who being gone out a Fuddling, they knew not what shift to make to draw a fresh Bath; and at last found they had no way left, but to make the Ladies Bath serve again: So that they were forc'd to deceive the Gentleman, by telling him there was an extraordinary Bath, preserv'd with Sweet-Herbs, for a Person of Quality, who had sent to bespeak the Room Hot; the time being relaps'd, they believ'd my Lady would not come, and that it was great pity to let it run off without use, which if he pleas'd to accept on, he might have, without Paying any more than the Common Rates of the House; the Gentleman very well pleas'd with so kind a proffer, very gladly consented to make use of it, and after he had Sweated a little, went into it, the Rubber fishing for the Herbs to Scowre the Gentlemans Skin, happen'd to feel something amongst 'em, that felt very soft and Pappy, who turning his Head aside, and smelling to his Fingers, found 'twas some unsavory Lees, which chanc'd to drop thro' the Bung-hole of that Mortal Cask which had before been rinsed in the same Water; the Rubber in a sad Agony began to be thoughtful of an Excuse, in case the Gentleman should discover it, fearing the affront might Agravate him to do him a Mischief; at last the Gentleman looking about him, saw the remains of her cleanly Ladyship in his Bath? *What a Pl—gue*, says he, *Is this Nastiness, that is Swimming amongst the Herbs?* Sir, says the Rubber, it is nothing but Italian Paste, which is accounted the most excellent thing to cleanse and make smooth the Skin Imaginable, and it is what my Mistress cannot afford to use but in an extraordinary Bath, which are paid for above the common Rates of the House. *Prithee, Friend*, says the Gentleman, *if it be so good for the Skin, Rub me well with it; but Egad*, says he, *in my mind it looks as like a Sir-reverence, as ever I see any thing in my Life.* Ay, Sir, says the Servant, *so it does; but it is an incomparable thing to wash with, for all it it looks so nastily; and is a compound of the richest Gums, and best Castle-Sope boild up together, that can be bought for Money.* Pray, says the Beau, *take a little Pains with me, and Rub me all over with it very Well. Who is it that makes it? I'll buy some for my Hands. It is made Sir,* replies the Rubber, *by a Gentlewoman in this Town, but where she Lives I cannot tell; my Mistress, were she within, could inform you: But she went into the City to Dinner, and is not return'd yet.* Thus my Comrade that attended him, by the good Management of his Tongue, brought off the Mischance cleverly without Discovery. The Perfumes and Sweet-Herbs in the Bath overpowering the Scent, that the Gentleman, tho' he Nos'd it, being amongst such a mixture of Effluvias, that it confounded his smelling, and render'd him incapable of distinguishing a fair Ladies Sir—nce, from the Excrement of a Civet-Cat; but rise out of his Bath extreamly pleas'd, and gave him that attended him Half a Crown for his extraordinary Care and Trouble, so march'd away with great Satisfaction.

Having thus concluded his former Story, he proceeded to the latter, *viz.* A Gentleman of Fortune one day lying under a shrewd suspicion

of

of Debt, was dog'd by a Bayliff into our House, who came to the door whilst the Gentleman was sweating, and ask'd for him, and one of our Rubbers by chance opening the door, happen'd to know his Calling, and comes in to the Gentleman and tells him a Fellow wanted to speak with him at the door, pretendingly from such a Gentleman of his Acquaintance, and that he knew him to be a *Bayliff*: The Gentleman thank'd him kindly for his Information, and put it into his head to get him in, and Torment him alittle in one of the hot Rooms; accordingly my fellow Servant went back to the *Moabite*, and told him that the Gentleman was within, and desir'd him to come to him: So conducts the *Debter-Snapper*, who was ready arm'd with his Legal Authority, into an Anti-Room of the Next Apartment to the Gentleman, where he bids him wait a little, and the Gentleman would come to him presently: In the mean while my fellow Servant came to me and the Stoaker, to consult after what manner we should punish him. I, like a good Projector of Unluckiness, told him my advice was for us to put on our Callico Gowns with the Hoods over our Heads, and disguise our Faces with burnt Cork as frightfully as we can, and Arm our selves with Fire-weapons out of the Kitchen ; so enter upon him altogether, seize him, and carry him into the hot-Room, and there torment him as we shall think fit. Accordingly we put our selves into this order, rush'd in upon him, and forc'd him into the hot-Room: The fellow coming in the Piazza-way, was wholly Ignorant what place it was, but took it by the front to be a Gentlemans House; but feeling the excessive heat, and seeing himself in the hands of so many ill-look'd Goblins, arm'd with a great Beef-Spit, Tongs and Fire-Fork, began to roar out like a stuck Bacon-Hog; and fancy'd himself in Hell. Then in a hoarse Voice, said I to my Brother Infernals, *First let us Bake him, and then Boil him*; To which my Comrade with the Spit, added, *And then I'll have him Roasted*. Which terrible Sentences, so frighted the *Disturber* of *Humane Quiet*, in this new State of Damnation, That he fell into a Swoon, and we were forc'd to put him into a cold Bath to fetch him to Life again. Who when he recover'd, look'd as Wild as a Lunatick at full of the Moon; and then cry'd out as much against the Cold, as he did before against the Heat. Upon which, we let run the Cock of Hot-water, till we had almost par-boil'd him: Then he fell into a Second Fit, that we thought fit to take him out of the Bath, and carry him into the Anti-Room for fear he should have Dy'd: Where we shav'd one side of his Head and Beard, and fix'd on a couple of Cupping-horns (which we sometimes use) upon his Fore-head; so carry'd him to the back-Door, and turned him a Drift: Who was so Rejoyced, that he found Redemption from the Devils Clutches, that away he run as fast as a Thief under a persute ; and after him all the Mob, and Boys, in the street, crying out, *A Mad Cuckold! A Mad Cuckold!* And telling the Gentleman what we had done, he return'd us hearty thanks, and was mightily pleas'd at our Unluckiness.

F I N I S.

THE
LONDON
SPY.

For the *Month* of *August*, 1699.

PART X.

By the Author of the Trip to *JAMAICA.*

LONDON,
Printed and Sold by *J. How,* in the *Ram-Head-Inn-Yard* in
Fanchurch-street, 1699.

Books Sold by J. How, *in the* Ram-Head-Inn-Yard *in* Fanchurch-Street; J. Weld, *at the* Crown *between the Temple-Gates in* Fleet-ftreet; *and* M. Fabian, *at* Mercers-Chappel *in* Cheapfide.

1. SOt's Paradife: Or the Humours of a Derby-Ale-Houfe: With a Satyr upon the Ale. Price Six Pence.

2. A Trip to *Jamaica*: With a True Character of the People and Ifland. Price Six Pence.

3. *Eclefia & Factio.* A Dialogue between *Bow-Steeple-Dragon,* and the *Exchange-Grafhopper.* Price Six Pence.

4. The Poet's Ramble after Riches. With Reflections upon a Country Corporation. Alfo the Author's Lamentation in the time of Adverfity, Price Six Pence.

5. The London Spy, the Firft, Second, Third, Fourth, Fifth, Sixth, Seventh, Eighth, and Ninth Parts. To be Continued *Monthly.* Price Six Pence Each.

6. A Trip to New-England. With a Character of the Country and People, both Englifh and Indians. Price Six Pence.

7. Modern Religion and Ancient Loyalty: A Dialogue. Price Six Pence.

8. The World Bewitch'd. A Dialogue between Two Aftrologers and the Author. With Infallible Predictions of what will happen in this Prefent Year, 1699. From the *Vices* and *Villanies* Practis'd in *Court, City* and *Country.* Price Six Pence.

9. A Walk to *Iflington:* With a Defciption of New *Tunbridge-*VVells, and *Sadler's* Mufick-Houfe. Price Six Pence.

10. The Humours of a Coffee-Houfe: A Comedy. Price Six Pence.

11. O Raree-Show, O Pretty-Show; Or, the City Feaft. Price One Penny.

All Written by the fame Author.

THE
LONDON
SPY.

HAVING now purified our Scorbutick Carcasses in a resemblance of *Purgatory*, tho' in a *Protestant Country*; and made our Skins, by Sweating, Bathing, Rubbing and Scrubbing, as smooth as an old Drum-head that had been long beaten, we satisfied the demands of the House, gratified our Groom for extraordinary Pains in dressing our dirty Hides, and then departed, finding our Bodies so refresh'd, and our Spirits so enliven'd, that we were weary of groveling upon the Surface of this gross World, and began to fancy, like the Flying Quaker, from the nimble motion of our Spirits, that we had got *Icarus*'s Wings, and were able at one flight to Translate our sublim'd Bodies into some Loftier Region, more suitable to our refin'd Natures, being as it were renewed by this Fiery Tryal, and cleans'd of all Corruptions.

From thence we adjourn'd to the Wits *Coffee-house*, in hopes the Powerful Eloquence, which drops from the Silver Tongues of the Ingenious Company that frequent this Noted Mansion, might inspire us with such a Genius, as would better fit the present Perfection, of our renovated Clay, now purg'd of all Impurities, being render'd proper Receptacles, for the most Discerning and Poetick Spirits. Accordingly up Stairs we went, where we found much Company, and but little Talk; as if every one Remember'd the old Proverb, *That a close Mouth makes a Wise Head* : And so endeavour'd by his Silence, to be counted a Man of Judgment; rather than by Speaking, to stand the Censure of so many *Cruticks*, and run the hazzard of losing that Character, which by holding his Tongue, he might be in hopes of gaining. We shuffled thro' this moving Crow'd of *Philosophical* Mutes, to the other End of the Room, where three or four Wits, of the upper Classis, were rendezvouz'd at a Table, and were disturbing the Ashes of the Old Poets, by perverting their Sense, and making strange Allegories and Allusions, never Dreamt or Thought on, by the Authors. Whereby they excused some Faults, which were really the Slips or over-sight of

the

the Poet, but made others so very gross, thro' Prejudice and Mis-con-struction, that none but *Criticks* of very little Judgment, or very much Ill Nature, could have Wrested the Sense of the Words, so much to the Injury of him that writ 'em. When they had show'd their Learning, as they thought, by Arraigning and Condemning, many of the old *Roman* Muses, they condescended so low, as to call some of our Modern Poets to stand the Test of their all-judging Opinions. Upon whom in brief they confer'd these Characters. One was a Man of Great *Judgment*, *Learning*, and *Fancy*, but of no *Principle*. Another was One that Had *Writ well*, and Could *Write well*; but Would not Write. A Third, never Writ but *One Good Thing* in his Life, that ever was taken Notice on; and that he *Recanted*. A Fourth, had a *Poetical Talent*, but it was hid under a *Philosophical Bushel*. A Fifth, was a Good *Latin Poet*, but had Sacrific'd his *Muse* to *Bacchus*, instead of Dedicating her to *Apollo*. A Sixth, had got a great deal of Credit by *Writing* of *Plays*, but lost it all by *Defending* the *Stage*. A Seventh, had got some Reputation by turning of *Old Ditties* into *New Songs*; but lost it all by turning a *Spanish Romance* into an *English Stage-Play*. An Eighth had got Honour by a *Dull Poem*, which his Brother *Medicus* Envy'd, and Vow'd he'd out-do him in Verse, as he hop'd also to be *Knighted*. Thus the Carping *Momus's* proceeded according to the *Criticks* Custom, never to let any thing, tho' well perform'd, escape their *Scrutiny*, to the Discovery of a Colourable Fault; nor any Character pass their Lips, tho' of the Worthyest Persons, without being tag'd with some Failings, on purpose to Eclipse the Brightness of that Lustre which arose from those Vertues, for which they are chiefly Eminent. And it may generally be observ'd of those who delight in Criticism, That they are so Curious in having the Maiden-Head of an Error, that if a better Judgment finds a fault, which has had the Good Fortune to Escape his Censure, he will, if it be possible, find out a Salve for that Sore, and Justifie the Author, Ever-here-after, in that Particular, and will make it appear, there is more Sense lies hid in those very Words, than in all the Book besides, tho' he knows what he defends, to be Arrant Nonsence; being usually so Conceited of his own Judgment, that rather than acknowledge, he had over-look'd an Errour, he will Justifie it not to be so: And of such a sort of *Critick*, of which there are Hundreds in this Town, as well as some at the next Table, I think it very proper in this Place, to give a Character. Accordingly, I dictated, and my Friend Writ.

A Modern *CRITICK*

Is a Compound of some Learning, little Judgment, less Wit, much Conceit, and abundance of Ill-Nature: Who wanting true Merit, aims to raise a Reputation, not by his own *Performances*, but by others *Failings*, which he takes more Pleasure to Expose, than he does to Mend: And Reads an Author as much in search of his *Faults*, as a Wise-man does of his *Knowledge*. Whoever Speaks Latin in his Company, must be as watch-ful of his *Words*, as a *Prince* is of his *Actions*; for if he once breaks *Priscians* Head, he must be forc'd to break the *Criticks* too, or else suffer him-self to be baited as bad as the *Tyger* at the *Cock-pit*. True *Spelling* and *Pointing*, he admires as the chief Ornaments in *Writing*; and always

minds

（ 5 ）

minds the *Senfe* much lefs than the *Orthography*. When ever he Repeats
Grave Verfe, he has more Turns in his Voice, and Changes in his Countenance, than a Young Preacher in his *Sermon* upon *Death* and *Judgment*.
And when he Reads a *Tragedie*, he out-mouths a *Player*, and corrects the
Stage with his agreable *Gestures*. Whoever talks of an *Author* within
his Reading, fhall be fure to be attack'd with thofe Places that remain
Doubtful and Obfcure ; which *Riddles* he Expounds and renders as Plain
(if you'l depend upon his *Judgment*) as that the Candle Eat the Cat,
or the Coach draws the Horfes ; and would not give a Farthing to
underftand any thing but *Difficulties*, which had puffled much Wifer
Heads than is own to truly find the meaning of. He's a Man that
feldom *Writes* any thing ; but when he does, is fo very *Nice*, that it's
carry'd as often to the *Corrector*, as a *Ladys Stays*, or a *Beau's Coat* to the
Taylors, before the *Typography* and *Orthography* is according to his Judgment. His *Talk* is ufually like a *Maze* or *Labyrinth*, for none but himfelf
has the *Clue* to find the Beginning and Ending of his Tedious Comments,
with which in all Companies he is very Troublefome. Whenever he
undertakes to Reconcile an *Abfurdity*, or Expound a *Myftery*, he ufually
does it with as much fuccefs as Phyficians when they Labour to un-
fold the Nature of fuch Medicines to the Patient which work by
Occult Qualities, who tire the Ears with a few uncommon Words, which
ferve among *Fools* as well as an Intelligible Explication. He is one that
is not *Wife*, but would very fain be thought fo , and takes as much Pains
to fit a Straddle upon other Mens Shoulders, as would raife his Reputation
to twice the Height, had he *Wifdom* enough to apply the fame Induftry to
a better Purpofe. His *Head* is a meer *Houfe of Correction*, his *Brains* are
the *Regifter* of other Mens *Faults*, and his *Tongue* the Unmerciful *Scourge*
that Punifhes them. He is the *Store-houfe* of other Mens *Infirmities*,
where feldom any thing is laid up but what the Authors are afham'd
off. They are the meer *Wafps* of the Age, who are furnifh'd only with
Stings, but yield no *Honey*.

Says my Friend, You have deviated much from the Character of a
true *Critick*, whofe bufinefs in the *Roman* time, was to Judge the Actions
and Works of Men, deliver'd to the Publick, by *Hiftorians*, *Poets*, *Philofophers*, and the like ; to examine the Probability, and Reafonablenefs
of former Tranfactions, as they are handed to us by our Anceftors,
to prevent their Impofition on Pofterity, and to Enquire into the Truth
and Ufefulnefs of all forts of Learning, and report their Opinions to
the World accordingly ; to expound and give their beft Senfe of all Am-
biguities and obfcure Paffages, which they find in any Author ; and thefe
were very Commendable and Serviceable Tasks: But yours is fuch a
Coniwobble of a *Critick*, I know not what to make on him. Why then
I'll tell you, faid I, I give not this as the Character of a real *Critick*,
but fuch a fort of a Mungril *Critick*, as he that you heard talk juft now,
who takes a Pride in nothing, but Snaping and Snarling at the little Slips,
and Unavoidable Failings of Authors, beneath the Notice of any Judicious
and Good-Natur'd Reader ; and would Die, were it not that thefe Petty
Studients in *Syntaxis*, who handle Mens Faults in Company, as a Jugler does his Balls, till they have made as many as they pleafe of 'em,
and think they cannot give greater Demonftrations of their Learning,
than in Publick, to difparage fuch Perfons, who have Ten times the

B Parts

Parts of themfelves, Foolifhly believing what ever they detraſt from others, they add to their own Reputation; and Fancy every Stain or Blemifh they can give to an Ingenious Mans Charaſter, is a heightening of their own Merit: Thefe are the Perfons of whom I have given this rough Sketch, who are only Cavillers, or Pretenders to *Criticifm*, and know nothing of the Matter. Nay, fays my Friend, if it be thofe you aim at, you have faid lefs than they deferve: I have obferv'd, fince I have fat here, I have heard thofe Gentlemen Judge very feverely of fome Modern Authors, who have not only Merited, but Enjoy a general Approbation and Applaufe, and have fo rafhly Condemn'd fome Writings, of an Ancient Worthy and Honourable Gentleman, as if they had Commiffion to take away Mens Reputations, without giving the leaft Reafon why, or an Account wherein They have forfeited their Credits.

At another Table were Seated a parcel of Young, Raw, *Second-Rate Beau's* and *Wits*, who were Conceited, if they had but once the Honour to dip a Finger and Thumb into Mr. *D——'s* Snufh-box, it was enough to infpire 'em with a true Genius of Poetry, and make 'em write Verfe, as faft as a Taylor takes his Stiches. Thefe were Communicating to one another the Neweft Labours of their Brains, wherein were fuch wonderous Flights, unaccountable Thoughts, ftrange Figures, Hyperboles, and Similies, and upon fuch notable Subjeſts, that to hear 'em read their Works, is at any time fufficient to Cure the Hippochondria, and turn the deepeft Melancholly into a Fit of Laughter. One plucks out a *Panegyric* upon *Orange-flower-water*; another, a *Satyr* againft *Dirty-weather*; a Third, produces a cleanly *Lampoon* upon nafty *Tobacco-Smokers*: a Fourth, a *Poem* in praife of fhort *Puff-Wigs*, together with the Ufe and excellency of *Paint*, *Powder*, and *Patches*: What I heard of thefe their moft admirable Flights, came too abruptly to our Ears for us to make a fair recital of any part worth the Readers perufal, or elfe I would have gladly Oblig'd the World with Copies of fome of the Wild Exuberancies of their Juvenal Fancies. But, however, one of them being (as I gueft by his Garb) a Young Officer, happen'd in plucking out fome other Papers, to drop this following Poem, which my Friend believing to include no great matter of Moment, imagin'd it would prove fome fuch bufinefs as we found it to be, fo took it flightly up without Notice; and taking our leaves of this Wit's Seffions-houfe, we brought it away with us; and finding fomething in it we believe may divert the Reader, we have prefented him with a Copy, it being

A Letter from a LAWYER in Town, to a New Married OFFICER in the Country.

L Etters in Profe, my Friend, are Common,
    As Pride in Prieft, or Luft in Woman.
Our Annual *Curfe of Long* Vacation,
To Bus'nefs giving a Ceffation,
Affords me time to thus Salute-ye,
And pay in Rime this Friendly Duty.

Not rightly knowing which is worse,
The Lawyers, *or the* Poets *Curse,*
Both Silenc'd with an Empty Purse.
For now our Pens, upon our Words,
Are grown as useless as your Swords,
We having but as little Writting,
As, God be thanked, you have Fighting.
You may draw Sword, so we may Pen,
To show our Tools of War, and then,
Like Fools, e'en put 'em up again.

But what a Pox is't I am doing?
Or where the Devil am I Going?
Now Pegasus *I've once bestriden,*
Methinks I Gallop like a D——n:
And pleas'd I'm in the Vein, Egad,
Blunder out Verse like any Mad.
Long as 'tis Rime, it's no great matter,
And Bombast, whether Praise or Satyr.
Mistake me not, and think I've Writ
To show my Parts, that is not it;
I'd not be Envy'd for a Wit.

For he that's Rich in Thought, is sure
To be in Friends and Pocket Poor;
For Wisemen will not Care to serve him,
And Fools would all be glad to starve him.
Wit carr's an Edg, few can abide-it,
And he that has it, ought to hide-it.
Such Weapons in a Mans Possession,
Scare the Unarm'd from's Conversation;
And is so far from b'ing Delightful,
It renders him that draws it, Frightful:
For no Man Cares for th' Company,
Of him that has more Wit than he:
Nor can he with Good will afford
The better Genius one Good Word.
So Dowdys *will no Praise allow*
To her, that has the Lovely Brow;
But will endeavour to Confute-ye,
She has more Faults by half than Beauty.
To Wits 'tis Fear that makes us Civil,
Just as an Indian *is to th' Devil.*

This Ignis Fatuus *in my Braines,*
That kindles up these Rambling Strains,
Makes my Head light as any Feather,
And leads me Wandring God knows whither.
But Poets, when we make Digression,
The Fault we supple by Confession;
And so excuse the wild Transgression.

I only meant to let you know
I'm Well, and hope that you are so,
With all the Merry Knaves oth' Pack,
Who Love the Fair, the Brown, the Black:
And rather than submit to Marry,
Fly still at Whore, as Hawk at Quarry.

Pray tell me how Lieutenant A——
Maintains his Vice with half his Pay:
Who has, I hope, by Good Direction,
Repair'd his Rudder of Affection;
And gain'd his Natural Complexion.
I fear it prov'd a Scurvy Jobb;
Bid him beware, least to'ther Rub,
Shou'd bring him to the Powd'ring-Tub.

I want to know if Captain Blunder
Is still the Country Wenches Wonder;
And how he shifts for Copulation,
To Oblige his Lustful Inclination.
I fear his Tail's so much his Master,
'Thas brought him under some Disaster:
For Bolus, Pills, and Sal Prunel,
(In which Repenting Sinners deal,)
Were sent among ye by Jack Staily,
To quench those burning Pains that aileye,
Which have possest, I plainly see,
Some Label of Mortalitie.

But hold! What is it I am doing?
I must not here appear too knowing;
Least you Arch Wags should turn the Satyr,
And say, I'm Skilful in the matter.

But now, dear Friend, I change my Strain,
And grieve to think weak Man so Vain,
That Resolutions made of Late,
Against a Matrimonial State,
Should not defend you from the Curse
Of Fools, for Better or for Worse.
Prithee now tell what means this Riddle,
That you should be so Fond and Idle,
T' eclipse the Freedom of your Life,
With that Dull Mournful Clog, a Wife?
What if she's Youthful, Rosh, and Fair,
And Virtuous too, she's still a Care?
These are but Chains that bind thee Faster,
And make Man's Plague the more his Master.
Since Married, I account Thee One,
Who his best Threds of Life has Spun;
And now his Miserie's just begun.

But use this Caution, thro' thy Life,
Slave not thy self to please a Wife,
Lest thro' o'er Fondness thou dost prove
A meer Anatomy *of Love.*

But since the Earthen Vessel, Man,
Whose Life's compris'd within a Span,
Is by his Nature Weak and Vain,
I must excuse your Over-sight,
Committed 'gainst your Reason's Light:
And since you're Catch'd in Loves Decoy,
I'll wish you, like the rest, much Joy*:*
Hoping your Choice has prov'd so Good,
That she's as Chaste *as you are Lewd;*
And then she could not be with-stood.

You know, my Friend, what can't be Cur'd,
It's said of Old, must be Endur'd;
Since that's your Case, I'll so Be-Friend-you,
As wish all Happiness Attend-you.

May she prove Just *(I hope she's* Fair)
Calm, Kind, and Good, as Angels are;
And may her sweeter Charms produce,
(When sprinkled with your Balmy Juice)
A Noble Fruit of Glorious use.

May your whole Lives be Harmonie;
Mutual your Loves, from Troubles Free;
And Dutiful your Progenie.

May she so Live, that all her Joys,
May prove her Merit, not her Choice:
And to compleat that Happiness,
I truly Wish you to Possess,
To your Fair Bride may you prove True,
And Good, to her, as she to you.

My Friend, with Gladness do I hear
You find your Spirits much too clear,
For Fens, and its Gross Foggie Air.

That you intend, within a while,
To Bless your own dear Native Soil,
And leave that Poisonous Croaking Isle
To Frogs, and Toades, Snakes, Evts, and Ants,
Its Native foul Inhabitants;
But e'er you come, take Care, and See
You send me a Retaining Fee,
In Cordial Nants, *or some such Liquor,*
To move my Spirits round the Quicker.

C

For Man's but Heaven's Water-Mill,
In motion kept by th' Glass or Jill;
And wanting Liquor must stand still.
Don't thro Oblivion, now Neglect it,
For I assure you I expect it.

This being in Rime my first Essay,
I've Jingled on a wondrous Way:
Pray Pardon my Prolixity,
A common Fault in Poetry.

Excuse me Friend, in what I Write t'ye,
And don't forget the Aqua Vitæ,
Is all I Beg, and so Good B'wi't'ye,

Having thus Diverted our Selves with the perusal of the foregoing Epistle, we steer'd our Course into *Bridges-Street*, with intention to see a Play. But when we came to the House, found (upon enquiry) that all the Wiser part of the Family of *Tom Fools* had translated themselves to *Bartholomew* Fair. After Strugling with a Long *Se Saw*, between *Pride* and *Profit*; and having Prudently consider'd the weighty difference between the Honourable Title of one of his *Majesties Servants*, and that of a *Bartholomew-Fair-Player*, a *Vagabond* by the Statue, did at last, with much difficulty, conclude, That it was equally reputable to Play the Fool in the *Fair*, for, Fifteen or Twenty Shillings a Day, as 'twas to Please Fools in the *Play-house*, at so much *per* Week. And indeed I think they made a very Commendable Result; for I think there's no more distinction between a *Kings-House-Player* and a *Countrey-Stroler*, than there is between a *Bull Dog* bred up in *Clare-Market*, and another Educated in his Majesties *Bear-Garden*: And as he is the most Valluable *Dog*, that runs Furthest and Fairest in, so is he the most Reputable *Comedian*, that gets most Money by his Fooling. For he that is a *Mountebank*, its no matter whether he keeps his *Stage* over against *White-hall-Gate*, or at *Cow-Cross*; for if the Means to Live be the same, it signifies little to his *Credit* in what Place they are put in Practice.

But, however, we were disappointed in what we propos'd; and were oblig'd to defer our intended Measures till another Opportunity. And considering it would be expected we should, according to the Month, take a Survey of the *Fair*, we took Coach, to escape the Dirt and the uneasiness of a Crowd, and adjourn'd thither. At the Entrance of which, our Ears were saluted with *Belsegar's* Concert, the rumbling of *Drums*, mix'd with the Intollerable Squeakings of *Cat-Calls*, and *Penny-Trumpets*, made still more Terrible with the shrill Belches of *Lottery Pick-Pockets*, thro' Instruments of the same Metal with their Faces, that had I not been foretold by my Friend, of the astonishing Confusions I must expect to meet with, I should have been as much frighted at this unusual piece of disorder, as *Don Quevedo* in his Vision, when he saw *Hell* in an Uproar. We order'd the Coachman to set us down at the *Hospital-Gate*, near which we went into a Convenient House to Smoak a Pipe, and over-Follies of the Innumerable Throng, whose Impatient Desires of *ry Andrew's* Grimaces, had led them Ancle-deep into Filth
and

and Naſtineſs, crowded as cloſe as a Barrel of Figs, or Candles in a Tallow-Chandlers Basket, Sweating and Melting, with the heat of their own Bodies, the unwholeſome Fumes of whoſe uncleanly Hides, mix'd with the Odoriferous Effluvia's that aroſe from the Singeing of Pigs, and burnt Crackling of over-Roaſted Pork, came ſo warm to our Noſtrils, that had it not been for the uſe of the Fragrant Weed *Tobacco*, we had been in danger of being Suffocated.

Small Beer, Bitter'd with Colloquintida, drawn by a Louſie-look'd Tapſter, with the Impudence of a Goal-Bird in his Face, a Bunch of Ruſty Keys hanging on one ſide of his Apron-ſtrings, to keep him in equal Ballance between a Bruſh that was hug'd under the contrary Arm, who Plagu'd us as Conſtantly with his impertinent *Do-you-Call Sirs*, every two Minutes, as ſurely as the Clock ſtrikes every Hour; till at laſt he had ſo affronted us with his over-dilligence, that we were forc'd to tell him we would Kick him down Stairs if he came any more till we call'd him; by which means we reſpited our Uneaſineſs, during our own Pleaſure.

The firſt Objects, when we were ſeated at the Window, that lay within our Obſervation, were the Quality of the Fair, Struting round their Ballconies in their Tinſy Robes, and Golden Leather Buskins; expreſſing that Pride in their Buffoonery Statelineſs, that I could reaſonably believe they were as much Elevated with the thoughts of their Fortnights Pageantry, as ever *Alexander* was with the Glories of a new Conqueſt; and look'd with as much Contempt from their *Slit-Deal-Thrones*, upon the admiring Mobility, who gazing in the Dirt at their Oſtentatious Heroes, and their moſt Superbitical Doxies, who look'd as Awkward and Ungainly in their Gorgeous Accouterments, as an Aldermans Lady in her Stiffen-body'd Gown upon a City Feſtival. When they had taken a turn the length of their Gallery, to ſhow the Gaping Crow'd how Majeſtickly they could Tread, each aſcended to a Seat agreeable to the dignity of their Dreſs, to ſhow the Multitude how Imperiouſly they could Sit. Than came the Conjurer of the whole Company, Merry *Andrew*, I ſuppoſe as much admir'd by the reſt for a *Wit*, as the fineſt Dreſs'd *Jilt*, amongſt 'em was by the Mob for a *Beauty*. As ſoon as he came to his ſtand, where he deſign'd to give the Spectators ſome Teſtimonies of his Ingenuity, the firſt thing he did, he gave a ſingular Inſtance of his Cleanlineſs, by blowing his Noſe upon the People, who were mightily Pleas'd, and Laugh'd heartily at the Jeſt. Then, after he had pick'd out from the whole Dramatic Aſſembly a Man of moſt admirable Acquirements in the Art of Tittle-Tattle, and fit to Confabulate with the Witty and Intelligible Mr. *Andrew*, he begins a Tale of a Tub, which he Illuſtrates with abundance of Ugly Faces and Mimical Actions, for in that lay the chief of the Comedy; with which the Gazers ſeem'd moſt to be affected. Between theſe two, the Clod-skull'd Audience, were Lug'd by the Ears for an Hour, the Apes blundering over ſuch a parcel of Inſignificant Nonſcence, that none but a True *Engliſh* unthinking Mob could have Laugh'd or taken Pleaſure at any of their Empty Drollery, the Inſippidneſs of which, Occaſion'd my Friend to think, that ever ſince the *Andrew* was Whipp'd for ſingeing his Pig with Exchequer Notes, and Roaſting him with Tallys, it has made St. Bar-

tholomew

tholomew Jefters afraid of being Witty, for fear of Difobliging the Government. For, fays he, fure this is the dulleft ftuff that ever was Spew'd out amongft the Rabble fince Heaven made them Fools, or ever any fuch Cox-comb in a Blew Doublet undertook to prove them fo.

The Epilogue of merry *Andrew's* Farce, was, *Walk in, Gentlemen, and take your places whilft you may have 'em*; *the Candles are all Lighted, and we are juft a going to begin*; then Screwing his body into an ill-favour'd Pofture, agreeable to his Intellects, He ftruts along before the Glittering Train of Imaginary *Heroes*, and their *Water-lane-Beauties*, leading them to play the Fool within-fide, in anfwer to his performances without; whilft fome, that had Money went in, and thofe that had none, walk'd off Equally Satisfied.

The outfide of the Droll-Booths being all Garnifh'd with the like Foollerie, we found nothing further amongft 'em worth Repeating: and being feated in a place where nothing elfe was to be feen, we were forc'd to remove from our Quarters, and hazzard our *Carcaffes* amongft the Crowd, and our *Pockets* amongft the Nimble-Finger'd Gentlemen of the Diving-Myfterie, or elfe we fhould fee nothing worth the pains we'd taken. Accordingly we paid our Reckoning, and button'd up our Pockets, as fecurely as a Citizen does his Shop-Windowes when his Family goes to Church; and fo Launch'd our felves into the Tempeftuous Multitude, amongft whom we were hurry'd along from the ground by a Stream of Rabble, into the middle of the Fair, in as little time as a forward *Beau* may make a *Fumbler* a *Cuckold*.

Thus we fwam down with the Tide, till we came to the Rope-dancers Booth, before we could find any Bottom; where (praifed be our Stars) we once more got fafe Footing upon *Terra-firma*, and ftood a little to behold the Agility of the Tumblers, whofe Pranks, were they fhown to a Whimfical Virtuofa, are enough to beget in him a new Syftem of Philofophy; and make him believe, that to walk only upon our Feet with our Heads uppermoft, is nothing but a Ridiculous Habit we have contracted from our Nurfes; and that it is as Natural for Mankind to run Races upon their Hands with their Heells upwards, if they would but Practice it. I was mightily pleas'd to fee the Women at this fport, it made 'em feem to have a due Sence of the Ills done by their Tongues, to Degrade which, they turned 'em downwards, giving the Preheminency to their more deferving Parts, for which Reafon they Practic'd to walk with their Arfes upwards, which indeed I think is but Juftice, for that part to be moft Honour'd that's moft Ufeful; and whether that be the Head, or the Tail of a Woman, I'll appeal to Marry'd Men, who I muft acknowledge to be the better Judges. Truly, fays my Friend, I think you are much in the right on't; for a Woman is a meer Receptacle, and to fee her ftanding on her Legs is as Unnatural a Pofture, in my Mind, as to fee a Pipkin upon the Fire with the Mouth downwards. Prithee, faid I, let's have done with this *Jack-Pudding's* Dialect, or People will think the Fair has infpir'd us with Bombaft. Come, fays my Friend, let us fling away Six-pence a peice, and fee what's to be done within-fide; methinks, fays he, there is fomething in this fort of Activity that is both Diverting

ting and Amufing. I readily Confented to his Propofal ; fo in we went, where a parcel of Countrey *Scrapers* were Sawing of a Tune: And a mix'd multitude of Longing *Spectators* were waiting with Impatience the beginning of the Show ; looking upon one another as fimply, as a Company fat down at a Table, that waits with an Hungry Appetite an Hour for their Dinner. At laft they put up a little *Dumplin-Ars'd* Animal, that look'd as if it had not been Six-Weeks out of a Goe-Cart, and that began to creep along the Rope, like a Snail along a Cabbage-ftalk, with a Pole in its Hand not much bigger than a large Tobacco-ftopper. This was fucceeded by a couple of Plump-Buttock-Laffes, who, to fhow their Affection to the Breeches, wore 'em under their Petticoats ; which, for decency fake, they firft Danc'd in : But to fhow the Specta-tors how forward a Woman once warm'd, is to lay afide her Modefty, they doft their Petticoats, after a gentle breathing, and fell to Caper-ing and Firking, as if Old *Nick* was in 'em. Thefe were follow'd by a *Negro* Woman, and an *Irifh* Woman ; as foon as the Black had Seated herfelf between the Crofs Poles that Support one end of the Rope, a Coun-trey Fellow fitting by me, fell into fuch an Extafie of Laughing that he Cackled again. *Prithee,* Honeft Friend, faid I, what do'ft thou fee to make thy felf fo wonderful Merry at? *Mafter,* fays he, *I have often-times heard of the Devil upon two Sticks, but never Zee it bevore in me Life. Bezide, Maffter, who can forbear Laughing to fee the Devil going to Dance?* When with much Art and Agility, fhe had exercis'd her well-Propor-tioned Limbs, to the great fatisfaction of the Spectators; the *Irifh-Woman* arofe from her Hempen Seat, to fhow the multitude her Shapes, whofe Shoulders were of an *Altas*-Built ; her Buttocks as big as two Bufhel-Loaves, and fhak'd as fhe Danc'd like a Bog or Quagmire · Her Thighs as Flefhy as a Barron of Beef ; and were fo much too big for her Body, that they look'd as Gouty as the Pillars in St. *Paul's*. Her Legs were as ftrong as a Chair-mans, her Calves being as Round, and as Hard as a Foot-Ball ; the fwelling of the Mufcles ftretching the Skin as Tort as the Head of a new-brac'd Drum. She waddled along the Rope, like a Goofe over a Barn Threfhold, till at laft, poor Creature, willing to fhow the Affembly the utmoft of her Excellencies, and putting Nature upon a Strefs, to Cut a Caper as high as a Hog-Trough, happen'd to ftrain her Twatling-Strings, and let fly an unfavory Sound, as Lowd as a Note of the double Curtil? *Wounds, my Lady,* (fays my Neigh-bour, the Countrey-man) *Have a Care you don no Fall, for by the Mafs, you made the Rope give a woundy Crack.* The Men Laugh'd, the Wo-men they Blufh'd : Madam Lump quitted the Rope with a Shameful Expedition, and as it is thought, did her Dancing Trunks much damage, By the Unfortunate Eruption.

This was fucceeded, by a Pragmatical Brother of the fame Quality, who mounted the Ladder next, in Order to afcend the Rope ; whofe Looks foretold fuch an unhappy Deftiny, that I was fearful of his Falling, left his Hempen Pedeftal fhould have catch'd him by the Neck ; he commanded the Rope to be alter'd according to his Mind, with fuch an affected Lordlinefs, that prefently I perceiv'd he was Mafter of the Apes, by his Imperious Deportment, and looking ftedfaftly in his Face, I remember'd, I had feen him in our Town, where he had the Im-pudence to profefs himfelf an Infallible Phyfician. Upon which, I afk'd

D

my

my Friend the meaning on't: *Poh*, says he, *I am sorry you are so Igno-rant*: Why we have Dancing *Physicians*, Tumbling *Physicians*, and Fools of *Physicians*, as well as Colledge-*Physicians*: *Nay*, and some of them too, if they will, can Play much stranger Tricks than you are aware on. But these Fellow's you must know, says he, are bred up between Death and Remedy; that, is Rope and Medicine; and as they grow up, if they happen to prove too heavy Heel'd for Rope-Dancers, or Tumblers, they are forc'd to learn first how to be Fools, and when once grown expert *Jack-Pudding's*, the next degree they Commence, is Doctor; so leave off their Painted Coat, and put on a Plush one. The Person that Danc'd against him, was the *German* Maid, (as they stile her in their Bill) with a great Belly, who does such wonderful Pretty things upon the Rope, having such Proportion in her Limbs, and so much Modesty in her Countenance, that I Vow, it was as much as ever I could do, to forbear wishing my self in Bed with her; She as much out-Danc'd the rest, as a *Grey-hound* will out-run a *Hedg-hog*, having something of a Method in her Steps, Air in her Carriage, moving with an Obervancy of Time, playing with her Feet, as if assisted with the Wings of *Mercury*. And thus much further, I must needs say in her Behalf, That if she be but as Nimble between the Sheets, as she is up-on a Rope, she's one of the best Bed-fellowes in *England*. Then Doctor, *Cozen-Bumpkin* mounts the Slack-Rope, and after he had lain down and Swung himself a quarter of an Hour, in his Hempen Hammock, he comes down, believing he had done wonderful things, honours the Mob, with a gracious Nod; slips on his Night Gown, to prevent catching Cold, and then up steps the *Negro*, to the top of the Booth, and began to Play at Swing Swang, with a Rope, as if the *Devil* were in her, Hanging sometimes by a Hand, sometimes by a Leg, and sometimes by her Toes; so that I found, let her do what she would, Providence or Destiny would by no means suffer the Rope to part with her. This Scene being ended, they proceeded to the Conclusion of their Enter-tainment, the Tumbling; which indeed was very admirable, to think that Use shou'd so strengthen the Springs of Motion, and give that Flexibillity and Pliablenes to the Joynts, Nerves, Sinews, and Muscles, as to make Man Capable of exerting himself, after so Mira-culous a manner. I could not but conceive it possible, from the strange-ness of their Tricks, to bring up a Child by Practice to Jump first off a Brick, than two, so-on to a Story; and at last from the Top of the *Monument*, without catching any more harm than a Cat. When we had seen all, and the Master of the Revels had bid us *Welcome*, my Friend ask'd me how I lik'd it? Truly, said I, as for the Tumbling, I am mightily pleas'd with it, but as for the Dancing, I have seen that in the Countrey, perform'd by *Monkeys*.

The Spectators being now dispatch'd with a hearty Welcome, we Squeez'd out of the Door as close as a Thimble full of Shot out of the Barrel of a Birding-piece; and instead of avoiding a Crowd, we were got out of the Frying-Pan into the Fire: Amongst whose Confused Hummings, nothing was distinguishably heard, but the shrill Cries of *Nuts* and *Damsons*. Thinking it the Prudentest way to take new Sanctuary as soon as we could, we Justled into a Booth where was to be seen a Dwarf *Comedy*, Sir-nam'd a *Droll*, which most commonly proves as

wonderful

wonderful a Monster as any's to be seen in the Fair: It was under the Title of that Curse of a Companion, *The Devil of a Wife*. Which occasion'd me to look round the Audience, to examine whether there was the same mixture of both Sexes as is accuftomary at such fort of Entertainments; but found quite contrary to what may be ufually obferv'd, that there were Ten *Men* to One *Woman*: The Sex, as I suppose, being so highly diftafted at the Title of the Play, that they thought it greatly inconfiftent with their Eafe and Intereft, to encourage such a Publick Difhonour done to the Authority of *Tirmagants*, who they account are the only *Amazon's* of Spirit, who support and defend the Reasonable Priviledges of their Sex from the Ufurpation and Incroachments of the Husband, to the great Abufe and Violation of the wholefome Laws of Matrimony, as they were long fince fettled by that Reverend Affembly of Grave Matrons, the Parliament of Women. The Booth notwithftanding was pretty full, but of Men, cheifly who had the Plain-Dealing Looks of good Sober Citizens, and I believe happen'd moft of them to be enflav'd under Petticoat-Government, and came hither to learn how to Tame a Shrew, and recover into their own Hands the Power and Authority of their Fore-Fathers, which they had in Vain furrender'd to their Wives upon the Terms and Conditions of Peace and Quietnefs.

By the time my Friend and I had Crack'd a quart of Fill-birds; and Eat each of us two Penny-worth of *Burgamy* Pairs, to keep our felves from Idlenefs, the Minftrels Scratching over a Concife Piece of Unintelligible Difcord, call'd a Flourifh, the Curtain was drawn up, and the Strutting Reprefentatives began their Foollery: At whofe performances I confefs, I was moft wonderfully pleas'd; for every thing was done to fuch a Perfection of Uncoothnefs, that had fo many Puppits, made of Sticks and Clouts, been but qualified with Speech, we could not have Laugh'd more heartily at their awkward and ridiculous Imitations; every one looking, notwithftanding his Drefs, like what he really was, and not like what he reprefented; that I fancy'd all the while they were Playing, I heard fome of 'em Crying *Flag-Broomes*, fome *Knives to Grind*, and others *Chimney-Sweep*: Whilft their Ladies were making up the Confort with *Buy my Cucumbers to pickle*; and, *Here's your rare Holland Socks, four pair for a Shilling*: For I am certain they had accuftom'd their Voices to fome fuch Cries, that had begot in their Speeches fuch unalterable Tones, that they are no more able to play a part without giving a relifh of their Calling, than a Fanatick Parfon is able to tell a Story in his Pulpit without *Humming* and *Hawing*. The whole Entertainment was the ftrangeft Hodg-Podg that ever was Jumbled togegether; and is an excellent Farce to pleafe an Audience of fuch Fools, who are apt to Admire that moft, which they leaft Underftand · For I'll engage they will find it fuch a piece of puzzle, that is harder to expound than one of *Patridges* Riddles, or Mother *Shiptons* Prophecies. We were forc'd to make our Patience as long as their Play, being wedg'd in on both fides, as clofe as a couple of City Cuckolds in *Guild-hall* at a Lord-Mayors Election; till at laft they made an end as abruptly, as they begun foolifhly; and let down the Curtain, which cut off the Communication between our Eyes and their Actions: fo, with the reft of the Crowd, we from thence departed.

Having

Having trefpaf'd like Mifers too far upon Nature; and fpent moft part of the day without giving our Bodies that refrefhment which was requifite to enliven our Spirits and preferve Health, we after a fhort confultation agreed to gratifie our impertinent Appetites with a Quarter of a Pig, on purpofe to be Fools in the Fafhion; in order to accomplifh our Defign, with a great deal of Elbow-Labour, and much Sweating, we fcrambled thro' the Throng, who came pouring into the Fair from all the adjacent ftreets, each ftream of Rabble contending to repel the force of its oppofite Current, who were ftriving like Tide and Stream to overcome each other. At laft, with as much difficulty as a hunted Buck gets thro a Wood with his Horns on, by Inch and Inch, we gain'd *Pye-Corner*, where Greafie Cooks ftood driping at their doores like their roafting Swines Flefh; with painful induftry each fetting forth in an Audible Voice, the Choice and Excellency of his *Pig* and *Pork*, which were running as merrily round before the Fire, as if they were ftriving who fhould be firft Roafted. Some Pigs hanging upon Tenters in the Shop Windows, as big as large Spaniels, half bak'd by the Sun Beames; and look'd as Red as the Thighs of a Country Milk-wench in a Frofty Morning. After we had look'd round us, to examine what Cook was moft likely to accommodate our Stomachs with the beft Entertainment, at laft we agreed to ftep into a large fhop were we had great expectancy of Good meat, and cleanly ufage, but had no fooner enter'd the Suffocating Kitchen but a fwinging fat Fellow, who was appointed Over-feer of the Roaft, to keep the Pigs from bliftering, was ftanding by the Spit in his Shirt; Rubing of his Ears, Breaft, Neck, and Arm-pits with the fame cloth he rub'd the Pig, which brought fuch a Qualm over my Stomach, that I had much ado to keep the ftuffing of my Guts from tumbling into the Dripping-pan; fo fcowring out again, thro an Army of Flies, incamp'd at the door in order to attack the Pig-fauce, we defer'd our eating till a cleanlier opportunity.

Note, That this is but a fmall part of what's intended on the Fair; and whatever is deficient here, fhall be fupply'd in the Next.

F I N I S.

THE
LONDON
SPY.

For the *Month* of *September*, 1699.

PART XI.

By the Author of the Trip to *JAMAICA.*

LONDON,
Printed and Sold by *J. How*, in the *Ram-Head-Inn-Yard* in
Fanchurch-ftreet, 1699.

1. SOt's Paradiſe: Or the Humours of a Derby-Ale-Houſe: With a Satyr upon the Ale. Price Six Pence.

2. A Trip to *Jamaica*: With a True Character of the People and Iſland. Price Six Pence.

3. *Eclefia & Factio.* A Dialogue between *Bow-Steeple-Dragon,* and the *Exchange-Graſhopper.* Price Six Pence.

4. The Poet's Ramble after Riches. With Reflections upon a Country Corporation. Alſo the Author's Lamentation in the time of Adverſity. Price Six Pence.

5. The London Spy, the Firſt, Second, Third, Fourth, Fifth, Sixth, Seventh, Eighth, Ninth, and Tenth Parts. To be Continued *Monthly.* Price Six Pence Each.

6. A Trip to *New-England.* With a Character of the Country and People, both Engliſh and Indians. Price Six Pence.

7. Modern Religion and Ancient Loyalty: A Dialogue. Price Six Pence.

8. The World Bewitch'd. A Dialogue between Two Aſtrologers and the Author. With Infallible Predictions of what will happen in this Preſent Year, 1699. From the *Vices* and *Villanies* Practis'd in *Court, City* and *Country.* Price Six Pence.

9. A Walk to *Iſlington*: With a Deſcription of New *Tunbridge-*VVells, and *Sadler's* Muſick-Houſe. Price Six Pence.

10. The Humours of a Coffee-Houſe: A Comedy. Price Six Pence.

11 O. Raree-Show, O Pretty-Show; Or, the City Feaſt. Price One Penny.

All Written by the ſame Author.

THE
LONDON
SPY.

BEING quite Surfeited with his Greafiness's Cleanliness, our *Jewish* Stomachs began to be as much avers'd to *Bartholomew-Fair-Swines-*Flesh, as a Court Lady is to Onion-Sawce, or a Young Libertine to Matrimony. That the fight of a Pig was as hateful to me for the Fortnight, as an *Easter-*Gammon-of-Bacon to a *Scotch* Pedlar, or *Christmas-*Porridge to an *English* Puritan. The Eagerness of our Appetites, being thus affwag'd without the expence of Eating, we fac'd about to the Wooden *Sodom,* and fuffer'd our felves to be carry'd back by an Inundation of Mobility, into the Body of the Fair: Where, in Compaffion to one of the Female gender, who was labouring in the Crowd, like a Fly in a Cobweb, I laid my hands upon my Friends Shoulders, and by keeping her between my Arms, defended her from the rude Squeezes and Joftles of the Carelefs Multitude: In which Interim, fhe, to give me a remarkable Inftance of her Gratitude, put her hand behind her and pick'd my Pocket of a good Handerchief, in return of my Civility. Who when fhe had done her bufinefs, Shuffl'd into the Crowd; and the next minute after, I difcover'd my Lofs; which as it was but fmall, begot but a Concern Proportionable. I could not without fome fhame, acquaint my Friend of the matter, expecting he would laugh at me for my over-care of my Lady, and carelefsnefs of my Self: Who accordingly ridicul'd my fmall misfortune; and told me, Smiling, You muft be as careful of Women in *Bartholomew-Fair,* as Countrey People are of Stags in Rutting-Time; for their accuftomary ways of rewarding Kindneffes, are either to take fomething from you you'd unwillingly part with, or give you, on the contrary, that which you would be glad to get rid of.

Having heard much of a Comedians Fame, who had Manfully run the hazard of Lofing that Reputation in the *Fair,* which he had got in the *Play-houfe*; and having never feen him in his proper Element, we thought the time might not be very ill fpent if we took a fight of another *Beft Show* in the *Fair,* for fo they all ftile themfelves, that we
might

might judge of his Performances. The Number of Kings, Queens, Heroes, Harlots, Buffoons, Mimicks, Priests, Profligates and Devils in the Ballcony, occasion'd us to believe, with the Crowd, that there were no less Varieties to be seen within, than there were Signs of without; for indeed we might Reasonably have thought, from their Numerous Appearance, that when they were all in the Booth, there would be but room for a Slender Audience. To help make up which, we put our Fools Pence into his Worships Pocket-Apron, with which Title the Mob honour'd the Master of the Booth, because (as they said) he had been a Justice of the Peace; and then enter'd the Pit, where several of the Top Quality of the Tickle-Tail Function sat Cracking of Nuts, like so many Squirrils; and looking round 'em for Admirers, that they might Kindle such Flames in some Amorous Spectator with their studied Looks and Ogles, that nothing should be able to quench but the Lushious Embraces of that Sweet Lady that had rais'd his Concupisence. Their prevailing Glances, I observ'd, soon took effect upon some Juvenal Gentlemen, whose Youthful Opinions of the Pleasures to be found in Love and Beauty, had render'd them, like Gunpowder, liable to be inflam'd with every sparkling Eye, as the other is to be blown up by the Casual touch of any Fire it shall meet with. The Baskets of Plumbs, Wallnuts, Pears, and Peaches, began now to be handed about from the *City-Bubble* to the *Suburbs-Jilt*; and Tittle-Tattles of Love were Bandied forwards and backwards, between the Tongues and Ears of those Amorous Frontiers of the Impatient Audience, who were forc'd to pacify themselves under their Longing Expectancies with Nuts and Damsons: Now and then brreaking out into *Bear-garden* Acclamations of *Show, show, show, show*; till at last, in answer to their loud-mouth'd Importunities, the Curtain was drawn up, and a Trunk-Breeches-King, in a Fools Cap, and a Feather in it, attended with his Cringing Nobility, some Court Jilts, and Two or Three Flattering Priests, which I suppose the Poet Thought to be as true a Representation of an Old *English* Court, as possibly he could think on. After these had entertain'd the listening Audience alittle with their Fustian Confabulations, they made their *Exeunt*, and the Scenes were shifted into a Library, where Fryar *Bacon*, by his Long Study, had Projected a Brazen-head, who was to Wall the Kingdom round with the same Mettle, had not the Devil catch'd him Napping, and broke his most wonderful Noddle into many Pieces.

The Priest grown Drowsie with much Reading, rub'd his Eyes, arose from his Elbow-Chair, and in my Opinion, seem'd, both by his Looks and Actions, much too Ignorant, as well as too Young, for such a Notable Undertaking. When he had Rav'd and Strutted about alittle with his *Magicians* Wand, like a *Hero* with his Truncheon in a Fit of Jealousie, he began, like a true Priest, to make large Promises to the People, of wonderful things which he very well knew would never come to pass: And after he had made a short Oration in praise of his *Brazen-head*; the Scene chang'd, and shut him up in his Study to Consult the Devil alittle further, how to bring his admirable Project to a Reputable Conclusion.

Then Enter'd the *Miller* and his Son *Ralph*. The Father I confess seem'd to be the same thing he imitated; and had a Countenance, so very

Pertinent

pertinent to his Profession, that he look'd as if (according to the Millers Maxime) his Conscience could dispence with taking five Pecks out of a Bushel. And as for his hopeful Progeny, who was the only Person we were desirous of seeing, I think he kept up to so true a behaviour of an *Ideot*, that it was enough to perswade the Audience, that he really was in Nature what he only Artfully represented. I could not but conclude, the Part was particularly adapted to his Genius, or he could never have exprefs'd the Humour with such agreeable simplicitie: But I fancy if he was to play the part of a *Wise man*, it would be quite out of his way, and puzzle him as much as it would a *Common-Whore* to behave herself in Company like a *Vertuous Woman*. There was nothing in the Part it self, but what was purely owing to his own gesture; for it was the *Comedian* only, and not the *Poet*, that render'd the Character diverting. To be plain, they both Acted and Became their Characters extreamly well; for I cannot but acknowledge, that I never saw any Body look more like a *Fool* than the *Son*, nor any Miller more like a *Cozening Knave* than the Father.

The next part of the *Droll*, that was chiefly diverting, was the *Country-Juftice*, whose Weaknefs and Indifcretion I fuppofe were defign'd to let the People know what ignorant Magiftrates have fometimes the administration of Juftice; and how common a thing it is for a Wife-man to Bow a Learned Head to an Empty Noddle in Authority. These were the chief of their Characters Jumbled confufedly together; with a Flying Shoulder of Mutton, dancing and finging Devils, and fuch like pieces of conjuration, by the Diabolical Friar *Bacon*. With whofe Magical Pranks the *Mob* were wonderfuly pleas'd, as well as greatly aftonifh'd. Having thus entertain'd us for about three Quarters of an hour, at laft with a moft fplendid Appearance of all their Lords and Ladies, they concluded their *Droll*. From amongft which glittering Affembly, one of the beft-mouth'd Orators fteps to the front of the Stage, and with a Cringing piece of formality, promifes the Audience to begin again in half an hour, as if they believ'd the people to be fuch Fools to fling away their Money fo unprofitably Twice in one day, when the feeing of them once is enough to tire any man of reafonable patience.

The Show being thus ended, my Friend ask'd me how I lik'd it? Truly, faid I, I think 'tis a very Moral Play, if the Spectators have fenfe enough to make a right ufe of it. At which faying, my Friend burft into a Laughter. Prithee, fays he, wherein lies the Morality of it? Why faid I, it will ferve to let us know how familiar a Prieft, notwithftanding his Holy Orders, may be with the Devil. How eafily the Clergy may impofe upon the Vulgar a belief of thofe things which never were nor can be. What a Blockhead may be a Juftice of Peace; how a Rich cunning Knave may have a Fool to his Son: How Old men love Young Bedfellowes; how a Woman will cheat her Father to oblige her Gallant; what Stratagems Lovers will Project to Accomplifh their Ends; and what *Jack*-Puddings men will make of themfelves to get a little Money. On my Word, fays he, you have made a rare ufe of it indeed. But I very much Queftion whether any Body elfe will be half fo much

B

the

the better for it; for it may be obſerv'd that *Bartholomew-Fair*-Drolls are like *State-Fireworks*, they never do any Body good, but thoſe who are concern'd in the Show.

From thence with much difficulty, we croſs'd over to the *Hoſpital-Gate*, being Jumbled about in the Crow'd like a couple of *Tories* at a *Whiggiſh* Election; over againſt which ſtood a very Comical Figure Gaping and Drumming, that his Beard wag'd up and down like an Aldermans Chin at a Lord Mayors Feaſt, when Chewing of a Gooſes Apron; and his Eyes rowld about like a Stallions at a Chriſtening, when he ſtands Godfather. Which occaſion'd ſome of the Ignorant Spectators, that ſtood crowding beneath, to cry out, *Lord, do but ſee how he ſtares at us, and Gnaſhes his Teeth as if he could eat us for looking at him.* On each ſide of him ſtood a Wax Baby, which look'd very Natural, inſomuch that it induced us to walk in and take a ſight of their whole Work; being much aſtoniſh'd at our firſt entrance of the Room, at the Livelineſs of the Figures, who ſat in ſuch eaſie Poſtures, and their Hands diſpos'd with ſuch a becoming freedom, that Life it ſelf could not have appear'd leſs ſtiff, or the whole Frame more Regular; the Eyes being fix'd with that Tenderneſs, which I apprehend as a great difficulty, that the moſt experienc'd of our Charming Ladies could not in an hours practice at her Glaſs, have look'd more ſoft and languiſhing. Whilſt we were thus viewing of the Temple of *Diana*, for under that Title they had diſtinguiſh'd their Show, up comes a Country Carter in his Bootes, Arm'd with his weapon of Correction, by which he Governs and Chaſtizes his five four-leg'd Subjects, belonging, as I ſuppoſe, to ſome Hay-Cart in the Market; as ſoon as the *Hobbadyboody* was brought to the door of the Room where the Figures were ſeated, he peepes in, and ſeeing, as he thought, ſuch a Number of Great Perſons, ſteps back and doffs his Hat, *Adsbleed,* ſays he, *I waant gooe in amang zo many vine Vouk, not I; what doſt ſend mau up to be made a game on? Pray gim mau my Money agan, vor I dount come here to be laugh'd at.* The Miſtreſs of the Show, with all the Arguments ſhe could uſe, had much ado to prevail upon the Fellow to go in; telling him wherein he was deceived; and that thoſe fine People, as he thought 'em, were only Waxwork which was the ſight that he was to ſee. That at laſt *Bumpkin* took Courage, and ventur'd into the Show-Room, but could not forbear making his Countrey Honours to the Babies, till he was ready to claw the Boards up with his Hobnails. When he had look'd round him, and pretty well feaſted his Eyes, he turns about to the Girl that ſhows 'em, ſays he, *They are all Woundy Silent. I pray you, Forzooth, can they Speak?* At which the Young Damſel fell a Laughing, ſaying, *You muſt Speak to 'em firſt, and then perhaps they'll Anſwer you.* With that the Loobily Ignoramus did as he was bid, crying to one of the Figures, *How d'ye Vorzooth? You in the Black-whood, Evaſth I'll give ye a Pwot en you'n Spake to me.* At which the whole Company burſt into a Laughter, which made the Fellow ſo angry, that in a paſſion he thus expreſt himſelf. *Adsheartly vounds, why what dye make a Gam at a body vor? A Plague Bran ye for a Pack of Zimpletons. Why I zee zome litte Vouk but O'er the Way, no higher than a Flaggon, I beleeve they are the Zons and Daughters of theſe Gentlevouk here, and they coud Tauk as well as I can* A Notable pert Gentlewoman ſtanding by him, ſays ſhe, *Well Countrey man, what would*

you

you think of that Lady you spoke to, for a Bedfellow? Ads my Loif, says he, *for all she looks so woundy gainly now she's drest, when she comes to pluck off her Paint and her Patches, and doff her vine Clouthes to come to Bed, she perhaps may look as Ugly as you do, vorsooth.* Which Clownish Repartee so dash'd the Lady out of Countenance, That her Blushes shew'd she had a modest Sense of her own Failings and Imperfections

Having satisfied our Curiosities with Arts nicest imitation of Human Nature, we return'd again into the Multitude, considering what next Folly we could commit, that would yield us any tollerable Diversion. To see more *Drolls* we thought would be as ridiculous, as 'tis for a couple of Sots to Stagger from Tavern to Tavern all day long, where the Entertainment is still the same, distinguishable by no difference but the *Name* and the *Sign*; so that we were quite tired with that sort of Fooling. And upon further consideration of the matter in debate, we at last agreed to spend an hour in a Musick-Booth. In pursuance of our design, we press'd thro the Crow'd, till we cross'd the Fair to the Norweststide; where *Musick-Houses* stood as thick one by another, as *Bawdy-houses* in *Chick-lane*; and at every door two or three hanging look'd *Scaramouches*, who, rather than to encourage People to *walk in,* were, as I imagin'd a means rather to afright 'em from entering, for fear of having their Throats Cut, or their Pockets pick'd by such an Ill-favour'd Gang of Raskally Rapskallions. But, however, hoping to fare as well as the rest of our Neighbours, we ventur'd into one of their Diabolical Academies, where we suppos'd all sorts of Wickedness were practic'd, for the good Instruction of unwary Youth, who are too apt to imbibe the poisonous Draughts that flow from these pernicious Fountains, to which we often owe the sorrowes of our Riper years; and never clear our foul Stomachs from those bitter belches which the venom they have once suck'd from these unwholsome Springs will ever leave behind it.

At our first Entrance, the Dancing in such several disguises, made it appear to me like a Rendesvouz of Gipsies upon the Election of a New King, or like so many strolling Beggars making Merry in a Barn. As soon as ever the Curtain was put by, and we approach'd the Bar, a crack'd Bell was Rung by a Weather-beaten Strumpet, dress'd up in White, as if she had been going to Beg some Rogue of a Gallant from the Gallows. No sooner had the untunable Alarm reach'd the Ears of the dispers'd Attendants, but a Frizzle-pated Suck-fosset with a Head bloated with much Tipling, as round as a Foot-ball, and an Indico Muckender hanging down to his Toes, according to the Mode of a *City-Beau-Dravel,* follow'd by half a dozen of his Dancing Scarecrowes, some in Masques as Ugly as the Faces of those who were without, all bidding us *Wellcome* in such hoarse Flux'd Voices, that their Speech sounded more like the Croaking of Ravens, or growling of the fourth string of a Crack'd Base, than like the Organs of Humane Utterance. Who seeing us look a degree above Common Customers, I suppose they were in hopes we would prove the greater Bubbles; and as a means to Encourage us to the greater Extravagancy, they Conducted us to the further End of their Fools-Paradise, and plac'd us upon the Hoistings (amongst *Cracks, Rakes* and *Bullies,* of the better Quality) which separate Apartment was exempt from the dishonour

of

of inferiour Liquors, and nothing fuffer'd to difgrace your Table beneath a half Crown *Whore*, or a half Crown *Flask*.

As foon as our Wine came, and we had fill'd out a Glafs, the Kettle-drums and Trumpets began to exprefs their willingnefs to oblige us; which was perform'd with that harmonious excellence, that no *Sowgelder* with his *Horn*, and *Cooper* with his *Adds* and *Driver*, could have gratified our Ears, with more delightful Mufick. This was fucceeded by a Confort of Fiddlers, with whofe Melodious Diddle-Diddle I was fo affected, that it made my Teeth Dance in my Mouth like a fit of a Quartan Ague. The next piece of Harmony that laid Siege to our Ears, was a moft admirable New Ballad, Sung in two Parts by feven Voices. I call'd the *Drawer*, and bid him ask them if they were not Singing the *Cat-Catch*, who brought me word *No*; and that it was a very fine Play-houfe Song, fet by the beft Compofer in *England*. Why then, faid I, pray tell your Songfters, they deferve to be whip'd at the Carts-Arfe for attempting to Sing it; and that I had rather hear a Boy beat *Round-Headed Cuckolds Come Dig*, upon his Snappers, or an old Barber Ring *Whittingtons* Bells upon a Cittern, than hear all the Mufick they could make. Which Meffage, I fuppofe, the Fellow was afraid to tell 'em, left they fhould Crack his Crown with the Bafe-Fiddle-Stick.

That we might have a Tafte of all their Varieties, the next Inftruments they betook themfelves to, were the Haut-boys, which are undoubtedly the beft Wind-Pipes in the World, Ill plaid upon, to Scare a Man out of his Wits; and I dare Swear would raife the Devil, the Father of all Difcord, much fooner than ever Fryar *Bacon*, or *Cornelius Agrippa*, could with their Diabolical Invocations. For my part, I declare their difproportion'd Notes, and Imperfect Cadencies, had fuch an effect upon my Ears, that I thought their Noife would have burft my Head in as many pieces as Gunpowder does a Granado Shell, and put my whole Microcofm into fuch a diforderly Trembling, that had they Tooted a little longer, I believe I fhould have been all dif-jointed: for fuch Mufick is enough to make any Mans Bones dance out of their Sockets; and put his whole body under a painful diflocation.

The harfhnefs of their Notes, having like a Ring of Bells, or a Peal of Cannon, Box'd our Ears into a Deafnefs, they now began to treat our Eyes with as taking an Entertainment; and prefented us with a Dance in imitation of a Foot-pads Robbery; and he that Acted the Thief, I proteft did it fo much like a Rogue, that had he not often commited the fame thing in Earneft, I am very apt to believe he could never have made fuch a *Jeft* on't; Firing the Piftol, Striping his Victim, and Searching his Pockets, with fo much Natural humour, feeming Satisfaction, and Dexterity, that he fhow'd himfelf an abfolute Mafter of what he pretended to. And I cannot forbear having fo little Charity as to fancy, that his laft Caper will be fo far off the Ground, that he will quite lofe his Breath before he comes down again,

The next that prefented her felf to our View was a Bouncing Beldam, who had as much Flefh on her Bones as a *Lincoln-fhire Heifer*; that her Hips, without the help of *Fardingales*, look'd as round as the Stern

of

of a *Dutch-Fly-Boat*, and her Buttocks trembled when she Stirr'd, like a *Quaking-Pudding*: And had she not been Lac'd up to the best advantage, her Skin would have hung down in Folds like the Hide of the *Rhinoceros*. The admirable Qualifications of this Lady, were to Dance with Glasses full of Liquor upon the Backs of her Hands, to which she gave Variety of Motions, without Spilling, expressing in her Exercise as much Prodigality, as if Riches, Fame and Honour, had been the Rewards of her Foolery, putting her Greasie Corps into a great Sweat, and Slav'd as much at her paultery Performances, as a fat Porter at *Nine-Pins*, in the *Easter-Holidays*, or a Brawny Milk-woman on a *May-day*, till at last having quite lost her Strength by an expence of Spirits, she was forced to conclude her Awkward Steps, and *Elephant* Capers, resting her unweildy Carcass on the nearest Bench, where she Panted like a Race Horse, that had won the Plate, or a Bear-dog after a Let-go, the Mob declaring their Approbation and Applause, by claping their Hands, and knocking their Heels, expressing thereby their own Satisfaction; as well as their Aprobation of the wabbling Squab, with whose Unpolished Saltation they were so highly Delighted.

The next Figure that appear'd, was a Youthful Damsel, who to render her more Charming, was dress'd up in her Holland Smock, and Fring'd Petticoat, like a Rope-dancer; having disarm'd most of the Swords Men in the Room, she Steps into the Center of the Booth and there began to handle 'em as dextrously as a *Welch Shoppardess* does her Knitting Needles, putting her self into a Circular Dance, wherein she turn'd as Merrily Round as the Flyer of a Jack, or as Nimbly as a Gig under the Scourge of a School-Boy; shifting her Swords, to all parts of her Face and Breast, to the very great amazement of Countrey Fools, and the very little danger of her own Carcase; when by her unalterable Circumflection, she had supply'd the defects and weakness of the Liquor, and made most of the Company Drunk and Giddy, with observing the Nimbleness of her Tail, which according to the *Knife-Grinders* Song, ran *Round, and around, and around-a*, she gave a stamp with her Foot, like a Doe-Rabbit after bucking, which serv'd as a Period to her Dance, which according to Custom, was rewarded with a Clap, being the true *Theatre* and *Musick-House* method of expressing Thanks or Approbations, which makes the Ladies belonging to both Places very apt to reward the Love of their Gallants after the like manner.

This was succeeded by abundance of Insipid Stuff, so very sorrily design'd, and so wretchedly perform'd, that instead of either Laughter or Delight, it begot in me nothing but Blushes, and Contempt, that I thought it an abuse to Humane Shape, for any thing that bore the Proportion of either Sex, to behave themselves so Ostentatiously Foolish, so Odiously Impudent, so Intollerably Dull, and Void of all Humour, Order or Design, that there is more Diversion in the Accidental Gestures of one Ape, than in all the Study'd Performances of the whole Company of pretending Vagabonds; we therefore think it not worth while to Trouble the Reader with any further Particulars, of their ridiculous poor Pedantick Fooleries, but leave 'em to a further Shameful Exposing of their own Ignorance, and give him a Rough Draught

C

of

of the Company, who cheifly frequent thefe Scandalous Nurferies of all Vice, Vanity, and Villany.

Some Companies were fo very odly mix'd, that there was no manner of Coherence in the Figure of any one Perfon and another: One perhaps fhould appear in a Lac'd Hat, Red Stockins, Puff Wig, and the like, as Prim as if going to the Dancing-School. The next a *Butcher*, with his Blew Sleeves, and Woollen Apron, as if juft come from the Slaughter-houfe. A third, a Fellow in a *Torkfhire* Cloth-Coat, with a Leg laid over his Oaken Cudgel, the Head of which being a Knob of the fame Stuff, as Serviceable as a Proteftant Flail, and big as a *Hackney* Turnep. Another in a Soldiers Habit, and look'd as Peery as if he thought every frefh Man that came in, a Conftable; thefe mix'd with Women of as different appearances: One, in a Straw-Hat and Blew Apron, with Impudence enough in her Face, to dafh a Begging Clergyman out of Countenance; and he that can Publickly ask an Alms in a Parfons Gown, if he has Title to wear it, one would reafonably think has Impudence enough to Face any Body. Another, Drefs'd up in Hood, Scarf, and Top-knot, with her Cloaths hung on according to the *Drury-Lane* Mode, as if fhe could fhake 'em off and leap into Bed, in the Twinkling of a Bed-ftaff. A third, in a white Sarfnet Hood, and a Pofie at her Bofome, as if fhe was come from the Funeral of fome good Neighbour, that Dy'd in Child-bed; and amongft the reft, a Girl of about a Dozen Years of Age, whom I fuppofe, they were early draging up in the wicked Ways of Shame and Mifery; that her Riper Years might in no meafure give her a Senfe of her Unhappinefs, and by Checking her in her Lewd Practices, render her but a daftard Sinner. Thefe were at one Table, and of one Society; and tho' feverally and Singularly dreft, yet I could do no other then Conjecture from their Carriage and Phyfiognomy, that they were under one and the fame Influence; and that their unlucky Stars had infus'd the like Evil Genius into every Perfon among 'em; for the Women Look'd like Jilts, the Men Swore like Pick-pockets, and both were as Drunk as Swine, and as Merry as Beggars.

Juft beneath us, on the fide of the Hoiftings, fat a Couple of Madams over a Stone Bottle of Ale, who by their want of Stays, the Airinefs of their Drefs, the Improvement of their Complexion by Paint, and the multitude of Patches, to add a gentle Air to their Servile Countenances, we could guefs to be no other than Ladies of that wretched Quality, whofe *Pride*, *Poverty*, *Leachery*, and *Lazinefs*, had reduc'd them under a Neceffity of expofing themfelves to Sale at a fmall Purchafe, for in came a Fellow, that I have heard Cry Brufhes, and *Moufe-Traps* about Town, and a Smith along with him, that I have feen hawk about *Iron Candelfticks*, and being almoft Drunk, their Brains ran on Coney-Catching, and they muft needs, after two or three awkward Scrapes and Compliments, beg the Ladies good Company to drink a Bottle of *Cyder*, which the willing Damfels, without any manner of Scruple, very readily comply'd with, fo they all remov'd to another Table, which they thought was more Commodious for their Entertainment, where the old Coxcombs Court to their Ladies, was fo fingular and Comical, that it made the whole Company Obfervators of their Ridiculous Behaviour, who at laft difcovering by the Peoples Tittering, they were become a Publick Jeft, agreed with their Miftreffes, as I suppose, to remove to some more Private Place convenient, for the finishing their Intrigue; but as they were Leading their Condescending Madams out of the Booth, with abundance of formal Ceremony, the Gallants, notwithstanding their Holiday Cloaths, being known to some of the Guests, were accosted as they made their *Exit*, with, *Will you buy a Mouse-Trap, or a Rat-Trap? Will you buy a Cloths Brush, a Hat Brush, or a Comb Brush?* That they sneak'd off with their Doxies, as much asham'd as a Perjur'd *Evidence* out of *Westminster-Hall*, or a *Puritan* out of a *Bawdy-House.*

At another Table sat a parcel of Rural Sots, who with the Gross Spirits of common Belch, were elevated to such a Pitch of Merriment, that they began to Talk Bawdy, like old Women at a Gossiping, and Swear Ads-hearthwounds, as fast as a Gamester Curses the Dice, when he meets with Ill Fortune, and show'd as many ungainly Postures over their Liquor, as a parcel of Swine made Drunk with *Hog-Wash.* These, to make their Ale run down more chearful, had got with them a Female Fidler, who had charg'd her Tun-belly'd Carcase, like the rest, with more Guzzle, than her Legs were able to carry, and behav'd her-self in Sight of the whole Company, with such Unaparallel'd Impudence in Singing Bawdy Songs with a Hickuping Voice, which she endeavour'd to improve with intollerable Scrapes upon her Crack'd Instrument, that I was afraid her Nauseous Behaviour, together with her Odious Discord, would have rais'd in me such an Aversion to both Women and Musick, that I should never hereafter, agree with the common Opinion, and esteem 'em as the Choicest of Blessings on this Side Heaven.

Then in came a couple of Seamen, in their Canvas Jackets, just step'd from on Board, to give themselves a Taste of the Fairs relishable Delights, expressing in their Looks such wonderful Satisfaction, that a *Bayliff,* at a Prize, or a *Butcher* at a *Bull-baiting,* could not have showd more signs of Gladness; at last one of them Order'd the Musick to Play an old *Wapping* Jig; and plucking out of his Pocket a clean white Handkerchief, which, I suppose, he borrow'd of his *Land-Lady* on purpose to Dance with, being no more able to Cut a Caper without that in his Hand, than a Fellow is able to Dance the *Morris* without his *Bells,* or a Beau Court a *Lady* without his *Snush-box* in his Hand; thus equip'd for the business, he steps into the middle of the Booth, and after he had made his Honours with as much Grace, as a Cow might make a Court'sie, he begins to Caper and Firk-it round the Room, entertaining us with so many Antick Steps, *Merry Andrews Postures,* and *Country Cuts* and *Shuffles* with his Feet, that no *Jack-Adams,* at *Clerkenwell*-Feast, or a Drunken *Ploughman* upon my Ladies Birth Day, could have been more Diverting; his Comrade crying out every now and then, *Gad ha Mercy Robin! Now* Kate *of* Dover's *step! Chear up my Lad! Ah bravely done Boy! Now for a Sea-Pye, and a Can of Phlip!* Thus he Jigg'd it about, with his greasie Hat in one Hand, and his Muckender in t'other, till he was out of Breath, like a *Thrasher* at a Wake when he Dances for a Favour; where he that Dances Longest is always allow'd to Dance Best. Having thus put a Period to his Wild Boree, his Companion met him with a Quartern of Brandy, and after he had Clap'd him on the Side for Encouragement, as a *Butcher* does his *Bull-dog,* instead of spitting in his Mouth, he refresh'd him with a

Cogue,

Cogue, and made him fit for t'other Let-go; who fiting down with his Arms on Kimboe, feem'd as Proud of what he'd done, as an *Admiral* that had beaten the French Fleet, or a *Mountebank* that had drawn a Tooth with a Touch, before a Multitude of Spectators.

What further lay within our Obfervation, were the fundry forts of Women who fat ready upon fmall purchafe to gratifie the Luft of every Drunken Libertine; fome very well dreft, and in Masks; who notwith-ftanding their appearance, were as ready at your beck as a Porter Plying at a Streets Corner; Others bare-Fac'd, and in mean Garbs, whofe Poverty feem'd equal with their Impudence, and that, fo fulfome and Prepofterous, that they are as great Antidotes to expel the Poifon, of Luft, as the Modeft Counterfeit Behaviour of a Cunning pretty Harlot, is a means to enforce defire, and beget a liking. A third, fort of Scoundrel *Strumpets* in *Blew-Aprons* and *Straw-Hats*, who by taking much *Mercury*, or the Loud bawling of *Oyfters* about the Streets, were as Hoarfe as a *Jackpudding* at the latter End of the Fair; thefe were Good Subjects to the Government, and Contribute more towards the Maintainance of his Majefties Foot Guards, than any People in the Nation, for every one has a Souldier or two at her Tail, of whom fhe takes as much Care, as a Bitch does of her Puppies.

Having here taken Notice, of moft of the Particulars that lay within our View, by paying our Reckoning, we purchas'd our Redemption from this Epitomy of *Hell*; and being now almoft Dark, we took a Turn round the outfide of the Fair, on the Back-fide of the Booths, where we found feveral Emblems of the Worlds Giddinefs: Children Lock'd up in Flying Pews, who Infenfibly climb'd upwards like Im-metorious State-Tools, who knew not whither they were going, but being once Elevated to a certain height, came down according to the Circular Motion of the Sphere they mov'd in; and being forc'd to decline from their Meridan Altitude, were reduc'd to the low Station from whence they firft took their Rife; reflecting on their paft Pleafure, with a bundance of diffatisfaction, Envying thofe who are got in their Room, and heartily bemoan'd their want of Money, or Favour, which remov'd them from their Poft.

Thefe Whirligigs, fays my Friend, may be very properly apply'd to the Common Fate of Great Men: For when a Man is once rifiing, it is not very difficult for him to rife to the Top, but 'tis Impoffible for him, as you may fee by thefe, to continue long at the fame Pitch; for the Intereft of him that Governs the Wheel, and the Politick Mo-tion of Affairs for Publick Safety, require fome to be Rifing, and others Falling: For this World is but Fortunes Well, and Mankind are the Buckets thereof, and it muft of Neceffity ever be fo, that the Winding Up of one, will be the Letting Down of another.

From thence we mov'd in the Stream, and pafs'd by a couple of *Poppet-fhows*, where *Monkeys* in the Ballconies, were Imitating Men, and Men making themfelves *Monkeys*, to engage fome of the weaker part of the Multitude, as Women and Children, to ftep in and pleafe them-felves with the wonderful Agility of their Wooden Performers; thefe

we

we pass'd by with as much Contempt as a Hungry *Taylor* at *Easter*, does a *Fleet-ditch* Furmity Woman, or a Prodigal Debauchee an old Mistress. We squeez'd on amongst the rest, till we came again to the *Hospital-Gate*, which we enter'd with as little Ease as a Good Christian, Impatient of his Dinner, gets out of the Church, when Sermon is Ended, till at last we came into the *Cloisters*, where we met such a parcel of Eagle-Ey'd Sparks, and heard such a Whispering and Humming of G——d D——mes, *She's a* Bitch, *and t'others a* Whore; *And that's a fine* Woman, *t'others a pretty* Creature; That I thought the People were all Mad, and that this Place was a *Bedlam* for Lovers. A Gentleman with a Red-face, who my Friend told me, was fam'd at all Gaming Ordinaries, for a wonderful Similizer, steps up to a very pert Lady, who I suppose, was not for his Turn, and claps his bare Hand in her Neck: *Dear Madam*, says he, *You are as Cold as a Cricket in an Icehouse*: She turning short about, look'd upon him, and reply'd, *If you Please to clap your Fiery Face to my Backside, 'twill be the ready way to warm me*: At which smart Return, all that heard it fell a Laughing: The Gentleman thinking it a little Inconsistent with his Honour, to be thus Put Upon, had a great mind to redeem his Credit, by adding, *Indeed Madam, I find Your Tongue's much Nimbler than the rest of your Members, for your Body moves like a Loaded Waggon up a Hill: Dear Sir*, says she, *You Look so like an Honest Gentleman, that I am bound in Gratitude, to return you at least an Empty Cart, for your Loaded Waggon; and as for the Hill, Pray Sir*, let it be Holbourn, *and I don't Question but your Good Life, in time may direct you to the Use and Application, of both*; *so Sir, your Humble Servant*. And away she step'd into a Raffling Shop, where some Civil Gentlemen follow'd her, and to reward her Wit, Loaded her and her She-Friend, that was with her, with Nick-nacks, and Guarded her into a Coach from the Insolence of the Town Cormorants, who had a wonderful mind to be Snaping at so fair a Bait.

This Rendesvouz of *Jilts, Whores*, and *Sharpers*, began now to be very full, insomuch, that the Sowr Breaths of Corrupt Carcases, and the *Turpentine* Belches that were ever and anon thrown into our Nostrils in the Crowd, were so offensive, that the Pumping of a *Derby-Ale* Cellar, or the removal of an old *Close-stool-pan*, could not have surpris'd our Sense with a more intollerable Nosegie. This we were forc'd to endure, or quit the Place, which we were unwilling to do, till we had made a more Nice Inspection into the Pomps and Vanities of this Wicked World. To further discover which, we went into one of the Shops, which we saw most Crowded, and as Poor Spectators, with willing Hearts and low Pockets, we stood in the Rear, and like Boretto Pentioners at the *Groom-Porters*, peep'd over the Shoulders of those that raffled, among whom, I observ'd, this Ridiculous Vanity, that whatsoever the Gentlemen won, they presented to the Fair Lady that stood next, tho as great Strangers one to another, as Doctor B——gs, and the *Whore* of *Babylon*. You are Insensible, says my Friend, of the Cunning that is us'd by *Sharpers*, to make this kind of Diversion turn to a good Account; that pretty sort of Woman, who receives so many Presents, to my Knowledge is Mistress to him who is now handling the Box, who has no other Business, but to improve such a lucky Minute to his Maintainance, and he seems you see, to be an utter Stranger to that Lady he's so kind to, and only makes her Mistress of his Winnings, purely to draw the other Gentlemen on to do the like, that what Presents they foolishly bestow on her, to Night, may serve to furnish his Pockets for the Hazard-Table, on the next Morrow.   D   Being

Being tired with this Paftime, we adjourn'd from thence, and crept up a Pair of Stairs as narrow and as fteep, as the Stone Steps of a *Bell-frey*, over which was Written in Golden Capitals in two or three Places, *The Groom Porters*; defign'd, as I fuppofe, for Fools to Underftand it was the Honefter Place, for his Name being there, and that they might as fairly fling away their Money at his Table, as in any Place in Chriftendom: When with the danger of our Necks, we had climb'd to the Top, we ftep'd into a little Room on the Left Hand, where *Lawyers Clerks*, and Gentlemens *Footmen*, were mix'd *Higgle-de-piggle-de*, like Knaves and Fools at an *Eaft-India-houfe* Auction, and were Wrangling over their Sixpences with as much Eagernefs, as fo many *Mumpers* at a Church-door on a *Sacrament Day*, about the True Divifion of a Good Chriftians Charity. Being quickly furfeited with the Boyifh Behaviour of thefe Callow *Rakes*, we mov'd from thence into the next Rooms, where a parcel of old Batter'd *Bullies*, fome with Carbonadoed Faces, and others with Pimpgennet Nofes, were feated as clofe round a Great Table as Country *Attorneys* in a Stage Coach, at the Conclufion of a Term; amongft 'em, here and there a declining Tradefman, who, I fuppofe, was ready to ftart into fome Foreign Plantation, and came hither, to acquire the Qualifications of a *Libertine*, that their Portion in this World may be a Merry Life, and a fhort: Curfes amongft thefe were as profufely fcatter'd as Lyes among Travellers, and as many Eyes lifted towards the Heavens in Confufion to their Stars, as there are in a Storm to Implore Safety: Money was tofs'd about as if a ufelefs Commodity, and feveral parts of the Story of the *Prodigal Son*, were here acted to a miracle. When Four had the Good Fortune to come before Seven, or Ten before Eight, the Breeches of the Lofers, were fo Nettled they were unable to keep their Seats, and could no more keep the Ends of their Fingers out of their Mouths, than a Porter when he plucks off his Hat, can forbear Scratching of his Head. The Dice had far more Influence upon, 'em than the Planets, for every Man Chang'd Countenance according to the Fortune of the Caft; and fome of them I am fure fhew, all the Paffions in half an Hour, Incident to Humane Nature.

He that made the moft obfervable Figure amongft 'em, was a *Butcher* in his white Frock, with a Head as large as a *Sarazens*, and Cheeks as plump as a *Sowgelder's* when he Proclaims his Profeffion by his Semi-circular Trumpet; his Beard tho' in Carnival time, was as long as a *Hackney* Writers in the middle of a Long Vacation, and look'd as Frowzy and Irregular as the Gyants Whiskers in *Guild-Hall*, who feems fo terrible to Young Apprentices. The Hair of his Head being as Greafie as the Fur of a Cooks Cap that wears one, and Shined with the *Pomatum* of *Beef* and *Mutton*, like a Satten Cap upon the Noddle of an *Independant* Teacher. I could not but take Notice, when ever he made his Stake, he cry'd, *Go again*, when he clap'd down his Money on the Board; which ferv'd me to Underftand he was a true *Hockly I'th' Hole* Sports-man, it being the fame expreffion they ufe to their Dogs, after the firft Let-go. I obferv'd he was attended with great Lucks enough to make us believe according to the Burlefque of *Ovid's* Saying, That Fortune favours Fat Folks, or that her Mope-Ey'd Ladyfhip, like a true *Sow*, was a great Lover of Blood, Filth and Naftinefs: When ever he handled the Dice, he had fo Lucky a Devile in the Box, or at his Elbow, that he very feldom threw out under three or four Hands holding in, which Occafion'd his peevifh Antagonifts to fet him with fuch Sowr Countenances, that no Lover that had loft his Miftrefs, or Client that had loft his Caufe, could have Contracted his Face into a more fretful Pofture; length of time having made this Diverfion as dull as the reft, we left the Lofers to recover their Loffes, and the *Butcher* to bring his Hogs to a fair Market, returning down Stairs with as much Care and Caution of Tumbling Head foremoft, as he that goes down *Green Arbor Court*-Steps in the middle of Winter. When we were got fafe to the bottom, being quite tir'd with the fundry Follies we had feen, and the Brain-breaking Noifes we

had

had heard, my Friend defir'd my Company into *Charter-houfe-Lane*, where he was Oblig'd to make a fhort Vifit to a Patient, leaving me at an Ale-houfe hard by to Divert my felf in his Abfence with a Pipe of Tobacco, which I did accordingly, and refrefh'd my felf with a Pot of Excellent Englifh Liquor, which was as Comfortable to my Pallat, after our Troublefome Survey, as a Down-Bed to the Gall'd Haunches of a weary Travellour. By that time I had light my Pipe, in comes a couple of Old Fellows, who look'd as if they were the Superannuated Servants of fome Great Man, who to exempt himfelf from the Charge of keeping 'em, when paft their Labour, and to reward the Faithful Service of their Youth, had got 'em into an Hofpital; they Seated themfelves down in the next Box, and Call'd for a Pot of warm'd Ale, over which, after they had Accommodated their Lanthorn Jaws with a Pipe of Tobacco, they began to bemoan fome great Oppreffions that were Impos'd upon 'em, by the Ruler of their Society, whom they Charg'd with thefe following Accufations, beginning their Complaint after this Sorrowful manner:

I Remember, fays one, Two Old Proverbs from my Youth, which, alas! I have found too True in my Age: New Lords, New Laws; *and,* When the Old One's gone, feldome comes a Better; *and Efaith Brother, as another Old Saying fays,* We have found both too true to be made a Jeft on; *for our allowance formerly, if any of us were Sick and out of Commons, was* Five Shillings *and* Eleven-pence *a Week, but now our Good Mafter, Providence reward him for his Kindnefs, has reduc'd us to* Four Shillings *and* Five pence; *which, let me tell you, Brother, is a great Abatement in fo fmall a Sum; and a very great Abufe of the Pious Defign and Charitable Good Will of the Donor: We likewife, when we were Sick, had a Bufhel of Coals per week, allow'd us, to warm our Old Nofes, under our Infirmities; but now are ftinted to juft half the Quantity, thanks to our Good Mafter, for his Chriftian Love and Kindnefs to us.*

Sometime fince, a Brother Pentioner was Sick, with a Violent Flux, from the middle of September, *to within* Ten days *of* Chriftmas, *in which time his Nurfe went feveral times to the Mafter, to obtain a Grant of the* Five Shillings *and* Eleven Pence *per Week, and a whole Bufhel of Coals, declaring that his fhort Allowance was not fufficient to Support him in his Low Condition. But notwithstanding all her reasonable Pleas and Importunate Solicitations on her Patients behalf, the Mafter would give no Ear to her Petitions, not taking into his Confideration the Coldnefs of the Weather, or Tedioufnefs of his Sicknefs.*

Befides our Diet is much Abated of our Ancient Allowance, neither is the Meat fo Good.

And notwithstanding thefe great Abufes, and Retrenchments, of us the Poor Pentioners, he has procur'd his own Sallary to be advanc'd, from Fifty *to* Two Hundred Pounds, *per Annum: Who keeps his Coach, and lives as Great as the Governour of a Town, inftead of the Mafter of an Hofpital; but withal gives this Example of Frugality, that he allows but half a Crown a Week, to his Trencher-Scraper, for his Coach-mans Diet, for which he is Oblig'd to afford him two Meales a day; therefore Judge you what the Poor Fellow gets by his Boarder.*

Some Years fince upon the Twelfth of December, *which is held as an Anniverfary in Commemoration of the Founder, the Reader being Abfent, upon fome Extraordinary Occafions, was difappointed by one who promis'd to Officiate for him, and the Congregation was difmifs'd without Prayers. Notwithstanding the Mafter was in Holy Orders, and at the fame time prefent in the Chappel.*

Indeed, reply'd the other, *'tis a fad thing we fhould be fo ferv'd; but fince we can't help it, we muft Content our felves, I think, with the Cold Comfort, of an Old Saying, viz.* What Can't be Cur'd, muft be Endur'd; *for Complaint without the Profpect of Redrefs, is like a Mans Venting his Anger towards another, by Talking to himfelf.*

By this time, my Friend came in, to whom I Communicated what I overheard, who made light of it, as if they were fuch Practical Abufes, as were fcarce worth Liftening to; faying, You never knew any Confiderable *Hofpital* in your Life, but the poor Pentioners live like common Seamen in an *Eaft-India* Veffel, whofe Allowances are fo fhort Home-wards Bound, they are but juft kept alive, in a Starving Condition, whilft the Officers grow Fat at a Plentiful Table, and Pinch Eftates in a little Time, by Abridging the Juft Dues of their Floating Society.

Thus heartily tir'd with our Days Ramble, we paid our Reckoning, and pofted Home to Bed, with as Good an Apetite to Reft, as a New Married Lover had to the Embraces of his Bride the firft Night, or a Hungry Ploughman, to a Plum Pudding on a Sunday, when he had Walk'd Three Mile from Church.

POSTSCRIPT.

POSTSCRIPT.

THe Wonderful *Eclipse*, which, according to the promises of *Astronomers*, was to bring the wicked World within *Ames Ace* of the Day of Judgment, tho Invisible to us in *London*, by reason of a Stinking Fog that arose from wreaking Dunghills, Distillers Fats, and Piping Hot Close-Stool-pans, which as the Learned say, could neither be rarified nor dispers'd till the Eclipse was over, by reason that the Beames of the Sun were intercepted by the Moones Body. Yet it is asserted by Letters from many Credible Persons in several Countries, *Who I hope are all well, as I am at this present Writing, praised be ——— for it*; That the *Eclipse* was seen by many Thousands, as plain as ever the Old Woman see the Needle in the Barn-door, who enquir'd (after she pretended to see the Needle) where abouts the Barn stood. But, however, to Confirm our Infallible *Planet-Peepers* in their Unerring Judgments, It was seen upon the Road by many Travellours, especially by Strolling Tinkers and their Budget-bearing Trulls, Scotch Pedlars, Gipsies, Vagabonds, and Cadators; who, if you clear but their Eyes with a Cup of humming Liquor, are able to see *Faries* Dance, *Spirits* Walk, *Witches* Fly, *Prodigies* in the Clouds, Blemishes in the Sun, and Worlds in the Moon; and since our *Star-gazers* on their behalf, have such Good Evidence to prove the matter of fact, I think we had as good put the Contest out of dispute, and agree with what they say, whose Business it is to know most of the matter. But as a further proof of the *Eclipse*, which, is still ridicul'd amongst some obstinate unbelievers, These following persons do say, or think, they see it as plain in the Town, as ever 'twas seen in the Countrey.

A *Vintner* behind the *Change*, being very desirous of making a clear discovery of this dangerous Interposition, got a piece of Clay, and bestow'd an hours time in stopping up the bottom of his Cullendar, all but the Middle Hole, thro' which he peepes from Nine till Eleven, and does think he see the *Moon* or a *Cloud* between the *Sun* and the *Cullender*, but cannot be positive which; and therefore his Evidence is of little Validity.

An *Upholsterer* in *Cornhill*, being Curious also of being as Wise as the rest of his Neighbours, carries a Looking-glass out of his Shop into *Stocks-Market*, and after he had Earnestly look'd for about half an hour, and had just obtain'd a small Glimpse of the *Eclipse*, a Porter coming by with a Heavy Burthen. by accident stumbled, and put the Corner of his Bundle between the Upholsterer's Neck and Shoulders, Knocks him down, breaks the Looking Glass, and the Porter recovering himself, march'd forward with his Load; up rises the fallen Gazer from the Ground, with nothing but the Frame and Back-Board in his hand; and shaking his Head at his Missfortune, thus express'd himself to the people, *Alas! Alas! I fear the Terrible Effects of this* Eclipse *will be very fatal to poor* England; *for if just a Glimpse of it shall bring a Man to this disaster, may Providence defend the whole Kingdom from its Malicious Influence.*

Happening to be in Company with a very famous *Astrologer*, I was willing to enquire a little into what Effects he thought this *Eclipse*, that had made such a bustle, would have upon that part of the World to which twas visible, more especially *England*. *Why*, says he, *because you ask me the Question Modestly, I'll Tell you, Master, I do understand from the Authentick Censures of* Albumazer *and* Ptolemy, concerning the Circumvolution of Celestial Bodies, which procure perpetual mutability in this Lower Reign, that this great *Eclipse* being at the new of the Moon, when she first puts on her Horns, does infallibly predict as many Cuckolds to be at *Horn-Fair* this year, as have been seen there this seven years. Many Litigious Law-Lovers this year will Sell their Coats to contend for the value of a Button; and the Lawyers prate the Fools into compliance by bringing them to poverty. The Poor will die this year faster than the Rich, because there is a Hundred of the one, to one of the other. The Fingers of Envy will pick out the Eyes of many a Mans Reputation, and the Affections of Women will be as easily gain'd and as hardly preserv'd as ever. To be plain, I believe we shall have much such another World on't, as we had last year, and so, I suppose we shall not differ in opinion.

F I N I S.

THE
LONDON
SPY.

For the *Month* of October, 1699.

PART XII.

By the Author of the Trip to *JAMAICA.*

LONDON,
Printed and Sold by *J. How,* in the *Ram-Head-Inn-Yard* in
Fanchurch-street, 1699.

Books Sold by J. How, *in the Ram-Head-Inn-Yard in Fanchurch-Street;* J. Weld, *at the* Crown *between the Temple-Gates in* Fleet-street; *and Mrs.* Fabian, *at* Mercers-Chappel *in* Cheap-side.

1. SOt's Paradise: Or the Humours of a Derby-Ale-House: With a Satyr upon the Ale. Price Six Pence.

2. A Trip to *Jamaica*: With a True Character of the People and Island. Price Six Pence.

3. *Eclesia & Factio.* A Dialogue between *Bow-Steeple-Dragon,* and the *Exchange-Grashopper.* Price Six Pence.

4. The Poet's Ramble after Riches. With Reflections upon a Country Corporation. Also the Author's Lamentation in the time of Adversity. Price Six Pence.

5. The London Spy, the First, Second, Third, Fourth, Fifth, Sixth, Seventh, Eighth, Ninth, Tenth, Eleventh, and Twelfth Parts. To be Continued *Monthly.* Price Six Pence Each.

6. A Trip to *New-England.* With a Character of the Country and People, both English and Indians. Price Six Pence.

7. Modern Religion and Ancient Loyalty. A Dialogue. Price Six Pence.

8. The World Bewitch'd. A Dialogue between Two Astrologers and the Author. With Infallible Predictions of what will happen in this Present Year, 1699. From the *Vices* and *Villanies* Practis'd in *Court, City* and *Country.* Price Six Pence.

9. A Walk to *Islington:* With a Description of New *Tunbridge-*VVells, and *Sadler's Musick-*House. Price Six Pence.

10. The Humours of a Coffee-House: A Comedy. Price Six Pence.

11. A Frolick to Horn-Fair. With a Walk from Cuckold's-Point thro' *Deptford and Greenwich.* Price Six-Pence.

All Written by the same Author.

THE
LONDON
SPY.

Aving heard of a fam'd *Coffee-house* in *Aldersgate-street*, where *Doctors* of the Body, who study *Machiavel* much more than *Hippocrates*, Metamorphose themselves into State Polliticians; and the slippery Tongue, of thoughtless *Mechanicks*, undertake to Expound the Mysteries of Scripture, by the Power of Grace without Learning; We were willing to refresh our Intellects with their improving Discourses; in which, tho' we had but little expectancy of discovering much of the *Innocency of the Dove*, yet we had some hopes of Inspecting a little further into the *Subtlety of the Serpent*. Thither accordingly we steer'd our Course, and enter'd the Ancient Fabrick, by Antiquity made Venerable, whose Inside was lin'd with as great a Number of *Geneva* Christians, as if they were met to Sign some Canting Address, to Cheat the Government into a good Opinion of their Loyalty, whose Zeal to the *Good old Cause* was so Legible in their Looks, as if they had Contracted their Faces into Lines and Shrivels by looking awry upon *Monarchy*. Some were very highly extolling the *Dutch* Government; setting forth the *Freedom* and *Prosperity* of all such People who flourish under the happy Constitution of a *Common-Wealth*. Others Commending the Conduct of all Affairs under the Protector-ship of *Cromwell*; and how far the Felicity of the Nation, in those Days, Exceeded the Present Happiness of the Kingdom, so much Boasted on by the Blind Lovers of *Kingly-Power* and *Episcopacy*. At last up starts a bundle of Verbosity, who I had seen often at a *Coffee-house* near the *Court of Requests*, tho' never here before, to my Remembrance, notwithstanding I have gone frequently to the House. He is not Tall enough to be a Compleat *Man*, nor Short enough to be a *Monkey*, having more Mercury in his Head, than there is in a Weather-Glass. His Tongue began to flutter about his Mouth, like a wild Bird trappan'd into a Cage; spitting out as much Venom against Monarchy, as ever was Spew'd up after a full *Stomach* at a *Calves-Head Feast*. His Voice is as untunable when he Speaks, as the Screaking of a Countrey Sign in a high Wind; that were a Blind-Man to hear him Talk, he might easily mistake the Sound to be the Whining of some Puppy that wants the Dug in his Dams Absence. He has one Rhetorical Excellency, which becomes him wonderfully, He will assert a Falsity to be Truth, with as Graceful an Impudence, as

ever

ever the *Salamanca*-Saviour of our Lives and Liberties did, when he affirm'd Don *John* of *Austria* to be a Tall Black Man, who was quite opposite to the Description. He is one who will never own himself in the Wrong, and yet is never in the Right; but takes as much Pleasure in the Justification of a *Lye*, as if he was Cut out by Nature to be a Plot-Evidence. What commonly he Reports is as distinguishable from Truth, as Copper is from Gold: Yet nothing does he bear with more Impatience than Contradiction. He has got the Secret History of King *Charles* and King *James*; also *Imago Regis*, and some other Fam'd Pieces of the Doctor's Scurrility, by Heart; and has acquir'd from thence, as rare a Knack of railing against Kings, Justifying the Martyrdom of King *Charles*, and Blackening the Race of the *Stewarts*, as if he was at first a *Maggot* bred in one of *Shaftsbury*'s T—ds, and afterwards became a *Wasp* with a Natural Propensity to *Sting* and *Wound* the Memory of so Unfortunate a Family. I thought it so Ungrateful to any Charitable Ear, to hear a Rattle-Headed *Prattle-Box* set up to Reform the Church, New Model the Government, and Calumniate the Best of Princes, that I no longer could forbear giving him such a Reproof, as I thought so vain a Babler did in Justice deserve. Which he so highly resented, that he grew as hot as a Botchers Goose, to press down the Nitty Seams of an Old Dublet; that I fear'd he would have burst out into such an Ungovernable Flame, which nothing would have quench'd but a Good Cudgel. My Friend and I, gave him no time to Cool, but still fed his Passion with a supply of sharp Reflections on his past Talk, till we had spur'd him at last to such a Pitch of Madness, that he boild up into such a Ridiculous Froth, as render'd him a Laughing Stock to the whole Company; boasting, what Interest he had in the *Parliament-House*, and how many *Ay's* or *No's*, were ready to serve him upon all just Occasions. We found our selves Obliged to Prosecute our Undertaking, to the utmost, for we had reason to believe, if we had laid down the Scourge, he would have taken it up, and have us'd it against us, with much less Modesty, and more Barbarity: So that being once engag'd, we were forc'd in our own Defence, to pursue the Battle to a Compleat Victory, which with much difficulty we obtain'd, that he leap'd up from his Seat, and ran away; Branding us as he went out, with the Name of *Papists*, for no other Cause, but that we would not suffer him to rail without Reason, Talk Nonsense, without Reproof, and tire the Ears of the whole Company, with nothing but Malicious Invectives, against the Pious Martyr, and his Sons whose Names are too Sacred, as being Princes, for the Utterance of so Vile a Tongue.

As soon as he was gone, I was Desirous of knowing what this Carcass-ful of Spleen, Ignorance, and Ill-Nature could be; and to satisfie my Curiosity, I enquir'd of a Gentlemen that sat next me, who I discover'd by his Talk had some Knowledge of him, and he told me, the chief of his Business was to sell Pictures by *Auction*. *Nay*, says my Friend, if he be an *Auctioneer*, he's the more Excusable; for Cozening and Lying, are the two most Necessary Talents of his Profession; and I'll warrant you, he puts 'em both in Practice, as often as he has Opportunity, because he would not willingly Lose 'em, for want of Using.

Lyars

Lyars their Odious Talents often Show,
That they by Practice more expert may Grow;
So Knaves and Nedlles, on this Point agree,
The more they're us'd, the Sharper still they be.

As my Friend and I, were reflecting between our selves, upon some of the Insolent Expressions of our Shatter-brain'd *Runegado*, a Merry Pleasant-Look'd Gentleman step'd into the *Coffee-house*, sits down, and whilst he was filling a Pipe of *Tobacco*, Entertain'd the Company with this following Intelligence, of a remarkable Breakfast provided by a Generous Vintner, on *Tuesday* the 24 *th.* in Order to Treat his Guests, on the following *Thursday* Morning, upon which Day, all Customers should be Free to Feast their Bellies, and you're Welcome Gentlemen; so that he as yet had only seen it Raw, an Account of which he gave us in a Witty Dialect, after a Comical manner, which I will Endeavour to Imitate, in hopes to Divert the Reader.

Gentlemen, says he, *I have seen such a Sight to day, would make a Spaniard change his Pace, and turn his Stately Steps into a Dog-Trot, to run after it; or make a Dutchman in surprise, pluck his Hands out of his Pockets, and hold 'em up, like an* Englishman *going to be Hang'd, to Praise the God of Plenty for Blessing his greedy Eyes with so wonderful a Feast, or put a* French-man *into as great Amazment, as the Snow did the* Bantum *Embassador, and make his whole Body move with admiration, like a* German *piece of Clock-work. And, Pray Sir,* says a Grave Gentleman, that sat by, *What would it make an* English-man *do, Nothing? Yes Sir,* answered the other, *it would make an* English-man *Whet his Knife, if it were Dress, and fall on without Grace, and Stuff his Belly till it was as hard as a Foot-Ball, before he would Rise from the Table. But, Sir,* says the Old Gentleman, *You'll forget, I am afraid, to tell us what it was; we want to know that, Sir. Why, Sir,* says he, *Then I'll tell you, It was a piece of Roasting Beef, but of such an extraordinary Size, that Ten Men might Ride upon't, without Incommoding themselves any other Way, than by Greasing of their Breeches, and but turn it upon its Back, and it would carry as many People within-side, as a* Graves-End-Wherry; *it was the whole Length of a Huge, Large, Long, Lincolnshire Ox, Fed up from a Calf, upon all Long Grass, that he might grow the Longer; there were no Scales at the Custom-House big enough to weigh it, but they were forc'd to Drive it down to* Wapping *in a Cart, and weigh it by an Anchor Smith's Stillyards, where they Weigh their Anchors, to discover the true Weight; it proving, upon exact Computation, to be Four-hundred and Fifteen Pound; which Magnificent Piece of Beef, notwithstanding its Ponderosity, will certainly, on the Day appointed, by some strong Jaw'd Men of the Law be taken up by the Teeth, without the assistance of the* Southwark-Sampson, *who breaks Carmens Ribs with a Hug, Snaps Cables like a Twine Thred, and draws Dray-Horses upon their Arses, with as much Ease as a* Westphalia *Hog can Crack a Cocoa-Nut? But, Pray Sir,* says Mr. *Inquisitive, How did they get it Home to the Tavern?* The Gentleman reply'd, *It was Kill'd in Butchers-Hall Lane, and removed from thence, by the Assistance of as many Butchers walking under it, as there are Porters under a Pageant upon my* Lord-Mayors-Day; *some of the Bloody Fraternity walking before, with their Cleavers mounted on their Shoulders, as so many Maces; and thus Convey'd it Home, in as much Triumph,*

B

as if it had been a Lord-Mayor, *going to Persecute the* Bakers; *attended with as many* Mob, *as the* Victuallers Corps *that Lay in State, when he was carry'd to be Buried with a Drawn Sword upon his Coffin, instead of double Chalk, and Tap-Tub.* Pray Sir, *said I,* Where is the Leviathan *of Beef to be Devour'd, that a Man may go view this Gluttonous Prodigy, before the Cooks have mangled it out of all Shape, with their* Bucks-Horn *Handled Scimitars?* Why Sir, *says he, At the* Kings-Head Tavern *at* Chancery-Lane-End, *where at this time the Honestest* Vintner *in* London *Lives; where the best* Wine *in* England *is to be Drank, and the stateliest piece of* Beef *in* Christendom, *is to be Roasted.*

Our Pipes being out, tho' we Imagin'd he might Illustrate the Story, Sir *Harry Blunt* like, with some few Advantages, yet we Believ'd in the main there was something in it worth our further Inspection. Upon which, we determin'd to Adjourn to the *Tavern,* where the Gentleman Reported this Extravagant Breakfast was to be Eaten.

Accordingly we Discharg'd our Reckoning, and made our *Exit,* and being Spurr'd on with the Conceit of this Amusing Whim, as the Gentleman had render'd it, by his Diverting Account, we stumbled along o'er the Pebble Stones, as fast as a *Penny-post-man,* or a *Temple Student* with a Bill into the City, to Receive his Quarterage, till we came to the Door of this happy Mansion; which according to the Report we heard, abounded with those Delights, were in other *Taverns* very difficult to be found: But met with such Crowds in Opposition, Some striving for Entrance, and others for an *Exit,* that we were forc'd to Struggle as hard for our Admittance, as a couple of be-lated *Beaus* do to squeeze into the Pit, when the Girl is to Sing a New Bawdy Song, or *Dogget* in *Love for Love,* is to Play *Son Benjamin;* but at last with no small striving we Shot the Entry into a Pav'd Yard, where we waited as Long for a Sight of the Demi-Carcass of the Beast, as a Gentleman in Adversity, does for the Sight of a great Man, when his Business is to Beg a Favour, or put him in Mind of a Promise he never intended to Perform: At last, in the Interchange of Comers and Goers, we slip'd into the Kitchen, where about a Dozen of the most Eminent *Jack-Winders* in *Fleet-street,* some in their Night-Caps and White-Aprons, like *Heathen Priests* going to Kill the Sacrifice; others with their Sweaty Hair ty'd back in a List Garter, that it might not hang in their Light, and hinder them in the Performance of the Difficult Task they had undertaken, which was to Spit this Unwieldy Monster, with such Mathematical Judgment, that it should run round by the help of a *Turnspit,* with as true a Poise, as the Sail of a Windmill in a fresh Gale; after they in Vain had Wounded the Back of Beef in sundry Places, either an *Ach-Bone,* a *Chine-Bone,* a *Blade-Bone,* or a *Rib,* standing in their Way, still deny'd Entrance to their Massy Weapon; that they Puff'd and Blow'd at their Fruitless Labour, like so many *Custom-House* Porters, Lifting at a Wooll-Pack; and at last sitting down, like a Jury of Inquest over a Dead Corps, they began to Consult of some new Measures, to force this Stubborn Piece of Mans-Meat, into a Submission of being Roasted: At last one of the Burgesses of the *Dripping-Pan* starts up, and wisely made this motion, to the rest of the Greazy Brother-hood, *My Honest Freinds and Neighbours, since we the Professors of, and Wellwishers to the Noble*

Art of Cookery, are Assembled together in our proper Element the Kitchen, *upon this Solemn Occasion, let us not be Baffled by the* Back-Bone *of an* Ox, *but let's stir up our Brains with the* Fire-Fork *of* Understanding, *and by the Flame of Reason, give fresh Light to our Judgments, that we may see to Spit this Pack-Saddle of Beef, or the Reflections of the Town will put us all upon the Rack, and every Sawcy Jack, will tumble our Reputation into the* Dripping-Pan. *I therefore declare my Opinion is, That we forthwith send for my Neighbour* Knockdowdy *the Smith, and his Man* Thump, *and by the assistance of them and their Sledges, we may Compleate our Task, in as little time, as a Man may boile an* Egg, *or melt a Pound of* Butter Juft as the whole Society of *Lick-fingers*, had with great Applaufe very highly approv'd of their Brother *Skimpot's* Advice, who fhould Crowd into the Cook's Territories, but a *Carpenter* Arm'd with a huge Mallet, as if Providence had fent him purpofely to their Affiftance, who undertook to do more Work with his Wooden Weapon at one Blow, than all the Cholerick Company of Unthinking Bunglers, were able to do with their United Strength without him. This Speech gave 'em frefh Courage, fo that every *Epicurean's* Minion ftarted up as Nimbly to his Bufinefs, as a Mafter of Anatomy at *Surgeons-Hall* to a Diffection, inftead of the Spitting, of a Dead Carcafs. The Underlings of the Sweating Tribe were appointed to fharpen *Broomftaves*; the Vintner having that Day broke all the *Kent-ftreet* Merchants, who came by the Door, that the Handles of their Ware might be Pointed into *Skewers* for his Beef, and the Broom be bound up into Brufhes, not to Sell to his Cuftomers, but to kindle that *Montanious Æfna*, at which this more aftonifhing Breakfaft, than ever was feen in *Heliogabalus's* Kitchen, was to be Roafted.

When with the Induftry of all the *Culinarian-Crew*, they had made a Thorough-Fare for the Spit, from the Right Buttock of the Beaft to the Left Shoulder of the Non-refifting Morfel, fuch Acclamations of Joy were Belch'd up by the Greafy Undertakers, as would have dafh'd a Mob out of Countenance, that Yelp out their Huzza's at a *Gun-Powder-Treafon Bonfire*; and he that was chief Leader of the Knights of the *Frying-Pan*, ftrutted about the Kitchen with his Arms on Kimbo, Puffing and Swelling, like *Drawcan-fir*, in the Rehearfal, after, with his own fingle Hand, he had Slain a whole Army; Crying out in a Majeftical Voice, *'Tis Done! 'tis Done! The Mighty Deed is Done!* Which Words were no fooner fpoke, but in comes *Raggoe-Raoy*, and after him a Neighbouring Brother Sloven, chief Prefident of the *Slap-Dabs*, who feeing the Noble Duke of *Carnis Bubalina*, trufs'd up to his good Behaviour on a Spit, containing as much Iron as, by Computation, would have made a Sheet Anchor, for one of *Julius Cæfar's* firft Rates, when the whole Fleet Rid in *Holborn Ditch*, upon his Landing in *London*, fell into fuch a wonderful Rage, to think they fhould be flighted, and not have timely Summons to appear at fo great a Solemnity, but lofe the Reputation of having any thing to do in fo remarkable an Adventure in their own proper Bufinefs, falling both into a mighty Paffion, with the Mafter of the Houfe, *One Vowing Revenge to the* Vintners *for his Sake, and that he would put no more* Sack *in his* Puddings *for a* Twelvemonth: *The other Swearing for ought he knew, he would ufe no more* Claret *in* Fifh-Sawce, *as long as he Liv'd, but would make the Knaves as humble to a* Cook, *as a* Tip-ftaff *is to a* Lord-Chief-Juftice. If every Brother *Coquus* was but of

his

his Mind, for the great Indignity he had put upon the Profeſſion, by Neglecting to Invite, not only two ſuch Neighbours and Cuſtomers, but Men ſo Eminent in the Generation they Live in, for Conquering all difficulties in the Noble Art of *Cookery*; who had Spit ſo many ſtately *Chines*, *Barons*, *Sides*, and *Sirloins*, and not to be at the Spitting of his Grace the *Duke*, when they had ſo juſt a Title, to be preſent at the Action: Well, it was ſuch an affront, that if they had him but at Home, in either of their own Kitchens, they would *Roaſt-him*, and *Toaſt-him*, and *Tumble-him* about in the *Dripping-Pan*, till they had made him a Greaſy Sop, fit for the Devils Eating. Having thus Vented their Paſſions, they both look'd Bluff upon the Bar, and turn'd out of the Houſe, in as Splenetick an humour, as if a *Sawce-Pan* of *Butter* had run to *Oyl*, the *Veniſon-Paſty* been over *Bak'd*, or the *Fat* faíl'n into the *Fire*.

The chief Operator and his Aſſiſtants, who were ſo very Joyful, they at laſt had overcome the greateſt of their difficulty, like Prudent Artificers, began now to Examin the Truth of their Work, and try whether it was pois'd with that Exactneſs as was Neceſſary, for the Eaſe of the *Turn-ſpit*; but found, like Notable *Conjurers*, that one Side was juſt as much too Heavy, by as many Pound as t'other was too Light; which now was no way to be Remedied, but by Chipping and Paring, till they had brought 'em to an Equality; which by that time they had Cut off as many Slivers as amounted to the Weight of about Fifty Pound, was finiſh'd effectually, with great Gladneſs and Applauſe.

Beef-ſtakes, we now obſerv'd, were as plenty about Houſe, as Yolks of Eggs in Brewing-time; which Encourag'd us, notwithſtanding the Hurry, to ſit down in the Kitchen, and take ſhare of the Superfluity, and alſo over our Flask to take Notice of the divers Humours, and Various Sentiments of the Numerous Spectators, who flock'd in and out, as faſt to behold the Novelty, as if it had been the Corps of an Old Woman laid in State, that had Hang'd herſelf for Love of a Young Fellow of five and twenty. Amongſt the reſt, in came an Old Gentleman, who look'd as Grave as a *Modern Philoſopher* in the Laboratory of an *Alchimiſt*; and that he might take a more ſatisfactory Survey of this Uncommon Eatable, which look'd as frightful upon the Spit, as the *Flying-Dragon*, upon St. *George*'s Spear, when he Reſcu'd the Damſel from the Teeth and Talons of the furious Monſter, after he had fumbled as long in his Pockets, as a *Hypocrite* does to find a Farthing for a *Beggar*, he at laſt pulls out his artificial Peepers, which he mounted upon the handle of his Face, that the wonderful Object might be thereby render'd the more Conſpicuous to his Sight; round which he walk'd with as much Circumſpection, as ever a prying *Virtuoſo* did round a Glaſs *Bee-hive*, to obſerve how the Winged Labourers work their *Honey-Combs*; telling the *Ribs*, meaſuring the *Length*, with his Crutch-headed *Cane*, gueſſing at the *Weight*, turning up the *Rump*, as the *Monkey* did the *Cats Tale*, when he ran the Spiggot in her *Fundament*, and at laſt holding up his Hands like a Belly-Saint, Craving a Bleſſing upon his Food, he broke out into this Joyful Rapture, *Look ye, d'ye ſee, Gentlemen, on the t'other hand, it may be, we are the happieſt Nation in the World; for let us but Conſider: D'ye hear me, what a Bleſſing of Providence it is as a Man may ſay, that ſuch a Glorious Sight as this, that is a Glorious Sight,*

I

I say, is to be seen amongst us, after so long a War; That let me tell you, had it continu'd till now, such a piece of Beef as this, without great Mercy, would have been a much more Graceful Sight than the fattest Alderman in London Then fell a Laughing at his Jest, till he brought himself into a Fit of the Phthisick, *which put a Period to his Learned Oration.*

The next Spectator, that was worth our Notice, was a kind of a Captain *Blustre,* who was so Brim full of Oaths, that he run over, like a *Southwark-Ditch* at a Spring-Tide; and I am apt to believe, were his Bottom to be fathom'd, he would prove as Filthy. *Why the Pox,* says he, to one of the Drawers, *Was your Master such a Fool to have the Head Cut off, which would have been so great a Grace to your* Pack-Saddle *Monster, that I'll warrant you, there's never a Cuckold about Town, but what would have had a Peep at him?* The reason Sir, says the Drawer, *That my Master had it Cut off was, Because the Range is not long enough to Roast it.* Cats Nouns, says the Gentleman, *your Cooks are all Blockheads, for they might have trust it as short with the Head on, as 'tis now without it.* How Sir? says the Master of the Roast, with great Indignation, *I have been a Student in the Art of Cookery, above this Twenty Years, and I do affirm Sir, that what you say is Impossible.* Then I do say, reply'd the Gentleman, *That thou art a meer Codshead of a Cook, and I can tell thee which way it may be done presently, if the Head had been on.* I'll hold you Sir, says the Cook, *The Price of the Beef, to a Pound of Kitchen-stuff, if the Head had been on, it must have requir'd so much the Longer Fire to have Roasted it.* No, no, says the Gentleman, *it had been but Joynting the Neck, and you might have brought the Head round, and have stuck one of the Horns thro' the Body, as you do the Bill of a* Wood-Cock; *what think you of that,* Domine Coquus? Efaith Master, says he, *I did not think of that; now you have put it in my Head, I don't question but I could have done it; but what should we have done with the Horn, that was next to the Fire?* For that, says he, *would have hung upon the Range, and have stop'd the going of the Meat.* That, says the Gentleman, *I Design for the Cook's Fees.* At which, the Company fell into a Laughter, which kindled such a Fire in the Cook's Countenance, that his Looks were almost sufficient to have Scalded all the Company out of the Kitchen.

By this time we had Eat a Stake, and Drunk up our Flask of Wine, and being quite tired with the Cook's Clutter, the Confusion of Tongues, the Hurry of the House, and other Inconveniences, that always attend such Publick Novelties: We adjourn'd to our own Homes, in order to dispatch some Domestick Business, which with reposing Nature, took us up our time, till *Thursday* Morning, upon which day this Liberal Entertainment was to be in a Roasted Readiness to Oblige the Guests.

When the Morning came, my Friend and I, having a great desire to discover what an Attractive Influence, such a Magnificent Piece of Beef, had upon the Good Stomachs of this Town, we resolv'd not to lose the Opportunity of Gratifying our Pallats, as well as Feasting our Eyes, and come in for our share of the Benefit, as well as the rest of the Town Epicures; and that we might also the better inform our selves, how the Whim took amongst those Tipling Gudgeons, for whom the alluring Bait was in chief design'd. When we came to the Door, we had more difficulty to get Admittance, then we had before; for as many

C

People

People were Crowding to see it at the Fire, as there were to see the Ox Roasted upon the Ice. When we had squeez'd side-ways thro' the Entry, with as much Pains as a Fat Man takes to shove his Guts thro' a narrow *Turn-stile*, we got into the Yard, where such a Litter of Drawers were scampering from *Cellar* to *Bar*, and from *Bar* to *Company*, that it was difficult to believe, the whole House could have entertain'd Guests sufficient to have requr'd such a Number of Attendance; as many Bells rattling at a time, as o'et a *Green-Birds*-Cage, when the Feather'd *Animal* (tho' it hates a *Cat*) Rings *Whittington*; the Servants all Puffing and Blowing like Grey-hounds after a Course, sweating like a Couple of Chairmen in the *Dog-Days*, who had just set down a Bulky Nobleman. The Kitchen being now as hot as *Guinea* at Noon-day, we concluded there we should be best Attended, being near the *Bar*, and the least incommoded for want of Room, could we but reconcile our Bodies to the extraordinary Heat, which we thought we could more easily endure, than many other Inconveniencies we should have found elsewhere. Accordingly, we ventur'd into the Kitchen, which at first Entrance, seem'd hot enough to have Bak'd a *Custard* in the middle of it, but seating our selves at a convenient distance from the Fire, and where we drew in a little Cool Breath at a Back-Door, we found our selves well setled in a pretty moderate Climate: The poor Carcase of the Beast was by this time so Lamentably Mangled by the Cuts and Slashes of the broiling Carvers, that had Sir *Courtly Nice*, or my Lady *Squeamish*, been to have taken a View of the Roasting Rarity, they would scarce have Long'd to have been Partakers of the Feast; for the Shoulders and the Ribs were soon stripp'd as bare of their flesh as if the *Tower-Lyons*, or the *Tygar*, had been just at Breakfast on't; and the Buttock, and more fleshy Parts, were Cut and Digg'd so full of holes and furrows, that it look'd as Disfigur'd, as the Carcase of a Goose, after a couple of Tunbelly'd *Church-Wardens* have had the Picking on't: Yet the Poor *Anatomy* Cock'd his Tail, as he ran round upon the Spit, like *Ralph's Dobbin* in a full Gallop; the Turn-spit so discolour'd with Sweat, Soot, Smoak and Ashes, that both him and his Cookery look'd as if one Devil was Roasting of another, letting fall so fast their greazy Tears, as if there was an Emulation between both, who should afford the most Dripping, the Cook and his Attendants were so very busie about the Carcase of the Beast, that every Round it took, it was at least two or three Pound the lighter.

By this time a Generous Plateful of the Good Creature was brought as a Present to my Friend and I, with all the rest of the Appurtenances at once, without the Trouble of Calling; which encouraged our Appeties, and gave us a better Liking to our Treat; which in Justice I must say, according to the old English way of praising Beef, was as Rich, Fat, Young, Well-fed, Delicious Meat, as ever was taken into the Mouth, masticated between the Teeth, and swallow'd into the Belly of a true English-man. By that time we had made an end of our Plentiful Commons, the Bones of the whole Carcass were pair'd as clean as the sharp whetted Weapons of the Blunt Dissectors could well Pick 'em, insomuch that the Vintner found himself, under a Necessity of sending for two *Barons* more, or half his Guests would have been disappointed of their Breakfast. For the *Templers* whose Business call'd them to *Westminster*, omitted their Accustomary Eating of *Roast-Beef* in *Hell*, and came Roaring in Crowds with

with such Devilish Stomachs, which the Exercise of their Lungs in the Hall, had made as insatiate as their Consciences, their Tongues, as fast as they came in, Pleading so very hard in the behalf of their Bellies, that nothing was heard but *Beef, Beef, Beef,* Threatening to Run all to the Devil presently, if the Master did not retain 'em speedily, by greasing their Stomachs as well as their Hands, with a Present of his Fat Opsonium, which he Promised 'em to do with all imaginable Expedition, and so Pacified 'em with good Words, till the next was Roasted. Having now well fraighted the Hold of our Vessels, with excellent Food, and delicious Wine, at a small Expence, we Scribled these following Lines with Chalk upon the Wall, so took our Departure from thence, and steer'd our Course to a more Temperate Climate.

To Speak but the Truth, of my Honest Friend Ned,
The best of all Vintners that ever God made;
He's free of his Beef, and as free of his Bread,
And Washes both down with a Glass of rare Red,
*   That Tops all the Town, and Commands a good Trade.*
Such Wine that will chear up the Drooping Kings-Head ;
And brisk up the Soul, tho' our Body's half Dead,
*   He Scorns to Draw Bad, as he hopes to be Paid:*
And now his Name's up, he may e'en lye a Bed ;
*   For he'll get an Estate, there's no more to be Said.*

Considering *Coffee* to be a Liquor that sits most easie upon *Wine,* we thought it our best way to Check the aspiring Fumes of the most Christian Juice by an *Antichristian-Dose* of *Mahometan Loblolly,* and to hear what News the Grizly Trumpeters of Fame's Reports, had rak'd up together from Credulous Noddies ; Who hear without *Attention,* believe without *Reason,* and affirm without *Probabillity.* Accordingly we went into a great *Coffee-House* by the *Temple-Gate,* where a parcel of Grave Men, were thickening the Air with the Fumes of their *Nicotianian Weed ;* we sat down amongst the rest of 'em, most of the Company, we observ'd, being as choice of their Words, as a Miser is of his Treasure ; each seeming as loth to open his Mouth, as the other is his Cabinet, which made me think they had either something extraordinary in 'em, that they lock'd up in *Pythagorian Silence ;* or else, that they were a parcel of Cunning Fools, who having a Sense of their Infirmities, were unwilling by their talking to discover their Ignorance : At last comes in an old *News-Hound,* who in Hunting after Intelligence, was at a great Loss, and enquir'd of the rest, if any stragling News had come that way. News, reply'd, a Jolly Red-Fac'd old Toper, *We have News enough, I think, to Comfort the Hearts of the whole City in the Days of Affliction: We may Remember when the Government of our Metropolis was fallen into the Hands of the Double-Refin'd Christians, the Honour of the City and the Grandure of the Mayoralty dwindled into the very Socket of Dissention, which extinguish'd the Ancient Glories of our Noble Town, and made 'em appear but a meer Snuff half drown'd in the Tallow of Hypocrisie ; but since Providence has restor'd the Church to the Chair, We see every succeeding Lord-Mayor gives us greater Instances of a General Regard to the publick Wellfare ; who instead of the Severe Execution of the Laws upon poor Wretches, who are already by their Miseries made the Objects of Pity, rather than of Punishment, extend their Charity to the Releas-ment,*

ment, as well as Relief, of Prisoners; and give Succour to the *Distressed, Fatherless and Widdows, instead of Uncharitable Confinement, and Unreasonable Correction,* to those Poor *Mendicants, who have not above Nine-pence or Twelve-pence a Week from the Parish, without Begging, to keep 'em from Starving.* Besides, says he, *Authority we see rightly given into the Hands of those Persons who have just Title to Receive and Execute the same, by being truly Qualified as the Laws require, prevent the Ignorant from Dissenting from the* Church, *and Alienating their Obedience from the true Worship of* God, *as well as from their Soveraign* Princes, *which Power given into the Hands of Dissenting* Magistrates, *have at all times Encourag'd:* When the Sword was carry'd to the Meeting-house, how Empty were the Churches, and Numerous the Congregations of the Saints? But since the Magistracy of the City *is given on the Right-side, who much better deserve it, the Churches are every where as full, as if true* Christianity of Late, *by the Industry of our Clergy, and Care of our* Magistrates, *had been greatly Advanc'd; and the Assemblies of the Over-*Righteous, *are grown so very thin, that it is verily Believ'd, if things succeed as they begin, the Dancing-Masters about this Town may in a little-time have Choice of Good Schools, at more Reasonable Rates than ever: And that I think, Boys, is much better News, than to see* Paul's Church *as Empty as a* Saturday's Change, *and the Meeting-House as full as* Westminster-Hall *in an Issuable Term.* Most of the Company agreeing rightly with the Old Gentlemans Sentiments, applauded him highly for expressing his Affections to the Establish'd Church. This serious Speech of the old *Cavalier's*, was a Key to the Hearts of all the rest, who began, after one had open'd, like a Pack of true *Beagles* at full Cry, to hunt down the Churches Enemies with all imaginable Speed; all expressing so venerable a Character of the Present *Lord-Mayor*, that few Magistrates have deserv'd, and scarce any Enjoy'd; so highly extolling him for his great Charity towards the poor Prisoners, and many other Commendable Acts of *Hospitality*; which has deservedly rais'd him to so high an Esteem among all Good Christians, that if no Mismanagement of his own, nor Calumny thrown by the Hands of Envy, shall futurely sully his present Reputation, when he resigns his Office he will leave behind him so worthy a Pattern of Authority, that will be a Puzzling Task for his Successors, tho' brave Men, to Imitate.

If any shall say, Want of Manners, *or* Sense,
　Have made me this Caution intrude;
I justly may urge, to excuse the Offence,
　To be Moral, is not to be Rude.

Who-ever to Popular Praises aspire,
　Must do't by much Trouble and Cost;
Tho' a very Good Name is so hard to acquire,
　Yet nothing's so easily Lost.
The Turns and the Changes of Fame *and of* Fate,
　To no Mortal Power Fore-known,
May raise us to Day, by Good-means, to be Great,
　Yet to Morrow may tumble us down.
May therefore your Prudence *and* Conduct *be such,*
　To add New Applause to your Name;
And raise such Esteem, that no Envy can touch,
　Or Malice deservedly blame.

Having

Having now wafted our time till about Nine at Night, we thought it a reafonable Hour to take leave of the *Coffee-houfe*, and repair to our own Lodgings, where my Bufinefs engag'd me to continue clofe, till the Triumphs of the City call'd me to make one of the Innumerable Multitude of Gaping Spectators. When the Morning came, that my *Lord-Mayor* and his Attendants were to take their Amphibeous Journey to *Weftminfter-Hall*, where his *Lordfhip* according to the Cuftom of his Anceftors, was by a Kifs of *Calves-Leather*, to make a fair promife to his Majefty, I equip'd my Carcafe in order to bear with little Dammage, the Hufflles and Affronts, of the Mannerly *Mobility*, of whofe wild Paftimes and unlucky Attacks, I had no little Apprehenfion ; and when my Friend and I, had thus carefully Shelter'd our felves under our Ancient Drabdeberries, againft their dirty Affaults, we ventur'd to move towards *Cheap-fide*, where I thought the Triumphs would be moft Vifible, and the Rabble moft Rude, looking upon the Mad Frolicks and Whimfies of the Latter, to be altogether as Diverting, (provided a Man takes Care of the Danger) as the Solemn Grandure and Gravity of the Former. When I came to the End of *Blow-Bladder-Street*, I faw fuch a Crowd before my Eyes, that I could fcarce forbear thinking the very Stones of the Street, by the Harmony of their *Drums* and *Trumpets*, were Metamorphos'd into *Men, Women,* and *Children*; the Ballconies, were hung with old *Tapftry*, and *Turky-work Table-Cloaths*, for the cleanly Leaning of the Ladies, with whom they were chiefly fill'd, which the Mob had foon Pelted into fo Dirty a Condition, with their Kennel Amunition, that fome of them look'd as Nafty, as the Cover-Cloth of a *Led-Horfe*, that had Travel'd from St. *Margates* to *London*, in the midft of *Winter*; the Ladies at every Volley quitting their Poft, and Retreating into their Dining Roomes, as Safer Garifons to defend them from the Affaults of their Mifchevious Enemies, fome Freting at their Daub'd Scarfs, like a Godly old Woman that had dropt her Bible in the Dirt, Sing'd her *High-Crown'd-Hat*, or broke her *Spectacles*; others wiping their New *Commodes*, which they had bought on purpofe to Honour his *Lordfhip*, expreffing as much Anger in their Looks, as a difappointed *Bride*, or a *Dutch Houfe-Wife*, when an *Englifhman* has blow'd his Nofe in her Parlour, the Windows of each Houfe, from the Top to the Bottom, being ftuff'd with Heads, Pil'd one upon another, like *Skulls* in a *Charnel Houfe*, all gazing at the Lobcocks in their Coney-Skin Pontificallibuffes, with as much Intention, as if an *Indian Prophetefs* had been Riding thro' the City, upon the back of a *Tyger*. Whilft my Friend and I were thus ftaring at the Spectators much more than the Show, the Pageants were advanc'd within our View, and fuch a Tide of Mob overflow'd the Place we ftood in, that the Women cry'd out for Room, the Children for Breath, and every Man, whether Citizen or Forreigner, ftrove very hard for his Freedom; for my own part, I thought my Intrails would have come out of my Mouth, and I fhould have gone fhotten Home, I was fo clofely Imprifon'd betwen the Bums and Bellies of the Multitude, that I was almoft fqueez'd as flat as a Napkin in a Prefs, and would have joyn'd with the Rabble with all my Heart, to have cry'd *Liberty, Liberty*. In this Pageant was a fellow, Riding a Cock-horfe upon a *Lyon*, but without either *Boots* or *Spurs*; as if intended by the Projector, to fhow how the Citizens Ride to *Epfome* on a *Saturday-Night*, to bear their Wives Company till *Monday Morning*,

Or elfe to let the Hen-peck'd Cuckolds know,
A Lyon's Tam'd more eafie than a Shrow.

D

At the Base of the Pedestal were seated four Figures, representing, according to my most Rational Conjecture, the four principal *Vices* of the City, viz. *Fraud, Usury,* seeming *Sanctity* and *Hypocrisie:* As soon as this was past, the Industrious Rabble, who hate Idleness, had procur'd a dead Cat, whose wreaking Puddings hung dangling from her torn Belly, cover'd all over with *Dirt, Blood* and *Nastiness,* in which pickle she was handed about by the Babes of Grace, as an innocent Diversion; every now and then being toss'd into the Face of some gaping Booby or other; and made him look of as delicate a Complection, as if his Cheeks had been Painted between a *Tom-T——Man* and a *Chimney-Sweeper.* By that time this sport had gone a little about, Crying out no *Squibs,* no *Squibs;* another Pageant aproach'd us, wherein an old Fellow sat in a Blue Gown, dress'd up like a Countrey *School-Master,* only he was Arm'd with a Sythe instead of a *Burch-Rod,* by which I understood this figure represented *Time,* which was design'd, as I suppose, to put the City in mind how apt they are to abuse the old Gentleman, and not dispose him to such Good Uses as the Laws of God, and the Laws of Man require, but trifle their time away, in those three Vanities, which were represented by the three Figures, under the Dome, viz. *False-hood, Pride,* and *Incontinency,* which are chiefly owing to the other four Figures, at the Angles, representing, as I suppose, the Cities *Imprudence, Impatience, Intemperance,* and *Inhumanity;* when this Pageant was pass'd, the Ingenious Rabble, had got a Leathern Apron, which they tyed full of *Sirreverence,* as hard as a *Foot-Ball,* and afterwards prick'd it full of Holes with a *Taylors Bodkin,* then flung it from one to another, it spewing it's Excrement thro' the Bee-holes, upon every Body it met with; the Mob, crying out, when it had hit any Body, All *Honey,* all *Honey.* By that time the *Plebeian* Gentry, had Diverted themselves about a Quarter of an Hour with this their Odoriferous *Sweet-Bag.* A third Pageant was advanc'd forward, which appear'd to the Sight much Richer than the rest, the chief Figure in it, Representing, as I imagin'd, a Lady of Pleasure, being Drest in much Costlier Robes, than the other Female Representatives, which may serve to let the City know, that *Whores* in this Wicked Age, to the great Dishonour of Vertue, wear richer Apparrel at the Expence of their Keepers, than Honest Women, and those three Maides that attend her, as her Servants, signifie the *Pride* of a *Concubine,* who will not be Content without three Servants, when the Lawfull Wife perhaps must be glad of one; and those four Figures that are plac'd beneath the rest, signifie the sad Calamities that attend the Conversation of Lewd Women, viz. *Want, Poverty, Shame,* and the *Gallows.* This Pageant is chiefly Dedicated to the *London Prentices,* at the Charge of the Society for Reformation. In every Interval between one Pageant and Pageant, the Mob had still a new Project to put on Foot. By that time they had got a piece of Cloath, of a Yard or more Square, that they dip'd in the Kennel, till they had made it fit for their purpose, then toss'd it about, it expanding it self in the Air, and falling upon the Heads of two or three at once, made 'em Look like so many *Bearers* under a *Pall,* every one Luging a several way to get it off his Head, oftentimes falling together by the Eares about plucking off their *Cover-slut.* By that time fourty or fifty of the heedless Spectators were made as Dirty as so many *Scavengers,* the fourth Pageant was come up, which was a most Stately Rich and Noble *Chariot,* made of Split-Deal and Past-Board, and in it sitting a Woman Representing (as I Fancy) the *Whore* of *Babylon,* drawn by two Goats, signifying her Lust; and upon the Backet of them two Figures, Representing *Jealousie* and *Revenge,* her Attendance, Importing the Miseries that follow her; and the Kittle-Drums and Trumpets serve to show that where so e'er she comes, 'tis with Terrour and Amazement.

The Rabble having Chang'd their Sport, to a new Scene of Unluckiness, had got a *Bullock's-Horn,* which they fill'd with Kennel-water, and pour'd it down People's Necks, and into their Pockets, that it run down their Legs into their Shooes, the Ignorant Sufferers not readily Discovering from whence the Wet came. When they had Exercis'd this new Invention, about a quarter of an Hour, the Fifth Pageant mov'd forward, wherein all sorts of Trades were Represented; a Man working a *Turning Engine,* as if he was Cutting of *Tobacco,* but often did not; a Woman Turning of a Wheel as if she Spun, but did not; a Boy as if he was Dressing of an Old Womans Head, but was not; which was design'd, as I suppose to reflect upon the Frauds and Falsities of the City Trades, and show that they often pretend to do what they do not, and to be what they are not, and will Say what they Think not, and Think what they Say not, and that the World may See, there are Cheats in all Trades.

The Bully Citts March'd after in a Throng,
Huzza'd by th' Mob, as Drum'd and Pip'd along;
Whilst Wise Spectators do their Pomp Disdain,
And with Contempt behold the Dragling Train.

The End of the First Volume.

The CONTENTS of the Twelve Parts of the First Volume of the LONDON-SPY.

The Contents of the Sixth Part.

The Contents of the Seventh Part.

The Contents of the Eighth Part.

The Contents of the Ninth Part.

The Contents of the Tenth Part.

The Contents of the Eleventh Part.

The Contents of the Twelfth Part.

On the Fifth of December next, will be Publish'd the First Part of the Second Volume of *The London Spy*, to be Continu'd Monthly.

THE
LONDON
SPY.

For the *Month* of *November*, 1699.

The Second Volume.

PART I.

LONDON, Printed and Sold by *J. How*, in the *Ram-Head-Inn-Yard* in *Fanchurch-street*, 1699.

Books Sold by J. How, in the Ram-Head-Inn-Yard in Fanchurch-Street; J. Weld, at the Crown between the Temple-Gates in Fleet-street; and Mrs. Fabian, at Mercers-Chappel in Cheapside.

1. SOt's Paradise: Or the Humours of a Derby-Ale-House: With a Satyr upon the Ale. Price Six Pence.

2. A Trip to *Jamaica*: With a True Character of the People and Island. Price Six Pence.

3. *Eclesia & Factio.* A Dialogue between *Bow-Steeple-Dragon*, and the *Exchange-Grashopper.* Price Six Pence.

4. The Poet's Ramble after Riches. With Reflections upon a Country Corporation. Also the Author's Lamentation in the time of Adverfity. Price Six Pence.

5. A Trip to *New-England*. With a Character of the Country and People, both English and Indians. Price Six Pence.

6. Modern Religion and Ancient Loyalty: A Dialogue. Price Six Pence.

7. The World Bewitch'd. A Dialogue between Two Astrologers and the Author. With Infallible Predictions of what will happen in this Present Year, 1699. From the *Vices* and *Villanies* Practis'd in *Court, City* and *Country*. Price Six Pence.

8. A Walk to *Islington*: With a Description of New *Tunbridge-Wells*, and *Sadler's* Musick-House. Price Six Pence.

9. The Humours of a Coffee-House: A Comedy. Price Six Pence.

10 A Frolick to *Horn-Fair*. With a Walk from Cuckold's-Point thro' *Deptford* and *Greenwich*. Price Six-Pence.

11. The First Volume of the LONDON-SPY: In Twelve Parts.

All Written by the same Author.

THE
LONDON
SPY.

THE Triumphs of the City being now paſt by, they drew after them the Mobility to our ſafe deliverance, my Friend and I clinging as faſt to a Poſt, as a *Bear* to a ragged Staff, to avoid being carry'd away by the reſiſtleſs Torrent of the Rabble; which if we had quitted our hold, would have inevitably happen'd, to the farther bruiſing of our Ribs, and the great pennance of our Toes; but on the contrary finding our ſelves as ſafe as a Politick Prince in the Rear of an Engagement, we began to conſider in what new Adventure we ſhould ſpend the remainder of the Day; and at laſt I remembred, I had oftentimes in the Countrey heard wonderful Tales and Tidings from *Higlers, Hawkers, Carriers, Drovers,* and ſuch like *Hobbadeboodies,* of ſeveral four-footed *Barbarian* Kings, with many of their Ravenous Subjects, who had for divers years been kept cloſe Priſoners in his Majeſties Palace and Priſon, the Tower of *London*; till their Hair was grown ſo long, it hung over their Eyes, like the Fore-top of a Parſons Mare, that goes ſix days to *Plow,* and the ſeventh to *Church*; and till their Nailes were improv'd to ſuch a terrible Extention, that the Keepers, by Relation, might as well venture to take a Bear by the Tooth, as to come within the reach of 'em, for fear they ſhould be worſe Scratch'd, then ever was poor Witch by her Languiſhing Sufferer, to diſſolve the Charm. The ſundry reports of theſe amazing Objects, together with many other Enticing Rarities, to be viſited at a ſmall expence within the Ancient Battlements of this Renown'd *Citadel,* which I had receiv'd from the Magnifying Mouths of ſome Boobily Bumpkins, who had ſtolen ſo much time from their *Waggons* and *Hay-Carts,* as to be Spectators of theſe ſurprizing Curioſities; had begot in me ſuch an earneſt Deſire of beholding theſe Forreign Monſters, and Domeſtick Engines of Deſtruction, with *Crowns, Scepters,* and many other Pompous *Knick-Knacks,* worth any great Mans Coveting, who prefers Grandure before Eaſe, and Riches before Safety; inſomuch that having prevail'd with my Friend, to Concur with my Propoſal, we determin'd to ſteer our Courſe towards this

ſtately

ftately *Magazine*, and fpend a little time in Viewing the Martial Furniture of that famous Garifon, which States-Men Dread, and the Common People Admire.

Having fo lately efcap'd from the Punifhment of a Crowd, we were very Cautious how we relaps'd into the fame Condition; for my *Lord Mayors Show* being paft over, the Mob began to divide their Main Body into diftinct Parties, a Divifion attending each feveral Company to their proper Hall, gazing at the Grave Noddies, who being perplex'd with either *Horns, Corns, Gout, Stone* or *Gravel,* hobbled after their *Hoitboys,* like the Great old Dons of the Law, when they Dance the Meafures in an *Inns-of-Court-Hall* upon the firft Day of *Chriftmas.* But we having hitherto very luckily avoided any Dirty Remembrances of the Rabble's Civility, notwithftanding we had been carelefsly drawn into fuch ill Company, which has been many a brave Mans Ruin, yet we (be thanked) recover'd our Freedom fiom their unlucky Hands without Damage but were fo fearful of falling a fecond time into their Clutches, that when ever we heard the *Waites, Drums,* or *Trumpets,* behind us, we ftarted forward with as much dread, as a couple of Church Mice would do from the Diapafon of *Paul's* Organ, for where-ever we heard the *Bagpipes,* we were affur'd the *Bears* were not far off; we thought our felves not free from the danger of fome Abufe, till we got thro' *Leaden-Hall Market* into fome of the back Lanes, for the Great Streets were the Channel of the Mob, who were very careful, as they mov'd along, to improve every handful of Dirt they could rake up to the prejudice of fome-body, or other. Crying, *All Fair, No-body, No-body* ; as they do in Frofty weather, when they break Windows at Foot-ball; the Perfon Injur'd having nothing elfe to do, but to bear his Wrong with much Patience; for Apprehenfion or Reprehenfion, will make 'em double the Mifchief. We found litttle worth our Obfervation as we pafs'd along, but many Merchants Houfes as ftately as Princes Palaces, and 'tis reported by fuch who have the Opportunity of being Judges of their inward Hofpitality, that their Houfe-keeping within, is anfwerable to their outward Grandure; which if it be, it's enough to make our Nobility Blufh, to fee themfelves out-done, in that Commendable Liberality, wherein the Honour and Splendor of a Great and Rich Man is moft Magnificently Vifible; Three or four of Qualities Coaches at one Door, two or three Chairs at another, as if the Courtiers were come into the City to Kifs the Merchants Wives, and borrow Money of their Husbands ; an old Game that has oft been Plaid, and will never be out of Fafhion whilft the City's Richer than the Court.

When we came upon the Hill, the firft Object that more particularly affected us, was that Emblem of Deftruction, the Scaffold, from whence Greatnefs, when too Late, has oft beheld the Happinefs and Security of Lower Stations; reflecting with a deep Concern on the fuddain Profperity and reftlefs Ambition which had brought 'em to that Fate, which the Contentment under a moderate Fortune, and a private Life, might have happily prevented; for he that fits too high in the favour of his Prince, is liable to be deliver'd up, upon Publick Diforders, as a Sacrifice to appeafe the Fury of the People; and he that Labours for a Popular Efteem, is always look'd upon by his Prince, to be a dangerous

Subject,

Subject, so that according to *Phœbus*'s Caution to his Son *Phaeton*, 'tis safest, to steer the Course of our Lives in a middle Station.

At a little distance from this *Memento Mori*, stood a very ragged Indigent Prophet, delivering with a thin pair of Jaws, a Shock-doggish-Beard, and a devout Countenance, the Doctrine of *Charity*, with a much Larger Congregation round him, than I have seen at Church, giving as serious Attention to their Mendicant Shepherd, as if every listening Member according to his Condition, design'd to Contribute something towards the Relief of their Distressed Lecturer, but before he had come to his Use and Application, a Blind Fellow, who had for many Years been one of the Hill Pensioners, takes up his Stand at a little Distance, and out of a Budget, which had as many Partitions as an old Country Cupboard, for his *Silver*, *Farthings*, short *Pipes*, *Tobacco*, and *Bread* and *Cheese*, &c. He pulls out a couple of little Flutes, claps one to each Corner of his Mouth, and with his Melodious Roundela's, drew off all the Audience from *Charity*'s poor Chaplain, leaving the *Ubiquitarian* Disciple in a wonderful Indignation; Calling after 'em as they mov'd off, in this manner, *Beloved, pray Beloved, stay a little, I am just a going to Conclude. Alas, alas, what a wicked Age do we live in, when Men shall forsake the Word of the Gospel, to follow a hobling Guide, and prefer the Tootings of a Blind Piper, before the Delightful Musick of Salvation.* But away went all the People, notwithstanding his reproof, to tickle their Ears with the Harmony of their dark Musician. The expectancy of the Paultry, instead of Spiritual Pastor, being quite Baulk'd the Multitude being drawn off without showing him one Example of their *Charity* amongst 'em all, he march'd Mumbling away in a great Fury with his Flock; Saying, just as he pass'd by us, *They were a Wicked Congregation that deserved to be Curs'd, and he would Pronounce an Anathema against 'em*: And looking over his Shoulder towards the People, breath'd out this Comical Execration, viz. *I wish your Ears were full of Birdlime, your Eyes full of Cats-piss, and your Mouths full of Sir-reverence, that you might all be Deaf, Dumb, and Blind, every time you stand to hear that Blind Hedg-bird Whistle, when you may bless your Ears with a good Sermon.* And having thus express'd himself, away he Rambled.

From thence we went into the first Gate of the Tower, where a parcel of Lazy Red-coates were Loitering about, like so many *City Bull-Dogs* at the *Poultry-Compter*. We were no sooner past the first Sentinel, but right before us, against the front of a little House, hung a strange sort of a Picture. My Friend ask'd me, what I thought it represented, or whether I had ever seen any Creature that was like it? To me it seem'd to be the Picture of some Rugged-Fac'd Mans Head, and after I had Compar'd it in my Thoughts, to every Body I could recollect, and all the Idea's I could form, I thought by its flat Nose, and Ill-favour'd Countenance, it was the likest the Unborn Doctor, the seventh Son of the seventh Son, in *More-fields*, of any thing that I ever saw in my Life. My Friend smiling at the Odness of my Fancy, undeceiv'd me, by telling me, 'twas a *Lyon*'s Head, hung out as a means to inform Strangers that comes to see the Tower, that *There* is the Royal Palace, where the King of Beasts keeps his Court, and may every day, at a proper distance, be seen at Dinner without danger; tho', like the *Czar* of *Muscovey*, if you

B

stare

stare at him too near, he'll be apt to do you a Mischief. This, says he, being the first sight, let us take it in it's Turn, and then you'll be better Satisfied.

Accordingly we went in, where the Yard smelt as Frowzily, as a Dove-house, or a Dog-Kennel: In their Separate Apartments, were four of their Stern affrightning Catships, one with a Whelp Presented to his present Majesty, of which the *Dam* was as Fond, as an old Maid when Married is of her first Child; One Couchant, another Dormant, a Third Passant Guardant, a Fourth, very fierce, was Rampant, being a Lyoness, and was as Angry when we Spoke to her, as a *Milk-Maid* when you cry, *Wo Ball*; she put out her Paw to me, which was tipp'd with such Ill-favour'd sort of Pruning Hook's, that sooner than she should have shaken me by the Hand, I would have chose to have taken *Old-Nick* by his *Cloven-foot*, and should have thought my self in less danger. One of the Keepers Servants, whilst he was showing us his Unruly Prisoners, entertain'd us with a couple of remarkable Stories, which because the *Tragedy* of the one, will render an Escape in the other Story the more Providential; I shall proceed to give 'em the to Reader in their proper Places, *viz.* That a Maid some years ago, being a Servant to the Keeper, and a bold Spirited Wench, took Pleasure now and then, to help feed the Lyon's, and Imprudently believing the Gratitude of the Beasts would not suffer them to hurt her, she would venture sometimes with extraordinary Caution, to be a little more familiar with them than she ought to be; at last either Carelesly or Presumptuously ventur'd too near their Dens, and one of the Lyon's Catch'd hold of her Arm, and Tore it quite off at the Shoulder, after a most Lamentable manner before any Body could come to her Assistance; killing her with a Gripe before he would loose her from his Tallons, till she was made a miserable Object of her own Folly, the Lyons Fury, and the Worlds Pity.

This Story he succeeded with another, wherein was shown as miraculous a Preservation of himself, contrary to the Cruelty the Lyon had before us'd to his unhappy fellow Servant, which he deliver'd after this following manner, *viz. 'Tis our Custom,* says he, *when we clean the Lyons Dens, to drive 'em down over Night thro' a Trap-Door into a lower Conveniency in order to rise early in the Morning, and refresh their Day-Apartments, by clearing away their Filth and Nastiness; and having thro' Mistake, and not Forgetfulness, left one of the Trap-Doors Unbolted, which thro' an Oversight I thought I had carefully secured, I came down in the Morning before Daylight, with my Candle and Lanthorn fasten'd before me, to a Button, with my Implements in my Hands, to dispatch my Business as was usual, and going Carelesly up into one of the Dens, into which a Lyon had return'd thro' the Trap-Door, and lay Couchant in a Corner with his Head towards me, the suddain surprize of this terrible Sight, brought me under such dreadful apprehensions of the danger I was in, that I stood fix'd like a Statue, without the Power of Motion, with my Eyes stedfastly upon the Lyon, and his likewise upon me; I expected nothing but to be Tore to Pieces every Moment, and was fearful to attempt one Step back, lest my Endeavour to shun him, might have made him the more Eager to have hasten'd my Destruction; at last he rouz'd himself, as I thought, in order to make a Breakfast of me; yet, by the*

assistance

assistance of Providence, had the Presence of Mind to keep steady in my Posture, for the reasons aforemention'd; he mov'd towards me without expressing in his Carriage either Greediness or Anger, but on the contrary Wag'd his Tail, signifying nothing but Friendship in his fawning Behaviour; and after he had star'd me a little time in the Face, he raises himself upon his two Hindmost feet, and laying his two Score Paws upon my Shoulders, without hurting me, fell to licking my Face, as a further Instance of his Gratitude for my feeding him, as I afterwards Conjectur'd, tho' then I expected every minute when he would have stripp'd my Skin over my Ears, as a Poulterer does a Rabbits, and have crack'd my Head between his Teeth, as a Monkey does a Small-Nut. His Tongue was so very rough, that with the few Favourite Kisses he gave me, it made my Cheeks almost as raw as a Pork Griskin, which I was very glad to take all in good Part, without a bit of Grumbling: And when he had thus saluted me, and given me his sort of Welcome to his Den, he return'd to his Place, and lay down, doing me no further Damage; which unexpected Deliverance hereto, occasion'd me to take Courage, that I slunk back by degrees, till I recover'd the Trap-door, thro' which I Jump'd, and plucking it after me, thus happily, thro' an especial Providence, escap'd the Fury of so Dangerous a Creature.

The under Keeper having thus ended his Stories, we proceeded to our further view of these *Beelzebub's Blood-hounds*, or *Lap-dogs* for a she-*Devil*. Two of them being Dead, and their Skins Stuft, one of them having been King *Charles's* Lyon, but had no more the fierceness in his Looks, that he had when he was Living, than the Effigies of his Good Master at *Westminster*, has the Presence of the Original; the other that was stuft, was said to be Queen *Mary's*, but made such a Drooping figure with his false Intrals, that it brought into my Mind an Old Proverb, with which I could not but agree, *That a Living Dog is better than a Dead Lyon.*

The next Ill Favour'd Creatures that were presented to our Sight, were a couple of pretty looking *Hell-Cats* call'd a *Tyger* and a Cat of *Mountain*, whose fierce penetrating Eyes pierc'd thro' my very Belly, to the sad Griping of my Guts, as if *Basilisk*-like, they could Kill at a distance.

In another Apartment, or Ward, for the conveniency of drawing a Penny more out of the Pocket of the Spectator, are plac'd these following Animals. First, a *Leopard*, who is grown as Cunning as a cross *Bedlamite* that loves not to be look'd at; for as he will be apt to Salute you with a Bowl of stinking Chamber-lye, so will the *Leopard* if you come near him, stare in your Face and Piss upon you, his Urine being as hot as *Aqua-fortis*, and stinks worse than a *Pole-Cat's*. The next Creatures we observed were three Hawk-Nos'd Gentlemen call'd *Eagles*: One Black, and another in Second Mourning, a Third with a bald pate as if he had been pulling a Crow, with his Two Comrades, and like unmerciful Enemies they had peck'd all the Feathers off his Crown, and left it as bare as a Birds Arse. Next to these were a couple of outlandish *Owles*, whose Mouths lay under their beaks like an Old Citizens under his Nose, who has rotted out his Teeth, with Eating Custard, at the Lord-Mayors Feasts. These *Owles*, besides Eyes as big as the Gladfes of a Convex-Lamp, had each of them Long Ears that grew like Horns, under which they look'd as venerably grave as a couple of Aged Aldermen.

The next part of the Show recommended to our Notice, were two preternatural Objects, being a *Dog* and *Cat*, Pupp'd and Kitten'd but with two Legs each: The former having a Bump upon his Head, which in derision to our high Crown'd Ladies, they are pleas'd to call a *Top-knot*. Prithee Friend, said I, to the Man that show'd 'em, what is it that you value those imperfect Vermin for? There's but little Satisfaction, I should think, in the Sight of such Ill-favour'd Monsters? *Sir*, says the Fellow, *whether you know it or no, these Vermin, as you are pleas'd to call them, are as highly Priz'd, and as well look'd after, as any Creatures in the Yard.* But pray Friend, said I, for what reason are they so Esteem'd? *Why, Sir*, says he, *Because they have but half their Number of Legs.* To which I answer'd, If that be all the reason, methinks they should take as much care to feed the Poor Humane Cripples, who were born with all their Legs, and have lost one half in the Nations Service, and are forc'd to seek their Bread where they can find it; I believe I see Twenty Begging upon the Hill as I came hither. *Ah Sir*, says the Fellow, *but they are no Rarities: Were it as uncommon a thing to see a* Soldier, *or a* Sailer *with but one Leg, as 'tis to see a* Dog, *or a* Cat *with* Two, *no question but they would Live as well, and be as much taken Notice on as these are.*

From thence we were remov'd into another Division, to see that alluring Creature so much talk'd on by the Old *Poets* call'd, *The Hyena*, which, as they report, has the Voice of a Man; and coming near a Cottage, would cry out like a Travelour in some distress, by which means he decoys the Shepherds out of their Houses, and afterwards, devours 'em; which whether it be Truth or Fiction, I could see nothing in the Creature to Determine.

Having thus paid Homage to the Kings of the Quadrupedes, and the Lofty Monarch of the Feather'd Kind; whose Ambition when at Liberty makes him Soar above all Terrestial Beings. We mov'd forward to the second Gate, where a parcel of Bulky Warders, in old Fashion'd Lac'd Jackets, and in Velvet Flat-Caps, hung round with divers colour'd Ribbonds, like a Fools Hat upon a Holiday, look'd as fierce as a File of *Artillery Ale-drapers* in *Buff*, when they are going to Besiege a Dunghill in *Bunhill-fields*, and play at Souldiers one against another, to please the Rabble. We had no sooner made a Nimbler step than ordinary, beyond the *Port-Cullis*; as Cautious Citizens do by the *Monument*, for fear it should Tumble upon their Heads, but one of these brawny *Beeff-and-Pudding-Eating-Janizaries* demanded, like a busie Constable at Midnight, whither we were going? Thought I, we are no sooner come from his Majesties *Lion's*; but we are fallen into the Clutches of his *Bears*; but did not dare to tell 'em so, for fear the *Bloody Colour'd Animals* would have fallen into a passion with me, and have spoil'd our Sight; but instead of that, inform'd 'em like an honest *Tell-troth*, our real business: They told us we could not be admitted to gratifie our desires without we took a *Warder* with us; which we found we were

forc'd

forc'd to consent to, or return back without the Satisfaction we propos'd. Upon which we order'd him to attend us, and had the honour of walking up and down the *Tower*, as great as a *Lord* committed for Suspicion of *High-Treason*.

The First thing we observ'd, when we were past the Gate, was a great *Brass Gun* painted over, of a Copper Colour; sure thought I, this was not done in a Jest, to let Folks who come in here see that *Guns*, like *Bells*, are as great *Turncoats* as those that command 'em, meaning *Parsons* and *Officers*; for the one will *Roar*, the other *Ring*, the Third *Preach*, and the Fourth *Fight*, for any Power that's uppermost: And 'tis verily believ'd by all people who have any Regard for that prevailing Principle, *Interest*, that they are all in the right on't.

The next place that fell in its Turn within our Notice, was the *Traitors-Gate*, where the fall of the Moat-Waters or the Cataracts on each side, made so terrible a noise, that its enough to fright a Prisoner that lodges within the hearing on't, out of the World before his time of Execution: the Passage being fortified by a parcel of Iron-Guns, which to me that understood 'em not, seem'd as old and as rusty as the hinges of the Gates of *Babylon*; but were, no doubt on't, in a good condition of giving a Sufficient Repulse to any Enemy that should attempt a violent Entrance.

We were from thence conducted thro' another Gate, upon an Ascent as steep as *Holbourn-hill*, tho' not so often dangerous; on the right hand of which stood a stately Square stone Fabrick, distinguish'd by the Name of *Julius Cæsar's Tower*; but must needs be as dark within side, as a Country *Bee-hive*, having but one Door, and never a Window that I could see, only a little *Slit* or Two, no bigger than the Mouth of a *Christmas-Box*, in proportion to its vast body; made so very close, as I conceive, to keep Fire and Gunpowder at their proper distance; left by an unhappy Conjunction of both, it should send more *Stones* into the City, than the *Shopkeepers Wives*, notwithstanding their *present want*, would know how to make good use of.

The next remarkable Place we came to, was the *Church*, whose Rugged Out-side appear'd with such Antiquity, that I dare engage the External Wall was far more reverenc'd by the True-Blew Protestant *Foot-Guards*, then all that could be heard or seen within-side.

A little beyond this Holy *Closet* of a *Church*, stood the famous *Armory*, now plac'd under a new and modish Name of *Arsenal*, of which I had heard such a General Applause, that I was particularly desirous of obliging my Curiosity with this Martial Entertainment; and accordingly order'd our Burly Guide to conduct us thither, who pursuant to our request, usher'd us up a stately *Stair-case*, where at the Corner of every Lobby, and turning of the Stairs, stood a *Wooden-Grenadier* as Sentinel, painted in his proper Colours, cut out with as much exactness upon Board, as the Good Housewife's with their Brooms, very usually set up in great Families, as good Examples for Servant Wenches, to make 'em mindful of their Cleanliness; but tho there were seve-

C ral

ªal Figures, yet the Painter, thro' the narrowneſs of his Fancy, had made their Poſtures, and their Faces ſo exactly alike, that it would be as hard for a *Moor-fields* Doctor, who Judges Diſtempers by Urine, to tell *Mares Piſs* from *Maids Water*, as it would be to diſtinguiſh one from the other, were they not differently poſted. When we came to the Top of the Staires, we were ſaluted, as I ſuppoſe, with two or three of the *Armorers Subſtitutes*; one amongſt the reſt, who I imagine was eſteem'd as their principal Orator, advanc'd before us, Cap in hand, with as much Ceremony as a *Dancing-maſter* uſhers the Parents of his *Pupils* into the School upon a *Ball-day*; beginning to tell us at our Entrance with an Audible Voice, the ſignification of thoſe Figures which firſt preſented to our view; having every thing as ready at his Fingers ends, as the Fellow that ſhows the Tombs at *Weſtminſter*, or as a *Savoy* Vagabond has the explanation of his *Raree-Show*: The firſt Figure at our coming in, that moſt affected the Eye, by reaſon of its bigneſs, was a Long Range of *Muskets* and *Carbines*, that run the length of the *Armory*, which was diſtinguiſh'd by a Wilderneſs of Arms, whoſe *Locks* and *Barrels* were kept in that admirable Order, that they ſhone as bright as a Good houſewifes *Spits* and *Pewter* in the *Chriſtmaſ-Holidays*; on each ſide of which were *Piſtols, Baggonets, Simiters, Hangers, Cutlaces,* and the like, Configurated into *Sheilds, Triumphal-Arches, Gates, Pillaſters, Scollopſhells, Mullets, Fans, Snakes, Serpents, Sun Beams, Gorgon's Head,* the *Waves* of the *Ocean, Stars* and *Garter,* and in the middle of all, *Pillars* of *Pikes,* and turn'd *Pillars* of *Piſtols*; and at the end of the *Wilderneſs,* fire Arms plac'd in the Order of a great *Organ*: This, ſays my Friend, is a kind of an Allegorical Emblem of a Wolf in Sheeps Clothing; for theſe Engines of Deſtruction, never plaid on to any purpoſe but in Wars, whoſe harſh and threatning ſounds Proclaim nothing but Wounds, Death, Diſcord, and Deſolation; to have their Miſchiveous Applications Diſguis'd under the Form and Figure of a *Muſical Inſtrument,* which breathes forth nothing but Peace, Innocence, Delight, and Harmony, is like putting the Devil into a Canonical Robe, or, as I ſaid before, a Wolf into Sheeps Clothing.

The next thing that our Expoſitor recommended to our particular Notice, were Sir *William Perkins's* Arms, taken under Ground at his Country-Houſe, as our Voucher told us, Pointing more eſpecially to Sir *William's* own *Carbine* and *Piſtols,* of which he made ſuch a terrible Story, that it would have frighted a Country Fellow from looking at 'em ; telling us they were ſcrew'd Barrels, *Heptagonically* bored. Why Friend, ſaid I, thou talkeſt as if thou Underſtandeſt Greek ; Prithee what is the meaning of that word *Heptagonically,* Oh Sir, ſays he, *it means a Barrel that will mould a Bullet into a Slug I don't know how many times Square, and will Kill as many Men again, and ſix times as far, as an ordinary round Barrel of the ſame Bigneſs.* We could not forbear Smiling at our Interpreter's Ignorance (who we expected would have told us the Barrel conſiſted of *Seven* ſides) anſwering him according to his Folly, and ſeem'd to be well ſatisfied with the account he gave us. Over the top of this Range of Treaſonable Implements, was plac'd a little *Braſs Blunderbuſs,* upon which he fix'd his Eyes, turning up the Whites like a Good Chriſtian at Prayers, ſhaking of his Head about half a dozen Times, like a ſorrowful Father about to reprove his Graceleſs Progeny, and then plucking one of his

Hands

Hands out of his Dutch Gloves, he pointed to it with a trembling Finger, and began to Open upon the Subject after this manner; *That Blunderbuss*, says he, *was design'd by the bloody Assassinators to have kill'd the King, which God of his great Goodness hath most happily prevented, bringing the Bloody Conspirators to condigne Punishment, and their Trayterous Weapons into the Power of that Glorious Prince whose Life they so basely fought; which are here (blessed be Providence) hung up in his Armory, as a perpetual Memorandum of his Majesties escape from the Hands of his Popish Enemies, to Gods great Glory, King William's Safety, and Englands Happiness.*

Our Little Holder-forth having done his Blundering Lecture upon the *King-killing Blunderbuss*, we remov'd from thence to another stand, where he shou'd us a parcel of *Dutch Fire-Locks*, with which the King landed at his first Coming to *England*, which was carry'd, I suppose by the *Monsters of Men* in *Bears-Skins* with *Sarazens-Heads*, Long Beards, and terrible Countenances, the report of which so frighten'd the Citizens of *London* and their Wives, that they were in as great a Consternation, as at the Midnight cry of the Coming of the *Cut-throat-Irish*.

Having thus taken a short view of the most renown'd *Armory* in *Christendom*, according to the Report of those who are far better Judges than my self, we return'd down Stairs with our Warder, who waited at the door to save his Legs, whilst we feasted our Eyes with that glittering sight, which was to him no Novelty : When we had descended the Grades, at the bottom door stood a *Bulky-frizzle-pate* (who, we might guess by his Fatness, could write himself no less than Servant to his Majesty) in a readiness to receive the accustomary Purchase-money for that sight which had given our Eyes an extraordinary Satisfaction.

Being now left to a further consideration of what we should see next, we took a little turn to deliberate upon the matter, but were forc'd quickly to make a result; for the *Tower-Rooks* began to flutter about us, like so many *Sales-men* about a Countrey Fellow in *Long-Lane*; only as the one asks whether ye want *Coat, Wastcoat*, or *Breeches, Will you buy any Cloaths*; so the other, after the same manner, and in much the same dialect, *Whether you will see the Crown, the whole Regalia, or the Kings Marching Train of Artillery.*

My Friend and I, considering the Marching Train of *Artillery* consisted of Great Guns, enough of which might be seen about the Tower without paying for't, made us think it scarce worth while to spend our Time and our Money to take a sight of those Threatning Potguns of Destruction, since all that could be said of them, if we had seen 'em, was, They cost the Nation a great deal of Money, were able to beat down Walls, would give a Devilish Bounce, and knock a Man on the Head at a great distance; so we agreed to pass by these, and adjourn to the Horse-Armory, whither we order'd our Guide to Conduct us accordingly. When we came to the Door, there stood ready to receive us two or three Smug-fac'd *Vulcans*, who were as Amiable in Complexion, as if, to make themselves *Infernal Beaus*, they had

powder'd

powder'd their frizled Locks with Lamp black ; and Beautified their Phyfiognomies with Kennel-water, the Lines of their Faces being fo pounc'd with Dirt, that, from the Shoulders upwards, they look'd like fo many Anticks heads in an Ale-houfe-Box, drawn in *Charcoal* by a Drunken *Painter*. After our Guide, who look'd in his Warders Robes, as if he had been cut out of a *Tapeftry-Hanging*, had given a Caution to the Smutty Interpreter of this Raree-Show, to tell us with deliberation the Names of his glitering Troop of Superficial Heroes, the Spokes-man introduc'd us amongft the Monumental Shells of our Deceas'd Princes, which only by the Induftry of common Hands fhin'd Bright in Memory of thofe that wore 'em. As we gently moved along, and view'd the Princely Scare-crowes, he told us to whom each Suit of Armour did belong Originally, adding fome fhort Memorandums out of Hiftory to every empty Iron-fides. Some True, fome Falfe, Supplying that with Invention which he wanted in Memory. He now and then endeavour'd to break a Jeft to divert his Cuftomers, but did it fo like an *Irifhman*, that I had much ado to forbear telling the Fellow what a *Fool* he was in endeavouring to be *Witty*. In our Circular progrefs round thefe Men of Metal, mounted on Wooden Horfes, we came to the Armour of *John* of *Gaunt*, fo famous for his Strength and Stature ; and indeed if his Coat of Defence was made fit for his Body, I believe he was as big as any of the Poetical Giants that Waged War againft Heaven: for on my Confcience a man may fpeak without Lying, that is I mean ftanding, that his Armour is near as big about, as the *Trojan Horfe*, as you may guefs by his very *Codpifs*, which was almoft as big as a *Poop-Lanthorn*, and better worth a Lewd Ladies admiration, than any piece of Antiquity in the *Tower*. As we were thus amongft the Reliques of our Ancient *Kings* and *Generals*. I could not forbear reflecting on fome Appearances before me, till I fancy'd my felf funk into Death's Subteranean Territories, where the *Juft* and *Wicked*, by the Impartial Skeleton, are equally refpected. Nor could I, without concern, behold, *Tyrants* and *Martyrs*, *Conquerers* and *Cowards*, *Lawful Princes* and *Ufurpers*, fhine equally bright by the Skill of an *Armorer*, in the Eyes of the Common People; when, if the Spots of Injur'd Blood were to ftain the Warlike Ornaments of fome who have long fince fpilt it, their Arms, which now look Bright, would appear of a Sanguine dye; and record to Pofterity thofe Cruelties which ought never to be forgotten. Whilft I was thus making my felf uneafy with thefe Melancholy Thoughts, we were advanc'd to the Armour of *Will. Sommers*, the Jefter, to which they had added an Ill-favour'd Face, with Horns upon his Head, and upon his Nofe a pair of Spectacles ; on which our Jocular Commentator was pleas'd thus merrily to defcant, *This Figure*, fays he, *reprefents that Drolling Gentleman* Will. Sommers, *who was Jefter to Harry the Eighth, he had the misfortune, poor Gentleman, to be in the Condition of many an honeft Cittizen even at this Day; That is, to have a very handfome Wife, who lov'd her Neighbours much better than her Husband, to which, like an honeft well-meaning contented Man, he would never give Credit, tho' he had been oft inform'd of her failings; and becaufe he was fo blind, like many a poor Cuckold in this Age, that he could not fee his Horns, which were Confpicuous to all others, he was prefented by a Noble-man who had kiffed his Wife, with a pair of Spectacles, to help his Sight, by which he afterwards difcern'd his Cuckoldom, which he here wears as a Memorandom to others in the*

fame

same Condition, to follow his Example. The next Subject he began to flourish upon, was King *Henry* the Eighth's *Codpiece*, which was lin'd with Red, and hung Gaping, like a *Turky Cocks Head* when he crys *Cobble*, or like a Maiden-head upon full Stretch, just Consenting to be Ravish'd · This, says he, *is the Codpiece of that Great Prince who never spar'd Woman in his Lust, or Man in his Anger; and in it to this Day remains this Virtue, That any Married Woman, tho' she has for many Years been Barron, if she sticks but a Pin in this Member-Case, the next time she uses the proper means, let her but think of her Tower Pin-Cushion, and she need not fear Conception.* From thence we pass'd by several Princes Armour, of which there was nothing deliver'd but a bare Name, till we had compleated our Round, and came again to the Door; where hung upon a Post the Armour of *King Some-body*, made in the fashion of a *Petty-coat*, in which, as our Dirty Oratour reported, he sometimes went a Masquerading, and when he had got such a pretty Lady as he lik'd, in a Corner, he us'd, says he, to whip it up in this manner, thrusting the Skirts all up in folds above the Belly, and under it appear'd a most Princely Scepter with which he ruled the Women, and made 'em do homage upon their Backs when ever he requir'd it.

This being the Conclusion of this *Warlike Opera*, we paid our Money, and made our *Exit*; our Stuttering Preambulator, turning his Head over his Shoulder, as a *Fox* that has Stole a *Goose*, ask'd us whether we would see the Crowns or no? *Marry*, said I, *Not I: Crowns are mighty things, that ought to be Reverenc'd at a distance · I have heard many a Wise Man say there's danger in coming too near 'em. Besides, if a Body should not make a Leg Handsomly, and Worship 'em as one should do; which a Country Clown, you know, can perform but awkwardly, they may think a Body stiff-Neck'd, and take one for a Disaffected Person to the Government.* Prithee, says my Friend, I thought you had more Wit than to be affraid of a fine thing , *why Prithee a Kings Crown is no Living Creature, it cannot bite thee.* I know well enough, said I, *it is not a Living Creature, nò more is a Kings Writ ; yet, I have known it Gripe many a Man to his Ruin; therefore I tell you, I don't Care to traft either any further than I cann't help it : And I'll warrant you our Conductor can inform us as well, as if at our Expence we had gone our selves to see 'em.* Upon which my Friend ask'd Old *Bluff-Jacket* what part of the *Regalia*, as he call'd it, was to be seen? Who told us there was the Royal Crown, and a new one made for the Coronation of the Late Queen *Mary*, and three others wore by his Majesty, with distinct Robes, upon several Occasions; also the Salt, Spoons, Forks, and Cups, us'd at the Coronation; which account we thought as Satisfactory from the Mouth of our Guide, as if our own Eyes were Witnesses of the matter, and so Cozen'd the Keeper of them of our Eighteen-pence a piece; which we thought would serve much better to Exhilerate our Souls, and Feast our Appetites, than to please our Eyes, and satisfie our Curiosities.

Having thus taken a remarkable View of most of the *Tower-Rarities*, in Respect to the Governour, we gave his House the Right hand as we came out, and rewarded the Warder with one of his Majesties Pictures in Silver, to his thorow Satisfaction, and so departed.

D

We

We now walk'd down upon the *Wharf*, where at the Entrance stood such a parcel of *Greenwich* Water-dogs, that I thought they would have Tore us in pieces before we could have Elbow'd our way thro' 'em. At last, with much difficulty, Sower Looks, and Negative Answers, we happily clear'd our selves of these Fresh-Water-Sharks, and took a pleasant Walk by the River side, where great Guns lay drawn into their proper Order ready to declare the Will and Pleasure of that Great Monarch who alone Commands their Voices, and gives their Sound Interpretation to the common People; for tho' the Loud-mouth'd Disputants, have but the Utterance of one Monosyllable call'd *Bounce*; yet does their Universal Language carry along with it such a Dint of Argument, that neither Logick, Rhetorick, or Philosophy, are able to withstand the force on't: About the middle of the *Wharf*, was a Stone Arch over the Passage to *Traytors-Gate*, where stood a Sentinel, who I observ'd, was very Careful no Body should lean upon it, or touch it, lest their Elbows or their Fingers should wear away his Majesties Free-stone; and to Piss against it, was a Crime that deserv'd Capping at least, except (like Swearing at a Precisians Club) for every such offence you would forfeit Sixpence to the Sentinel; so that I found it was held much better by the Guards, that a Good Subject bursts himself, than they lose the Advantage of a ridiculous and Shameful Custom, which oftentimes frights Fools out of their Money, and serves Wisemen to Blush at.

We walk'd round the *Tower*, and came again upon the Hill, where Mumpers, Soldiers, and Ballad-singers, were as busie at *Chuck-farthing* and *Hussle-Cap*, as so many Rooks at a Gaming Ordinary, wrangling and Squabbling about the fowlness of their Play, like so many knavish Pettifoggers in the *Kings-Bench-Walks*, about the unfairness of their practice. From thence we rambled into a remote part of the Town, which my Friend told me was as much *Incognito* to many thousands in *London*, as it was to me before ever I came into't: There was as many turnings and windings in and out of every street, as I believe could be contain'd in fair *Rosamond*'s Bower; and that which made me the more astonish'd was, we could walk by forty or fifty Houses, and not see an Ale-house; which was a greater sign of a Sober Neighbourhood, than I had observed before, since I came to *London*. As we were thus wandering carelesly about, on the other side the way, we saw a Door very finely Painted, which allured us to cross the Kennel, and give our Eyes the Satisfaction of taking a nearer view of what Mr. *Painter*, as we thought, had put up at his door to stand the censure of the Publick; but when we came over, we found according to our first apprehension, such a parcel of strange Hieroglyphicks, that would have puzzled an *Egyptian Magi* to have told the meaning of 'em. There was a *Goat* and a *Scorpion*, a *Fish* and a *Centaur*, a *Ram* and a *Crab*, and many other such-like Whims, at which we could not forbear Laughing. At last, reflecting more seriously upon the Whim, we found it to be a Representation of the *Twelve Signs*; from whence we presently concluded no less than an Eminent *Conjurer*, or some strange foretelling *Star-Peeper*, could be Lord of that House, whose Door was so gloriously set off with such a Number of Constellations: As we were thus spending our conjectures upon that Inhabitants Profession, out comes a Figure at the

door

door with such a malignant Aspect, that a great-belly'd Beggar woman, as she ask'd him for a farthing, turn'd her head, I observed, another way, for fear her looking in his Face might cause the Child to be like him ; one Eye look'd upwards, and the other downwards, as if he was Stargazing with one Eye, and minding his way with the other: What he was, we know not, but the House look'd as if a Conjurer liv'd in't, and the Man look'd as if he was bewitch'd. I ask'd my Friend the name of that Place, and he told me 'twas *Prescot-street*.

Pray, says my Friend, take Notice of yonder Tavern, at the sign of the *Green-Monster* ; that Tavern, says he, has ruin'd almost as many *Vintners* as Sir *Base-ill-fiery-Face*. I have known three or four break out on't ; whether for want of Trade, the knavery of the Merchant, or mis-management, I know not: The first indeed had a very handsome Wife, but very Jiltish, and suppos'd to be very kind to the Person that set her up ; who when he had once gratified his Lust at a great expence, vexing at his Folly when he had coold his Courage ; resolv'd, like a true Letcher, to turn his Lust that could not last, into a Revenge that should ; and accordingly brought Ruine upon the whole Family ; the Husband running away to *Ireland*, leaving the poor Woman to shift for her self, with nothing but what God sent her ; which she has since trusted into the Hands of a Draper, but what use he makes of it, you may easily Judge. Truly said I, I commend the Woman for trusting what her Husband left her with, in the hands of such a Trader, who when he is never so much tired with her, cannot at last, without great dishonour to the Linnen-Drapers Trade, leave her without a Smock to her back : Which is very commonly the Fate of Women who unhappily enter into such Illegal Contracts.

From thence, like Roving Pirats, who coveted no Harbour, we sail'd about we cared not whither, till meer accident, and our own motion, without shaping any Course, brought us into a street which both my Friend and my self were equally strangers to, in which we espyed a very sumptuous *Tabernacle*, by its being built so distinguishable from the House of the Lord, according to the Form of *Solomons-Temple*, that we were very desirous of knowing which of the Buzzing Sectaries made use of it for a Hive, wherein to work (with fear and trembling) the Combs of their Devotion, which I very much fear'd yeilded more Wax than Honey ; and meeting in our way with a down-right honest sort of a Fellow, I ask'd him, *What he call'd that street?* He told me, *Penitent-street?* I ask'd him further, *If he knew any peculiar reason why it was so Christen'd?* who answer'd me very roughly, *Because it was built*, he suppos'd, *for a parcel of deep Sinners to live in, and they call'd it by that Name, to put 'em in mind of Repentance. Who does this Meeting belong to?* said I, *A wicked Congregation*, says the Fellow: *Prithee*, said I, *who is their Teacher? The Devil, Sir*, says he. *I mean*, said I, *Who is it that Preaches, or holds forth here?* Oh ho, says my Respondent, *now I overstand yee* : Why they call him *Ca—sa—sa ca—lamanca Doctor*, I think, says he ; or *by such kind of a hard Name, which I cann't remember* ; tho I have seen him and heard him often ; *but as for my part, he does so whine when he speaks, that I had as live hear a Capon Crow, as hear him Preach* ; and as for his Face, on my Conscience, I think

he

be has a Chin to't as long as the handle of my Pick-ax: *Honest Friend*, said I, I thank jee, we'll trouble you no farther, for I know the man well enough by your Description, Good-buy to you. Nay, said I to my Companion, since my old Acquaintance, the Doctor, has fallen so luckily in my Way, according to my old Custom I must give him a Taste of my kindness.

> *Gods People sure, are once again run Mad,*
> *To chuse so sad a Soul to be their Teacher;*
> *No Nation such a Saviour ever had,*
> *Or Christian Congregation such a Preacher.*

> *His Doctrine, sure, can be no more than Farce;*
> *What Fools can follow such a vile Instructor?*
> *Perjur'd V—— who adores an A—s;*
> *Which since he does, mine A—s upon the Doctor.*

FINIS.

THE
LONDON
SPY.

For the *Month* of *December*, 1699.

The Second Volume.

PART II.

𝕿𝖍𝖊 𝕾𝖊𝖈𝖔𝖓𝖉 𝕰𝖉𝖎𝖙𝖎𝖔𝖓.

LONDON, Printed and Sold by *J. How*, in the *Ram-Head-Inn-Yard*, in *Fanchurch-Street*, 1701.

THE
LONDON
SPY.

THE merry *Christmas* Carnival being now come on, when the good Housewife makes her Husband Eat his Dinner upon a Trencher, to preserve her new Scour'd Plates in their shining Beauty, and Pinches the Guts of her Servants for the preceding Week, that her Windows may be splendidly adorn'd with superstitious Greens, and that her Minc'd-Pies and Plumb-Porridge may be Richer than her Neighbours. We Rambled from the Reverend Doctors boarded Theatre, who being lately Disgusted at the Ingratitude of his Audience, has divested 'em of their Cushion and Pulpit-Cloath, which he had before Presented them with, and has left 'em as Lost Sheep, to run headlong to Destruction without a Guide.

Being now got quite out of our Knowledge, we wandred about like a couple of Runaway Prentices, having confin'd our selves to no particular *Port*, *Uncertainty* being our *Course*, and meer *Accident* our *Pilot*. Every Street we pass'd thro' smelling as strong of *Roast-Beef* and *Rosemary*, as *Pye-Corner* does of *Pig* and *Pork* in the wicked Season of St. *Bartholomews*. Journey-men and Prentices we met every where as thick as Fools in *Cheapside* flocking to S——m's Lottery : The former to Collect their *Christmas-Box-money*, and the latter to see themselves Cozen'd out of their Foolish Expectancies. Every Ale-house we came at was serenaded with a Drum, to thunder their Rattle-headed Customers into a Humour of spending their Pence like *Asses*, which they had got like *Horses*. Every now and then we came to a common Vaulting-School, where peeping in, we saw Drunken *Tarpaulins* and their *Taudry-Trulls* Dancing to a *Scotch* Bagpiper, or a Blind Fiddler ; where, according to Mother *Shiptons* Prophecy, there were seven Women to one Man; and at least seventeen *Strumpets* to one that had *Modesty* enough in her looks to be thought otherwise. Sometimes meeting in the Street with a Boats-Crew, just come on shore in search of those Land-Debaucheries which the Sea denies 'em : Looking like such Wild, Staring, Gamesome, Uncooth Animals, that a Litter of Squab *Rhino-cerosses*,

cerosses, drest'd up in Humane Apparrel, could not have made to me a more ungainly appearance; so Mercurial in their Actions, and Rude in their Behaviour, That a Woman could not pass 'em, but they fell to Sucking her Lips like so many *Horse-Leaches*; and were ready to Ride her in the open Street, as if they were absolute Strangers to all Christian Civility; and could have committed a *Rape* in Publick, without a sense of Shame, or fear of Danger; quarrelling with one another, who should have the first Kiss, like so many Wanton Puppies after her Proud Ladyship, Snarling and contending who shall be next happy in her Beastly Favors. Every Post they came near, was in danger of having its Head broke; for every one as he pass'd by, would give the Senceless Block a bang with his Oaken Cudgel, as if they wish'd every Post they met with, to be either the *Purser* or the *Boatswain.* The very Dogs in the Street, I observ'd shun'd 'em, with as much Fear and Aversion, as a *Loitering Vagrant* would a Gang of *Press-Masters,* being so Caution'd against their Ill Usage by the stripes they have formerly receiv'd, that as soon as ever he sees a Seaman, away runs the poor Cur, with his Tail between his Legs, to avoid the danger of the approaching Evil. I could not forbear Reflecting on the Prudence of such Parents who send their Unlucky Children to Sea to *Tame* and *Reform* 'em; which I am well satisfied is like sending a Knave into *Scotland,* to learn Honesty; a Fool into *Ireland,* to learn Wit; or a Clown into *Holland,* to learn Breeding, by any of which Measures, they that send 'em may be sure that instead of mending the Ill Habits they have contracted, the first will return more *Wild,* the Second more *Knavish,* the third more *Foolish,* and the fourth a greater *Clown.*

By the time we had made these Observations and Reflections on those *Maritime* kind of *Monsters,* who had little more to show they were *Men,* than that they walk'd Upright, we were straggl'd into *Wappen*; and being pritty well tired with our Walk, we went into a *Publick-House* to refresh our selves with a Sneaker of Punch, as being the most likely to be the best Liqour that end of the Town could afford us: The first Figure that accosted us at our Enterance, was a Female *Wappineer,* whose Crimson Countenance, and duble-Chin, contain'd within the borders of a White Callico Hood, made her fiery Face look in my fancy, like a round red hot Iron glowing in a Silver Chavendish; The rest of her Body being in proportion to her Head, bore so Corpulent a grace, that had a Bag of Cotten, or a Wooll-Pack been lac'd into a pair of Stays, adorn'd with Petecoats, and put upon Stilts it would have made a Figure of such Similitude to her person, that the best Wax-worker, or Carver in *Christendom,* could not have represented her in either of their Arts, with truer Dimentions, or greater Likeness. My Friend having a Sword on, I observed to him she was most respectful, asking him, in a Voice as hoarse as a Boatswain aboard a Kings-Ship, *What will you please to drink, Noble Captain* ? Believing she could distinguish a Commander from an interiour Tar as well by his Sword, as she could a *Monkey* from a *Jack-a-napes* by his Tail. After we had answered her question, she had soon prepar'd us a little Bowl of her Spiritual *Diapente,* which, for want of better, we were forc'd to dispence with. Up in the Chimney-Corner sat a great hulking Fellow Smoaking a short Pipe of Stinking Tobacco, looking as Me-

lancholy

lancholy upon the Fire as a Female Wretch does upon *Smithfied* Piles when she is brought thither to be Burnt for High Treason. By and by in comes my Landlady, and like a true Lover of Industry, begins to read him a Lecture against Laziness, tormenting the Ears of the poor dejected Water-rat, with a severe Reprehension, after the following manner; *Why how do you think, John, in your Conscience, I am able to maintain you in this Lazy life that you lead? Thou knowst I have no Money, God help me, but what I work as hard for as any Woman in the Parish; therefore, John, it behoves thee to consider I am not able to let thee lie upon me in this condition. Why what a Rope ails you Mother?* reply'd the Fellow. *Why you wou'd not have the Conscience to turn me a Drift now I have spent all my money on Board you, before I have got me another Voyage. You are as hasty with a body to turn out, as a Boatswain in a Storm. Why, but John,* reply'd the Landlady, *d'ost thou think to get a Voyage by Smoaking in the Chimney Corner? No,* says John, *but how do you think a man can look out without a penny of Money in his Breeches? I swear by the Pursers honesty, I had as live step up to furle the Main Saile in a Gust of Wind, without a Knife in my Pocket.* To which reply'd the old Beldam, *Why I would not have thee think what I speak is out of any ill will to thee; for I hope thou thinkst I am willing to do any thing for thee, as far as I am able: Here, there is Sixpence for thee, and prithee John go and look out, and don't fling it away idely. For consider these hard times 'tis a great deal of Money.* He takes the Sixpence, thanks her; and She thus continues, *There are several Ships going out, bound to the* West-Indies, *that want Men; and I know thou art as able a Seaman as ever walk'd between Stem and Stern of a Ship, that any Commander will be glad to Enter thee. As for that, Mother,* says he, *I can speak a Proud word for my self, there is ne'er a part of a Seaman, from the Splicing of a Cable to the Cooking of the Kettle, but what I know as well as the Boatswain. Well, Mother, wish me good Luck, I'll go see what I can do, as the Gunner said to the Cooks Daughter.* She wish'd he might prosper in his endeavours; and away he went.

I could not but reflect on the unhappy lives of these Salt-water kind of Vagabonds, who are never at home, but when they're at Sea, and always are wandering when they're at home, and never contented but when they're on Shore. They're never at ease till they've receiv'd their Pay, and then never satisfied till they have spent it: And when their Pockets are empty, they are Just as much respected by their Landladies (who cheat them of one half, if they spend the other) as a Father is by his *Son-in-Law*, who has Beggar'd himself to give him a good Portion with his Daughter.

Whilst we were thus busying our Brains with thoughts relating to the condition of a Seaman, in steps another of the Tarpauling Fraternity, with his Hat under his Arm, half full of Money, which he hug'd as close as a *School-Boy* does a *Birds-Nest*. As soon as ever he came into the Entry, he sets up his Throat like a Country *Bridegrom* half drunk, so overjoy'd at his prize, as if he was as little able to contain himself under the Blessing of so much Money, as the Bumpkin was under a Foresight of those Pleasures he expected to find in the Embraces of his New Married Hug-Booby. *Ounds, Mother,* says our Marine *Cæsus where are you?* She hearing his Tongue, thought by his lively expressing himself, he had brought good News; came running with all speed

to

to meet him, crying, *Here am I, Son* Bartholomew; *You're Welcome ↄ shore. I hope your Captain and Ships Crew are all well. By Fire and Gunpowder, I don't Care if they be all Sick. Why we are paid off in the* Downs, *and I am just come up in a Hoy. I hope I can have a Lodging with you, Mother?* Ah ha *Child! Do'st think I won't find a Lodging for one of my best Children?* In answer to which, he innocently returns this Compliment, *Sure never any Sea-faring Son of a Whore had ever such a good Mother upon shore as I have. Ounds, Mother, let me have a Bucket full of Punch, that we may Swim and Toss in an Ocean of good Liqour, like a couple of little* Pinks *in the Bay of* Biscay. *I always said,* said she, *thou wert my Best Boy: Well, I'll go and prepare thee such a Bowl, that every Cup thou drink'st on't, shall make thee wish for a* Loving Sweetheart. *Now you talk of that, Mother, how does Sister* Betty? *She's very well,* says old *Suck-Pocket; Poor Girl, she'll be at home presently; I expect her every Minute. I believe she has ask'd after you a thousand times since you have been on Board. I dare swear she would be as glad to see you as if you were her Husband.*

In this Interim, whilst she was mixing up a *Sea-Cordial* for her adopted Sea Calf, John happens to return from his enquiry after a Voyage. *Lackaday,* John, says his Landlady, with a seeming sorrowful Countenance, *Here's the saddest accident falln out since you went abroad, that has put me to such a Puzzel, I know not how to order my Affairs, unless you will let me beg one kindness of you.* What a Pox, says John, *I'll warrant you now 'tis to lie upon that Lousie Flock-Bed that lies upon the Boards in the Garret.* Why truly John, *I must tell thee I have one of the best Friends I have in the World, just come on shore; and if you don't oblidge me, I shall be put to a sad Non-plus. Here,* John, says the old Wheedling Hypocrite *here's to thee; Come, drink; 'tis a Cup of the best Brandy, I'll assure you. Here* John, fill a Long Pipe of Tobacco: *Well, Son* John, *you say you'll let your Mothers Friend have your Room, Child, won't you? I don't care, not I,* says the Foolish Lubber, *he may ha't and he wool, I think I han't long to stay with you; I know now I have spent my Fifty Pound with you, you want to be rid of me.*

By this time the Bowl was just begun between Mother and Son; and who should step in, in the lucky Minute, but Sister *Betty*; and there was such a wonderful Mess of Slip-Slop lick'd up between Brother *Bat* and Sister *Bet*, that no two Friends met by accident in a Foreign Plantation could have express'd more Joy in their Greeting: But as soon as ever the *White-Chappel* Salutation was over, Mrs. *Betty* I found began to exert some further Arguments of his kindness, than just barely Kissing, and ask'd him, What had he brought his Sister *Betty* no present from Sea with him? *Yes,* says he, *I have sure. I can as soon forget the Points of my Compass, as forget my Sister* Betty: *As good a Girl as ever was kist in a Cabbin, or lost her Maidenhead in a Hammock. I told thee if ever I came home again I would present you with a Ring, and there's Money to buy it.* How now, Hussie, crys the Mother, *how dare you put your Brother to this Charge, you forward Baggage you? Pray give it him again, you'd best, or I'll Ring you, Marry will I, Minks.* The Daughter well acquainted with her Mothers Hypocrisy, replies, *I did not ask him for't, that I did not. I won't give it him, that I won't. As long as he gave it me, I will keep it, that I will: Why should'nt I?*

By

By this time our Punch was exhausted; and remembring we had heard of a Famous Amphibeous House of Entertainment, compounded of one half *Tavern*, and t'other *Musick-house*, made us willing to dedicate half an hour to what Diversion we might there meet with. Accordingly we left the old *Subtile Beldam* and her young *Jilting Fricatrix*, to empty the Fools Cap of his Nine Months Earnings, and send his *Hat* and his Pockets to Sea again, as empty as his Noddle.

As soon as we came to the Sign of the Spiritual Helmet, such as the High Priests us'd to wear when they bid defiance to the Devil, we no sooner enter'd the House, but we heard Fiddles and Hoitboys, together with a Hum-drum Organ, make such incomparable Musick, that had the Harmonious Grunting of a Hog, been added as a Base to the ravishing Concert of Caterwauling Performers, in the height of their extasie, the unusualness of the sound could not have render'd it to a Nice Ear more Engaging. Having heard the Beauty and Contrivance, of the Publick Musick Room, as well as other parts of the House, very highly Commended, we agreed to first take a view of that which was likely to be most Remarkable. In order to which we ascended the Grades, and were usher'd into a most stately Appartment, Dedicated purely to the Lovers of *Musick*, *Painting*, *Dancing*, and *t'other thing too*. No Gilding, Carving, Colouring, or good Contrivance, was here wanting to Illustrate the Beauty of this most Noble Academy; where a good Genius may Learn with safety to abominate Vice; and a bad Genius, with as much danger to Practice it. The Room, by its compact Order and costly Improvements, looks so far above the use its now converted to, That the Seats are more like Pews than Boxes; and the upper-end being divided by a Rail, looks more like a *Chancel* than a *Musick-Loft*. That I could not but imagine it was built for an *Oaten* Meeting-house, but that they have for ever destroy'd the Sanctity of the Place by putting an Organ in it, round which hung a great many pretty Whimsical Pictures, more particularly one, wherein was describ'd the solemnity formerly us'd at *Horn-Fair*, which, at first, I took (till I was undeceiv'd) for an Assembly of Grave Citizens, going to deliver a Petition to a Court of Common Council, to desire 'em to make a By-Act, or an Act by the by, to prevent Cuckold-making. There were but few Companies in the Room; the most Remarkable Person was a Drunken Commander, who plucking out a handful of Money, to give the Musick Sixpence, dropt a Shilling, and was so very Generous, that he gave an officious Drawer, standing by, half a Crown for stooping to take it up.

The Master finding we were much pleas'd with the Order and Beauty of his Room of State, was so Civil to ask us to see his House, whose kind offer we very readily Embrac'd, following him into several Cleanly and Delightful Rooms, furnish'd for the Entertainment of the best of Company; and to render 'em the more Diverting, had so many Whimsical Figures Painted upon the Pannels, that you could look no way but you must see an Antick, whose Posture would provoke Laughter as much as the *Dumb Man* in the *Red-Cap*, when his Brains are agitated by a Cup of Porters Comfort. When he had show'd us the most Costly Part of his Tippling Conveniency, he brought us into the Kitchen, which was Rail'd in with as much Pomp, as if nothing was to be Dress'd in it, but a Dinner

for

for a Prince. Over-head hung a Harmonious Choir of *Canary-Birds*, Singing; and under them, a parcel of *Sea-Gulls*, Drinking; who made such ordinary Figures, in so fine a Room, that they look'd as homely as a *Bantam Ambassador* in one of the Kings Coaches. From thence he Usher'd us down Stairs, into a *Subteranean* Sanctuary, where his *Sunday* Friends may be Protected from the Insolence of *Church-Wardens*, who every *Sunday*, like *Good Christians*, break the *Sabbath* themselves, to have the Leatchery of Punnishing others for the same Fault. Round this *Sots Retiring-Room*, were Painted as many Maggots as ever crawl'd out of an old *Cheshire Cheese*, in one Pannel a parcel of drunken Women tormenting the Devil, some plucking him by the Nose, like St. *Dustan*; some spewing upon his Worship, and others endeavouring to piss his Eyes out; and many other such like Whimsies. But the most remarkable of all, was the *Bonana-Tree*, which bears a very Evil Fruit, of which Women are most wonderful Lovers: Beneath its Umbrage are a great Number of the kind Sex, Contending for the Wind-falls; and some are so unreasonable, that notwithstanding they have gathered up more than they are able to stick in their Girdles, yet exert the utmost of their strength in endeavouring to shake the Tree: Some measuring what they had pick'd up, with their Spans, to try whether the Size was standard; others quarrelling for those of the largest Growth, like so many Sows for a great Apple; in which Condition we left 'em to dispute the matter, and return'd up Stairs, where we drank a Quart of good Red, thank'd the Master for his Civility and so departed the House, which may very justly be stil'd by such who love good Wine, and a Pleasant Room to sit in, *The Paradise* of Wapping.

Proposing but little more Diversion at this end of the Town, we thought it our best way to be returning Homewards; accordingly we fac'd about, and to make our Walk the more Pleasing, we chose a different Path to what we had before Travel'd, which brought us, after a little Rambling, to the *Danes* Church; it seeming, by the out-side, to be a very Regular and Commodious Building: Which put me upon an Enquiry of my Friend, whether ever he had seen the inside? Who told me *Yes*; and that it was a very Neat and well Compact Tabernacle, but the Congregation to whom it appertain'd, were such a parcel of poor Wainscote Fac'd Christians, they were enough to scare an English Parson out of the Pulpit were he to ascend amongst 'm; and Stunk so of Pitch and Tar, that as soon as ever I had clap'd my Nose into the Church, I thought my self between Decks. Their Uncomb'd Locks, Tobacco Breaths and Sea-faring Apparrel, adding such further Fragrancy to the former, that no Nest of Rats that had taken Sanctuary in a *Cheshire-Cheese*, could have smelt more Frowsily, And further, says my Friend, it is as Vainly as Rediculously Reported, That the Church is Cover'd with one intire Leaf of Copper, without Joynt or Sodder, which was cast in *Denmark*, but how they stow'd it on Ship-board to bring it over, and how they brought it from the Water-side to the Church, and how at once they rais'd it to the Roof, neither the Inhabitants of the Square, or any Body that reports it, could ever yet inform me: For granting it were True, the Demensions must be so large, and the Ponderosity so great, that it would require in the Performance such wonderful Art and Industry that would be worth Discovering.

From

From thence we Rambled on, like a couple of Sweetners in search of a Country Gudgeon, who thro' greediness of gain, would bite at his share in a drop'd Half-Crown, a gilded Ring, or Rug and Leather, till we came to a Heathenish part of the Town distinguish'd, as we found by Enquiry, with the applicable Title of *Knock Varges*, adjoining to a *Savoury* place which, in Ridicule of Fragrant Fumes that arise from Musty Rotten old Rags, and Burnt Old Shoes, is call'd by the sweet Name of *Rosemary-Lane*; where such a Numberless Congregation of Ill-Favour'd Maukins were gather'd together with their Hand-Baskets, That we thought a Fleet of *French* Protestants had been just arriv'd; and were newly come on Shore with Bag & Baggage, to implore the Charity of *English* well disposed Christians, to shelter them from the terrible Persecution of *Rags*, *Lice*, and *Poverty*. But upon a true Inquisition into the meaning of this Tatter'd Multitude being assembled in this surprizing manner, we were inform'd, by a little draggle-Tail *Flap-Cap*, it was *Rag-Fair*, held every day from between two and three of the Clock in the afternoon, till Night: where all the Rag-pickers about Town, and such as swop Earthen Ware for old Apparrel, also the Cryers of *Old Sattin*, *Taffaty*, *or Velvet*, have recourse, to sell their Commodities, to *Cow-Cross* Merchants, *Long-Lane* Sharpers, and other Brokers, who were as busy in Raking into their Dunghills of old Shreds and Patches, and examining their Wardrobes of decay'd Coats, Breeches, Gowns, and Petticoats, as so many Cocks upon a pile of Horse-Dung, Scraping about the Filth to find an Oat worth Picking at; or like a Parsons Hogs on a Monday Morning, routing about a Church-yard to find a S———nce worth biting at.

The adjacent Magistrates, we were inform'd, had us'd the utmost of their endeavours to suppress their Meeting, but to no purpose; for their *Number* bids defiance to all Molestation, and their *Impudence* and *Poverty* are such, that they fear neither Goal nor Punishment. You may here see the very scum of the Kingdom in a Body consisting of more *Ragged Regiments*, than ever, I believe, were muster'd together at any other Rendezvouz since the Worlds Creation. Its a rare place for a Miser to lay his Letchery at a small expence; for Twopence will go as far here in Womans Flesh, as half a Crown at Madam *Quarles*, and with much less danger of Repenting his Bargain. Its a very Healthful part of the Town, to cure Lazy People of the Yellow Jaundies; for Body-Lice are so plenty, that I dare engage they may have them without buying. It's a good Market for Country Farmers to buy their Scarecrows at; for let them but Bargain with the Rag Women to dress 'em up some *Maukins* in imitation of themselves, they need not fear but fright the Birds out of their Corn, and the Hogs out of their Pease-field; for I observed every Dog that came by scowr'd thro' 'em with as much expedition as an offending Soldier that runs the Gantlet thro a Regiment. Some of them, who by many years industry, having conquer'd the difficulties of this World, and rais'd themselves to the prodigal pitch of Twenty Shillings before-hand, were crept into little Huts and Holes, about as big as a Dog-kennel, and Lorded it over the poor Street-sitting-Vagabonds, like a Country Justice of Peace over his poor Neighbours. The Women that cry *Pancakes*, and the Girls that cry *Diddle, Diddle, Dumplins ho*, were wonderful busy amongst 'em; and several little Ale-houses are already crept in amongst 'em, to ease 'em of their pence as fast as they

C

can

can raife 'em by the Sale of their Commodities; The Flefh of the Inhabitants, as well as the Market-People, look'd of fuch a dingie Compleἔtion, as if Dame Nature had mix'd kennel dirt with her Clay, as Bricklayers do with their Mortar, to make it bind the fafter; or elfe as if frefh water was as fcarce in the Neighbourhood as 'tis in *Antego*. All Strangers that came by look'd about 'em as if frighted; and like us, till they were better fatisfied, thought they had fallen into a Congregation of Vipers, who look'd as if the good and bad Angels were fharing their interefft in this World; and in order to feparate the Righteous from the Ungodly, the Devil had drove his Parcel to this end of the Town, where he had drawn 'em together, in order to Embarque for his Infernal Territories; for it would amaze any body at firft fight, to think what fuch a Number of poor Wretches could do together, unlefs like Seamen in a long Calm, they were going to draw Cuts about devouring one another. The chief Cuftomers were Mumpers, and People as *Ragged* as themfelves, who came to barter *Scraps* for *Patches*; obferving it was a very Currant Swop to chang *Food* for *Rayment*; that is, fuch needful Repairs as a Beggars Breeches may want between the Legs, or his Coat at Armpits or Elbows. Some Rags I obferv'd were parcel'd out for better purpofes, and would not be difpos'd of to any but ready money Cuftomers: Many of their Stocks were fo very fmall, that, I found Twopence, or Three-pence, were accounted, amongft fome of them, confiderable Takings. Yet this obfervation I made, That amongft all that I beheld, as I pafs'd thro' 'em, I faw not one melancholy or dejeἔted Countenance amongft 'em; but all fhowing in their Looks more Content and Chearfulnefs than you fhall find in an *Affembly* of Great and Rich Men on a Publick Feftival. From whence we may Reafonably Conjeἔture, that *Poverty* is commonly attended with fuch a Carelefs Indifference, that frees the Mind from refleἔting on its Miferies. For undoubtedly were thefe defpicable Paupers, but to let the unhappinefs of their Circumftances once affeἔt their thoughts, and become an Objeἔt of their Confideration, it would have fuch a melancholy Effeἔt upon their Spirits, as would be foon legible in their Looks, and difcernable even in their Aἔtions, which would want that Vigour and Vivacity neceffary to perform whatever they undertake

As we were thus Defcanting upon the Ragged Sons and Daughters of Neceffity, a formal Figure pafs'd by us, in an Ancient Plate-Button'd Suit, with an old fafhion'd Silver Hilted Sword, tuck'd up to the Waft-Band of his Breeches, in a long Wig, buckled up in fmall Rings, as if, like an old Cavaliers Whiskers, every Hair had been turn'd up with Gum-water, the Curles hanging all as ftiff as a Pigs Tail, and as regular as the Worm of a Bottle Screw, his Hat as dufty as the top of a Sluts Cup-board, and his Hands and Face look'd as rufty as an Old Negleἔted Piἔture, that had lain feven Years in a Garret full of Rubbifh; as he Waddled by us in great hafte, he gave my Friend the Civility of his Hat, which was by us return'd; but looking after him, obferv'd he had left the Print of his Fingers where he had handled the Brims, as plain as a *Chimney-Sweeper* could have done, if he had clap'd a *Meal-Man* upon the Shoulders; but taking Notice of his Complefance, I ask'd my Friend, if he had any acquaintance with him? Who told me, he had feen him fometimes at the *Green Dragon* Tavern, but had little knowledge of him, any other than

that

that he had heard several Odd Stories of him, from some who use the House, that are much better acquainted with him: He is very Famous among those that know him, for Three Slovenly Neglects, *viz.* He very seldom Washes his Hands, or Face; very rarely Brushes his Hat; and never Combs his Wig but when he goes to Church, which is not above Once in a Twelve-Month; for he is a Man of no extraordinary Principles, but one who has run thro' a great many Cunning Professions without success, as *Merchant, Brewer, Lawyer, &c.* and failing in all, is at last, thro' a Natural Propensity to exert his Wits, turn'd *Sharper.*

By this time we were got into *Goodmans-Fields,* where passing by the *Little Devil Coffee-House,* my Friend gave me such a large Encomium both of the *People* and their *Punch,* That I, like himself, was unwilling to let slip so good an opportunity of Refreshing my Intelects, with a little of that most Edifying Liquor; which if Compounded of good Ingredients, and Prepar'd with true Judgment, Exceeds all the Simple Potable Products in the Universe. At our first Entrance of the Publick Room, we found a Jolly Company blessing one another o'er a plentiful Bowle of this Corroborating Creature, whose Excellencies were visible in the very Looks of its Lovers: The Worldly Air of their Countenances, being chang'd into a Heavenly Chearfulness. This pleasing sight gave me great encouragement to walk up Stairs; where in a Room neat enough to entertain *Venus* and the *Graces,* we were in a Minutes expedition supply'd with an *Indian* Goblet of their Infallible Cordial, which in half an hour, had carry'd off the Dregs of our Flegmatick Constitutions, and so sublim'd our Thoughts, that we found our selves Elevated above the Pitch of Humane Conversation: And having the Company of our Landlord, and a Friend or two of his, as Jolly as himself, the Cup pass'd round in a Circle, as an Emblem of Eternity, till at last I was so highly inspir'd by the Noble Virtues of our *Nectar,* that I had much ado to forbear thinking I was in a State of Immortality. And that which added much more to our Felicity, and crown'd the Pleasures of our Liquor, were these following Advantages, My *Landlord* was *good Company,* my *Landlady good humour'd,* her *Daughters charmingly pretty,* and the *Maid* tollerably *Handsome*; who can Laugh, Cry, say her *Prayers,* sing a *Song,* all in a Breath; and can turn in a Minutes time to all the Sublunary points of a Female Compass: Yet thus much I must say in her behalf, that she's obedient to her Mistress, and obliging to Company, and I dare swear, as far as a Man may guess by outward appearance, she'll prove an exellent Bed-fellow to him that has the luck to Marry her.

After we had throughly awaken'd our Drowsie Brains with a sufficient Quantity of this unparallell'd *Punch,* my Friend Writ the following Verses.

In

In Praise of *PUNCH*.

Immortal Drink, whose Compound is of Five,
  More Praise do'ſt thou deſerve, than Man can give;
A Cordial that ſupports the Troubled Heart,
And do'ſt infuſe new Life, in ev'ry part:
  Thou clear'ſt our Reaſon, and inform'ſt the Soul,
And makes us Demy-gods, when o're a Bowl,
Inſpir'd by thee, we're rais'd to ſuch a Pitch;
That things beyond Mortality we reach,
Such as without thy Pow'r no Stag'rite e'er could Teach.
Had our Forefathers but thy Virtues known,
Their Foggie Ale to Lubbers they'd have thrown;
And Stuck to thee, who gives the Soul a Sight
Of things that Study ne'er could bring to Light.
Which if they had, I may with Reaſon ſay,
Our Great Great Grandſires might have ſeen this day;
Had they th' Effects of this Di'pente ſeen,
Five would have ſure the Golden Number been.
Let Muſick Judge thy Harmony alone,
A Fifth's a Concord, but a Seventh's none.
Therefore thou ſurely doſt excel in Heaven,
And Juſtly takes the upper Hand of Seven.
Thou Friendſhip knit'ſt, and do'ſt the ſame Preſerve;
They who Neglect thee, do not Live, but Starve:
Slight thoſe great Benefits they might Poſſeſs,
Which Wine cann't Equalize, or Words Expreſs.
Thou clear'ſt all Doubts, and driv'ſt away all Care,
And mak'ſt Mankind ſhow truly what we are;
When to thy Pow'r we chearfully ſubmit,
And round the Bowl, thy flowing Confines, ſit,
We Paradice Regain, and Re-injoy
That happy State, which common Ills Deſtroy.
The Sober Muckworms, who thy Name abuſe,
And with Contempt thy Jolly Cups refuſe,
Are Ploding Knaves, who're fearful to betray
Some baſe Deſignes they are about to Play;
And therefore without Danger cannot Truſt,
Evils with thee, that art Divinely Juſt.
Thou art the Key to humane Heads and Hearts,
O'er thee, the Modeſt, Witty, ſhow their Parts.

Thou

Thou pat'ft new Vigour into Life's old Springs,
The Poet Rhimes, and the Mufician Sings;
The Artift does his Rules and Means difclofe,
The Lawyer Feelefs tells you what he knows.
The Parfon quits Divinity and Drinks;
At all our little Slips and Failings Winks;
Nor tells you what he has Read, but truly thinks.
The Virgin all her Coynefs lays afide,
And hears a Love Petition without Pride,
* Shewing thofe Faults, before by Art fhe hid.*
The Wife, will by her true Behaviour fhow,
Whether fh'as Horn'd the Goodmans Head, or no;
The Subtile Widow, will her Love fet forth,
And frankly tell you, what fhe's truly worth.

*   In thee one Virtue more, I muft commend,*
Of Liquors, thou'rt the only Womans Friend;
'Twill make the Youth, his utmoft Pow'r exert,
And the old Fumbler, play the young Mans Part.

To thee, my only Miftrefs, could I Raife,
An everlafting Monument of Praife.
For thus much may I juftly fay in fine,
Thou haft an Excellence furpaffing Wine,
And art the only Cordial that's Divine.
* Therefore to know this mighty Truth I want,*
If a Saint firft made Punch, or Punch firft made a Saint.

We now return'd back again to our buzzing Metropolis, the City; where Honefty and Plain-Dealing were lay'd afide, to purfue the wonderful Expectancies fo many Thoufands had from a mixture of Projectors *Knavery* and their own *Folly.* The *Gazett* and *Poft-Papers* lay by Neglected; and nothing was purr'd over in the *Coffee-houfes* but the *Ticket-Catalogues:* No talking of the *Jubilee,* the want of a current Trade with *France,* or the *Scotch* Settlement at *Darien;* nothing buzz'd about by the Purblind Trumpeters of State-News, but *Blank* and *Benefit. My Son had Five Pounds in fuch a Lottery, but got nothing; my Daughter,* fays another, *had but Five Shillings, and got the Twenty Pound Prize.* People Running up and down the Streets in Crowds and Numbers, as if one end of the Town was on Fire, and the other were running to help 'em off with their Goods. One ftream of *Coachmen, Footmen, Prentice-Boys,* and *Servant-Wenches,* flowing one way, with wonderful hopes of getting an Eftate for Three Pence. *Knights, Efquires, Gentlemen,* and *Traders,* Marry'd *Ladies, Virgin-Madams, Jilts, Concubines,* and *Strumpets,* Moving on Foot, in Sedans,

D   *Charriots,*

Charriots, and *Coaches*, another way; with a Pleafing Expectancy of getting Six Hundred a Year for a Crown.

Thus were all the *Fools* in Town fo bufily imploy'd in running to one *Lottery* or another, that it was as much as *London* could do, to conjure together fuch Numbers of *Knaves* as might Cheat 'em faft enough of their Money. The Unfortunate crying out as they went along, *A Cheat, a Cheat, a Confounded Cheat, nothing of Fairnefs in't*. The Fortunate, in Oppofition to the other, *Crying, 'Tis all Fair, all Fair, the Faireft Adventure that ever was Drawn*: And thus every body, according to their fuccefs, expreffing varioufly their Sentiments. Tho' the Loofers, who may be faid to be in the Wrong of it to venture their Money, were moft Right in their Conception; and the Gainers, who were in the Right of it, to their Opinion of the matter: For I have much ado to forbear believing that *Luck in a Bag*, is almoft as Honeft as *Fortune in a Wheel*, or any other of the like Projects. Truly, fays my Friend, I confefs I cannot conceive any extraordinary Opinion of the Fairnefs of any *Lottery*; for I am very apt to belive, when ever fuch a Number of *Fools* fall into a *Knaves* Hand, he will make the moft of 'em; and I think the *Parliament* could not have given the Nation greater Affurances of their efpecial regard to the Well-fare of the Publick, than by fuppreffing all *Lotteries*, which only ferve to bouy up the miftaken Multitude with Dreams of Golden Showers, to the expence of their Money, which with hard Labour they have Earn'd; and often to the Neglect of their Bufinefs, which doubles the Inconveniency. The Gentry indeed might make it their Diverfion, but the common People make it a great part of their Care and Bufinefs, hoping thereby to relieve a Neceffitous Life; inftead of which, they plung themfelves further into an Ocean of Difficulties. What if one Man in Ten Thoufand gets Five Hundred Pounds, what Benefit is that to the reft, who have ftruggled hard for Fools Pence to make up the Sum, which perhaps falls to one who ftood not in need of Fortunes Favours

Prethee, fays my Friend, let's go to *Mercers-Chappel*, and fee how the Crowd behave themfelves there: Ten to one but we fhall find fomething or other that may be Diverting to our felves, and worth rendering to the Publick. Accordingly we directed our felves thither; to which Rendezvous of Adventurers, as well as our felves, abundance of *Fools* from all parts of the Town were flocking; none fhewing a Defparing Countenance, but all expreffing as much hopes in their Looks, as if every one had had an affurance from a *Moor-fields Conjurer* of having the great Prize. Some being thoughtful how to Improve it, fhould it fo happen; fome, how happily they'd Enjoy it; Women, what fine Cloaths they'd Wear; Maids, what handfome Husbands they'd have; Beaus, what fine Wigs they'd Wear; and Sots, what rare Wine they'd Drink; the Religious, what Charitable Works they'd do; and young Libertines, what fine Whores they'd keep. In the Porch, or Entry of the *Hall*, was a Bookfellers-Shop; where they Sold the Printed Benefits, for which the People were fo Impatient, that there could not be more clawing

ing amongſt Mumpers at a Noblemans Gate, (when he goes out of the Town) at the diſtribution of his Charity. With much ado we crowded into the *Hall*, where *Young* and *Old*, *Rich* and *Poor*, *Gentle* and *Simple*, were mix'd higgle-de-piggle-de, all gaping for a Benefit, like ſo many Fortunes Minions, waiting for a Windfal from the Blind Ladies Golden Pippin Tree, whilſt the Projector and the Honourable Truſtees ſat Laughing in their Sleeves, to ſee fair Play dealt out to the attentive Aſſembly, whoſe avaritious Hearts went a Pit-a-Pat at the Drawing of every Ticket.

Every now and then, when a Benefit aroſe, ſome impatient Novice or other crying out, *That's mine*; buſſling up to the Truſtees, producing his Ticket to prevent that Fraud, which, tho' he had ventur'd his Money, he was fearful might be Practicable amongſt 'em. It ſometimes proving that the Adventurer had miſtaken his Number, or the Number that was Drawn to the Benefit, which unhappy Miſtake would be ſuch a diſappointment to 'em, that their ſilly Looks would render 'em a Laughing-ſtock to the whole Congregation of Fortunes Courtiers, every one equally big with the hopes of being the only Favourite.

My Friend and I having no pretence, or title to be rank'd, by any accident, in the number of the Fortunate, having Ventur'd nothing in their plauſible piece of Uncertainty, thought it not worth our while to ſpend any further time amongſt 'em, but concluded to march about our Buſineſs, and leave the numerous Sons and Daughters of Fortune, to flatter themſelves with the vain hopes of their Mothers kindneſs. Going, when we came out, to a neighbouring Coffee-Houſe, where we ſmoak'd a Pipe, and conſulted of ſome *New Meaſures* to take in our next *Spy*; which having agreed on, we retir'd home, where I ſcribled o'er the following Lines upon *Lotteries*, with which I ſhall conclude.

W Hat ſundry Projects the Ingenious find,
    T' Allure and Cozen Avaritious Fools;
    And draw the Common People, who are Blind,
    In all their Stratagems to be their Tools?

The hopes of ſuddain Wealth, does moſt deceive,
    When 'tis from Labour and from Danger free;
    Let but the hopes be plauſible you give,
    And moſt Men will with your Deſigns agree.

For all men love Proſperity and Eaſe,
    And when its Proſpect they with Safety have,
    Tho' at a vaſt long Diſtance, yet 'will pleaſe,
    More ſurely him, whom Want does moſt Enſlave.

This made the Lott'ries with the Crow'd prevail;
    The Odds, tho' great, they never mind to Scan;
    As long as each among the Num'rous All,
    Has equal hopes to be the happy Man.

The

The vaft Deduction, for the Pains and Charge,
Of Ten per Cent, in Reafon is too great;
And where the gain in Juftice is too Large,
The very Profit is alone a Cheat.

Thoufands, 'tis plain, would foon have been Undone,
Had the late Act much longer been delay'd;
Where many fuffer to enrich but one,
All fuch defigns are in their Nature bad.

All loofe vain Projects ought to be debar'd;
Which are of Evil to the Publick known,
Wherein Projectors have a large Reward,
For doing what had better ne'er been done.

This is enough to prove they hurtful are;
Since amongft all the Adventurers you meet,
To one who has reafon to believe 'em Fair,
A thoufand fhall cry out, A Cheat a Cheat.

He that Projects, or Models the Defign,
Like the Box-keeper, *certain is to Win:*
In Lott'ries *'tis the fame as 'tis in* Play,
The Knave's *the* Vulture, *and the* Fool's *the* Prey.

F I N I S.

THE
LONDON
SPY.

For the *Month* of *January*, 1700.

The Second Volume.

PART III.

LONDON, Printed and Sold by *J. How*, in the *Ram-Head-Inn Yard* in *Fanchurch-street*, 1700.

Books Sold by J. How, *in the* Ram-Head-Inn-Yard *in* Fanchurch-Street; J. Weld, *at the* Crown *between the* Temple-Gates *in* Fleet-street; *and* Mrs. Fabian, *at* Mercers-Chappel *in* Cheapside.

1. SOt's Paradise: Or the Humours of a Derby-Ale-House: With a Satyr upon the Ale. Price Six Pence.

2. A Trip to *Jamaica*: With a True Character of the People and Island. Price Six Pence.

3. *Eclesia & Factio.* A Dialogue between *Bow-Steeple-Dragon,* and the *Exchange-Grashopper.* Price Six Pence.

4. The Poet's Ramble after Riches. With Reflections upon a Country Corporation. Also the Author's Lamentation in the time of Adversity. Price Six Pence.

5. A Trip to *New-England.* With a Character of the Country and People, both English and Indians. Price Six Pence.

6. Modern Religion and Ancient Loyalty: A Dialogue. Price Six Pence.

7. The World Bewitch'd. A Dialogue between Two Astrologers and the Author. With Infallible Predictions of what will happen from the *Vices* and *Villanies* Practis'd in *Court, City* and *Country.* Price Six Pence.

8. A Walk to *Islington*: With a Description of New *Tunbridge-VVells,* and *Sadler's* Musick-House. Price Six Pence.

9. The Humours of a Coffee-House: A Comedy. Price Six Pence.

10 A Frolick to *Horn-Fair.* With a Walk from Cuckold's-Point thro' *Deptford* and *Greenwich.* Price Six-Pence.

11. The First Volume of the LONDON-SPY: In Twelve Parts.

12. The First, Second and Third Parts of the Second Volume, of the *London-Spy,*

All Written by the same Author.

THE
LONDON
SPY.

A S a Fair *Town-Miss*, of a Twelve-Months standing, when she has surfeited the Appetite, of those *Debauchees* who are always ranging after Novelty; and render'd herself *Contemptible*, by being too *Common*, puts on a dark Fore-top, blacks her Eye-browes, changes the Mode of her Dressing, her Lodging, and her Name, and sets up for a *New Creature*; so we, for fear of falling under the same Fate, have thought fit to vary a little from our Former Method, in hopes to preserve the same Liking to our Design, which we believe the World has hitherto had, from the Encouragement it has given us to continue our Undertaking. Our chief Alteration will be to Treat more upon *Men* and *Manners*; opening the *Frauds* and *Deceits* practicable in many Trades, also of the sundry sorts of *Conversation*; With *Moral Reflections* on the same. *Characters* of *Trades*, and those that follow 'em. And *Remarks* upon all Occurrences worth Notice. In pursuance to which Method, I shall begin with *Victualers*, showing their usual *Rise* and means of *Success*. And also shall lay open their *Pride, Sawciness,* and *Ingratitude*; which either most Men have, may, or will find, by their own experience.

Of Victuallers.

In Times of *Sobriety*, when *Ale-houses* were as scarce as *Churches*, not above one in a Parish; when any Tradesman was undone by the *Levity* of his *Wife*, the *Disobedience* of his *Children*, by *Fire*, in either *House* or *Codpice*, or any other Losses or Crosses incident to a Man in this World; upon his humble application to the Magistrates of the Ward, or Precinct wherein he liv'd, they would Grant, or procure him to be Granted, a License to sell Ale, that he might be doing something to defend himself and his Family from being burthensome to the Parish. And being unhappily fallen into a peevish Temper, by reflecting on his Misfortunes; he was usually distinguished in his new Employment, with some of the following
ing

ing Nick-names and Titles, as *Alderman Snarl, Captain Rufty,* Sir *John Tun-belly, Efquire Gruff, Doctor Grunt,* or the like; being look'd upon no other than an old *Crack'd-Fiddle,* fit for every Merry *Prattle-Box* to Play upon. Neither could the good Woman, (whofe Bufinefs it was to draw the Tipple, and who kept her Shoulders warm with a piece of an old *Blanket* inftead of a *Night-Rail*) avoid being new Chriften'd by fome Drunken Godfather or other, by the Name of *Mother Huff, Mother Damnable,* the *Witch* of *Endor, Dame Saucy, Goody Blowze, Gammer Tattle,* or the like. But now the World, like a Man advanc'd from *Poverty* to *Profperity,* is fo ftrangely alter'd, That as foon as a Tradefman has got a little Money by the Bufinefs he was bred to, obferving the fluency of *Fools-pence,* the *Lordlinefs* of *Victuallers,* the *Lazinefs* of their *Lives,* the *Plenitude* of their *Purfes,* and *Welfare* of their *Families,* is refolv'd to Thrive upon his Small Stock at the fame Rate; and purfue the hopes and profpect of growing Rich with the fame Expedition. Accordingly takes a Houfe well fituated for his purpofe; where, in a few years time, behaving himfelf at firft very humble, he breaks half his Acquaintance of his former Trade with coming to fee him; Advancing himfelf in a little time to fome petty Office of the Parifh; with which he begins to *Swell,* and look as *Stiff* and as *Prodigal* as an *Alderman* after *Knight-hood.* From thence, in a little time, dignified with the Office and Title of Mr. *Church-Warden*; with the very Conceit of which, he is fo puff'd up, That during the poffeffion of the Church Keys, he thinks himfelf as great as the *Pope*; and meafures a Foot more in the Wafte, upon his firft Entrance into this *Parochial Authority,* than he did in feven years before he was chofen to't. His Wife muft now be call'd *Madam*; his Sons, *young Mafters*; and his Daughters *Miffes*; and he that falutes the old *Lickfpiggot* with any other Title than Mr. *Church-Warden,* runs the hazard of Paying double Taxes, befides the Forfeiture of his good Looks, Friendfhip, and Converfation, for as long as he lives afterwards; without Providence, by fome Cafualty, brings him back to his firft Humility; which is to be done by no other way than *Poverty.* He now begins to leave off his Colours, and to get the print of his Apron-Strings out of his Coat, that, as he walks along the Streets, it would be a hard matter to guefs at his Profeffion, were it not for the many Rings on his Fingers, and the Stiffnefs of his Gate.

His own Houfe now is not big enough to hold him: Befides, he begins to have fuch an Averfion to his own Liquor, That he hates *Malt-Drink* as bad as a *Grocer* does *Plumbs,* or an *Apothecary Phyfick. Wine* is the only Cordial that will go down with him, which he Purchafes with the Pence of thofe *Poor Sots* who are Guffling *Belch* at his own *Ale-houfe,* to maintain him at the *Tavern.* He expects great Reverence from all his little Neighbours; and will Loll againft the Door-cafe, and fwing his Bunch of little Keys half a dozen times round his Finger, before he will Anfwer a poor Neighbour a Civil Queftion. Thofe who were the firft Inftruments in procuring him a *Trade,* are as much out of his Memory, as a Womans *Firft Husband* when fhe's in *Bed* with a *Second*; efpecially if they Tick Sixpence with him, he puts on as pleafing an Afpect, as the Devil did when he look'd over *Lincoln.* If he that has fpent *Fifty Pounds* in his Houfe, asks to *Borrow a Crown* of 'im, his Wife made him fwear not above three Days ago,
that

he would never lend Sixpence again as long as he Liv'd or elſe he would have don't with all his heart. If any Perſon, tho' a good Cuſtomer, owes him any thing, and happens by extraordinary Buſineſs to be retarded from coming to his Houſe as uſual, there is a Verbal Hue and Cry publiſh'd after him preſently, among all his Acquaintance that are Cuſtomers; as thus, *Pray how does Mr. Such a one do? We have not ſeen him this Age. I remember the time when he us'd to think mine the beſt Beer in the Pariſh; but now, I ſuppoſe, he has found out ſome that he likes better: Indeed I take it very unkind of him. I never gave him any occaſion to leave my Houſe, as I know on. I am ſure he had always good Drink for his Money; and if he came without, I never refus'd to truſt him, as my Bar-board can teſtify; and my Meaſure is as large as any Body Sells. I wonder we ſhould loſe his Company thus.* Yet other heavy-headed Dunces can ſit and hear this, and not conceive they would ſay as much by them, were they under the like Circumſtance; but ſit and Guſſle down ſix times more than does 'em good, to the *Injury* of their *Bodies*, and *Impoveriſhment* of their *Pockets*, to make a parcel of *peremptory ingrateful Scoundrels* their *Maſters*; who with Conduct and good Husbandry, they might keep at Staffs-end, and force them to uſe that *Modeſty* and *Civility* as becomes their *Servile Station*. Some few indeed there are, who having the advantage of an Education above the Employment they have taken upon 'em, know how to treat every Body with ſuch a proportion of reſpect as is due to their *Quality*, or *Appearance*: Being of another mold, *Generous* and *Obliging*, and quite oppoſite to that *Mercenary Bruitiſh* Temper, with which moſt of 'em are poſſeſt, either by *Nature* or *Acquirement*: Such who have no more manners than (to uſe the *Hog-Grubbers* ſaying) that he knows no difference between a Porters two pence and a Gentlemans, ought I think to have none but Porterly-Cuſtomers; and he that knows how to bid a *Porter* give place to his Betters, deſerves a good Trade from Gentlemen. There are three ſorts of *Victuallers*, all differing very much from each other, according to the ſeveral Parts of the Town wherein they are ſituated. At *Wappin*, and that way, they Lord it over the people like a *Boatſwain* over a *Ships Company*; and look as bluff upon their Tarpaulin Gueſt as a *Mate* when firſt made *Commander*, or a *White-Fryars Printer* over a Gang of *Ballad-Singers*. In the *City* he is hail Fellow well met with any of his Cuſtomers on this ſide a *Common-Council-man*; but to all above, he is forc'd to pay a deference, and bow as low to the *Deputy* of a *Ward*, as a Countrey *Inn-keeper* does to the *Sheriff* of a County. And at *Charing-Croſs*, you ſhall find 'em ſo very humble and obliging for ev'ry two pence they take, that a Gentleman *Foot-Soldier*, or a *Lords Footman*, ſhall have as many Bows and Cringes from the Maſter and his Family, over the Drinking of a Pot, as a *French Dancing-Maſter* ſhall give the Miſtreſs of a *Boarding-School* when ſhe gives him half a piece for his Days Teaching. Whether it be *Poverty*, living amongſt Courtiers, or being bred Gentlemens Servants, and ſo kick'd and Cuff'd into good Manners by their Maſters, I'll leave the Reader to determine. There are ſcarce any of theſe ſundry ſort of Malt-Penſioners, (excepting ſome few ſuch as aforementioned) but what if you uſe their Houſes conſtantly, ſhall think you an intail'd Cuſtomer, and ſhall uſe

you

you worfe and refpeff you lefs, than they fhall the penurious *Niggard* that fpends a Penny once in a Week, and begs a bit of Toaft into the Bargain. Therefore the beft Method the Reader can ufe to avoid the *Infolence* and *Ingratitude* of thefe Mungril fort of Chriftians, is to aff purfuant to the advice of an experienc'd Toper, which is never to ufe any one Houfe long; but obferve this maxim, *When you find the Dog begin to wag his Tail upon you, 'tis time to feek for a new Tipling Office*; or it's Ten to one, if you have been a Cuftomer long enough for the *Spaniel* to be acquainted with you, but you will find the *Mafter* grow *Slighting*, and the *Servants Impudent*. And fince the Vitioufnefs of the Age has occafion'd every Parifh to abound with fuch great Numbers of thefe morofe mercenary foul fat-feeding unneighbourly *Cormorants*, I will proceed to give you a further Charaffer of one of the Worfer fort in Verfe, which I defire the Reader to accept on, as follows.

The Charaffer of a Common *Viffualler*.

THE *Monfter that progreffively is Bred,*
   To raife his Fortune by the Tippling Trade,
   (As oft they are) fhould be of Sparious Race,
Begot by Chance, without the Bounds of Grace:
Born of fome Luftful Wench, who could not ftay
Till Fortune flung a Husband in her way;
Firft Drop'd, and then Preferv'd at Parifh-Pay.
Or elfe brought up on Pack-Horfe from the North,
Born there of Parents who were nothing worth;
Sent up to Town, as Thoufands were before,
To Nick and Froth, and learn the Double-Score.
The Northern *Sharpnefs in his Rural Face,*
Soon recommends the Stripling to a Place;
Where, by fome thriving Country-man, he's taught
To Cheat the Gueft in ev'ry Quart a Draught.

Thus when a Seven-years-progrefs he has made,
And learn'd each Knavifh Myff'ry of his Trade,
Some labouring Drudge with Twenty pound he meets,
Who longs to dance the Shaking of the Sheets;
With her he couples, and improves her pence,
With his own hoarded Fool's Benevolence;
Who great as Kings, when drunk do often grant,
Thofe Boons to Tapfters, *which themfelves moft want.*
Then takes a Houfe, hangs up a Yorkfhire *Sign,*
New paints the Door-cafe, makes the Lettice fine.

Thus enter'd, fuch fharp Meafures does he take,
By which he Thrives whilft Twenty Tradefmen Break.
At firft Induftrious, as an an Indian Slave,
Clofe, as a Mifer; *Cunning, as a* Knave;
Humble and Fawning, as a Pedlars Cur;
And to each Cobler, *anfwer's,* Coming Sir.

His

His Bread *and* Cheese *he frankly does impart;*
And ev'ry thing is done with all his heart.
Porters *are* Welcome *near the* Fire *to fit,*
And may command; the Varlet *can fubmit.*
Without offence Red-herrings *they may broil,*
And tattle o'er their Pot *a wondrous while.*
Himfelf can on a Neighb'ring Errand *run;*
What e'er you ask for, in a trice is done.
If Guefts *defire to keep 'em up till late,*
Both without Grumbling will their leifure wait;
No Frowning from the Tike, *or maundring from his* Mate.

   Thus are they careful to oblige at firft;
But as they Thrive, *like* Currs, *they grow more Curft.*
Full Cellars *and full* Pockets, *change the Scene;*
And make the Lout *a Prince, his* Drab *a* Queen.
The Cobler *then muft at a diftance keep,*
And Porters *with their* Hats *in hand muft creep.*
No Frape *muft hover o'er the* Kitchen Fire;
They no fuch paultry Company Defire:
Sit up, you Fellow; move your Seat, you Clown;
And let my Mafter fuch a one fit down.
Pray troop; I keep a Publick Houfe, 'tis true;
But do not light my Fires for fuch as you.

   In comes a Neighbours Servant *for fome* Ale,
Pray dafh it with a little drop of Stale:
I've brought no Money, you muft fet it down:
The Maid's *thus anfwer'd by the Surly* Clown,
Pray tell your Mafter I fhall draw no more,
Until he comes, or fends to clear his Score;
I'd rather in my Cellar keep my Beer,
Then fend it out on Truft I know not where.
Perhaps fome Neighbouring Tradefmen *next appear;*
Where fhall we be to Drink a Pot of Beer?
Can't we go up? No, Marry, *fays the* Quean;
None has been up Stairs, fince the Room was clean.
Here Boy the *Bell,* or elfe the *Kitchen, fhow;*
Good Gentlemen I'm fure have fat below.
Nay, if we can't go up, we will not ftay;
I'll warrant we'll find houfes where we may.
We do not want your Cuftom; you miftake:
Pray troop, one Swallow *won't a* Summer *make.*

   Thus is the bafenefs of their Nature fhown.
No fooner Profperous, but Imperious grown:
By Wealth *made Sawcy, by Misfortune Cow'd;*
When Poor, *too* humble; *and if* Rich, *too* Proud.

Of *Astrologers*, and *Wisewomen*.

No Common *Errors*, *Frauds*, or *Fallacies* in the World, have so far subdued the Weaker, and consequently the Greater part of Mankind, as the *Juggles* and *Deceits* practicable in a parcel of pretending *Astrologers*; who undertake to resolve all manner of Lawful Questions, by Jumbling together those distant Bodies, in whose *Nature*, or *Influence*, they have just as much knowledge as a Countrey *Ale Woman* has of *Witchcraft*, or a *German Jugler* of *Necromancy*. In the first place, I have had an opportunity of examining several Nativities Calculated by those who have had the Reputation of being the best Artists of this Age: Wherein I have observ'd Sickness, length of Days, and all other Fortunate and Unfortunate Contingencies assign'd the Native, have been as directly opposite to what has happen'd thro' the whole Course of their Lives, as if the Fumbling *Star-groper* had rather, thro' an Aversion to *Truth*, study'd the *Rule* of *Contraries*, that he might always be found in the *Wrong* on't.

In the next place, Their Method in deceiving People who come to enquire about *Stolen Goods*, is such a bare-fac'd ridiculous piece of Banter, that I wonder any Creature that bears Humane shape, can be so stupidly Ignorant, as not plainly to discern the Impositions that are put upon them by their Canting *Albumazer*: Who, in the first place, enquires about what time, and after what manner the things were Lost; and what strangers they had then in the House? From whence he reasonaby, infers, whether the *Spoon*, *Cup*, *Tankard*, or whatsoever it be, was taken away by a common *Thief*, or stolen by a *Servant*, or Person that uses the House, or whether conceal'd by the Master or Mistress, to make the Servants more careful. If his Conjecture be, That it was taken by a common Thief, he describes a Swarthy, Black, Ill-looking Fellow, with a down-look; or the like: Most Wisely considering, That such sort of Rogues are seldom without a Gallows in their Countenances. Telling withal, that the Goods were pawn'd and will scarcely be recoverable, without they take the Thief speedily in order to effect which, he will give them his best directions; which the Credulous *Ignoramus* desires in Writing, for fear he should forget; which the Sower-look'd *Conjurer* gives accordingly, after the following manner: Go a *Quarter of a Mile* North, *from your own Dwelling, and then turn* Easterly, *and walk forward till you come to the Sign of a Large Four-Footed Beast; and Search within three or four doors of that Sign, and you will go near to take, if you go soon enough; or else hear of the Person, who is of a middle Stature and in poor Habit*. Away goes the Fool, as well satisfied with the Note, as if they had the Rogue by the Elbow; and if by any accident they do hear of the Thief, all is ascrib'd to the wonderful Cunning of their *Wizzard*: But if on the Contrary, he believes it to be taken by a Servant, or any Body that uses the House, he bids 'em hab nab at a venture, *Go Home satisfied, for they shall certainly find the Spoon, &c. in three or four days time, hid in a private hole, in such a part of the Kitchen, or he'll make the Devil to pay with those that have it, and force them to bring it in open shame and disgrace at Dinner time, and lay it down upon the Table in Sight of the whole Family*. Away goes the Person
well

well satisfied with what their *Ptolomist* had told 'em; and declares to every one in the House how the Thief was threaten'd, and after what manner the Spoon should be found within the time appointed, or else woe be to them that has it. This frightful Story coming to the Ears of the Guilty, brings 'em under such dreadful Apprehensions of the *Conjurers* indignation, if they do not lay what they've taken within the time, according to his Direction; that the first opportunity they have, they will place it to the utmost exactness, in whatever Hole or Corner he has appointed for the finding it. And this is the very Reason why in such sort of cases People so oft recover things that have been missing in their Houses, according to the Doctors Directions; which the *Ignorant* look upon to be all *Devilisme* and *Conjuration*; or if the Master, or Mistress, has conceal'd any thing from their Servants, to make 'em more careful, they are also ready to observe the dictates of the Cunning Man, that the Servants may believe what was missing was really stoln, that they might be more watchful of things in their Trust, to prevent the like Mischances for the Future. So that in this particular part of their Profession, there may be something said from the consequence of it, in the Behalf of their *Wizardly* sort of Policy; it being a means oftentimes of bringing those petty Thefts to light, which would otherwise lie undiscover'd, to the prejudice of the Loser. But as to their pretended knowledge in matters beyond the View of Common Reason, it is all a *Cheat*; and I am sorry this present Age should give such Evidence of it's Weakness, as to encourage such a parcel of *Illiterate* and *Scandalous Deceivers* of the common People, to flourish and live publickly Great, by such base and unjustifiable means, as casting *Figures*, telling *Fortunes*, Selling *Charms*, or *Sigills*, or the like.

The further *Frauds* of whose Practises I shall more pleasingly detect in these following Stories, some of which I can warrant as Truths from Persons of my own Acquaintance.

There is now living a famous *Wise-woman* in *Whitechappel*, who is a great Pretendress to this *Gipsie's Art* of *Fortune-telling*, who has acquir'd such wonderful Credit and Reputation amongst Servant Wenches and poor *Ignorant* People, that she has Forty or Fifty Sixpenny-Fools every Morning to attend her, most Women; some to know when they should be *Married*; some big with Child, who had lain with so many, they wanted to be resolv'd which was the right Father; some married Women, whose Husbands were at Sea, or in Foreign Plantations, who came to know whether she could give 'em any glad Tidings of their *Deaths*, or no; some to know whether they should be prosperous in their Marriage, Voyage, or Business in hand, or not; others about Stollen Goods, and the like. An Ingenious Married Gentlewoman, having heard much of *Mother Telltroth's* Fame, and giving but little Credit to common Reports, being hard to believe that Providence had made any of her Sex so much Wiser than she should be, resolv'd to let her own experience determine, whether the Woman was a *Witch*, or that her followers were all *Fools*; and accordingly has recourse to her abode, where she thrust herself in amongst the rest of the Querists, who where thronging in, like so many Spectators, to see a devout old Woman that had hang'd herself for Religion. Every one took their turns to be resolv'd, like

C

Customers

Cuftomers at a Chandlers; *Firft Come, Firft ferv'd* ;or like *Smiths* and *Coblers*, at a *Twopenny Barbers* waiting for the Chair : At laft it came to the Gentlewomans turn to apply herfelf to the Oracle ; and drawing near to the Elbow Chair of Infallibility, fhe gave a low Court'fie, as a Type of her Ignorance, as well as fubmiffion, and told her the chief of her Bufinefs was to be fatisfied when Providence would Blefs her with a Husband; The moft knowing Prophetefs, after fhe had Ogl'd and Examin'd her Phyfiognomy, with a very penetrating Circumfpection, the Lady keeping her Countenance, fhe told her the Man was yet unknown to her which fhe fhould very certainly Marry within a few Weeks, by whom fhe fhould have three Children; and then Bury him, and Marry a Second Time foon after, very much to her Advantange as well as Satisfaction; and fhould live very comfortably with him to fo great an Age, that fhe fhould be forc'd to walk with a Stick. *Sure Forfooth*, fays the Gentlewoman, *you muft deal with the Devil, or how fhould you know all this?* Indeed, Child, replyed the *Sorcerefs*, thou art miftaken; what I tell thee is purely from my Art. *No, No*, fays the Querift, *it muft be certainly from the Devil ; for he's the only Father of Lies, and I'll fwear, you han't told me one word of truth yet, for I have had a Husband this Nine years, and have Seven Children by him, all Living at this prefent : Therefore your Art, Forfooth, at this time has wonderfully fail'd you.* Pray, fays the old Gipfy, let me fee your hand once more. Upon a review of which, fays fhe, I fee I was miftaken; for I find now thou haft a Husband, but he's fuch a very little one, that 'tis as much as ever I can do to difcern his Significator in thy Palm. In which particular fhe happen'd to guefs right, for her Husband was a very little Man; which put the Lady into an Extravagant fit of Laughter: Who being well pleas'd with the cunning of the Old *Baggage*, went away confirm'd in her opinion, That there was nothing in her pretended Skill, but meer Guefs and Subtility.

A Country Gentleman not long fince being in Town, happen'd to be ftrangely infatuated with an opinion of *Aftrology* ; and refolving to venture fome Money at the *Royal Oak Lottery*, had recourfe to a Famous old *Planet Jugler*, giving him a Guinea to affign him a Lucky hour for his purpofe aforementioned: Who, according to their accuftomary way of Cozening, erected a Scheme, and after he had made himfelf half pur-blind, by poring upon his Jimcrack, and Jumbling together a parcel of Figures to amaze the Querift, he pofitively prefixes a certain time wherein he fhould be Fortunate. The Gentleman purfuant to the *Star-gropers* directions, puts Twenty Guineas into his Pocket, and away he goes to attack the *Devils Treafury* ; where, according to his Oracles Prediction, he met with fuch great Succefs, that he brought off a Hundred pound of the *Oak's* Money; returns to his Conjurer with a full affurance of breaking the Lottery in a little time; prefents the old Fox with ten Guineas, and defir'd he would confider of another Time wherein he might again be Fortunate; the old Shark very greedily fwallow'd the Golden Bait; and made him large promifes what the Stars fhould do for him; bidding him call again about Two or Three days hence, and he fhould have time to be more exact in his Calculation. The Gentleman goes home wonderfully pleas'd: and returns to his Prophet *Bubble-Blockhead* according to appointment, who prefixes him another Night, wherein he fhould be furely profperous.

rous. Away goes the Gentleman a Second time; flush'd with an affurance of the Golden Fleece ; but had not been long at Play, but his Stars by their Retrogradation brought him under a Neceffity of fending his Man home for more Money, which he was forc'd to repeat two or three times before the *Oak* fhut up ; That for the Hundred pound he had won, he had now loft Two; and began to be as angry with the Heavens and the Stars, as a young *Poet* that had loft his Miftrefs. Going back to his Deceitful *Ptolomy* in a wonderful Rage; telling him he and his Stars were a couple of Lying Confederates : And for ever after became as great an Enemy to *Aftrology*, as a *School-Boy* is to a Birch-rod after a found flogging.

The Third Story I fhall entertain you with, tho' it be fomewhat ftaler then the former, yet being applicable to my purpofe; I think it may be admitted without exception, *(viz.)* On *Southwark*-fide there liv'd a famous Student in thofe two fraternal Sciences, *Phyfick* and *Aftrology*; who to deceive people with more facility and affurance, had feveral Bells Plac'd in his Study above Stairs, the Ropes of which hung down the well of a dark Staircafe, one fignifying Loft Sheep, another Cloaths ftole off the Hedge, another ftray'd or ftollen Horfes; which were the chief things people had recourfe to him about : So that a Man who attended the Door, us'd firft to fift 'em what they came about; and fo at once rung for the Doctor and difpatch'd intelligence at the fame inftant.

It happen'd once that a *Butcher* having loft fome Sheep out of the Neighbouring Marfhes, came to requeft a caft of the Doctors Office, believing he could put him in a way of recovering his ftraid Weathers. Accordingly goes to his Houfe, where at his firft Entrance, the Servant ask'd him his Bufinefs, who readily without miftruft, told the Fellow his mifchance; who bid him not be difmay'd, for the Doctor without doubt would do him Service in the matter. *He's a little bufy,* fays he, *in his Study, but however I'll venture to Ring for him* ; and tingles the Sheep-Bell, upon which down comes the Doctor, having put on his *Fur-Cap* and conjuring Countenance, that half frighted the poor *Sheep-biter*. At his firft Appearance, *How, now, Friend,* fays he, *I'll warrant you have loft fome Sheep, and you want me to give you tidings of 'em. Yes, Noble Doctor,* fays the Fellow. *Come,* fays the Doctor, *walk into my Parlour,* and I'll endeavour to give you Satisfaction. The *Butcher* follows the *Doctor,* and happen'd to have with him a *Bull-Dog,* who crept under one of the Chairs, that no body minded him, the Servant according to Cuftom in fuch matters, had recourfe to his Wardrobe of *Shapes,* and dreft himfelf up in a *Bulls-hide,* waiting his Mafters Conjuring *Romile,* to fummons him to appear. The Doctor after he had talk'd a little with the Butcher about the bufinefs in hand, bid him befure to fit ftill and not be frighted at any thing he faw ; for nothing fhould hurt him, and after he had made a large Circle, he gives the Devil his Cue to make his terrible Entrance ; the Butchers Dog being of a true *Bear-garden* breed, feeing the appearance of a Bull, makes a fair run, feizes the Doctor's Familiar, and makes him roar like what he reprefented ; the Conjurer rifing in a great Paffion, *Ounds, what d'ye mean ? Take off your Dog, you Rogue ; take off your Dog.* The Butcher Smoaking
the

the Cheat, *Not I, by my troth, Doctor; I know he's as good as ever Run;*
Let 'em fight fair, Doctor: If you'll venture your Devil, I'll venture my Dog:
That never was poor Devil so mauld by a Hell-hound in this World
before. The Doctor being glad to pay the Fellow for his Sheep, to
lock up his Tongue from dispersing the detection.

Pursuant to the *Method* I propose, I shall also conclude this and eve‑
ry distinct *Trade,* or *Profession,* with a short Character in Verse.

Of a *Cunning-Man.*

POOR *Taylors, Weavers, Shooe-makers, and such,*
  Little in Trade, and think they know too much,
  Are the chief Senseless Bigots that advance
A Foolish Whim to further Ignorance;
Bouy'd up by Chance-Success, would things fore-know;
Aim to be wise, and still more foolish grow;
Peep twenty years at Stars, at Sun and Moon,
And prove themselves but Idiots when they've done.
Then finding by Experience they are lost,
In that True Knowledge *which they fain would boast,*
They draw in Fools to pay for th' Time their Study Cost.
All their whole Art consists in Barren Words,
Meer Sound, *but no* true Argument *affords;*
On a faint shadow do they all rely;
What few believe, and none can justify.
Mars, by Heroick Actions, got a Name;
Venus, by Beauty, and her Whoredom, Shame;
Mercury, for Speed was famous, and for Theft,
And now most bad when by himself he's left:
Good, if well mix'd, like Hair amongst the Loom;
If not, he's fatal to the Native's Doom:
So to the rest such influence they ascribe,
As we, they say, by Nature's course imbibe.
'Tis true, the Persons whence the Name's deriv'd,
Were Whores, and Thieves, and Heroes, whilst they liv'd,
But these bright Planets, which surround the Earth,
Had the same Force and Pow'r before their birth:
E'er they were Christen'd, they were still the same,
At first a part o'th' Universal Frame,
And do no influence borrow from an empty Name.
Mars can no Heroe by his Aspect make,
Nor Venus force a Virgin to forsake
Her Vertue; nor can Mercury prevail
On happy unstain'd Innocence, to steal:
No, no, 'tis Education make us fit
To Virtuous Live, or to base means submit.
All their pretended Impulse is a Quacking Cheat.
Only upheld by Knaves, believ'd by Fools;
The first the Workmen, and the last their Tools;
All their Pretences are but empty show,
Wise would they seem, but still they nothing know.

Instead

Instead of Reason, which all Art defines,
Their Brains are fill'd with Planets, Orbs, and Signs:
Their Knowledge little, their gray Hairs but green;
Their Learning less, and their Profession mean:
Their Conversation dull, each senseless word,
Is humbly paid to some Ascendant Lord:
A Globe's their Sign; in Alleys do they dwell;
And tho Fools think they've Conference with Hell,
To all things know, yet little Truth can tell.

A Modern *Reformer* of *Vice*: Or, A Reforming *Constable*,

Is a Man most commonly of a very Scandalous Necessity, who has no way left, but *Pimp* like, to Live upon other Peoples *Debaucheries*. Every Night he goes to Bed, he prays heartily that the World may grow more *Wicked*; for one and the same Interest serves him and the Devil. He always walks Arm'd with a Staff of Authority, Seal'd with the Royal Arms; and all Wise People think the fellow that carrys it a great *Blot* in the *Scutcheon*. He searches a *Bawdy-house*, as a *Church-Warden* does an *Ale-house*, not to punish *Vice*, but to get Money. He squeezes *Whores* as a *Thief-Catcher* does *Highway-Men*, takes from 'em the Fruits of their Iniquities; making them twice as wicked as they would be, by putting them upon fresh *Villanies* to keep themselves from Starving. He brings no Woman to punishment for her *Ill-Courses* but for want of Money; and she that Whores for Pleasure more than Profit, is sure oftenest to be Whipt for't. They are a sort of unlucky Bird-Catchers, and every naughty House their Net; the Whores their *Decoy-Birds*, that allure others into their Trap, and are freed themselves from that danger they have brought the Innocent into. They are the only Encouragers of what they pretend to suppress; Protecting those People, for Bribes, which they should Punish; Well knowing each Bawdy House they break is a Weekly Stipend out of their own Pockets. Meet 'em when you will, you shall never find any one in their Custody above a *Flat-cap*, or a *Cinder-wench*; who because their Rags won't pawn for a Dozen of Drink, must be made an example of. She that has the prudence to Whore with half a Crown in her Pocket, may Sin on without danger, whilst the poor needy Wag-tail must be cautious how she kisses at Ill Hours, in Ill Houses, or in Ill Company, left she be carried to *Bridewell*; where instead of being Reclaimed, she is harden'd, by her indelible shame, in her Miserable state of Wickedness. The only good they've done, they've put a sort of Socket-Money upon Whoring; and themselves are the Collectors of the Tax: By which Reason the price of *Venerie* is advanc'd, which makes it the more practised, for the cheapness of a Commodity always throws it out of Fashion; and things easily purchas'd, are very seldom minded. Of all people I know, I think their Imployment is most like the Dog-whippers of a Church, whose business is to watch the Tails of every Proud Bitch and Lascivious Puppy, from commiting an indecency; They are Wicked Servants to a pious Society, who have undertaken to insure the Nation from Vice; and their Business is to run up and down Town, to Quench Peoples Lust, as the Steel-cap Salamanders do to extinguish Fires.

D
The

The Suppreffing of *Vice*, and Reforming of *Manners*, is, in the Society, a moft commendable Undertaking; But, except they take care to regulate their Officers, and prevent the daily Abufes they commit, which are every where complained of; I fear the Ill management of their Mercenary People imployed, will be an injury to their Project, and bring a very good Defign under a great Difreputation, and hinder many Perfons from giving Encouragement to that Noble Work, which they would otherwife think worthy of their Affiftance: But whilft a parcel of Loofe Fellows, and felf-ferving Profligates, are imployed to fearch after, and detect thofe who are fcarce worfe than themfelves, it is reafonable to believe the *Innocent* will be often injur'd, and the Wicked practices of vitious Perfons conceal'd from the Magiftrates, who have a Will they fhould be brought to light, and a Power to punifh 'em, did not *Bribery* to inferiour Officers Protect 'em in their Lewdnefs; who make it their Bufinefs not fo much to fupprefs bafe Women, and thofe Sanctuaries they now daily act their *Vices* in with fecurity, as they do to go Snacks with thofe infamous Beldams, who make it their Lively-hood to Encourage and Shelter Mercenary Strumpets in their Wickednefs, and preferve 'em from the punifhment of the Laws, which they would otherwife more commonly fall under. There are many imploy'd, who are of Scandalous Fortunes, and defperate Characters; who are very converfant with, and Protect the very *Libertines* they fhould bring to Punifhment; Who undertake their Office thro no good Principle, but only thro a Mercenary End of Twelve Shillings a Week Sallary, whofe Confciences are fo corrupt, that for Twelve more, they would upon occafion, Swear they heard the *Dumb-man* in the *Red-cap* fwear Fifty Oaths, and that they fee the *Sober Gentleman* that drinks nothing but *Water-Gruel*, as Drunk as ever they fee a Foot-Soldier in a *Bawdy-Houfe*, or a Porter in a *Brandy-Shop*. I cannot forbear taking Notice of a poor Fellows faying, as I was paffing along the Street; *I'll warrant*, fays he, *they thought they had much reform'd my Manners, when they made me pay a Shilling for an Oath, when I had never another in the World; but Ifack, I was pretty even with them, for I went home, and telling my Wife what had happen'd; we fet foot to foot, and curs'd the Conftable for Two Hours by the Clock, and that was our Satisfaction for going Supperlefs to Bed.*

Vice, 'tis true, is grown to a Great and Lamentable Pitch in this Wicked Age we live in; but whilft a parcel of Loofe and Mercenary Fellows are continued in Office, who are as Wicked and Prophane themfelves, as the Profligate Wretch they look after, there will appear, I doubt, but flender figns of a Reformation. Of fuch fort of Conftables or Informers as thefe, there being many imploy'd about this Town, I fhall proceed to give you a further Character in Verfe.

Informing *Conftables*, and other *Informers*,

DO moft thro' Int'reft, *and but few thro' Zeal,*
Betwixt the Laws, and the Offender deal.
Poor Sinners may their Perfecution fear,
As Cozening Bakers *do a ftrict* Lord-Mayor.

But

But the Gay Curtezan, who Trades for Gold,
That can but grease a Palm, when she's in hold,
No Justice need she dread, or Bridewel fear;
But without danger Sin from Year to Year.
Or need the Money'd Libertine e'er see
The Awful Brows of Stern Authoritie:
But Drink and Swear, till weary of his Vice,
Would he Sin on at an Informers Price:
Who choose their Pious Office for its gain,
To dwell upon the Sins of other Men:
Not with a good intent, to Vice reclaim,
Or bring Offenders into open shame.
Few do we see that are Examples made,
But the poor Strumpet or the starving Blade;
Who wanting Money, do the Scourge endure;
Not punish'd for their Vice, but being Poor.

Vice deserves Publick Punishment, 'tis true;
But those that live upon the Ills I do,
And on my Failings for their Bread rely,
Do what good Morals cannot justify.
If the poor Harlot shall her Soul betray
For Money, which Informers take away,
To let her go, it is the Worlds belief,
Th' Receiver's full as guilty as the Thief.

If I by chance am Drunk, or should I Swear;
The Man that does against me Witness bear,
Purely to share the Money in my Purse,
I'm bad 'tis true, but such a Knave is worse:
If what he does, is with a true intent,
Of bringing Vice to Shame and Punishment,
And well considers if himself be free.
From all those failings he condemns in me;
If not, 'tis not true Zeal, but Impudence;
For him t' accuse th' Offendor of Offence;
The Hangman more may say in his Defence.
Those Vermin who for Interest do engage,
To dabble in the Vices of the Age;
By subtle means draw silly Creatures in,
And Devil-like, first Tempt 'em to the Sin:
No sooner gain'd the Wanton Dames consent,
But Drag the Wretch away to Punishment;
Lest she has Money, or if none, agree
To pawn her Cloaths to purchase Liberty.
Such are the Scum that do the Town infect,
Much worse than those they're hired to detect:
Some loose Shabroons in Bawdy-Houses bred,
By Others Vices like their Own are Fed.
A Scoundrel Crew, that o'er the City swarm,
Who by false Accusations do more harm

To Guiltless Persons, fearful to dispute,
Than all the forry Jilts they persecute.
If heedless Youth in an Ill-house they find,
Drop'd in as strangers, and no Ill design'd,
Void of Offence, yet loxibe to be let go,
Fearing their Masters or their Friends should know:
What is it less in him that takes the Fee,
Then picking Pockets by Authoritie?
What Moral Zealot justly can afford,
To Mercenary Shammocks one good Word,
Who live by filthy means, like Flies upon a T——d.

Comical Accidents and Occurences,

A Weſt-Country Graſiers Son, coming up with ſome of his Fathers Cattle, and being a Stranger in the Town, happening to ſtraggle croſs *Smith-field*, from his Inn, to Drink a Cup of Ale at a Townſmans Houſe, ſat ſo Long, and ſo Late, that he had made himſelf Pot Valiant with his Countrymans Liquor; and inſtead of Croſſing the Rounds to his Lodging, did, for want of a Guide, Stagger down *Hoſier-Lane*; and unhappily follow'd his Noſe down *Snow-Hill*, till he came to the *Ditch-ſide*, where feeling the Rails he thought in the Dark, he had been at the Rounds in *Smith-field*, and ſpending ſome time in groping for a Place to go thro: At laſt breaks out in a Paſſion, *Ads-heartly-wounds, I think the Devils run away with the Turnpike. I believe I muſt be forc'd to Skip over at laſt:* And accordingly lays his Hand on the *Railes*, and over he Jumps into the *Ditch*; but by good Fortune fell into a Lighter of Coles, where getting but little harm, according to the old Proverb, he gets upon his Legs, and began to Rave like a *Bedlamite.* *A Pax take you for a Pack of* Lonjon *Rauges, d'ye leave open your Trap Doors to catch Country Vault in your Cellars?* Then flinging about the Coles, cry'd, *Ads-heart either let me out of your Cole-hole, or I'll break all thy Windows and Thump and Veaz thee, and make thee Vart again, Vor a Vity Vaut Veaſon thou*

—The *Weavers* have already received ſuch Encouragement from the great hopes they have of the *Bill*'s being paſt, for the prohibition of all wrought Silks, and Calicoes from *India*, that for this week paſt, they have Solemnly proteſted, notwithſtanding it is Lent, againſt Eatof *Stale Sprats, Rotten Red-Herrings*, and the *Cuttings* of *Salt-Fiſh*; and are already advanc'd to the buying of *Bullocks Pettstoes, Napper Nulls, Grunters Muns*, and the like. Nay, further, it was obſerv'd laſt Market-day, that an Eminent Maſter of the Shuttle in *Spittle-Fields*, who has not above Twelve in Family, bought in *Norton Folgate* a ſtone and a half of good *Cow-Beef*, to the great wonder and amazement of the Butcher: So that it is generally believ'd on all Hands, if the *Eaſt-India* Company puts not a Spoke in their Cart, they will ſhift off their Poverty in a little time, which they have long groan'd under, and will to the whole *Nations Satisfaction*, as well as their *Own Happineſs*, be ſeen in a *Flouriſhing Condition.*

F I N I S.

THE
LONDON
SPY.

For the *Month* of *February,* 1700.

The Second Volume.

PART IV.

LONDON, Printed and Sold by *J. How,* in the *Ram-Head-Inn*
Yard in *Fanchurch-street,* 1700.

A

Books Sold by J. How, *in the* Ram-Head-Inn-Yard *in* Fanchurch-Street; J. Weld, *at the* Crown *between the* Temple-Gates *in* Fleet-street; *and* Mrs. Fabian, *at* Mercers-Chappel *in* Cheapfide.

1. SOt's Paradife: Or the Humours of a Derby-Ale-House: With a Satyr upon the Ale. Price Six Pence.

2. A Trip to *Jamaica*: With a True Character of the People and Ifland. Price Six Pence.

3. *Eclefia & Factio*. A Dialogue between *Bow-Steeple-Dragon*, and the *Exchange-Grafhopper*. Price Six Pence.

4. The Poet's Ramble after Riches. With Reflections upon a Country Corporation. Alfo the Author's Lamentation in the time of Adverfity. Price Six Pence.

5. A Trip to *New-England*. With a Character of the Country and People, both Englifh and Indians. Price Six Pence.

6. Modern Religion and Ancient Loyalty: A Dialogue. Price Six Pence.

7. The World Bewitch'd. A Dialogue between Two Aftrologers and the Author. With Infallible Predictions of what will happen from the *Vices* and *Villanies* Practis'd in *Court*, *City* and *Country*. Price Six Pence.

8. A Walk to *Iflington*: With a Defcription of New *Tunbridge-Wells*, and *Sadler's* Mufick-House. Price Six Pence.

9. The Humours of a Coffee-Houfe: A Comedy. Price Six Pence.

10 A Frolick to *Horn-Fair*. With a Walk from Cuckold's-Point thro' *Deptford* and *Greenwich*. Price Six-Pence.

11. The Firft Volume of the LONDON-SPY: In Twelve Parts.

12. The Firft, Second Third, and Fourth Parts of the Second Volume of the *London-Spy*.

All Written by the fame Author.

THE
LONDON
SPY.

MY Companion having given me the common civility of a *London* Inhabitant to a *Countrey* Friend, or Acquaintance, (*i. e.*) shew'd me the Tombs at *Westminster*, the Lions in the *Tower*, the Rogues in *Newgate*, the Mad people in *Bedlam*, and the Merchants upon the *Change*; with the rest of the Town-Rarities, worth a Countrey Fool's admiring, began about a Month since (I suppose) to be tir'd of his Office; upon which, like a *City Sophister*, to a *Country Cousin*, he Apologiz'd for his Departure; and so left me, saying he would wait upon me as often as the present urgency of his Affairs would permit; and if any thing worth Notice occur'd to his knowledge, he would communicate the same; or if he could not spare time to give me his Company, he would dispatch Intelligence by Letter: So that arm'd with his good Instructions, and all necessary Cautions I shifted off my Rural Bashfulness, and began to so embolden my self in a little time by strange Conversation, that I could call a careless *Drawer* Blockhead, Kick a Sawcy *Tapster* on the Breech, Swear Z—ds at a *Hackney-Coach-man*, or sit down amongst *Aldermen* in a *Coffee-house* without plucking off my Hat. When I first left my Mate, I thought my self in as disconsolate a Condition, as a Widdow for the first Month after the loss of her Husband: but I, like the Mourning Dame, found such new Diversion as quickly obliterated my old Friend, and soon made me as easie without his Conversation, as the Goodwoman is without her Bed-fellow.

Being thus left to range the Town by my self, like a *Man-hater* that Lov'd no Company, or like the *Hangman*, that could get none; I happen'd near the *Change* to step into a Tavern-Kitchen, where I found seated at a Corner-Table, a Knot of Jolly, Rough-hewn, Ratling Topers, who look'd not as if they were Born into the World, but Hammer'd into an uncooth Shape, upon *Vulcan's* Anvil; whose Iron-sides, and Metal-colour'd Faces seem'd to Dare all Weathers, spit Fire at the Frigid-Zone, and bid Death defiance: Bumpers of Canary went round as fast as the one could Drink and his Neighbour fill; and a stander-

by

by might have eafily gueft by their ftreakab'e Meafure, that every Glafs
had been a Health to an Emperour. I foon found by their Dialect,
they were *Mafters of Ships: Chear up my Lads, pull away, fave Tide ; come
Boys, a Health to* Moll Bifchet *the Bakers Daughter, that Swore a Sea Cheft
was as foft as a Feather-Bed.* Then handling the Quart being empty, *What
is fhe light? You, Sir, that's next, haul the Barline, and call the* Coopers-
mate: The Drawer being come, *Here, you Fly-blown Son of a* T–d, *take
away this Damn'd Crank Bitch and Ballance her well. Pox take her, there's no
ftowage in her Hold. Have you ne'er a Larger Veffel?* With fuch fort of ftuff
was I diverted for a little time, till an Old Gentleman coming into
the Kitchen, whofe grave and venerable Head being Froft-nip'd with
Age, was Bleach'd as white as Snow, his Silver hairs, which fhould have
been a fence to his Weather-beaten Ears, being fo very thin, that they
might be more eafily numbred then his Infirmities ; happening to approve of my fide of the Fire, he fat down near me, and call'd for his
half pint of that Golden colour'd Cordial over which our Fathers us'd
to number up their Juvenal Pranks, and make themfelves Merry with
Reflections on their paft Happinefs : And when he had meafur'd out
a moderate Dram of his Ages only comfort, after a very curteous manner he prefents his Service to me, whofe Compliment I return'd with
refpect due to his Gravity, but could not forbear fancying he was
too Complefant to be a Rich Citizen ; and that Misfortune had taught
him to be very civil to a Stranger ; For it may be generally obferved,
That a Thrifty Trader takes a Pride in being furly, and feldom is
burthen'd with more Manners than a *Rhinoceros.* After we had chang'd
Two or three words about *What News? What's a Clock? Methinks its
Cold to Day?* and the like, I obferv'd the old Gentleman when he had
difcover'd our Neighbouring Company by their talk to be *Commanders
of Ships,* look'd at 'em with as much malice as a Man under fufpi-
cion of Debt would at a Gang of *Officers*; every Glance feem'd to call
'em a pack of Knaves ; and at laft his paffion grew fo high, that I found
by the trembling of his Lips he was fallen into his Soliloquies ; and, I
believe was the Truth known, he was curfing 'em as faft within himfelf, as a *Country-Hag* does a *Farmers-Hogs,* when he denies her a Pitcher
of Whey, or a Difh of Cheefe-curds.

Whilft the old Gentleman feem'd to be under this perturbation of
mind, one of *Neptune*'s Sun-burnt Subjects, trufs'd up in Troufers of old
Sail-cloth, was ufher'd into the Kitchen by a Drawer, in order to deliver Melancholy Tidings, as he thought, to Father *Grifle.* Who I foon
underftood had been drawn in to hold a Fourth Part of a Veffel, to whom
the *Boatfwain* was difpatch'd with all expedition from *Deal,* to bring this
following intelligence, which after two or three Marine Scrapes and Congies, with a fhaking Head, like a Paralitical Alms-man, and a Countenance as fad as a Prieft in *Denmark* that has loft his Genitals, he begins after this manner. *Ah, Sir, I am beloth to let you know what I am
come on purpofe to tell you: I am fent as the Embeffeler of fad fad News indeed. Prithee Friend, fays the Gentleman, What is't, if my Family be but
fafe, and my Houfe not on Fire, I thank my Stars I fhall not be much frighted
let it be what it will; for I have been us'd to fo much bad News from Men
of your Calling, that I have not receiv'd a comfortable word from that unlucky Element you belong to, this four Years. I never fee a Seaman come to-*

wards me, to Speak to me, but I always fancy he's as ill an Omen to my Family, as a Raven that flies over my House, and Croakes three times in his passage; tho' now I know not what News thou canst bring me, that will Trouble me; therefore such as it is, Prithee, Friend, let's hear it. Ah, Sir, says the Fellow (blowing his Nose and wiping his Eyes) The poor Betty's lost : Coming into the Downs, a Storm of Wind sprang up at N. W. and by W. as God would have it, enough to blow the Devil's Head off. We made our Larboard Tack, and Ply'd to Windward, work'd like Dragon's, and did all that Men could do to save her, but could not Weather the Goodwin, in which Sand, to our great Sorrow, as well as your Lamentation, she lies now Bury'd. There let her Lye, says the old Dad, till Dooms-Day. Here's to thee, Friend, with all my Heart : 'Tis the best News thou could'st have brought me; for if the old Bitch of a Betty had surviv'd the danger of the Seas much longer, I believe she, and the Master together, would have brought me to the Parish. I hope, says he, I shall be a Warning to all Fools how they are drawn in by a pack of Knaves, to meddle with such Business that is out of their knowledge. My Shares cost me two hundred Pound, and not one prosperous, but three bad Voyages for it; brought her Owners in Debt, and now at last lost upon the Goodwin. Good Buy t'ye, Good Mistress Betty, I am heartily glad to hear you're at bottom : For, Efaith I believe if thou hadst not sunk, in a little time I shou'd. No more Long Bills for Refitting, no Masters long Accounts for Repairs of damage sustained in a Storm. No, no, if ever they hook in the old Fool again to make Ducks and Drakes with his Money in Salt water, I'll give 'em leave to draw a Rope thro' his Guts, and tye him to a Cable to make a Buoy on : For I find Merchants are a pack of Sharpers, Masters of Ships, a parcel of Arrant Knaves, A Vessel but a doubtful Confident and the Sea a meer Royal-Oak-Lottery. Having thus said, he paid for his Nipperkin of Canary, and away he went. I staying a little while after him, to observe the Behaviour of the Salt-water Emperours, from whose Ridiculous Talk, and more Ridiculous Actions, I drew this following Character.

Of a Master of a Vessel.

A Brawny Lump, that scarce knows good from ill,
Fatted on Board like Hogs, with Peas and Swill:
Affects a Hoarseness as a vocal Grace;
Churlish his Carriage, and Austeer his Face:
Lusty his Limbs, and Rusty is his Skin;
A Bear without, and a worse Beast within.
If Married, sure a Cuckold; and if not,
A gen'rous Cully to each Wapping Slut.
At Sea an Emperour, at Land a Slave;
A Fool in Talk, but to his Owners Knave.
Ty'd, when on Shore, to a huge Silver Sword;
And Struts about in Wapping like a Lord.
With Jilt in Musick-house, he's pleas'd and glad;
When Sober Surly, and in Liquor mad.
A Bulky Carcase, with a Slender Soul:
But stout as Julius Cæsar, o'er a Bowl.
In Company Pragmatical and Rude.
Humble to's Owners, to his Seamen Proud.

In

In *Calms* or *Storms*, he *seldom* Prays, but Swears;
Starving and *Drowning* are his only *Fears*;
And never thinks of Heaven beyond the Stars.
Mercator, *and his* Compass, *are his Guides*;
By them alone he thinks he safely Rides.
A Prosperous Gale he Looks for, as his Due;
He thanks no God, Religion *never knew*;
And is no more a Christian, *than a* Jew.
At Land altho' an Idiot, when at Sea,
None must presume to be so Wise as he.
Talk Reason, and your Arguments deny'd;
He Swears you nothing know of Time or Tide.
His Words are Laws, he's there a Soveraign Lord,
An Aristotle's *but an Ass on Board.*
The Burgoo Novice, bred 'twixt Stem and Stern,
That knows to Splice a Line, or Spin Rope-Yarn,
Shall by King Tar-Arse more respected be,
Than an Erasmus, or the Learned'st be.
His Head's an Almanack, which Men may find
Fill'd up with Tydes, the Weather and the Wind;
Suns Declination, Changes of the Moon,
And how to know in India *when its Noon.*
A Ship he takes to be the only School,
And really thinks a Land-Man is a Fool.
When warm'd with Punch, and his Mundungus Weed,
He Praises Briny Beeff and Bisket Bread;
Contemns Land Dainties, and the Bed of Down,
And Swears a Ship's more pleasant than the Town:
So Prisoners, long confin'd, would fain prevail,
With Freemen, to believe their stinking Goal
Affords more satisfaction to the Mind,
Than all the Pleasures they at Large can find.
All that the Sea-Calf has on Shore to Boast,
Is how he sav'd his Ship from being Lost;
Which the Unthinking Dolt, thro' Infolence,
Ascribes to his own Art, not Providence.
The most that to his Honour can be said,
Of a Tarpaulin *Rabble he's the Head*;
And Monarch of a Wooden World tis true;
But such an one as makes most Land-Men Sp——w.
Let him Rule on: His Famish'd Slaves Command,
Dreading each Storm that Blows, each Rock and Sand;
Rather than such a King, *I'll Subject be at Land.*

From thence I went to a *Coffee-house*, where I had appointed my Acquaintance to meet with me at certain Hours in the Day; and there I found a Letter from my Friend, to request my Company to Supper at a Private-House in the City: Where a Gentleman had provided a Commodious Entertainment for us, and some others of his Friend's that Evening.

When the Hour assign'd for our Meeting came, I accordingly went, pursuant

fuant to my Friends Directions, where I found a Jolly Company Aſſem-
bled, whoſe Looks ſufficiently d ſcover'd their Affections to the good
Creature, that I had no Reaſon to Miſtruſt any Obſtruction of our Mirth
from the Appearance of the Perſons. Amongſt 'em, were two *Country-Par-
ſons*, and a Notable Sharp *Town-Quaker*, who I had a Reaſonable Foreſight would produce ſome good Diverſion, as ſoon as our Cups, and
the Seaſon of the Night, had made us fit Inſtruments of each others Felicity.
I ſhall not tire you with a Bill of Fare, but in ſhort a very plentiful Supper we had, to the great Content of the Founder, (it being ſerv'd up in
ſuch admirable Order) as well as to the Satisfaction of the Gueſts. When
we had tired our Hands with ſtopping our Mouths, to aſſwage the fury
of our Appetites, and one of the Parſons had put a Spiritual Padlock
upon the Mouths of the Company, and gave a holy Period to our Fleſhly
Suſtenance for that Evening; a magnificent Bowl of *Punch*, and ſome
Bottles of Right *Gallick* Juice, were handed to the Table, which receiv'd,
as the Glaſs went round, a Circular Approbation. Our Stomachs craving
Hearty ſupply of Wine for the Digeſtion of our Fiſh, made us at firſt
pour down the Liquor in ſuch plentiful Streams, that it ſoon put our
Engines of Verboſity to work, and made us as Merry as ſo many School-
Boys at a Breaking-up, o'er a Batch of Cakes, or a Diſhful of Stew'd Pruins.

At laſt we came to a Good-looking Soldiers-Bottle of Claret, which at leaſt
held half a point extraordinary, but the Cork was drove in ſo far, that
there was no opening on't without a Bottle-Screw, ſeveral attempted with
their Thumbs and Fingers, to remove the Stubborn Obſtacle, but none could
effect the difficult Undertaking; upon which, ſays the Donor of the Feaſt,
*What is no-body amongſt us ſo Provident a Toper as to carry a Bottle-Screw about
him:* One cry'd *No.* Another *No, Poize on't,* he had left his at home. A
third, *never carry'd one*; and ſo 'twas concluded no Screw was to be had. The
Parſons being all this time ſilent, at laſt ſays the Lord of the Banquet
to his Man, *Here take it away*; tho' I Proteſt, ſays he, *Tis a fine Bottle, and
I'll warrant the Wine's better then Ordinary, its ſo well Cork'd; but what ſhall we
do with it? We cannot open it. You muſt take it down I think; tho', I Vow
'tis a great deal of Pity, but Prithe bring us up ſome more Bottles that may not
Puzzle us ſo.* The Oldeſt and Wiſeſt of the Parſons, having obſerv'd the
Copious Dimenſions of the Bottle, and well knowing by Experience that
ſound Corking is always an Advantage to good Liquor, *Hold, hold, Friend,*
ſays he to the Servant, who was going out with the Bottle, *I believe I
may have a little Engine in my Pocket that may unlock the Difficulty*; and
fumbling in his Pockets, after he had pluck'd out a *Common-Prayer-Book*,
an old *Comb-Caſe* full of Notes, a Two-Penny *Nutmeg-Grater*, and made a
remove of ſuch kind of Worldly Neceſſaries, at laſt he came to the matter,
and out he brings a Bottle-Screw, which provok'd not a little Laughter thro
the whole Company. *Methinks, Friend,* ſays the Quaker, *A* Common-
Prayer-Book *and a* Bottle-Screw, *are improper Companions, not fit to Lodge
in one Pocket together. Why doeſt thou not make thy Breeches afford 'em different
Apartments?* To which the Parſon made this Anſwer, *Since Devotion gives
Comfort to the Soul, and Wine in Moderation, Preſerves the Health of the
Body, why may not a Book that Inſtructs us in the one, and an Inſtrument
that makes way to the other, be allow'd, as well as Soul and Body, for whoſe
good they were intended, to bear one another Company?* But, *Methinks, Friend,* ſays
the Quaker, *A* Bottle-Screw *in a Miniſters Pocket, is like the* Practice of
Piety

Piety, *in the Hand of a* Harlot ; *the one no more becomes thy Profeſſion, than the other does hers.* To which the Parſon reply'd, *A good* Book *in the hand of a* Sinner, *and an* Inſtrument *that does good to a whole* Society, *in the hand of a* Clergy-man, *I think are both very Commendable*: *and I wonder why a good man ſhould object againſt either.* I am very glad, ſays the Quaker, *thou takeſt me to be a good man* ; *then I hope thou haſt no reaſon to take any thing till that I have ſpoken?* Nay, hold, ſays the Parſon, *I did not deſign it as a Complement to thee, for to tell thee the truth, I do not think thee near ſo good as thoſe who I believe thou haſt but a bad Opinion of* ; meaning, as I ſuppoſe, the Church Clergy. To which reply'd the Quaker, *Thou may'ſt ſee, the Government has a better Opinion of us, than it has of thoſe People who I imagine thou meaneſt, or elſe they would never have made our Words of equal Validity with your* Oaths. *Therefore I think we have Reaſon to be look'd upon as the moſt honeſt People in the Kingdom.* In anſwer to this, ſays the Parſon, *I remember a Fable, which with as much Brevity as I can, I will repeat to the Company in anſwer to thee.*

Once upon a Time, when the Lyon found there were many diviſions amongſt his Four-Footed Subjects, in ſomuch that he could not, without ſome difficulty, preſerve Peace in his Dominions, and allay the Grumblings of each diſaffected Party: But amongſt all the Factious Beaſts in the Forreſt, the *Aſſes* were moſt obſtinate, and would never change their pace, in Obedience to thoſe wholeſome Laws provided againſt their hum-drum ſlothfulneſs. The Lyon conſidering they were a Serviceable Creature, notwithſtanding their Formality, and would bear any Burthen without complaining, let them have but their own ways, and go their own pace, thought it very neceſſary to make a Law that every *Aſſe* ſhould have his own will, which they would always have before, in ſpight of all the Laws againſt it: and in anſwer to their Petition, that they ſhould not be oblig'd to go ſhod like Horſes, but with this proviſio, That if ever they Trip'd, or ſtumbled, they ſhould be ſoundly Whip'd for their fault. A little time after the commencement of this Law, an *Aſs* meeting with an *Horſe*, could not forbear boaſting what great Favourites the *Aſſes* were at Court, upraiding the *Horſe* with being Iron-ſhod, and how they by the Law were made free to travel upon their own Natural Hoof, which is much more eaſie ; you are miſtaken, ſays the Horſe, ſhooing makes us walk more Upright, and tread with more Security. And pray, Friend *Aſs*, remember this amidſt your Benefit, that you muſt be Whip'd if you ſtumble, as well as we.

Upon the application of this Fable, the whole company burſt into a Laughter, to the great diſcountenance of our merry *Ananias*, who had nothing left but Bluſhes for a reply. But having a great deſire to be even with his Antagoniſt, lay ſo very cloſe upon the Catch, that the Parſon was forc'd to put a Guard upon his Tongue, leaſt he ſhould give him an advantage to recover his Credit. Till at laſt, in a ſilent interval, the Glaſs coming two or three times quick about, made the Parſon neglect to take off his Wine with his uſual expedition, and ſet it down before him ; which the Quaker obſerving, ask'd him what Countrey-man he was? The Prieſt return'd him a Satisfactory Anſwer. *Didſt thou not lately hear of a great Living that was vacant in thy County, computed to be worth about Four hundred Pounds a Year?* Upon which the Parſon began to prick up his Ears, and enquired where abouts it was, never minding his Glaſs.

Glafs. Truly fays the Quaker, I cannot tell directly where it lies, but *I can tell thee 'tis in vain to enquire after it, for it is already difpos'd of to an Eminent Perfon of thy Function, who is now in this Town, and of whom I have fome Knowledge. At a Coffee-houfe where he ufes, I happen'd to hear him highly commending the Hofpitality, and good Houfe Keeping of the late Incumbent. It being, fays he, indeed fo plentiful a Benefice, that he might well afford it. And I hope, fays he, that I fhall not be backward in following his Example.* The Parfon fhowing great dif-fatisfaction in his looks, that fuch a Living fhould fall, and be difpos'd on, without fo much as his knowledge, not knowing but his own intreft might have been fufficient to have carry'd it. The Quaker he proceeds all the while in praifing the Orchards, Gardens, Barns, Stables, fine Rooms, large Kitchen, noble Parlour, convenient Buttery, &c. which fet the Parfon fo on gog, that he Liften'd and Gap'd, as if he would have catch'd it in his Mouth. But at laft, fays the Quaker, I heard him very much complain of one great inconveniency indeed, and that was the mifplacing of the Wine-Cellar, for which reafon he would have it remov'd, *Why where did the Cellar ftand,* fays the Parfon? *Juft under the Pulpit,* fays the Quaker, *and he look'd upon it to be a great Fault, to Preach over his Liquor.* The Parfon, who had let his Glafs ftand Charg'd all the time of the Story, readily took the aplication. *I confefs,* fays the Parfon, *I very unadvifedly left a Blot in my Tables, and you by chance have hit it; and now you've done, it ferves only to verifie the old, Proverb, That Fools have Fortune.* This unexpected retort of the Parfon, quite dumb-founded the Quaker and added a great deal of Pleafure to the Company. Our merry difpofed Friend took Breath, after this fparring blow a confiderable time, fitting as filent as a young Swearer before his Father; Endeavouring as much to hide his Faillings, as the other does his Vice.

By this time the ftock of Wine upon the Table being exhaufted, we began to apply our felves to the *Punch,* which upon the Wine we had already drank, foon put our Spirits into a frefh ferment; and made us now, like Gamfters in a Cock-pit, all bawling and betting on the behalf of one fide or t'other. Infomuch that with one impertinent Queftion or other, they had almoft put the Parfon into a paffion, during which uneafinefs, his *Yea-and-Nay-*Adverfary ask'd *him what he thought a* Quaker *to be?* The Parfon, a little angry they had begun to teafe him, made this refponfe, *A* Quaker fays he, *is fome of old Nicks Venom, fpit in the Face of Gods Church, which her Clergy cannot Lick out with their Tongues, or Rub off with their Claws: Therefore the Church makes a Virtue of Neceffity, and ufes them as Ladys do their black Patches, for fools to magnifie its Beauty.* Indeed Friend, fays the Quaker, *thou talkeft as if the Liquor had difturb'd thy Inward Man. Prithee tell me who thou thinkft was the firft Quaker, that thou fpeakeft with fuch Prophannefs againft fo good a Profeffion?* The firft Quaker, fays the Parfon, who after a very fhort Deliberation anfwer'd, *Balaam.* Balaam, fays the Quaker, *How doeft thou make that out?* It's plainly fo, fays the Parfon, *Becaufe he was the firft that ever gave his Attention to hear an Afs hold forth.* The whole Company expreft by their Laughter an Approbation of the Jeft; and it was concluded on all Hands, that it might reafonably pafs for a good Punch-Bowl Anfwer.

The Potency of the Liquor, and the Weaknefs of our Brains, had now drawn our Mirth to the Dregs, that we were more in danger of

C
falling

falling into Diforder, than we were of Recovering our almoft ftupified Souls to their paft Pitch of Felicity: Several of the Company having wifely fubmitted their Diftemper'd heads to that great Phyfician, Sleep, who can alone Recover the Patients Giddy-Brains of his Epidemical Feaver. At laft down drop'd the *Body* of *Divinity*, in the drowfie Condition of a *Weak Brother*, and left the *Quaker* one of the Survivers, who with great Joy brandifh'd a Triumphant Brimmer round his Head, as a Trophy of the Inebrious Victory he had gain'd over a Father of the Church.

My Friend and I, thought it now high time to be moving off, left *Bacchus* and *Morpheus* together, fhould clofe our Eye-lids, as they had done fome others; and make us become as Troublefome to the Family as the reft: Accordingly we made the Gentleman a Compliment for his kind and Liberal Entertainment, and took leave of the Company, which we left in Chafe of their Sences, fome Snoaring, and fome Talking, that they made as good Mufick as a parcel of Giddy-Headed Sportfmen at the Winding up of a *Venifon* Feaft. My Friend and I (our ways lying different) parted at the Door, and retired each to his own Lodging; but when I got home, and in my Chamber, the Witty Repartees, and pretty Converfation of the Parfon, fo run in my Head, that I could not go quietly to Bed till I had Communicated to Paper the following Defcription of a Merry *Levite* in his Cups, viz.

> *When* Bacchus *once the* Prieft *Subdues,*
>   *With his prevailing Liquor,*
> *The* Man, *in fpight of Art, breaks loofe,*
>   *Abftracted from the* Vicar.
>
> Sober, *he kept the Formal Path;*
>   *In's* Cups *was not the Same-man;*
> *But Reel'd, and Stagger'd in his* Faith,
>   *And Hickup'd like a* Lay-man.
>
> *A many pretty things he fpoke,*
>   *Deferving our attention;*
> *Not Drofs of Saints to feed a* Flock,
>   *But of his own Invention.*
>
> *Yet whether Truths faid o'er his* Glafs,
>   *Of which I took great notice,*
> *Were or in* Vino Veritas,
>   *Or 'n* Verbo Sacerdotis,
>
> *We could not tell; yet Praife was due,*
>   *But unto which to give it,*
> *I vow I know not, of the two,*
>   *The* Liquor, *or the* Levite.
>
> *His Scarlet Cheeks, Inflam'd with Drink,*
>   *Together with his Whist-Head,*
> *Made him appear juft like a* Link,
>   *When at one end 'tis Lighted.*

He

He Drank in Earnest, broke his Jest,
  No Scripture Phrases utter'd;
The Man he play'd, and not the Priest;
  Thus put the best side outward:

Till Drownd at last in Bacchus *Streams,*
  The Prophet's weak condition,
Lull'd him to Sleep, to Dream strange Dreams,
  Or see some wond'rous-Vision.

Having thus Exonerated my Brains of that troublesome Excrement which the Liquor had begot in the Guts of my Understanding, I pluck'd off Natures Disguise with as much Expedition as a Young Bride-groom, and leap'd into Bed, tho' I had no Matrimonial Drudgery to anticipate my Rest, but gently slid into a sweet Sleep, without burthening my Thoughts with Reflections on the Cares of a wicked World, or my own past Miscarriages, where I Enjoy'd the silent Refreshment of an uninterupted Repose till next Morning: When waking at my usual Hour, I made a new Resurrection for the Day; and sliping on my Breeches over my Nakedness, in Imitation of our first Parents *Fig-leaves*, I re-fitted my self for a Walk, in as little time as a Beau spends in Powdering his Periwig. When I had thus Wash'd me and Comb'd me, and put my self in a Cleanly Condition of Appearing abroad; I determin'd to give my self an Hour or two's Breathing in *Grays-Inn* Walks, in order to cary off the Dregs of the *Antedays Debauchery:* Accordingly I steer'd my Course to the Lawyers Garden of Contemplation, where I found (it being early in the Morning) none but a parcel of Superanuated Debauchees, hudled up in Cloaks, Frize-coats, and wadded Gowns, to preserve their old Carcases, from the searching sharpness of *Hampsted* Air; creeping up and down in Pairs and Leashes, no faster than the Hand of a Dial, or a Country Convict walking to Execution; some Talking of Law, some of Trade, some of Religion, and some of Politicks, Arguing the matter in Hand, with so warm a Zeal in Defence of their Opinions, that I thought every now and then, some of the feeble Peripateticks would have made a Combat of Skeletons, and have rattled their old Bones together, in order to deicde the difference with their Hands, which their Tongues could not determine. After I had taken two or three Turns round, I sat my self down in the Upper Walk, where just before me upon a Stone Pedestal was fix'd an old Rusty *Horizontal Dial*, with the *Gnomen* broke short off, a Bullet Headed *Boglandor* coming up into the same Walk, at last enter'd the Bow or Half-Moon, where I sat, and the Dial stood; and after he had spent near a Quarter of an Hour, *Be me Fait,* said he, *E did never see such a ting id me Lifesh.* I *pray ye, Dear-Joy, E gray vat ish de ush of it?* I could not forbear smiling at his Ignorance; and told him 'twas a *Sun-Dial,* to shew the Hour of the Day. *I pray,* said he, *will ye tell me vat it ish a Clock den?* It being a Cloudy Morning, and the Sun quite Obscur'd, I Reply'd, It could not shew the Hour unless the Sun shone out. *Ub bob bou,* says he, *erra be Chreesht den it ish not half so gude as a Vatch, vor dat vill show ush de Hour widdout Shunshine.* And away he shuffl'd upon an *Irish* Trot, seeming to be as much Conceited with his Expression, as if he had

spoke

spoke like a *Ben Johnson*. The Ignorance of the common *Irish*, have rendred them a Jest in all Nations, tho' amongst the Gentry, there are many brave, and well qualified Persons, of which the present Age has produc'd sufficient Testimonies. Therefore, as the fore-going Story will opportunely introduce a Character of an Illitterate Silly *Irish* Peasant, the following peice of *Micro-Cosmography* is only intended upon the most Ignorant of 'em, abstractly consider'd from all such of the same Countrey, who have had the Advantage of a better Education.

The Character of an *Irishman*.

He is commonly a huge Fellow, with a little Soul; as strong as a Horse, and as silly as an Ass; very Poor, and very Proud; Lusty, and yet Lazy; Foolish, but yet Knavish; Impudent, but yet Cowardly; Superstitiously Devout, yet Infamously Wicked; very Obstinate in his Faith, but very loose in his Morals; a Loyal Subject to his Prince, and an Humble Servant to his Master; for he thinks 'tis his Duty, to make a Rogue of himself at any time, to serve the One; and a Fool of himself at any time, to Oblige the Other; that is, to Back a Plot, or make a Bull. He's the fittest Calf in Christendom; he has a Natural Propensity to Pimping, and at his first coming into *England*, most certainly Lists himself into a Whores Service, and has so much a Day out of her Earnings to be her Guard *de Cor*, to protect her in her Vices. His next degree of Ascension, is to be a Bayliffs follower, so that by catching Strumpets by the Belly, and Creditors by the Back; he makes a Decent shift betwixt Pimping and Bumming, to Sing *Hall-la-loo* over *Usquebaugh*, and think himself as great as an *Indian* Emperour over a Bottle of *Rum*; he has as great a Veneration for his Sword as a *Spaniard*; he'll do nothing that's mean, without it, nor any thing that's Brave with it; yet no Man readier to draw it, to show his Forwardness to Fight; and none more glad to put it up, to show his Willingness to let it alone. Tho' Born within Mud Walls, and a Stranger to the Horn-Book, he's no less than a Gentleman; and if once in the Army, tho' no more than a *Powder-Monkey*, no less a Title will Content him, than to be Captain *Mac Some-body*; he has as little kindness for his Native Country as a *Scotchman*; when once he's come out of it, seldom Cares for returning. We cannot say in Conversation, he's a forward Man, for he generally Talks backwards, begins what he has to say at the latter end, and seldom comes home to the beginning, but ends in the Middle: He's an unfit Servant for a Family, where they Eat much Peas-Porridge; for tho' a very Windy Fellow himself, he has a great Aversion to a Fart. He is often under the Misfortune, in *England*, of bemoaning the Loss of a Country-man, for the Law usually every Month disposes of one of them, to keep the Gallows from Cobwebs. He's much of the Nature of *Pumpkins*, Thrives best within filthy places; base means to Live, he Loves most; and Honesty's a Soil that wont agree with him; he is never well, but when he's an Ill-man; and the worse he grows, the better Man he thinks himself: He's a rare Messenger to be sent of a Fools Errand; for tho' he bears the Image of a Man, he performs his Actions like a Horse without Thought or Reason. To conclude, he's a Coward in his own Country, a Lusty Stallion in *England*, a Graceful Footman in *France*, a good Soldier in *Flanders*, and a Valluable Slave in our *Western* Plantations, where they are distinguish'd by the Ignominious Epithet of *White Negroes*.

By

By that time I had digested this Character in my Thoughts, as I sat Musing by the Dyal, I found by the sundry *Turkish* and *Arabian* Sca-lamouches, who were Gracing the Walks with their most Glittering Appearances, that the Beaus began to Pose, and come forth in their Morning Plumes, in order to attract the Eyes of some Mercenary *Bellfay's*, by whose Airy Freaks, and distinguishable Graces I could perceive they would more easily be subdued by the prevailing Pow'r of a Guinea, tho' offer'd by a Wither'd Hand, belonging to an Ill-shap'd Carcass, then be tempted with the Charms of any Ostentatious Owle, who had Empted his Pockets to cover his Back with the Gay Ornaments of a *Peacock*. The sundry sorts of unusual Figures I beheld, transported my Thoughts beyond the Equinox, and made me fancy I was Travelling in some strange distant Territories, where Men Unpolish'd show the Rudeness of their Natures, by the Un-coothness of their Garbs, some having cover'd their tender Skulls with Caps in the fashion of a *Turkish Turbant*, and with such Gaudy Figures wove into their Gowns, that they look'd at a small distance, as if they had been frigthed out of their Beds by Fire, having not time to Dress, and had wraped themselves up in Tapstery Hangings, and Turky-work Table-Cloths in a Fright, as the readiest shift they could make to cover their Nakedness; others had thrust their Calves-Heads some in Baggs like Pudding-Pokes, and some in Caps fashion'd like an Extinguisher, and hung down half way their Backs, that made 'em look like Pages to some strange Ambassador, come from *Terra Incognita*, on purpose to let *England* see what Ridiculous Garbs are wore by the Devil knows who, at the very Fundament of the Universe; these were Masqueraded in Morning Gowns, of such Diversity of Flickering Colours, that their dazling Garments look'd like so many Rainbows, wove into a *Scotch Plad*; and look'd so Extra-vagantly Vain, and Foppish, that certainly had they not been influenc'd by some Giddy Brain'd Young Girls to have discredited their Masculine Natures, with this Female kind of Prodigality, the Thoughts of Men could have never Entertain'd such Butterfly-Conceptions as to Imagine any Reasonable Creature so Silly to Worship or Admire the Person of a Man, because they see him in a Fools-Cap or Fools-Coat; as if it added an Excellence to his Proportion, to have all the *Colours* in *Heraldry* Blazen'd upon his Back, or as if he thought it a peice of Plain-Dealing, to discover to the World by a *Taudry Outside* his *Inward Vanity* and *Emptiness*, that no-body might expect more in his Conversation, than to oblige their Eyes with a *New-Fashion*, or hear a Verbal Panegyrick upon some *French-Taylor*. Tis pity but Pedestals were erected in the Garden for the *Novices* to mount on in several Disguises, and there fix themselves in their *Fencing*, and *Dancing-School Postures*; and they'd serve rarely for Antick Images, to adorn the Walks; and no Question but the Painted things, according to the End they Propose by their Finery, would be wonderfully Gaiz'd at by the Ladys, and be thought worthy of each Strum-pets Admiration. For the Readers further satisfaction, I will let him more plainly see what sort of Animal I mean, by Summing up his Out-side and Inside in a brief Character.

A *Beau,*

Is a *Narcissus* that is fallen in Love with himself and his own Shadow. Within Doors he's a great Friend to a great Glass, before which he ad-

D   mires

mires the Works of his *Taylor* more than the whole Creation. Without Doors he adores the Sun like a *Persian*, and Walks always in his Rays tho' at Midsummer, to please himself with a moving Copy of his own Proportion. His Body's but the Poor Stuffing of a Rich Case, like Bran to a Lady's Pincushion; that when the outside is Stript off, there remains nothing that's Valluable. His Head is a Fools Egg, which lies hid in a Nest of Hair: His Brains are the Yolk, which Conceit has Adled. He's a stroling Assistant to Drapers and Taylors, showing every other Day a New Pattern, and a New Fashion. He's a walking Argument against Immortality: For no Man by his Actions, or his Talk, can find he has more Soul than a Goose. He's a very Troublesome Guest in a Tavern; and must have good Wine chang'd three or four times, till they bring him the worst in the Cellar before he'll like it. His Conversation is as intollerable as a Young Councel's in Term-Time, Talking as much of his *Mistresses*, as the other does of his *Motions*; and will have the most Words, tho' all that he says is nothing. He's a Bubble to all he deals with, from his *Whore* to his *Perriwig-maker*; and hates the sordid Rascal that won't Flatter him. He scorns to condescend so low, as to speak of any Person beneath the dignity of a Noble-man; the Duke of such a Place, and my Lord such one, are his common Cronies, from whom he knowes all the Secrets of the Court, but dare not impart 'em to his best Friends because the Duke enjoyn'd him to Secresie. He is always furnish'd with new Jests from the last New Play, which he most commonly spoiles with repeating. His Watch he compares with every Sun-Dial, Swears it corrects the Sun; and plucks it out so frequently in Company, that his Fingers go oftener in a Day to his Fob, than they do to his Mouth, spending more time every Week in showing the Rarity of the Work; than the Man did in making on't; being as forward to tell the Price without desiring, as he is to tell you the Hour without asking; he is as constant a Visiter of a Coffee-house, as a *Drury-Lane* Whore is of *Covent-Garden Church*; where he Cons over the News-Papers with as much indifference, as the other Prays; Reading only for Fashions sake, and not for Information. He's commonly of a small standing at one of the *Universities*, tho, all he has learnt there, is to know how many Taverns there are in the Town, and what *Vintner* has the handsom'st Wife. Tho' his Parents has given him an expensive Education, he's as Dumb to *Rhetorick*, as a Fool to Reason; as Blind to *Philosophy*, as an *Owle* in the Sunshine; and as Deaf to Understanding, as a Priest to Charity. He often hopes to pass for a *Wit*, by calling other People *Fools*; and his fine Apparrel is his only Armour, that defends him from Contempt. He's a Coward amongst *Brave-men*, and a *Brave-Fellow* amongst *Cowards*; A *Fool* amongst *Wise-men*, and a *Wit* in *Fools* Company: All that I know he's good for, is to give a poor Fellow a Dinner that will do him Homage; and help to serve the turn of an insatiate Woman instead of a D——d.

By this time I had finish'd the *Picture* of my *Beau*, the *Bellfa's* in their Morning-Gowns and wadded Wast-coates, without Stays, began to flow as fast into the Walks, as Whores into the eighteen-penny Gallery at the third Act, tripping about in search of their Foolish Admirers like so many Birds on a *Valentine's-Day*, in order to find a Mate; I was mightily pleas'd at the various diverting Scenes, with which I was en-

tertained

tertain'd in this Natural Theatre, where I had so large an opportunity of observing the Vanity of both Sexes in a greater Perfection, than the *Drama* by faint imitation is capable of representing. I cannot here make so good a use of it as I would do, because I am oblig'd to take Notice of something of greater Moment. I shall therefore only give you a short Character of a *Modish-Lady* in Verse, and so quit the Walks to pursue my further intention.

> *Pride, Beauty, Prattle, Leachery, and Conceit,*
> *Airy Deportment, and the want of Wit ;*
> *Small Waste, Plump Buttocks, and a Face Divine ;*
> *Wretchedly Foolish, and extreamly fine :*
> *At* Hackney, Stepney, *or at* Chelsea *Bred,*
> *In Dancing perfect, and in Plays well Read ;*
> *The only Daughter of some Trading Fop,*
> *Train'd half in School, and t'other half in Shop ;*
> *Who nothing by her Parents is deny'd,*
> *T' improve her Charms, or gratifie her Pride.*
> *Spoil'd by her Fathers Fondness and his Pounds,*
> *Till her Wild Fancy knows at last no Bounds :*
> *Impatient of Extreams, with Pride half Craz'd,*
> *Then must her Head a Story higher be rais'd ;*
> *In her next Gawdy Gown, her Sweeping Train,*
> *Is order'd to be made as long again ;*
> *All things must vary from the common Rode,*
> *And reach a Size beyond a Decent Mode.*
> *Thus Monstrously Adorn'd, to make a show,*
> *She Walks in State, and Courtsies very low,*
> *And is a proper* Mistress *for the* Fool *a* Beau.

From thence I took a Turn into the City, where People were running about with as much concern in their Countenances, as if they had receiv'd News of the *French* Landing, or that an Army of *Irish Papists*, had taken Possession of *Stocks-Market* in order to Massacre the *Protestants*, and Plunder the *City*.

At last I went to *Jonathan's Coffee-house* by the *Change*, to enquire into the meaning of this strange Disorder : Where I saw a parcel of Men at one Table Consulting together, with as much Malice, Horror, Anger and Dispair in their Looks, as if a new Pestilence had Sprung up in their Families, and their Wives had run away with their Journey-Men to avoid the Infection. And at another Table, a parcel of Merry Hawk'd Look'd Blades, Laughing and Pointing at the rest, as if with abundance of Satisfaction, they Triumph'd over the others Affliction. At last upon a little Enquiry into the matter, I found the Honest Brother-hood of the *Stock-Jobbers*, were in a Lamentable Confusion, and had divided themselves into two parts, *Fools* and *Knaves*. A few of the Latter having been too Cunning for a great many of the Former ; had drawn-in some Two, some Three, some Four, or Five Hundred Pounds deep, to the Ruin of many, and the great Disadvantage of the rest, who having been under the Reputation of *Knaves* all their Lives-time, have at last, by the Unexpected Success of an Unlucky Project, Undeceiv'd

the

the World at Once, and prov'd themſelves the Errantſt *Fools* in the whole City : And for the Readers better Information, I have drawn one of theſe Sublunary Buſie Bodys into a Brief Character, with which I ſhall Conclude.

A Stock-Jobber

Is a Compound of *Knave, Fool, Shopkeeper, Merchant* and *Gentleman.* His whole Buſineſs is Tricking ; when he Cheats another, he's a *Knave* ; when he ſuffers himſelf to be Out-Witted, he's a *Fool* ; he moſt commonly keeps a Viſible Trade going, and with whatſoever he gets in his Shop, he makes himſelf a Domeſtick Merchant upon *Change,* by turning *Stock-Adventurer,* led on by the mighty hopes of Advancing himſelf to a Coach and Horſes, that he may Lord it over his Neighbouring Mechanicks. He's as great a Lover of Uncertainty, as ſome *Fools* are of the *Royal-Oak-Lottery* ; and would not give a Farthing for an Eſtate got without a great hazard. He's a kind of a *Speculum,* wherein you may behold the Paſſions of Mankind, and the Vainity of Humane Life ; to Day he Laughs ; to Morrow he Grins ; is the third Day Mad, and always Labours under thoſe Twin Paſſions, Hope and Fear ; riſing one Day, and falling the next, like *Mercury* in a *Weather-Glaſs* ; and cannot Arrive to that Pitch of Wiſdom, as to know one Day, what he ſhall be the next: He is never under the Proſpect of growing Rich ; but at the ſame time under the Danger of becoming Poor, and is always to be found between *Hawk* and *Buzzard* ; he Spins out his Life between *Faith* and *Hope* ; but has nothing to do with Charity, becauſe there's little to be got by't : He's a Man whoſe great Ambition is to Ride over others, in order to which he reſolves to Win the Horſe or Loſe the Saddle.

F I N I S.

THE
LONDON
SPY.

For the *Month* of *March*, 1700.

The Second Volume.

PART V.

LONDON, Printed and Sold by *J. How*, in the *Ram-Head-Inn Yard* in *Fanchurch-street*, 1700.

Books Sold by J. How, *in the* Ram-Head-Inn-Yard *in* Fanchurch-Street; J. Weld, *at the* Crown *between the* Temple-Gates *in* Fleet-street; *and* Mrs. Fabian, *t* Mercers-Chappel *in* Cheap-side.

1. SOt's Paradise: Or the Humours of a Derby-Ale-House: With a Satyr upon the Ale. Price Six Pence.

2. A Trip to Jamaica: With the Character of the People and Island. Price Six Pence.

3. *Eclesia & Factio.* A Dialogue between *Bow-Steeple-Dragon,* and the *Exchange-Grashopper.* Price Six Pence.

4. The Poet's Ramble after Riches. With Reflections upon a Country Corporation. Also the Author's Lamentation in the time of Adversity. Price Six Pence.

5. A Trip to New-England. With a Character of the Country and People, both English and Indians. Price Six Pence.

6. Modern Religion and Ancient Loyalty: A Dialogue. Price Six Pence.

7. The World Bewitch'd. A Dialogue between Two Astrologers and the Author. With Infallible Predictions of what will happen from the *Vices* and *Villanies* Practis'd in *Court, City* and *Country.* Price Six Pence.

8. A Walk to *Islington:* With a Description of New *Tunbridge*-VVells, and *Sadler's* Musick-House. Price Six Pence.

9. The Humours of a Coffee-House: A Comedy. Price Six Pence.

10 A Frolick to Horn-Fair. With a Walk from Cuckold's-Point thro' *Deptford* and *Greenwich.* Price Six-Pence.

11. The Dancing-School. With the Adventures of the *Easter*-Holy-Days. Price Six Pence.

12. The First Volume of the LONDON-SPY: In Twelve Parts.

13. The First, Second, Third, and Fourth Parts of the Second Volume of the *London-Spy.* Price Six Pence Each.

All Written by the same Author.

THE
LONDON
SPY.

HAVING receiv'd a Note from my Friend, to meet him at the Sign of the *Dolphin* in *Lombard-street* ; which Fish, by mistake of the Painter, is render'd more like a Crooked Billet, than the Creature its design'd to represent : At the time appointed I accordingly went, where my Friend over a Penny Nipperkin of Molossas Ale, sat ready to receive me. When an accustomary Salutation had pass'd between us, it being about the time when strolling Pastry Cooks, who keep their Shops in their Baskets, pay their Visits to their Customers, we began to Consult about our Dinner, being posted in a very convenient House for that purpose ; At last, agreed to Coroborate our Bodies with a Slice of that Martial Venison, Beeff, fit Food for either *Saint, Soldier, or Sailor*, the King of Meats, and the most delicious of all Dainties, saith, S —— the Poet, and *Marriot* the Counsellour. When we had suppress'd our Hunger, the most Powerful of all Appetites, and tir'd our Jaws with tedious Mastication, we began to fall into talk about our Neighbouring *Scavengers*, whose Houses are the Lay-Stalls of that filthy dross which *defiles* the *Virgin, Corrupts the Priest, Contaminates* the Fingers of the *Judge*, is the Cause of every Ill, and the very Seed of Humane Misery ; it's the mistaken Happiness of Mankind, which brings with it, where so e'er it comes, a Thousand Curses worse than Poverty. Prithee, says my Friend, don't rail so against *Money*, it's a Task becomes no body but a Mendicant, who is always endeavouring to put other People that have it out of Conceit with it, that they may the more willingly part with it to those that want it ; there's a great deal to be said in the behalf of Money, and if you were but to hear a Rich Parson preach a Lecture upon it according to his real Sentiments, he would teach you, perhaps, to have as good an Opinion of it as e'er an Alderman in the City. You must consider our Ancestors had as great a Veneration for this sort of Dirt, as you call it, as the present Age can possibly bear towards it ; as you may find by the excellent Virtues they ascribe to it, in their Old Sayings, *viz.*

Money

Money anfwers All things. Money makes the old Wife Trot. Money makes the Mare to go. What Words won't do, Gold will; and a great many other Adages I could recollect with a little thinking, which would fhow fufficiently that our Fore-Fathers were as much given to Value this *Root of all Evil*, as fome term it, as any of our Modern Mifers can be. Therefore if you'll take Councel of a Friend, Inftead of Slighting it, endeavour to get it; and never rail againft it, till you are affur'd you have enough to ferve your Turn. To defpife Riches when they are out of your Power, favours more of Envy than Philofophy; but to feem not to Value Wealth, when you have it in poffeffion, is an Argument of Generofity.

I thank'd him for his Inftructions, which were a little out of my way at prefent to put in Practice; and then began to enquire of him what method thofe great Dealers in Money chiefly take, for the Improvement of fuch mighty Sums which were trufted in their Power. In anfwer to which, my Friend gave me this following Information: The beft of their Harveft, fays he, is now over; ever fince the alteration of the Coin, has put a period to the Project of Diminution, their Trade has been in a declining Condition; but they have, moft of them, fo feather'd their Nefts by the old Treafonable *Snip-Snap*, that they have no occafion to fear the greateft Difadvantages their Trade can fall under. As an Argument of their Dealings in that Profitable Affair, I will give you a Convincing Inftance of my own Knowledge, *viz.* I had in the very heat of thofe myfterious times, a Bill upon an Eminent Banker not far off, to receive Twenty-five Pounds; and waiting in the Shop till he had difpatch'd his Bufinefs with fome other Perfons who were ftept in before me, in comes a Spark in a good Camlet Cloak Lin'd with Red, Sword, Long Wig, and Beaver Hat, and gives the Banker a Bagg of Money, defiring him to lay it by for him, and he would call for it on the morrow Morning; which he took from him, and laid it down upon a Seat on the other fide of the Counter; the Perfon that brought it becoming his Habiliments but awkardly, like the Tinker in *Jevern's* Farce put into the Lords Apparel, occafion'd me to take more than ordinary Notice of his Face; which I was affur'd I had often feen, but could not, till he was gone, recollect where; at laft fully fatisfy'd my felf, about a Twelve-month before he was a *Cobler* at *Weftminfter*, who had mended me many a pair of Shooes, and run of many an Errand for me, I then Lodging within three or four Doors of where he kept his Stall; in which he us'd to be as Merry over his work, with the Ballade of *Troy Town*, as ever was Country Dame over her *Spinning-Wheel*, or a Mufical Bumpkin with his *Jews Trump*. When he had told over the feveral Sums, and fatisfy'd the Demands of the firft Comers, fhowing as much double-handed Dexterity in telling of Money, as a *Hocus Pocus* can well fhow in the Conveyance of his Balls, I then accofted him, and fhow'd him my Authority for another Sum, which he was ready to pay upon Sight of the Bill, as if he was never better pleas'd then when he was getting rid of his Money; and taking up the Bag my old Acquaintance had left, attempts to pay me in fuch fcrupulous and Diminutive Pieces, that I thought nothing but a *Knave* would offer to pay,

or

or a *Fool* be willing to receive. Upon which I refus'd to take it, he urg'd the Money was passable, telling me that a Gentleman left it with him but just before; which he thought, I suppose, I had not observed. Pray, said I, what was that Gentleman who left it here? He answering me an *Essex* Gentleman of Six or Seven Hundred Pound a Year. Said I, I see the Person that left it, and if he be worth such an Estate you speak of, he has got it in a very little time, for within this year and a Quarter, he has Soled me a pair of Shooes for Sixteen-pence, and I am sure he had not Land enough then to raise a Bunch of Carrots in, or Money enough to spare to buy the Seed; therefore I fancy you are mistaken in your Man. O dear, Sir, says he, your Eyes are strangely deceiv'd, he's a very worthy Honest Gentleman, I have had Money of his in my Hands, at times, this seven years. But howveer, Sir, if you don't like this Money, I'll see if I can look you better. And with that goes and finds me out good Market Money to my Content; which I suppose, I should have had some difficulty to have got, had it not been for my accidental Discovery.

Well, said I, but this Golden Age is past, and what Methods do they take now to improve their Cash? The chief advantage, says he, that they now make, is by supplying the Necessities of straitened Merchants and great Dealers, to pay the Customs of Goods imported, rather than they should fall under the discredit as well as disadvantage of being run into the Kings Ware-house; or by assisting of 'em in the Purchase of great Bargains, or the like; for which they make 'em pay such unreasonable Extortion, that they devour more of the Merchants Profit than Snailes, Worms and Magpies do of the Farmers Crop, or the Gardiners industry. In relation to which, I'll inform you of a pretty Disappointment that lately happen'd to one of these Unconscionable Usurers, who insisted upon a very extravagant Gratuity for the Loan of a considerable Sum, to a very Eminent Merchant; which take as follows.

A Person of Quality having made a Topping Banker in *Lumbard-street* his Cashier, having occasion to talk with him about some *Pecuniary* Affairs, order'd his Coachman to drive him to his Shop, where he found the Banker talking very busily with a Merchant: The Banker, in respect to his Quality, came immediately to his Coach side, to know the Gentlemans Pleasure, who desir'd him to first dispatch his business with the Person he was before talking to, and he would tarry in his Coach till he had done, for he was in no great haste. Upon which the Banker retiring into his Shop, they proceeded on the matter in Hand, which was about lending the Merchant a Sum of Money, who was very unwilling to come up to the Bankers Unreasonable demands for the use of it, which the Merchant requir'd but for one Month; the Banker being well acquainted with the present Necessity of the Merchant for Money, tho' a very Rich Man, and a great Dealer, stuck close to his first Proposals, and would abate him nothing of the Extortion he requir'd; which occasion'd 'em at last last to talk so warmly about the matter, that the Gentleman over-heard their Discourse; and calling his Footman,

whisper'd

whisper'd him, and bid him Dog the Gentleman till he had fix'd him, and bring him an Account where he left him, to *Lloyd*'s Coffee-house. The Merchant being very unwilling to comply with the Bankers Avaritious Terms, went out of his Shop in a Huff, and told him he would see what he could do elfe-where, before he would fubmit to fo inhumane an Exaction. As foon as he was gone, the Footman obferv'd the Commands of his Mafter, who after he had talk'd a little with the Banker, bid his Coach wait till he walk'd over to *Lloyd*'s, where in a little time his Footman brought him Intelligence, that the Gentleman he order'd him to follow, was gone into a great Houfe, in *Mincing-Lane*, which he believ'd was his own Habitation; becaufe when the Door was opened to him, he went readily in, without asking the Servant any Queftions. Upon which the Gentleman fteps into his Coach, and orders the Footman to direct the Coach to the Houfe, where the Gentleman order'd his Man to Knock, and ask the Servant that fhould come to the Door, whither their Mafter was within, who anfwer'd *Yes, but that he was juft fat down to Dinner.* The Gentleman bid the Servant not difturb him, but defir'd to walk into a Room, and he would ftay till he had Din'd. Upon which, they fhow'd him into a Parlor, where he waited but a little time before the Merchant, upon his Servants Information, came to him. The Gentleman finding it to be the fame Perfon, ask'd him if about an hour fince, he was not treating with fuch a Banker about fuch an Affair: He told him, *Yes, he was:* And feem'd to be furpriz'd the Gentleman fhould know any thing of the matter. Who, to make the Merchant eafie, difcover'd by what means he became acquainted with what had pafs'd between him and the Banker; Expreffing himfelf to the Merchant after this manner, *I have,* fays he, *In the Bankers hands you were talking to, between three and four Thoufand Pounds, and if he can think it fafe to Truft part of my Money in your hands for the fake of an Unreafonable Advantage, I don't know why I may not Truft you as well my felf upon more Reafonable Terms; he pays me no Intereft, and I cannot think him an Honeft Man that will be fo fevere with another, in whofe hands I have reafon to believe he think his Money fafe, or elfe he would not Venture it at all, tho on the moft Advantageous Conditions. Therefore fince he was fo hard with you, if you will let me know what Sum your Occafion requires, I will give you my Note upon the fame Perfon to pay you the Money, which you fhall ufe for any Reafonable time without a Penny Intereft or Gratuity.*

The Merchant, amaz'd at fo Generous an Offer from a Stranger, expreft himfelf in all the thankful Acknowledgements imaginable, gladly accepting of his Kindnefs, telling him Six Hundred Pounds would do his Bufinefs, for that three or four Ships were come in, on Board of which he had confiderable Effects, and that the Money was to help pay the Cuftoms. The Gentleman accordingly, as the Merchants Straits requir'd, draws him a Bill upon the Banker for Six Hundred Pounds; and afterwards found fuch agreeable Honefty from the Merchant, that he drew all his Money out of the Bankers Hands, and put it into the Merchants, by which means he is now become one of the Richeft Men and greateft Merchants; in the City, and the Banker loft a good Friend, to his great Injury, as a juft reward of his Covetoufnefs.

Thefe

These Base and Unchristian-like Impositions, are so very Practicable amongst Bankers and Money Scriveners, that Mr. *D. J.* Lecturer of St. —— Parish, thought it his Duty to reprove 'em Publickly in *Lombard-street* Church, for their abominable Usury and Extortion, which they so highly resented, being touch'd to the Quick, that instead of Reforming their Jewish and Unlawful Practices, they protested against his Doctrine, like a parcel of Incorrigible Sinners, and turn'd the Consciencious Priest out of his Lectureship, for the faithful discharge of his Holy Function; who gave 'em a very Notable, tho' Unwelcome Reprehension, in his Farewell Sermon, choosing these Words for his Text, *Am I therefore become your Enemy, because I told you the Truth?* Therefore since to the utmost of my Power I have enlightened your Understanding of these City-Money-Jobbers, I hope you will Sum up a short Character of one of them in Verse, to Oblige the World; and I make no doubt, but 'twill be very acceptable: Which, according to my Friends request, I have done for the further satisfaction of the Reader.

The Character of a *Banker.*

Himself, a Scavenger, his House the Cart,
Where Plodding Men throw in their Drossy Pelf;
   Thus like a Farmer, he from Rich mens Dirt,
Raises a happy living to himself.

   With others Cards, a Cunning Game he plays;
They stand the hazard, whilst he gains his Ends;
   He Borrows still, and still no Interest Pays;
And ne'er without a damn'd Extortion Lends.

   Tho' Proud and Stately, whether Rich or Poor,
Is to all Men, except himself, unknown;
   Amidst his Borrow'd Treasure, he's no more,
Then Slave to others Riches, not his own.

   His Dealings are so dark a Mystery,
No Man can truly tell, tho' ne'er so wise,
   Whether he thrives, or that he honest be,
Until the Black-palm'd Miser breaks or dies.

   With one Mans Money he another pays;
To this he Cuts, and to the other Deals,
   Small Accidents his Credit oft decays;
Then Farewel Fingers, God have Mercy heels.

   The Beggars Curse him as they pass his door
Envy the heaps of Riches which they see;
   Beg but in vain, then wish the Banker Poor,
Who rowles in Wealth, but has no Charitie.

Great

Great Sums each day are on his Counters told,
And Piles of Bags his Fetter'd Trunks contain;
But yet for all his Silver and his Gold,
He's but the Mimick of a vast Rich Man.

I having a Relation in Town, who about Twelvemonths since had the Courage, in spight of Cuckoldom, to suffer a Parson to rob him of his Native Liberty, and bind him fast with Fetters of Matrimony, to Mans Misery, a Wife; and the first Fruits of their Drudgery being lately, crept out of its Original Habitation into this World of Affliction, the Joyful Father, bringing me the glad Tidings of my new Squab Relation, very closely Solicited me to do the Pennance of a Godfather, that the little Epitomy of the Dad might be craftily cleans'd from the Sin of his Birth, and the iniquity of his Conception. I wanting Ill-nature enough to resist his Importunities, submitted to his Request; and engag'd for once to make my self a Witness to the little Infants admittance into Christianity, and stand as a *Tom Doodle* for an hour or two to be banter'd by a Tittle-Tattle Assembly of Female Gossips. The time appointed for the Solemnization of this Ancient piece of Formality being come, after I had put on a clean Band, and bestow'd two Penny worth of Razoridge on the most fertile part of my Face, whose Septuary Crop requir'd mowing, away I trotted towards the Joyful Habitation of my Friend and Kinsman; but with as aking a heart as a Wise man goes to be Marry'd, or a Broken Merchant comes near the Counter. At last I came to the Door, which I pass'd by backwards and forwards three or four times, as a bashful Lover does by his Mistresses Lodging, before I had Courage enough to enter; fancying every time I went up to the door, I heard a Confusion of Womens Tongues come thro' the Keyhole, which struck with such a violence upon the drum of my Ear, 'twas ready, when I listen'd, to knock me Backwards. At last I pluck'd up a Spirit like a City Draper going to Dun a Man of Quality, and gave a Tap at the Door, which brought Nurse *Busie-body* to give me admitance, who introduc'd me into a back Parlour, and call'd her Master, of whom I enquir'd after the Welfare of the Woman in the Straw, who answered me, according to the old Phrase, *As well, God be thanked, as can be expected for a Woman in her Condition.* I told my Kinsman how I dreaded the Fatigue I was bound to run thro', who heartily pitied my Condition, and advised me to put on the best assurance I could: Telling me he was equaly oblig'd to be a Part'ner in my Sufferings; for that he expected to be Tongue-teas'd by that time the Wine had gone a little about, as bad as a Man that had beat his Wife before a whole Jury of Matrons. The Women, Heaven be prais'd! were usher'd up stairs, so that I was in no great danger of having my Ears stretch'd upon the Rack of Verbosity, till the Sacerdotal Administration of the Sacrament was over.

By this time in came my Brother *Nuncupator*, who was to stand the Beats with me; and after we had made our selves a little Acquainted, by enquiring of each other *what News*, and the like; we began to look forward, and consider of the difficulties we were to run thro'. *Poh,*
says

says he, *Never fear, I'll warrant you we'll deal with 'em well enough, let me alone to bring you off, I have been us'd to't. This is sport,* says he, *That I have been at so often, that I believe half the Children in the Parish call me Godfather. I am as well known to all the Gossips hereabouts, as St. Austin is to the Parson, or Amen to the Clark. Do but take my method amongst 'em, and you will gain their Hearts for ever, and be accounted as pretty a Man by 'em as ever came into Womans Company, or listen'd to the Tattles of a Female Convention; that is, Before you highly praise the Fair Sex, and speak very Honourably of the State of Matrimony, Rail soundly against all those Jealous Pated Coxcombs that abuse their Wives, tho' with good Reason; and declare every Man that thinks himself a Cuckold, deserves to be made one; and that it is always Mens own Faults that they are so. Before remember a Womans Freedom is an Argument of her Honesty; and that the still Sow eates all the draught; that Women ought to have the Liberty of Drinking a Cheruping Cup as well as Men; and that she may go into a Tavern with another Man besides her Husband, and may be very honest for all that; and that she may like another Mans Company, for his good humour, Merry Jests, and witty Conversation, without doing an Ill thing, or abusing her Husband. Tongue the Old Women when you Kiss 'em, and suck the Lips of the young ones like a Horse-leach. If you hear a Woman Rail against her Husband, before you second her, and say he's a very morose Man to use so good a Woman after so ill a manner. Before you preach up Female Authority, that a Husband ought to mind nothing but his Trade, and let the Wife alone to govern the Family. That no Woman who wants Children by her Husband ought to be blam'd if she raises Seed with discretion by another, since it takes off from her the reproach of being Barren, and from her Husband the scandal of a Fumbler. Not forgetting the old saying,* There's no harm done when a good Child's got. *Follow but these instructions, and Lard your Talk now and then with a little Waggery wrapt up in clean Linnen, and you need not doubt but you will find your self as acceptable a Man amongst 'em, as if they had heard that Nature had bestow'd as great a Fools Blessing upon you, as ever they desir'd to partake of.*

I thank'd him kindly for his Serviceable Documents; and was mighty well satisfied I had so experienc'd a Partner to assist me at the Solemnity, not fearing but so good an Example would be a means of carrying me cleverly thro the whole Ceremony without Baulk or Discountenance. By this time in came the Parochial Sprinkler, with *Amen* at his Heeles; who were usher'd up Stairs amongst the Assembly of Help-meets. Now thought I, the Curtain's ready to be drawn, and the show will begin presently. Whilst I was thus thinking, down comes Nurse to desire us to walk up, who had so adorn'd her wither'd Countenance with Tapelac'd Head-clothes, that her Weasel Face look'd as disproportion'd to her Commode, as a *Tom-Tits* Egg put into an Owles Nest. Having a Stollup lac'd Hankerchief round her Neck, that look'd as old Fashion'd as if *Eve* had spun the Thred, and made the Lace with the same Needle she sow'd her Fig-leaf Apron with. Having round her a white Holland Safe ty'd down behind with Tape, that she look'd all over as white as the very Ghost in *Bateman.*

As soon as we came into the Room, and had bow'd our backs to the old Cluster of Harridans, and they in return had bent their Knees to

C

us,

us, I sneak'd up to the Parsons Elbow, and my Part'ner after me; and there I stood as demurely as if I had just turn'd *Jew*, and was going to be circumciz'd before all the Company. The Parson plucking out a little Pocket-Tool belonging to his Trade, began in Solemn-wise the usual Preface to the Business in hand, whilst old Mother *Grope* stood rocking of the Bantling in her Arms, wrap'd up in so rich a Mantle, as if both *Indias* had club'd their utmost Riches to furnish out a Noble covering for my little Kinsman, who came as callow into the World as a Bird out of an Egg-shell. At last the Babe was put into my hands to deliver, tho' not as my Act and Deed, to the Parson, who having consecrated some *New-River Water* for his Purpose, wash'd away Original Sin from my new Nephew, and brought him amongst us Christians into a State of Salvation. But when my froward Godson felt the cold Water in his Face, he threaten'd the Priest with such a parcel of Angry Looks, that if he had been strong enough I dare Swear he would have serv'd him the same Sauce, and under the same ignorance would have return'd him but little thanks for his Labour. After we had join'd together in a Petition for the good of the Infant Christian, the Religious part was concluded; and now Kissing, Feasting, and Jocularity were to follow in their Proper Places, I left it to my Part'ner to be the leading Man, resolving to be a true Copy of his Impudence to the utmost of my Capacity.

The first Example he set me was to kiss the Godmother, who had a very passable Face and tollerable Mein; and as for her Age, I believe she was near upon the Meridian. I follow'd his directions to a Tittle, and Kist so very close, that I am confident the inside of her Lips could do no less than take off an impression of her Teeth, as deep as a Child leaves when he bites a Mouthful of Bread and Butter. As soon as ever the Parson had refresh'd his Spirits with a Bumper of Canary, dedicated to the Woman in the Straw; and the Clark had said Amen to his Masters good Wishes after the like manner, each of 'em accepted of a Paper of Sweet-meats for his Wife or his Children, and away they went, leaving the rest of the Company behind to make a rehearsal of the good old Customs always practicable at these Neighbourly sort of meetings. The next piece of Lip-Exercise my Part'ner set me, was to make a Regular Service of Kisses round the Room, keeping such exact time in the discharge of this Ceremony, not daring to stay too long in a place for fear the rest should have taken it ill, that if he had but smack'd as he kist, he would have kept much the same Measure, and have made much the same Musick as a Church Clock that clicks every Quarter of a Minute. By that time he had ended his first Ceremonious Essay to please the Ladies, and had swept off with his Lips the dry Scurff, which loosly hung upon the Muzzles of the old Women, and had suck'd a Virmilion Colour in the Lips of the Young ones; I began to succeed him in the Drudgery of Osculation, which I went about with as ill a will as a Security pays a Debt he never Drank for; tho' there were two or three as tolerable Temptations as a man would desire to meet with, between a pair of Iniquity Counsell-keepers; yet the publick formality of the

matter,

matter, so took off the pleasure of Lip-Leachery, that instead of a Satisfaction, I thought it but a very troublesome and ridiculous piece of ancient Superstition : One old woman having the Palsie in her Head, happened by a sudden resolution of the Sinews which Govern the under Jaw, to snap my under Lip in between her Gums, that had it not been for shame, I had cry'd out; but as Providence would have it, she had ne'er a Tooth, or else I believe she had spoild my Kissing for a Fortnight; this accident has begot in me ever since such an aversion to the Kissing of old Women, that I sincerely Protest, I had rather Kiss Twenty Young ones, twenty times a piece, than to run the like hazzard of having my Lips disfigur'd. The next part we agreed to Perform, was a very Costly piece of Ceremony ; which was to pay our Acknowledgements to Mother *Bawdy-Flirt*, who brought the little Prisoner out of his dark Dungeon, into Light and Liberty; and so on to Nurse *Caudle-Cook*, who thro' Greedyness of the Present, gave my Fingers such a Mercenary Gripe, as if she had mistaken my Hand, and thought she had got fast hold of the Rudder of my Affections. Having very orderly proceeded thus far without a Baulk, I was glad I had overcome this, the most difficult part of my Journey, as a *Pilgrm* going to the *Jubilee* is, that he has past the *Alps*. The greatest Uneasiness that remain'd now, being only a little Tittle-Tattle, which I did not doubt but the Wine would inspire me with Courage enough to Cope with. When this was over, the next piece of Folly that my Kinsman was guilty on, in Submission, I suppose, to his Wifes Vanity, was to Usher the Assembly into the next Room, where was a very good hot Supper ready upon the Table, and two or three dozen of several sorts of Wine, to Entertain their Ladyships, who before they sat down, the Parsons Business forcing him to take an Early Leave of the Company, and I having the most Canonical Countenance, the Gossips pitch'd upon me to Bless the good Creatures ; and to tell you the Truth, being at a Nonplus for a Grace, and thinking it a Scandal to Acknowledge it, I was forc'd to Blunder out one *Ex-tempore*, as well as I could, for fear of being taken for a Heathen ; which, because of the Newness of it, I'll present it to the Reader.

Bless the good Ladys and good Food,
   That Heav'n has set before us ;
And may we Men prove all so good,
   The Women may adore us.

May these thy Fruitful Dames Live long,
   Grow ev'ry day more Handsome ;
And may their Husbands prove as strong
   I'th' Back as second Sampson.

May they Dance Merryly each Night,
   Without a Pipe or Tabour,
And Mother Midnight bring to Light,
   The Fruits of all their Labour.

God

God save the King, and send quite thro' the Realm,
Men may Obey, and Women Rule the Helm.

This Lucky thought so Oblig'd the whole Congregation of Tattle-Baskets; that I found by the satisfaction they exprest in their Countenances, scarce a Woman in the Company could forbear claping me; and the good Wives falling to, as eagerly as so many Livery Men at a Hall Feast, were all so ready to help me with a choice Bit, that I had a Plate Pil'd up in half a minute, enough to have Feasted a whole Family of French Protestants just Landed. As soon as the Edges of our Hungry Appetites were taken off, and our Mouths were a little at Leisure to imploy the Glass, and give way for our Tongues to express our Sentiments: The Women were presently so wonderful busie in Drinking the Chaplains Health, that they had like to have forgot the Sow and her Pig, if it had not been for the Womans Oracle, the Midwife, who put 'em in Mind of it. By that time three or four Glasses had wash'd away their Counterfeit or acquir'd Modesty, which restrain'd 'em from that Freedom of the Tongue which their Natures prompt them to, we had as great a Jargon of confus'd Talk arose amongst us, as ever you heard amongst a Crowd of Female Neighbours gather'd at a Womans door that had just hang'd herself; talking as much of the Ill-qualities of their Servants, and good Humours of their Childrens, as a parcel of Countrey Gentlemen got over a Tub of double Ale, do of their Dogs and their Horses. When ever they talk'd of any of their own Sex that were not present, a Man that had been wholly unacquainted with the Conversation of Women, would have thought they had been setting forth the Faults and Infirmities of some She-Devil; and that nothing which bore Humane Shape and Nature, could have been liable to so many Odious Imperfections; who 'tis very likely was much handsomer, and more Vertuous, then the Ill-natur'd she, who had accumulated such a Number of Defects and Vices, and laid 'em to her Charge, who was not present to justifie herself against 'em: The Failings of their Husbands also, was a great Subject of their Discourse, with now and then a Whisper, which I suppose, was touching some Secret Disabilities, or Neglects, which were not Proper or Consistent, tho' with the most free and Unrestrain'd Modesty, to Speak in Publick.

At last a great Talk arose about such a Woman, who had been Marry'd two years, and not proving with Child in so long a time, had lately made an Elopement from her Husband with a Courtier, who had got her close in his Lodgings at *Kensington*, even to the Distraction of the poor Cuckold, who offers to take her again, but that she wont Live with him: *Fy upon her*, says old Mother Tumble-Tuzzy, *for a Naughty Woman; if she had taken my Advice, I am sure it had been better for her; if things were as she told me, I am sure she had no great Reason to Complain; but in short, I don't believe she Lov'd her Husband, for if she did, she would never have done so by him: I'll Swear I pitty the Man with all my Heart; I look upon him to be as Honest a Man as any dwells in the Parish; and indeed I believe he Lov'd*

his

his Wife very well. Ay, indeed Neighbour, much better than such a Minx deserv'd. Why so Madam? says a third; Why should you Rail against the poor Woman behind her Back; she might have Reason enough to do what she did, for ought you know. Reason! Marry hang her, says a fourth; What Reason could she have to bring herself under this Scandal, and her Husband poor Man, under all this Shame and Sorrow? If she could not be Contented with what the good Man could give her, there are Journey-Men and Prentices enough in the House, that she need not have been such a Slut to have ran away from him. O fye, says another, Why sure you would not have had her Disgrace herself with so mean a Thing as a Servant, would you? Servants reply'd a former! Marry come up, my dirty Cousin! How little you make of Servants! As if 'twas impossible a Prentice or a Journey-Man could have a longer Nose than his Master. You see the Court Ladies they have Wit enough to be Content with their own Coachmen and Footmen; and not come into the City to expose themselves: Besides, a Servant looks upon it to be so great an Honour, that he will take thrice the Pains to Oblige a Woman, as a Man will that's her Equal, for which reason Quality have Sence enough you see to chuse such Men for their Gallants as are much beneath 'em, because they will have 'em more at their Beck: And since we follow their Fashions, I don't know but 'twould be better for us, if we follow'd their Examples too. Nay, truly Neighbour, says the other, I must confess there is something of Reason in what you say: But indeed, I think 'tis a burning Shame, that a Man who knows how 'tis with him, should be so Foolish to Marry a Woman, and bring her to these hardships; for they ought to Consider, that's the Truth on't, we are Flesh and Blood as well as they.

In this sort of hopeful Tittle-Tattle, they tired their Lungs, and wasted their Time, till they were most of them got as Boozy, as so many Bumpkins at a Wake, or Tipling Loyalists upon the Kings Birth-day. The Merry Dames by this time, having at one sitting pretty well fill'd their Carcases, and empty'd their Minds, they began to call upon me their Chaplain, to give 'em a Discharge; which put me to a second Nonplus, believing they had drank themselves at Supper past all Grace; but found my self mistaken, forgetting that Hypocrites are always most Devout, when they are Maudlin: Finding I had no way to avoid the Office, I made a shift to Blunder thro' this Ceremonious piece of Thanksgiving, after the following manner:

Our hearty Thanks we humbly Pay,
    For th' Blessings we have tasted;
L—d send such Christ'nings every Day,
    That we may thus be Feasted.

We Bless thee for each merry Dame;
    And her good Conversation;
O bring 'em Yearly to the same
    Blest End of their Creation.

May they abound in Girles and Boys,
    Yet still and still be Kiss-on;
That we may meet and thus rejoice,
    To make each Babe a Christian.

D

Bless

Bless all good Women in their Married State,
Make their Pains easie, and their Pleasure great.

This so obliged the Assembly of Fruitful Matrons, that I dare swear I might have pick'd and chose, as the Turk does in his Seraglio. I was now esteem'd as the prettyest, Wittyest, and best humour'd Gentleman, that ever they were in Company with in their Lives; and what a Thousand Pities it was I should be a Batchelour, every one offering to help me to a Wife, that I began to be afraid they would have made a *Priest* of the *Midwife*; and have Marry'd me in spight of my Teeth, before I could get safe out of their Company. I dare swear if we had had but a fair Opportunity, my Part'ner and I might have made as many Cuckolds as ever were made by a couple of *Church-Wardens* during the whole time of their Office; and they have generally as great a Command of the Parish, as any Men that dwell in't, except the Parson.

This generous Entertainment we had hitherto had, was not sufficient to Plague my poor Kinsman enough, and to Gratify the Ridiculous Prodigality of the good Woman in the Straw, it being the first Testimony of her Fertility: But after all this, the Extravagancy must be Sum'd up with a Service of Sweet-meats, which every Gossip carry'd away in her Hankerchief; then were my Brother Witness and I forc'd to conclude all with a Final repetition of Old *Judas's* Ceremony, and so sent 'em packing home to their own dear Spouses, to tease their Ears with a rehearsal of their Welfare. What now remain'd for me to do, was to go up stairs to wish my *Bed-ridden* Relation much Joy of her new Christian, and to receive Thanks for the Trouble she had put me to: I kist the good Woman, with a good Will enough; but having no great kindness for a Creature so newly Calv'd as my little Kinsman, I could not salute him but with as indifferent an Appetite as I did the Old Woman; for *Bull-Veal* so very Young, and *Cow-Beeff* so very Old, are two sorts of Flesh I could never heartily approve on; for I always fancy the one's a little too Tender, and smells of the *Cask*; and the other a little to Tough, and smells of a *Coffin*.

Having now struggled thro' every Difficult part of these accustomary Formalities, I had nothing to do but to thank 'em for our liberal Entertainment, wish the Woman well again, and both much Happiness in their Male-Offspring, and so take my leave, which I did accordingly; and was as greatly over-joy'd when I got out of the House, as ever Convict was that had broke Goal, or detected Pick-Pocket that had escap'd a Horse-pond.

When I came to my Lodging, I began to consider what further use I could make of the sundry passages, and pleasant humours, I had observ'd amongst this Female Congregation; and at last agreed with my self 'twas a rare opportunity to take off a true impression of a Gossip; which I desire the Reader to accept of.

The

The Character of a Gossip.

SEven Years in Wedlock first she must have spent,
And must have made her Spouse as long Repent,
That such a Curse was e'er from Heaven sent.

By Nature made to Team, to Tease, and Vex;
No longer Happy than she can Perplex;
Lustful t'wards Men, and Envious to her Sex.

Homely, Disdainful, Talkative, and Proud;
Foolish, Self-will'd, too Stubborn to be Bow'd;
Fiery as Light'ning, and as Thunder Loud.

A Junket-Foll'wer, and a Friend to Wine;
Who to her Betters will no place Resign;
And hates the *Gossip* that appears more Fine.

Of her own Faults she others does Accuse;
Her Neighbours Failings are her chiefest News;
And railes against that Vice she most pursues.

Her Spight at ev'ry Well-bred She, takes Aim;
The Modest Woman is a close sly Dame,
Who tho' she Opens not, yet Hunts the Game.

She's the still Sow that Drinks up all the Draught,
Tho' so Reserv'd in Tongue, she's Loose in Thought;
And is the most suspected to be Naught.

If Handsome, then the Envious Tatler cries,
Her Face is well enough, sh' as pretty Eyes;
But has an ugly Fault, else People Lies.

What I have heard, I'm very loth to Speak;
Besides all that, she gives her Cheeks the Lick;
And is as Ill-Condition'd as *Old-Nick*.

Were I a Man, such Beauty I'd Adore,
As should be only Nat'ral, and no more;
For she that Paints, will doubtless be a Whore.

Beauty's but Fancy, Silly Boys Pursue;
Men Love a Woman that is Just and True;
She's only Handsome, that will Handsome do.

She Blames the Dame that like herself is Free,
Who Loves good Liquor, and much Company;
One *Gossip* with another can't agree.

To Drink a Merry Cup, she holds no harm,
And finds in *Brandy* such a Secret Charm,
It chears her Heart, and keeps her Stomach warm.

Abroad

Abroad she Walks to see, and to be seen;
And if the good Man asks her where sh'as been;
With a Gallant, *Tom-Coney*, and what then?

Fools must ask Questions, I'm your Wife, 'tis true;
But am of Age, and know sure what I do;
Can Go and Come, without the leave of you.

Art jealous, Love? You need not be affraid,
Had you a Wife like such a One, Egad,
You then indeed might fear an Aking Head.

But I (as God well knows my heart) despise
The very thought, (altho' she knows she Lyes,)
B'ing Maudlin, then to please the Fool she Cryes.

Thus Charms the Man with her Dissembling Spell;
A Thousand Lyes can in a Moment tell;
And when she pleases, make things ill or well.

Thus she the Breeches wears, and Rules the Roast;
Of which she does at all her meetings boast;
The Man's no more, God help him, than a Post.

She tells how all things on her Care depends;
She Buys and Pays, she Borrows and she Lends;
Hoards what she pleases, what she pleases spends.

None could his ugly Humours bear but she;
Besides, she's sure he cannot but agree,
She understands the Trade as well as he.

She pleases Customers much better far;
He oft Neglects his Shop, he does not Care;
Pounds would be often lost, were she not there.

Believe me, Neighbour, he's so Peevish grown,
E'er since he has been Troubl'd with the *Stone*,
That 'twould be happy for him he was gone.

Poor Man! I pitty him with all my Heart,
And wish I could but ease him of his Smart;
He cannot say but I have done my part.

Thus can she *Lye, Dissemble*, and be *Drunk*,
Rail at Tobac; yet for the Tooth-Ach Funk
And wants no odious Symptoms of a *Punk*.

May my Throat meet a *Halter*, or a *Knife*,
Or any way, good Heaven, dissolve my Life,
Rather than Plague me with so damn'd a Wife.

F I N I S.

THE
LONDON
SPY.

For the *Month* of *April*, 1700.

The Second Volume.

PART VI.

LONDON, Printed and Sold by *J. How*, in the *Ram-Head-Inn Yard* in *Fanchurch-street*, 1700.

Books Sold by J. How, *in the* Ram-Head-Inn-Yard *in* Fanchurch-Street; J. Weld, *at the* Crown *between the* Temple-Gates *in* Fleet-ſtreet; *and* Mrs. Fabian, *at* Mercers-Chappel *in* Cheapſide.

1. SOt's Paradiſe: Or the Humours of a Derby-Ale-Houſe: With a Satyr upon the Ale. Price Six Pence.

2. A Trip to *Jamaica*: With a True Character of the People and Iſland. Price Six Pence.

3. *Ecleſia & Factio*. A Dialogue between *Bow-Steeple-Dragon*, and the *Exchange-Graſhopper*. Price Six Pence.

4. The Poet's Ramble after Riches. With Reflections upon a Country Corporation. Alſo the Author's Lamentation in the time of Adverſity. Price Six Pence.

5. A Trip to *New-England*. With a Character of the Country and People, both Engliſh and Indians. Price Six Pence.

6. Modern Religion and Ancient Loyalty: A Dialogue. Price Six Pence.

7. The World Bewitch'd. A Dialogue between Two Aſtrologers and the Author. With Infallible Predictions of what will happen from the *Vices* and *Villanies* Practiſ'd in *Court*, *City* and *Country*. Price Six Pence.

8. A Walk to *Iſlington*: With a Deſcription of New *Tunbridge*-VVells, and *Sadler's* Muſick-Houſe. Price Six Pence.

9. The Humours of a Coffee-Houſe: A Comedy. Price Six Pence.

10 A Frolick to *Horn-Fair*. With a Walk from Cuckold's-Point thro' *Deptford* and *Greenwich*. Price Six-Pence.

11. The Dancing-School. With the Adventures of the *Eaſter*-Holy-Days. Price Six Pence,

12. The Firſt Volume of the LONDON-SPY: In Twelve Parts.

13. The Firſt, Second, Third, Fourth, and Fifth Parts of the Second Volume of the *London-Spy*. Price Six Pence Each.

All Written by the ſame Author.

THE
LONDON
SPY.

Deeper Concern hath scarce been known, to affect in general the Minds of Grateful and Ingenious Men, than the Melancholy surprize of the Worthy Mr. *Dryden*'s Death hath occasion'd thro' the whole Town, as well as all other Parts of the Kingdom, where any Persons of either Wit or Learning have taken up their residence; wheresoever his incomparable Writings have been scatter'd by the Hands of Travellers into Foreign Nations, the loss of so great a Man must needs be Lamented amongst their Bards and Rabbies; and 'tis reasonable to believe the commendable Industry of Translators has been such, to render several of his most accurate Performances into their own Language, that their Native Countrey might receive the Benefit, and themselves the Reputation of so Laudable an Undertaking: And how far the Wings of Merit have convey'd the pleasing Fruits of his exuberant Fancy, is a difficult Conjecture; considering what a continual correspondence our Nation has with most parts of the Universe. But it is reasonable to believe all Christian Kingdoms and Colonies, at least, have been as much the better for his Labours, as the World is the worse for the Loss of him; those who were his Enemies, while he was Living (for no Man lives without) his Death has now made such Friends to his Memory, that they acknowledge they cannot but in Justice give him this Character, that he was one of the greatest Schollars, the most Correct Dramatick Poet, and the best Writer of Heroick Verse, that any Age has produc'd in *England*; and yet, to verify the old Proverb, *That Poets, like Prophets, have little Honour in their own Countreys*, notwithstanding his Merit hath justly Intit'led his Corps to the most Magnificent and Solemn Interment the Beneficence of the greatest Spirits could bestow upon him; yet it is credibly reported the ingratitude of the Age is such, they had like to have let him pass in private to the Grave, without those Funeral Obsequies suitable to his Greatness, had it not been for

that

that true *Brittish* Worthy, who meeting the Venerable Remains of the neglected Bard passing silently in a Coach unregarded to his last Home, ordered the Corps, by the Consent of his few Friends that attended him, to be respited from so obscure an Interment; and most generously undertook at his own Expence, to revive his Worth in the Minds of a forgetful People, by bestowing on his Peaceful Dust a Solemnial Funeral answerable to his Merit; which Memorable Action alone, will Eternalize his Fame with the greatest *Heroe's*; and add that Lustre to his Nobility, which time can never Tarnish, but will Shine with equal Glory in all Ages, and in the very Teeth of Envy bid defiance to Oblivion. The Management of the Funeral was left to Mr. *Russel*, pursuant to the Directions of that Honourable Great Man, concern'd chiefly in the Pious Undertaking.

The first Honour done to his deserving Reliques, was Lodging 'em in Physicians Colledge; from whence they were appointed to take their last Remove, the constituted day for the Celebration of that Final Office which Living *Heroe's* perform in respect to a Dead Worthy, was *Monday* the 13th of *May*, in the afternoon: At which time, according to the Notice given, most of the Nobility and Gentry now in Town, assembled themselves together at the Noble Edifice aforesaid, in order to Honour the Corps with their Personal Attendance. When the Company were met, a Performance of Grave Musick, adapted to the Solemn occasion, was Communicated to the Ears of the Company by the Hands of the best Masters in *England*; whose Artful Touches on their soft Instruments, diffused such Harmonious Influence amongst the attentive Auditors, that the most Heroick Spirits in the whole Assembly were unable to resist the Passionate force of each dissolving Strain, but melted in to Tears forthe loss of so Elegant and Sweet a Ravisher of Humane Minds, and notwithstanding their undaunted Bravery, which had oft Scorn'd Death in the Field, yet now by Musick's Enchantment at the Funeral of so great a Poet, were soften'd beneath their own Natures, into a Serious Reflection of Mortality.

When this part of the Solemnity was ended, the famous Doctor *G—th* ascended the Pulpit, where the Physicians make their Lectures, and deliver'd, according to the *Roman* Custom, a Funeral Oration in *Latin* on his Deceased Friend; which he perform'd with the great Approbation and Applause of all such Gentlemen that heard him, and were true Judges of the matter: Most Rhetorically setting forth those Elogies and Encomiums which no Poet hitherto, but the Great *Dryden*, could ever truly deserve. When these Rites were over in the Colledge, the Corps, by Bearers for that purpose, was Handed into the Hearse, being adorn'd with Plumes of Black Feathers, and the sides hung round with the Escutcheon of his Ancestors, mix'd with that of his Lady's; the Hearse drawn by six stately *Flanders*-Horses; every thing set off with the most useful Ornaments to move regard and affect the Memories of the Numberless Spectators, as a means to Encourage ev'ry Sprightly Genius to Attempt something in their Lives, that may once render their Dust Worthy of so Publick a Veneration. All things being put in due order, for
their

their Movement, they began their Solemn Proceſſion towards *Weſtminſter-Abby*, after the following manner.

The two Beadles of the Colledge in Mourning Cloaks and Hat-bands, with the Heads of their Staffs wrapt up in Black Crape Scarffs, followed by ſeveral other ſervile Mourners, whoſe buſineſs was to prepare the way that the Hearſe might paſs leſs liable to interruption; next to theſe mov'd a Concert of *Hoitboys* and *Trumpets*, Playing and Sounding together a Melancholly Funeral March, undoubtedly Compos'd for that particular Occaſion; (after theſe, the Undertaker with his Hat off, Dancing thro' the Dirt, like a Bear after a Bagpipe. I beg the Readers Pardon for foiſting in a Jeſt in ſo improper a Place, but as he walk'd by himſelf within a Parentheſis, ſo I have have here plac'd him, and hope none will be offended) then came on the Hearſe, as before Deſcrib'd, moſt Honourably attended with abundance of Quality in their Coaches and ſix Horſes, that it may be juſtly reported to Poſterity, No Ambaſſador from the greateſt Emperour in the Univerſe, ſent over with the moſt Welcome Embaſſy to the Throne of *England*, ever made his Publick Entry to the Court, with half that Honour as the Corps of the Great *Dryden* did in its laſt *Exit* to the Grave. In this order the Nobility and Gentry attended the Hearſe to *Weſtminſter-Abby*, where the Quire, aſſiſted with the beſt Maſters in *England*, Sung his *Epicedium* and the laſt Funeral Rites being perform'd by one of the Prebends; he was honourably interr'd between *Chaucer* and *Cowley*; where, according to report, will be Erected a very ſtately *Monument*, at the expence of ſome of the Nobility, in order to recommend his Fame, and preſerve his Memory, to all ſucceeding Ages.

The Cauſe of his Death being very remarkable, it will not be improper in this place to take notice of it, as a means to put the World in mind of what ſlender Accidents are ſufficient to change the State of Man, and hurry him into the Dark Somewhere of Eternity: The occaſion of his Sickneſs, was a Lameneſs in one of his Feet, ſpringing from ſo trival a cauſe as the Fleſh growing over one of his Toe-nails; which being neglected, begot a ſoreneſs, and brought an inflamation into his Toe, and being a Man of a groſs body, a flux of humours falling into the part, made it very troubleſome, that he was forc'd to put himſelf into the Hands of an able Surgeon; who foreſeeing the Danger of a Mortification, adviſed him to part with the Toe afflicted, as the beſt means to prevent the ill conſequence likely to enſue; which he refus'd to conſent to, believing a Cure might be effected by leſs ſevere means than the Loſs of a Member; till at laſt his whole Leg Gangreen'd, which was preſently follow'd by a Mortification, ſo that nothing remain'd to prevent Death, but an Amputation of the Member thus putrified; which he refuſed to conſent to, ſaying, He was an old Man, and had not long to Live by the Courſe of Nature; and therefore did not care to part with one Limb, at ſuch an Age, to preſerve an uncomfortable Life to the reſt; and therefore choſe rather to ſubmit to Death, which in a little time after, according to the foreſight of his Surgeons and Phyſicians, did unavoidably happen. Having thus given the Reader the manner of his Death, as well as the order

B of

of his Funeral, I could not withhold my Muse from presuming to attempt an *Elegy* or *Funeral-Song*, in respect to the memory of so Worthy an Author, whose Name and Works will out-live Time, and stand up with Eternity.

To the Pious Memory of the most Sublime and Accurate Mr. *John Dryden*.

TO those Blest unknown distant Regions, where
   Great Pindar, Homer, and sweet Virgil Live,
The Immortal DRYDEN's fled, and justly there,
His Nervous Poems does with theirs compare,
   Whilst more discerning Gods to Him the Laurel give.

May Envy let His Dust in Quiet Sleep;
   And Fame Eternal in his Volumes dwell;
Whilst Chaucer's Sacred Tomb his Ashes keep,
Ages shall o'er his Golden Writings Weep;
   And thus the melting Force of his strong Lines shall feel.

Great was his Learning, and Sublime his Thoughts,
   Powerful his Numbers, Matchless was his Wit;
Num'rous his Excellencies, few his Faults;
And those he plac'd as Foiles and Beauty-Spots,
   To give more sprightly Lustre to the Lines he Writ.

His Soul was sure some God wrap'd up in Clay,
   From Heaven descended, to Inform Mankind;
Whose mighty Genius did no Time delay;
But most Industriously Improv'd each day,
   To shew the World the Beauties of his fruitful Mind.

No Ancient Muse, in Greece or Room e'er bred,
   Could Sweeter, or more God-like Strains impart;
The Heav'nly Soul's unborn that can Exceed,
Those soft Enchantments in his Verse we Read;
   Where we find Nature heighten'd with the purest Art.

Envious Competitors, the worst of Foes,
   His Pen hath Conquer'd, that they can't but own
He so excell'd in Poetry and Prose,
That each great Task indisputably shows,
   None was like him inspir'd, his Equal's yet unknown.

The chiefest Glory of his Native Land,
   Whose Soul such large Angelick Gifts possest,
'Twas hard to think that any Humane Hand,
Could such Bold Stroaks, such Lofty Flights command;
   Yet harder to determine what he Writ was best.

Satyr

Satyr and Praise flow'd Equal from his Pen,
  Dramatick Rules, no Shakespear better knew;
The Stately Epick and the Lyrick strain,
In each he had so excellent a Vein,
  That from the best of Judges admiration drew.

Great King of Verse, whose Merit rais'd thee high;
  And won thy Brows fresh Lawrel Crowns each Day;
Thy works immortal are, and cannot dye;
Why not thy self exempt from Fate, O why;
  Unless the World's unworthy of thy longer stay?

Or was it 'cause thy Soul was so Divine,
  The Barren Earth could not her Fruits reward;
Or that the Power and Beauty of each Line,
Made thee, the Author, like a Deity Shine,
  And that the Gods foresaw, like them, should'st be ador'd!

Or did the Slights of an ungrateful Age,
  Hasten th' aspiring Soul to take its Flight;
And leave this worthless sublunary Stage,
Where Pride and Lust does Mortal Minds engage,
  And keep the Giddy World from doing Merit right.

What call'd thee hence, or whither thou wilt soar,
  None but Eternity it self can tell,
We know for Mankind thou canst do no more,
But Heaven for thee has its best Joys in store,
  To recompence those Tasks thou hast perform'd so well.

Let ev'ry Pen more worthy of the Theme,
  Thy Elegy or Epicedium Sing,
The Mournful Verse may equal the Esteem,
The Learn'd and Witty shou'd express for them,
  Who did to Humane Knowledge such Improvements bring.

Great Soul! No Pen less Powerful than thy own,
  Can thy deserv'd Immortal Praise set forth,
Which Time will magnify now thou art gone,
As ev'ry Age successively comes on;
And to Mankind discover by degrees thy Worth.

Could Dust be sensible within the Grave,
  How Joyful would thy Peaceful Neighbours be,
Such Venerable Company to have,
Whose meritorious Works will surely save
  Thy Mem'ry from decay to all Eternity!

Chaucer

Chaucer and *Cowley*, gladly would Reserve
Thy *Frozen Clay*, into their *silent Tomb*;
Desiring their *Applause* with yours might Live,
In hopes your *Fame*, *Eternity* might give
To theirs, and that your *Laurels* might together Bloom.

Since Fate, to *Wishmans Grief* hath call'd thee hence:
It justly to thy *Absence* may be said,
No *Grecian Bard* e'er show'd such *Excellence*;
None has so well bestow'd such *Reams* of *Sence*,
As the Great *Dryden* hath; but now alas, he's Dead.

For such an *Universal Loss* sustain'd,
May the best *Sorrow* thro' the *World* be shown;
Let ev'ry thing in *Nature* be Constrain'd
To *Weep*; let *sullied* dy'd Clouds distance lend,
And flaming Orbs above their *Fiery Tears* drop down.

I shall now return to *Chancery-Lane* end, where I stood to see the Funeral pass by, observing there some Passages of *Hackney-Coachmen* and the *Mob*, worth delivering to the Reader. The great Number of Qualities Coaches that waited for the Hearse, to put the *Hackney* Whore-drivers out of their Bias, that against the *Kings-head-Tavern* there happen'd a great stop, occasion'd by a Train of Coaches which had block'd up the narrow end of the Lane, obstructed by an intangled number of moveable Bawdy-houses, who waited to turn up the same narrow Gulph, the others wanted to go out of; some with their Poles run into the Windows of another Coach, wherein sat *Bawd* and *Whore*, or *Mother* and *Daughter* squeaking out for the Lords sake, that some merciful Good Man would come up to their assistance.

One Impudent Corrector of Jades Flesh, had run his Pole against the back Leather of a forgoing Coach, to the great dammage of a *Beau's* Reins, who peeping out at the Coach-Door, with at least a fifty Ounce Wig on, swore Damn him, if he came out he would make as great a Slaughter amongst Hackney Rogues with his Sword, as ever *Sampson* did amongst the *Philistines*, with the Jaw Bone of an Ass. Whilst he was thus Cursing and Swearing like an old Sinner in a Fit of the Gout, his own Coachman flinging back the Thong of his Whip in striking at his Horses, gave him such a Cut over the Nose, that he Jirk'd in his Head as if he had been Shot, not knowing from whence the blow came, that he sat raving within his Leathern Territories, like a mad Gentleman Chain'd down to his Seat, in order to be carry'd to the famous Doctor *N——ns* to be Cur'd, not daring to look out, for fear after the like manner he should a second time pay for his peeping. The Coachmen all the while saluting one another with such Diabolical Titles, and confounding one another with such bitter Execrations, as if every one was striving which should go to the Devil first: attacking each other

with

with such a Volley of Oaths, that if a parcel of Informers had stood by as Witnesses to their Prophaneness, and would have taken the advantage, there would scarce have been one among'st 'em, but what had Swore out his Coach and Horses in half the Time of the Disorder. At last, by sundry Stratagems, Painful Industry, and the great Expence of Whip-Cord, they gave one another way; and then with their Hey-ups, and ill-Natur'd Cuts upon their Horses, they made such a ratling over the Stones, that had I been in St. *Sepulchers* Belfrey upon an Execution-Day, when the Prisoners Bell Rings out, I could not have had a more ungratefull Noise in my Head, than arose from their Lumbring Conveyancies.

No Sooner had these dispers'd themselves towards the several Places they were bound to by their Fairs, but one of the Prize-Fighting Gladiators, from *Dorset-Garden-Theatre*, where he had been exercising the several Weapons of Defence, with his bold Challenger, upon a clear Stage, without Favour, was Conducted by in Triumph, with a couple of Drums to Proclaim his Victory, attended with such a parcel of Scarrified Ruffains, whose Faces seem'd to be as full of Cuts as a Plow'd Field is of Furrows, some their Countenances chop'd into the form of a *Good-Fryday* Bun, with Cuts cross one another, as if they were mark'd out for Christian Champions: Others having as many Scars in their *Bear-Garden* Physiognomies, as there are marks in a Chandlers Cheese Scor'd out into Pennyworths. These hem'd in with such a cluster of Journeymen Shooemakers, Weavers and Taylors, that no Bailiff from an Inns-of-Court Bog-House, or Pickpocket carrying to be Pump'd, could have been Honour'd with a greater Rabble of Attendance. Tho' this, the Victorious Combatant, came off with Flying, yet 'twas with Bloody Colours; for by report of the Mob, like a true hardy Cock, he won the Day after he had lost an Eye in the Battle. They mauld one another stoutly, to the great Honour of themselves; and Fought out all the Weapons, to the great satisfaction of the Spectators. I think it will not be amiss, if in this Place I present the Reader with a Character of a Prize-Fighter, it being properly enough introduced; I have therefore thought fit to put it into Lyrick Verse as follows.

> Bred up in th' Fields near Lincolns-Inn,
>   Where Vinegar Reigns Master;
> The forward Youth does there begin,
> A Broken-Head to Lose or Win,
>   For Shouts, or for a Plaister.

> For North, or West, he does Contend,
>   Sometimes his Honour Loses,
> Next Night his Credit is regain'd,
> Thus Fights till harden'd in the End,
>   To Bloody Cuts and Bruises.

When

When at his Weapon grown expert,
By Bangs and rough Instruction,
To make a Tryal of his Heart,
At Sharps he does himself exert,
And Dallies with Destruction.

Proud of his Courage and his Skill,
No Champion can out Brave-him,
He dares to Fight, yet Scorns to Kill,
He Guards so Well, and Lives so Ill,
That few know where to have him.

He Glories in his Wounds and Scars,
Like any Flanders Soldier,
And as one Talks of Forreign Wars,
The t'other Boasts of Hockly Jars;
Wherein no Man was bolder.

He Fought before some Duke or Lord,
With hardy Tom the Weaver;
And Cut him off the Stage at Sword;
The Duke his Manhood to reward,
Presented him a Beaver.

With Lies he tells his Bloody Feats,
And Bounces like a Bully;
Tho' all his Prizes were but Cheats,
Yet when he with a Coward meets,
He knows he has a Cully.

Thus backs in Jest, and finds at best,
But little Money coming;
And when his Youthful Days are past,
His only refuge is at last,
To follow Theft, or Bumming.

The Town having receiv'd Notice by an Advertisement in the *Post-Boy*, of a great Cause to be try'd on the following *Wednesday*, at the Kings-Bench-Bar at *Guild-Hall*, between one of St. *Hugh*'s false Prophets, who can fore-tell more in an Hour than will prove true in an Age, *Plaintiff*; and another famous Student in the Cœlestial Sciences, most highly Learn'd in the Language of the Stars, *Defendant*; the former having *Secundum Artem*, pursuant to the Old Custome of Almanack-makers, most closely attack'd the latter, about several profound Points in the Mystery of Astrology, in which many Fools put more Faith, than they do in the Twelve Articles; and Wisely knowing a Volley of Scurility, where Scoundrells are to Judge of the Battel, would do no more Execution
against

against a rising Competitor, and wound the Reputation of such an Adversary far deeper than the dint of Argument, drawn from the Rules of Art, assisted by sound reason; thought it therefore his safest Method to stuff his Almanack as full of hard Calumny and Ill-words, as the Art is full of Fallacy and Lying ones, accordingly began the Quarrel in Publick, in as pretty sweet obliging Language as ever *Billings-gate* Termagant bestow'd in Anger, upon a provoking Sister in the Turbulent Times of *Herrings, Sprats,* or *Mayerl*-Season, as if Sense and Manners were incongruous with Star-fumbling; and *Railing* and *Lying*, were the Two supporters of *Astrology.*

This malicious sort of Treatment from his predicting Brother Philomath, so animated the Defendant, that he could not forbear flinging off all Modesty and Patience, resolving to contend with his new Enemy at his own Weapon, Scurrility; and give him a true Taste in return of his Complements, of those stabbing Abuses which none but the worst of Men could give, or the best of Christians pass by without Notice: Accordingly he arms his *Ephemeris* with such a Justification of himself, and whetting his Ill-nature upon the very Grindstone of Revenge, chew'd his Words, as spightful Enemies do their Bullets, till he he'd made 'em so very rough and Ragged, that wherever they entred they made the Wound incurable. The Defendant having the best end of the Staff, and being vex'd, exercising his Weapon with more Cunning and Dexterity, so mauld his Opponent, that 'tis thought, had he had any in his Skull, he would have knock'd his Brains out. Being thus so hard set, he was forc'd to a very dishonourable retreat, in so much that he began to consider his Money was a better security than his Wits; and the Law a much better refuge under this Defeat, than *Ptolomy* or *Copernicus*; accordingly commences a Suit with his Antagonist, by Arresting him in an Action of Scandal, laying his Damages five Hundred Pounds, for the loss of a *Good-Name,* which he never enjoyed.

The Day being appointed for Tryal, amongst the rest of the Fools, my curiosity must needs lead me to hear the matter determin'd; when I came into the Hall, all the fortune-telling Wise-acres in the Town, both Male and Female, were drawn in a cluster from all the By-Allies in *More-fields, White-chappel, Salisbury-Court, Water-lane, Fleet-street,* and *Westminster*; who, I perceive, notwithstanding their Skill in Conjuration, by which they pretended to tell Fools their Fortune, and help the Credulous ignorant to lost Spoons, Thimbles, and Bodkins, yet could not by their Art foresee which of the two contending *Plannet-Peepers* were most likely to obtain the Victory.

Several great Counsel were Fee'd on both sides for the Tryal, looking upon the ordinary means which other People use, as the best security in such Cases, to be much more safe than a dependance on the Stars, to discover by their aspects what should be the Issue of the great difference between 'em. Several of the Councel were Conning over the Almanacks, wherein they had set forth the Vertues and Merits of each other, to such

an

an admirable Perfection, that I perceiv'd by the Looks of the Lawyers, they were so affected with the Cause, that I believe, had it been try'd, it would have given the Court as much Diversion as the Ridiculousness of a Fool in Contention, or the Banter of the Councel could have possibly afforded. Publick Notice of the Tryal having been given in the *Post-Boy*, great Numbers of Well-wishers to the Mathematicks had recourse to the Hall, in order to give Attention; that there was much more staring at the *Conjurers* as they Walk'd, then there was at the *Two Giants* as they stood; which sufficiently shows the former are the greater *Monsters* in the Eyes of the People: But as 'tis common for Astrologers to make Fooles of that part of the World that will give them any opportunity, so indeed they serv'd us, who came with an expectancy to hear them made Fools themselves in a Publick Court, who had made so many in a Kingdom. But a little before the Cause was to be call'd in, I suppose thro' the Prudence of some Friend or other, who was willing to prevent their being further expos'd, they were advis'd to Endeavour at some agreement. Whereupon some Terms of Accommodation being propos'd, they stop'd the Tryal, and adjourn'd to a Neighbouring Tavern to the great Disapointment of the Court, as well as Company.

I being curious to know what end they made of the Matter, follow'd into the same Tavern, and took up my sitting in the Publick Kitchen where I had been but a little time, before a parcel of approv'd Students in Physick and Astrology came in, whose Looks were as Legible to a Man of Common Reason, as the Neck Verse is to the Ordinary of *Newgate*; for by Contracting their Faces into Ill-Looks, to render themselves more terrible to Silly Wenches, and such sort of Ignorant Creatures, who give Credit to their Delusions, they had by Time and Practice fram'd such a Diabolical Air in their Crabbed Physiognomies, that no body can well guess 'em any thing but Conjurers by their Countenances. As 'tis generally observable, when several of the same Profession are in Company together, the main Topick of their Discourse must be something relating to their own Art, Trade, or Mystery; for most People take a Pleasure in Talking of what Business they are most Conversant with; so it Prov'd by these the Deceivers of Humane Ignorance, who were standing up very highly for their Art, and what wonderful things might be, as well as had been done, therein.

A Gentleman sitting next 'em in the Kitchen, who I suppose had but a very slender Opinion of these *Egyptian* kind of Juglers, took upon him now and then to slip in a Word amongst 'em, that so puzled the matter in hand, that the whole knot of Wizardly *Cacodæmons* were almost Dumb-founded. Yet they would peremptorily assert that things might infallibly be foretold by the Stars: and that the incredulity of those Persons who oppos'd Judicial Astrology, proceeded only from their Ignorance; and if they would but study it as much as they have done, they would be throughly convinc'd, that a certain foresight of things to come might be read in the great Library of the Heavens, as certainly, as the change of Weather might be fore-told by a Weather-
Glass

Glass. Upon which the Gentleman, having seen 'em in the Hall, surpriz'd 'em with this following Question, *viz.* Pray, says he, *Do you think it possible by the Art of Astrology to tell me if I am Robb'd, what's become of the Thief? Yes,* answers one, *We can, and direct you by our knowledge in the Stars, which way you shall find him.* I am very well satisfy'd now, reply'd the Gentleman, *You must either be a Pack of Deceitful Knaves, or a parcel of very Silly Fools; for if you are able to tell me, by Consulting your Planetary Friends, what sort of a Man hath done me wrong, and which way I shall find him, when he's fled from Justice; What's the Reason you cannot discover such Persons which the Government have truly describ'd ready to your Hands, and have given you the Advantage of their Names too, with an Assurance sometimes of Five Hundred, sometimes a Thousand Pounds Reward, for the great Service you would do the Nation to apprehend such Persons, which every good Subject ought to be Industrious to find out and bring to Justice; therefore 'tis plain, if you will pretend to make a Serviceable Discovery to an Ignorant Subject for half a Crown, and may have a Thousand Pound to serve the Government with the same Facility: 'Tis a great Argument you are Juggling Knaves, to undertake the former, and Couzen People of their Money, or else that you are Errant Fools to neglect the latter, wherein your Recompence may be eight Thousand times as great, for very little more than the same Trouble; for between Half a Crown and a Thousand Pound, there is just the same Disproportion.*

This put all the Star-Gazers to a great Non-plus for an answer; which the Gentleman observing, took a further advantage of their Weakness, and apply'd himself to 'em again, after this manner, *I suppose, Gentlemen,* says he, *You are Waiting here in order to hear by and by, how the Cause will go between the two famous Conjuring Antagonists.* No Sir, says one, I *find you are no Astrologer by your guess; the Tryal is put off by Consent till next Sitting, in order to an Accommodation:* But I suppose, Sir, reply'd the Gentleman, *You came with an expectancy of hearing it Debated this very Day?* Yes, Sir, says one of them, *We did so:* Why then, Sir, says the Gentleman, *You Astrologers may be out of your guess, as well as other People, or else why could you not foresee by your Art how the Cause will go, or if you came to day to hear it determin'd, you'd be all made Fools on.* Because, says one, *We took the Report as a granted Truth, and never Consulted the Stars at all about the matter:* Truly, reply'd the Gentleman, *If you had, I believe you would have found your selves as much the Wiser, as he that Consults* Cornelius Agrippa, *about raising a Homunculus; and so farewel to you.*

When he had made his *Exit;* my Sober Reflection on what he had said, whilst I was seriously wasting a Pint of Wine, and a Pipe of Tobacco, drew these following Lines into my Head; which being applicable to the matter in hand, I have given to the Reader.

> *Little their Learning, less their Sence,*
> *Who put in Stars such Confidence,*
> *As think those Senseless Bodies can*
> *Govern the Life and Fate of Man.*

D

How can we boast our State is free,
If under such Necessity?
That Beings quite inanimate,
The will of Man shou'd actuate;
And unlearn'd Dunces should foretell,
Who shall do ill, or who do well;
Predict our Fortunes, when 'tis known
The Jugler ne'er could tell his own.
If they such mighty things could do,
As prove their blind Conjectures true,
And make it manifest in Print,
Wise-men might think there's something in't.
Instead of that, their Prophecies,
To one true word, have Twenty Lyes;
And what by guess they do foretell,
Each Prudent Man foresees as well.

For Fools to think the Sun, or Moon,
Can help 'em to a stollen Spoon,
Or that, to ease the Losers Grief,
The Planets will declare the Thief;
The Novice may as well believe,
The Scissars turning with the Sieve,
As pin their Faith on Conj'rers Dreams,
Of Planets, Houses, and their Schemes;
Which the Fox seems to put in use,
Only to colour his abuse,
And keep the Clyents thoughts in Play,
Till he has study'd what to say;
And tho' an Art he does profess,
Yet chiefly what he says is Guess,
By which he does Fools Pockets pick,
Who think him Cunning as Old-Nick.
The Truth he tells 'em is no more,
Than what he sifts from them before;
Who Aw'd by his affected Look,
And Scrawles within his Conj'ring Book,
Forget the insight they have gi'n-him,
And think at last the Devil's in him.

A Wag that had sustain'd a Loss,
And coming to a Wizards House,
Some nasty Sloven, or else Slut,
Had at his Threshold eas'd a Gut;
The Conj'rer coming to the Door,
In mighty passion Curs'd and Swore,
That if he knew who 'twas had laid it,
He'd make 'em Rue the Day they did it;
Nay, says the Man, if you've no way,
To tell who did your Door bewray,

I'll e'en again put up my Purse,
For you can't help me to my Horse.
Would all like him consider right,
They'd bid Astrology good Night.

The Referree's, for want of an Umpire, which the Plaintiff would not admit of, could bring the matter to no manner of Conclusion, so that the accommodation propos'd was quite render'd ineffectual; and the next Sitting, in favour of their being Astrologers, their Cause was call'd on by the Court, about Eleven a Clock at Night, when the Moon and Stars were in their greatest Glory, and bore domination in Sol's absence, within our Horrison; both Parties put great Confidence in the present position of the Heavens; and according to the Astrological Judgment, they had both made of the Stars, neither could find pointing towards 'em, such an evil Direction, but that each had equal hopes from the propitious Aspects of the Planets, of overcoming his Adversary, but could not thorowly determine, by the surest Rules of their Art, who should have the best on't; one trusted so very much in the Stars, that his Friend had much ado, to perswade him to Fee Councel, which occasion'd some of the Wizardly Fraternity, to conjecture that he expected the Planets should have pleaded for him. The Plaintiff erecting a Scheme a little before Tryal, found by the position of the Heavens the Judge would be the Lord Ascendant, in this matter, and that the Jury were the Twelve Signs, towards which the Planets of the Law, the Councel, were to direct their influence, and accordingly took care to prudently secure, by the interests of Sol, the very Mars and Mercury of the Laws, to give his Cause their assistance, whilst the Defendant had engag'd none but Saturn on his part, to bid Defiance to his Adversary.

All things being put in as good Order as they were able; the Verbal Engagement, was begun so strenously, on the Plaintiffs behalf, who according to the Custom of such like Wars, always makes the first onset, that a stander-by might have easily foreseen, who would gain the Victory, without the Rules of Astrology. The Nimble Weapons of Offence and Defence, being almost tir'd with long pleading, in many foregoing Causes, made not half the Pastime the Audience expected; who were apprehensive of hearing the two Conjurers bandy'd about the Court from one to another, by their Bantring Advocates, and that they had chose to make the weighty difference of their wrangling Clients but the Court's diversion, which the lateness of the Night, and the weariness of the Councel, it was suppos'd prevented, to the great disappointment of many young Students, as well as old Practicers in the Noble Art of Pump and Wheedle, to which in this capacious Town there are of both Sexes an abundance of not only Pretenders, but real Artists; in half an hours time, from the beginning of the debate, the the business without much trouble was brought to a determination; the Plaintiff, however his Stars favour'd him, obtaining a Verdict, the com-
pasionate

paffionate Jury not knowing but some time or other it may be their own Case; giving him Five Pound damage for the great Abuses he had very honeftly deferv'd by a juft Provocation.

The decifion of this Controverfie prov'd very unlucky to both Enemies, for they were neither of them well fatisfied with the Juftice done both Parties, the *Plaintiff* being very angry his damage was no more, and the *Defendant* very much difpleas'd they had given him fo much; fo that the Jury would have had a very hard Task to have pleas'd both, fince they were fo unfortunate in their Concurrence they could content neither.

> *When Conjurers their Purfes draw,*
> *And like two Blockheads go to Law,*
> *They fhow by fuch Expenfive Wars,*
> *There's little Wifdome in the Stars;*
> *And that they Act, who know the Heavens,*
> *Like us, by Sixes and by Sevens;*
> *For if one Wizard had forefeen,*
> *The other fhould the Battel win,*
> *He'd cry'd Pecavi, and not come,*
> *Before a Judge to know his Doom;*
> *I think from thence the World may fee,*
> *They know by th' Stars no more than we.*

F I N I S.